INTRODUCTORY ASTRONOMY

INTRODUCTORY ASTRONOMY

NICHOLAS A. PANANIDES
Bakersfield College

ADDISON-WESLEY PUBLISHING COMPANY

Reading, Massachusetts
Menlo Park, California
London · Don Mills, Ontario

This book is dedicated to those students who truly are interested in understanding the universe.

Preface

The past decade has witnessed an unprecedented growth in astronomy which has been brought about by the many new developments in the sciences and by space exploration. Unmanned space vehicles have gone to the vicinity of Venus, Mars, and beyond and have sent back valuable data about the planets and space. On July 20, 1969, Neil Armstrong became the first man to land on another celestial body—the moon—while millions of people on the earth watched in tense expectation. Since the first landing, television has made the average man a member of each flight to the moon. He has traveled with the astronauts through space, walked with them as they explored the strange world of the moon, and shared their hopes, fears, successes, and failures.

Astronomy has taken on a new excitement and relevancy for the average man. It is no longer an esoteric science that is totally divorced from the everyday life of most men. The marked increase in the enrollment of college astronomy courses by nonscience students indicates how deeply astronomy has captured the popular imagination. Very few students in these courses plan to become professional astronomers; most of them are there to gain an insight into the basic concepts of astronomy. It is the responsibility of our colleges, especially the liberal arts and two-year community colleges, to teach astronomy as a vital element in a progressive society and to provide the foundation that will allow the student to intelligently appreciate the events occurring in space.

Introductory Astronomy is an attempt to fill a long-existing gap. Most introductory textbooks have been written for the professional. Overly complex material that is of little value and interest to the nonscience student has been introduced, basic concepts have been inadequately explained, irrelevant material has been introduced, and a scientific and mathematical background on the part of the student has been unduly assumed. These have produced unnecessary confusion and frustration. *Introductory Astronomy* provides a rigorous introduction to astronomy in a language that is easily understood by the nonscience student. The material is not so elementary that it insults his intelligence, nor so difficult that it makes him lose interest in the subject. Nothing has been assumed except the student's interest. Astronomical concepts are discussed in the clearest possible language, and all new terms are defined before they are used. Mathematical concepts are kept at a minimum, and when introduced, are explained in depth. Clarity is the touchstone that has been employed throughout the text. Since the study of science is no easy task for the average nonscience student, *Introductory Astronomy* was written in the belief that the road can be made less difficult and more interesting if the guideposts are clearly and simply presented. Only after the basic principles have been comprehended will the real beauty of astronomy reveal itself.

The text is designed primarily for use in a one-semester or a one-quarter course; however, it may be used as the basic text in a two-semester or two-quarter course by those instructors who desire to supplement the text with their own material, other readings, and observations. This text is the result of the author's experience in teaching a one-semester astronomy course at Bakersfield College for twenty-seven years, and a one-semester navigation course at the University of Michigan for four years.

The text presents the historical development of astronomy, what basic astronomical ideas and concepts were developed, and why they were accepted. The discussions are closely related to the abundant illustrations which should make the text easy to read and understand. This should allow the instructor to devote more time to classroom discussion, and if he desires, to introduce the social and philosophical aspects, thereby enriching the course.

The appendixes provide a practical guide for viewing the sky. Astronomy is not simply a set of concepts and facts; it is also the beauty and excitement of observing the celestial bodies. Since many introductory astronomy courses do not provide adequate observing time to acquaint the student with the sky, the appendix on constellations is constructed so that the student, with minimal assistance from the instructor, can begin to observe and study the stars intelligently.

I am greatly indebted to several astronomers who have read parts of the manuscript and have made many valuable suggestions. I want to thank Dr. Billy A. Smith and Bruce Fitzpatrick for reading the entire manuscript and for making perceptive comments and helpful suggestions. Every effort has been made to eliminate typographical and factual errors; however, for those that I have overlooked, I alone am responsible. I am particularly grateful to those astronomers and institutions who have provided the excellent photographs, especially to Mike Donahoe, NASA Ames Research Center, and Paul L. Wenger, NASA Jet Propulsion Laboratory for their cooperation and patience in selecting and providing the many beautiful photographs of space exploration. I also am very grateful to Mrs. Electra Paulick for typing the manuscript, to Mrs. Miriam Paine for her indispensable aid in proofreading, and to my son Dean for his editorial help. I would also like to thank the Addison-Wesley production staff for their capable, generous, and enthusiastic assistance in making this book a reality. Finally, I want to thank my wife, Ethel, for her patience and understanding in maintaining a normal home in the midst of a chaos of notes and papers while the manuscript was being written. Without the generous and capable assistance of these many friends and colleagues, the completion and publication of the book would have been impossible.

Bakersfield, California
September 1972

N. A. P.

Contents

Contents

Contents

1
Early Astronomy

1.1 ANCIENT ASTRONOMY

The night sky, with its impenetrable darkness broken by small dots of flickering light, has had an unceasing fascination for man. Primitive man must have been perplexed and thrilled by the continual rising and setting of the sun, which marked the ending and the beginning of darkness, the ever changing and yet unchanging faces of the moon, the myriad bright stars disappearing each day with the coming of the light, and the beautiful Milky Way stretching across the sky like a great luminous river. Through fear, awe, and curiosity man gave meaning to these mysterious objects and events by weaving around them myths and superstitions. He worshipped the sun, moon, and planets as gods because he believed that their lives mirrored human existence and exerted a persuasive influence and control over human destiny. As man pondered what he saw, astronomy, the oldest of the sciences, was born.

The stars, which were considered to be the lesser gods, appeared to be fixed to the inside of a large inverted bowl. Later, this concept was extended to that of a sphere with only one-half of its surface visible at any one time. With the passing of time, the entire star sphere appeared to rotate about an axis that passed through the north pole star, which was the only star that remained stationary in the sky. All the other stars appeared to rise above the eastern horizon, follow an arc across the sky, and set below the western horizon. Since all the stars appeared to remain stationary in relation to one another and to be arranged in definite groupings, primitive man traced the outlines of the men, women, and objects found in his religion. When he had established a number of these pictures, which he called constellations, the sky became a friendly domain, and the stars were no longer terrifying lights.

As primitive man continued to observe the heavens, he began to acquire knowledge about the celestial objects, which he used for the practical purposes of determining direction, position, and time. Later, this information became the basis for the development of astronomical thought. Long before man had invented instruments for measuring the passing of time, the sun, moon, and stars served as clocks. By observing the sun's daily motion of rising in the east, reaching its highest position above the horizon, and setting in the west, he established the moments of sunrise, noon, and sunset, and the intervals of day and night. He established the cycle of the seasons when he recognized that the sun's path differed every day (Fig. 1.1). In the winter, the sun appeared to rise in the southeast, follow a low path in the sky, and set in the southwest. At noon, when the sun was low in the sky, objects appeared to cast long shadows. In the summer, the sun appeared to rise in the northeast, follow a high path in the sky, and set in the northwest. At noon, when the sun was high in the sky, objects appeared to cast short shadows. On the first day of spring and autumn, the sun appeared to rise directly in the east and set directly in the west. When the length of the mid-day shadows were decreasing, it was spring and time to prepare the land for planting; when the length of the shadows were increasing, it was autumn and time to harvest the crops. As primitive man recognized the continuous cycle of the moon's changing shape, he used its motion and that of the sun to count the passing of the days, months, and years.

By permission of Johnny Hart and Field Enterprises, Inc.

1.2 CHINESE ASTRONOMY

As early as 4000 B.C., the Chinese ushered in the first important period in the history of astronomy, that of ancient astronomy. This period also included the astronomy developed by the great civilizations in the region of Mesopotamia and Greece.

Although the authenticity of some of the Chinese records has been questioned, most scholars recognize the Chinese as the first astronomers. As early as 2000 B.C., they made systematic observations of celestial

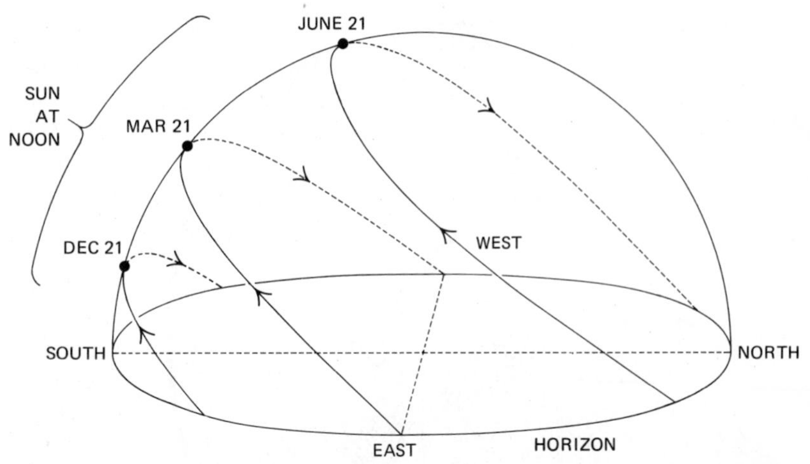

Fig. 1.1 Seasonal paths of the sun. In winter the sun rises in the southeast and sets in the southwest. In spring it rises in the east and sets in the west. In summer it rises in the northeast and sets in the northwest. At noon it is in the lowest position above the horizon in the winter and in its highest position in the summer.

bodies, determined the length of the year to be $365\frac{1}{4}$ days, established constellations which were used to guide them in their travels, and developed a calendar which enabled them to predict the beginning of the seasons. The Chinese were able to predict solar and lunar eclipses; however, on occasions they made mistakes or failed to predict an eclipse. One such occasion was recorded in the third century B.C., when the court astronomers, Hi and Ho, were put to death for neglecting to predict a solar eclipse which occurred while they were attending a garden party.

It appears that the Chinese were the first to recognize that the moon moves eastward in relation to the stars and takes approximately 28 days to complete one revolution around the sky. This is revealed in one of their myths which tells that the moon has 28 wives and spends one night with each as it moves around the sky. To keep track of the moon's position and the passing of time, they divided the moon's path into 28 stations, each about 13 degrees in length, the distance that the moon travels each day.

Although the Chinese did not understand the nature of comets, they kept accurate records of their appearances, including Halley's comet of 467 B.C. They also kept records of the appearance of "guest stars," which

we know as novae. These stars suddenly and unexpectedly burst into brilliance thousands of times greater than normal so that they are clearly visible in the daytime sky. One such star recorded by the Chinese was the Great Nova of 1054, which appeared in the constellation of Taurus the Bull. The remnant of this great explosion is believed to be the Crab Nebula (Chapter 13.7). While Chinese astronomy was quite impressive, its influence on western astronomy was not great because of China's isolated geographical position.

1.3 MESOPOTAMIAN ASTRONOMY

Ancient astronomy also flourished in the region known as Mesopotamia, around the great fertile valleys formed by the Indus, Tigris, Euphrates, and Nile rivers. These were the Indian, Babylonian-Chaldean, and Egyptian civilizations.

Indian astronomy has come down to us in legends. Their astronomical concepts were based primarily on imagination, religious beliefs, and preconceived ideas. One of the most interesting is their concept of the universe. The Buddhists believed in a round earth that was falling continuously in space; however, no one was able to detect its motion—a fact which allowed the

Fig. 1.2 The Hindu concept of the universe. Mount Meru, the earth, and the infernal regions were carried by the tortoise, the symbol of force and creative power. It rested on the great serpent, the emblem of eternity. The three worlds were the upper region, the residence of the gods; the intermediate region, the earth; and the lower, or infernal, region. At the summit of Mount Meru, which was supposed to cover and unite the three worlds, was the triangle, the symbol of creation. (Photograph from The Bettmann Archive, Inc.)

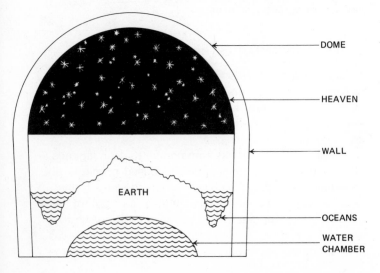

Hindus to believe that the earth was supported by four elephants that stood on the back of a large turtle resting on a coiled snake. (Fig. 1.2). Since these animals were included in their religion and were considered sacred, the Hindus believed that they were involved in the support of the earth.

The great civilizations that flourished between the Tigris and Euphrates rivers were the Babylonian and the Chaldean. The Babylonian came first and was later absorbed by the Chaldean. The history of these civilizations is recorded on numerous clay tablets that have been discovered in many areas of Mesopotamia. On one Babylonian clay tablet (from about 2000 B.C.) were recorded the movements of Venus and the omens associated with it. On a Babylonian boundary stone (from about 1200 B.C.) three people are shown with the symbols of the sun, moon, and Venus over their heads. The sun represented a goddess; the moon, a king; and Venus, his daughter. The Babylonians were one of the few of the ancient people who gave the moon male attributes.

According to the Babylonian concept of the universe (Fig 1.3) the earth, which was enclosed by a wall and supported a dome where all the celestial bodies were located, rested on a chamber of water.

An interesting Chaldean clay tablet was engraved with three concentric circles divided into twelve sectors with thirty-six areas. In each area, the name of a constellation and a number was recorded. No one has been able to decipher these inscriptions; however, astronomers believe that the tablet represents some form of a calendar. From these records, we know that the Chaldeans gave the names which we still use today to many of the star groupings: Gemini the Twins, Scorpius the Scorpion, and Taurus the Bull.

Fig. 1.3 The Babylonian concept of the universe. The earth, which rested on a water chamber, was enclosed by a wall supporting a dome where all the celestial bodies were located.

The Chaldeans were able to predict solar and lunar eclipses, observe the position and motion of the planets, record the appearance of meteors and comets, and measure the passing of time. In spite of these accomplishments, Chaldean astronomy never reached a high state of development because they lacked the knowledge of geometry. Moreover, there was no practical need for astronomy because the nature and structure of the universe was fully explained in their religion. Although the Chaldean priests had a tremendous background in astronomy, they simply used it as a means of establishing the dates of their religious festivals and as the basis for astrology. Since the motions of the sun, moon, and the planets were predictable, they believed them to be supernatural and to exert great influence and control over human destinies.

The Chaldean concept of the universe was a star-studded semispherical dome in continuous motion above the earth. The dome and the earth were completely surrounded by an envelope of water which at times fell upon the earth.

1.4 EGYPTIAN ASTRONOMY

Early Egyptian astronomy was primitive, naive, and based on preconceived ideas. During their 2000-year history, the Egyptians developed several concepts of the universe. A mural from the tomb of Rameses VI, who reigned about 1000 B.C., shows that one of the early concepts was anthropomorphic, that is, the sky, earth, and air were given human attributes (Fig. 1.4). The Egyptian goddess of the heavens, Nut, arched her body over the earth, which was represented by a man. Between them was a child, which represented the air. According to one legend, sunset occurred when Nut swallowed the sun each evening, and sunrise occurred when she gave birth to it each morning. In another legend, a river which was traversed daily by the sun god Ra in his boat flowed over the arched body of Nut. At sunset, the sun god Ra disappeared below the earth into the realm of the dead, and at sunrise he was reborn above the earth. A much later and more realistic concept pictured the universe in the shape of a rectangular box

Fig. 1.4 The early Egyptian anthropomorphic concept of the universe. (Yerkes Observatory photograph)

with Egypt located at the bottom center and surrounded by great mountain ranges. The sky was represented by a flat ceiling with holes in it and was supported by four great mountain peaks; the stars were lamps of different sizes, shapes, and colors. The sky river which flowed through the mountain ranges was traversed daily by the sun god Ra. When his boat disappeared behind a mountain peak, it was sunset—the signal for the gods who stood on top of the ceiling to lower the lamps by means of cables through the holes in the ceiling. This is how the Egyptians explained the appearance and disappearance of the stars.

From the writings of the Greek historian Herodotus (about 450 B.C.), we learn that the astronomical accomplishments of the Egyptians were many and great. They recognized and named many of the bright stars and constellations. As early as 2500 B.C., they determined that the length of the year was 365 days, which they eventually divided into twelve equal months of thirty days each with the exception of the last month, which was allotted the five extra days. They also discovered that the year was short one day every four years, and to compensate for it they introduced the leap year. Although the days and nights were divided into twelve hours each, the length of the hour varied with the seasons to account for the differences in the length of the day.

The Egyptians used the sun dial in the daytime and the water clock at night to mark the passing of time. They constructed calendars which they used to predict future astronomical events. Even though their geometry was advanced to a fairly high degree, it was not used as a tool in the development of astronomy, but rather in the resurvey of the lands that were flooded periodically by the Nile river. Another deterrent in the development of Egyptian astronomy was that since astronomical knowledge was considered sacred, all observations and information about it were kept secret within the priesthood. This was done to preserve and restrict to the priests the activity of making astrological predictions.

1.5 GREEK ASTRONOMY

Our first knowledge of Greek astronomy appeared in the Homeric poems written during the ninth century B.C. According to Homer, the ancient Greeks believed that the earth was a flat, circular disk; the sky, a spherical dome. Since the five planets, visible to the unaided eye—Mercury, Venus, Mars, Jupiter, and Saturn—appeared to wander in relation to the stars, they called them "Planetes," which means "wandering stars." Mercury and Venus, which always appear near the sun, confused the Greeks, who believed that each was two separate bodies: when they were following the sun, they appeared as evening stars; and when they were leading the sun, they appeared as morning stars. The Greeks also recognized meteors and comets. They called the meteors "falling stars" because they believed that the sporadic streaks of light were stars falling from the sky. They called the comets "Kometes," which means "long-haired," because the comets' tails resembled long, flowing hair.

The ancient Greeks observed that the sun appeared to move eastward approximately one degree each day in relation to the stars to make one complete revolution around the sky every year, and to pass through the same constellation at the same time each year. They detected these motions when they observed the sun setting each evening with different stars in the background. They plotted its path, which they called the ecliptic, among the stars. The band of constellations through which the sun passed was called the zodiac (Fig. 1.5). The band is about 18° wide, and its center line is the ecliptic. Since the sun appears to move eastward in relation to the stars, the star sphere appears to move westward faster than the sun, which causes the stars to appear to rise and set about one degree of arc, or four minutes of time, later each day (Chapter 6.7).

The Greeks became the first scientific astronomers when they separated their preconceived ideas and religious beliefs from science. They were interested in finding the solution to the problem of the nature of the universe, and in their attempt to find it they applied reason and logic. Greek science, aided by geometry, became an intellectual discipline which attempted to coordinate and understand the basic facts that it discovered. Modern science had its inception in the Greek mind. The generalizations which they developed from daily experiences gave satisfactory explanations of many natural phenomena.

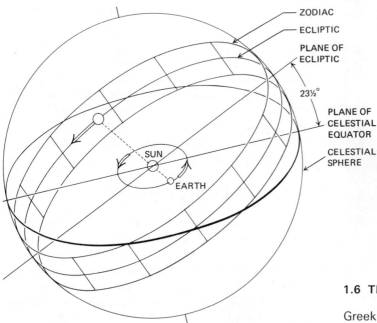

ZODIAC
ECLIPTIC
PLANE OF ECLIPTIC
23½°
PLANE OF CELESTIAL EQUATOR
CELESTIAL SPHERE
SUN
EARTH

Fig. 1.5 The celestial sphere. The celestial equator is a projection of the earth's equator; the ecliptic is the apparent path of the sun; and the zodiac is the band divided into 12 equal parts, each named after a constellation.

1.6 THE IONIAN SCHOOL

Greek astronomy comprised several schools of learning. The four most famous in early Greek history were the Ionian, Pythagorean, Academy, and Lyceum. The fifth great school flourished in the Hellenistic period at the Alexandrian Museum. Let us take a brief look at the philosophy and science of each of these great schools.

The Ionian school, whose science was developed around geometry, was founded by Thales of Miletus (about 624–547 B.C.). His place in the history of astronomy rests on his great achievement of predicting the total solar eclipse which occurred on May 28, 585 B.C. during the battle between the Medes and the Lydians. This was an astonishing feat because it was difficult to accurately predict the occurrence of a solar eclipse, since the available knowledge of eclipses failed to take into consideration the concept of parallax (Chapter 11.1).

Thales proposed a solution to the nature of the universe. He taught that water was the cause of all things in the universe; it was the primary element and

By permission of Johnny Hart and Field Enterprises, Inc.

motion, as pieces were being broken off to form the things in the universe. When the universe was formed, the "apeiron" separated into two parts, one consisting of hot particles and the other, cold. The cold particles became the earth, which was surrounded by the hot particles in the form of a sphere of flames. Eventually the flames were caught in a whirlpool of air which formed into circular tubes enclosing the flames and surrounding the earth. A hole in each tube permitted the flames to appear as the sun, moon, and stars. In this primitive theory, Anaximander attempted to explain that the revolution of the celestial bodies around the earth was produced by the rotation of the tubes and that eclipses occurred when the holes of the sun and moon were either partially or completely closed.

1.7 THE PYTHAGOREAN SCHOOL

Pythagoras was born in Samos about 560 B.C. He left Greece for political reasons and emigrated to the Italian peninsula where he established his school. Although the philosophy of the Pythagoreans was based on mysticism, they believed that knowledge was acquired through logical insight and that numbers were the substance of all things.

The astronomical philosophy of the Pythagoreans was established by three of its greatest members—Pythagoras, Philolaus, and Parmenides. They developed a geometrical concept of the universe which had ten concentric spheres (Fig. 1.6). The center of the universe was occupied by the central fire. The sun, moon, earth,

the source from which the three basic elements—air, earth, and fire—were derived. The tiny particles in each of these three basic elements combined in different ways to form all the things in the universe. His theory was based on the false assumption that water is the primary element and the false generalization that it is the source of all things. However, Thales was not altogether wrong, because his philosophy was based on the generalization that one substance was the building block for all the other substances.

Anaximander (about 611–546 B.C.), who was one of Thales' pupils, disagreed with his teacher about water being the primary element. He believed that all things in the universe were formed from an "infinite" mass, which he called the "apeiron." Although the "apeiron" was never defined, it was considered to be in continuous

Fig. 1.6 The Pythagorean concept of the universe consisted of ten concentric spheres. The center was occupied by the central fire. Each celestial body occupied its own sphere. The counter-earth always occupied a position between the earth and the central fire.

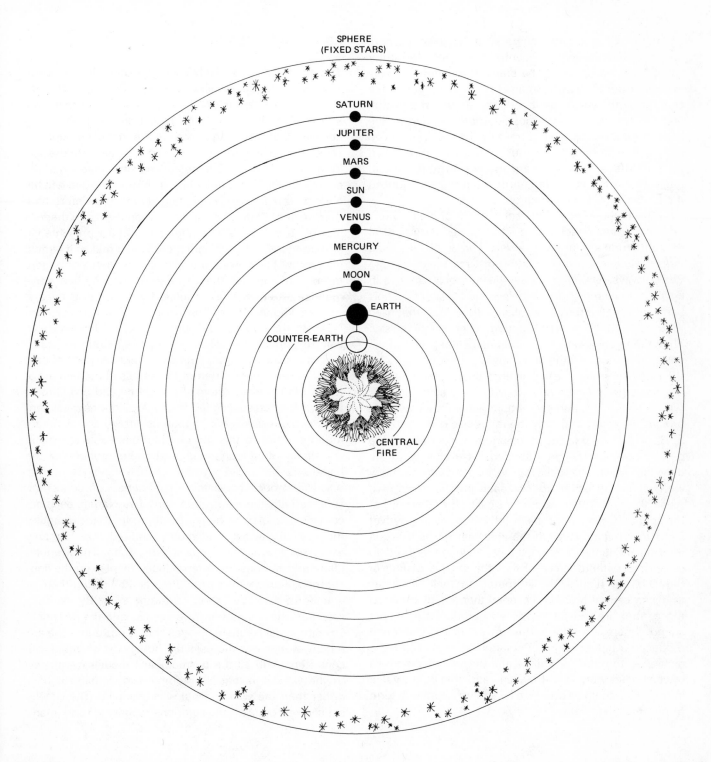

SPHERE
(FIXED STARS)

SATURN

JUPITER

MARS

SUN

VENUS

MERCURY

MOON

EARTH

COUNTER-EARTH

CENTRAL
FIRE

counter-earth, and five planets each occupied a sphere and revolved around the central fire. The fixed outer sphere was occupied by the stars. The central fire was invisible from the earth because of the presence of the counter-earth which, as it revolved around the central fire, always maintained a position between and in line with the earth and the central fire. The earth revolved around the central fire once every day and always had the same face turned toward the fire. With respect to the sun and the stars, the earth rotated and produced the intervals of day and night.

The Pythagorean spherical concept of the universe resulted from observations that gave astronomical thought a tremendous push forward. The Greeks observed that in Greece the constellation of Ursa Major the Big Bear always remained above the horizon, whereas in Egypt it appeared to move below the horizon for short periods of time. From these observations, they theorized that the earth is a spherical body floating within the sky. They then concluded that the fundamental shape of the celestial bodies and the sky itself is spherical.

When Pythagoras discovered that the strings of a lyre could produce the third, fourth, and the fifth octaves with ratios of $\frac{1}{2}$, $\frac{4}{3}$, and $\frac{3}{2}$ by subdivision with a moveable bridge he noted that only the four basic numbers of 1, 2, 3, and 4 occur in the ratios and that their sum is the perfect number 10. He extended his discovery to the universe which, he believed, is in complete harmony with all the celestial bodies, each producing its own musical sound. This concept was called the "harmony of the spheres" and was probably influenced by the myth of Orpheus, which conveyed the idea that music exerts a magical influence over all things. Pythagoras tried to prove (but without success) that the musical sounds of the celestial bodies are attributed to their distances from the central fire. He reasoned that a body closer to the central fire moved slowly and produced a deeper sound, whereas a body farther away moved faster and produced a higher sound. Pythagoras believed that the distances from the central fire and the sounds produced by the bodies were in arithmetical ratio, that is, any value in the series could be obtained by adding a common term to the preceding value.

1.8 THE ACADEMY

The Academy was established in Athens in the fourth century B.C. by the Greek philosopher Plato (about 428–348 B.C.), who as an idealist rejected the observational and experimental approach to astronomy because he believed that the world which we experience through our senses is an apparition and that the real world exists in the form of ideas. The objects of the visible world are simply copies of the real objects that have existed in the perfect state from the beginning of time. It is unfortunate that most of Plato's astronomical concepts and theories are found in his dialogue *Timaeus* and are presented in a literary style of poetic imagery which makes it almost impossible to translate into definite factual information. In spite of this, his theories and philosophy had a tremendous influence on scholars for nearly 2000 years.

As knowledge of the geography of the earth increased, the Pythagorean concept of the universe gave way to a theory proposed by Eudoxus (about 408–355 B.C.), a disciple of Plato, which is known as the "Spheres of Eudoxus." In his attempt to express in mathematical terms Plato's ideas about the motions and positions of the planets, he succeeded in developing a new concept which expressed the apparent irregular planetary motions. Prior to this, no one had been able to explain the direct, stationary, and retrograde motions of the planets.

His model consisted of a series of concentric spheres with the sun, moon, and five planets each occupying its own sphere. To reproduce the irregular motions of the sun and moon required three spheres each; for the planets, four spheres each. The irregular planetary motions were reproduced by placing the concentric spheres within each other and revolving them at a uniform rate, but about different axes. By carefully selecting the orientation of each axis and the rotational velocity of each sphere, he was able to reproduce the apparent motions of the celestial bodies. This model was consistent with all the cosmological models developed by the Greeks in that all attempted to explain the how rather than the why of what was observed. The Greeks simply reproduced the motions observed and made no attempt to reproduce the actual conditions. The "Spheres of Eudoxus" was modified and refined by Callipus (about 370–300 B.C.) and by Aristotle (about 384–322 B.C.) by adding more spheres to the celestial bodies.

1.9 THE LYCEUM

The Lyceum was established in Athens about 344 B.C. by Aristotle, the great logician and the most famous of all Greek philosophers. His greatest contribution to astronomy was his thorough and critical analysis of the concepts of previous philosophers and his presentation of personal views.

In opposition to Plato's beliefs, Aristotle accepted the validity of the senses. The observable phenomena constituted the real world, whereas ideas and concepts were merely the essence of the phenomena. Although Aristotle employed logic as his key analytical tool, he used the observable world as his starting point. He wrote that everything on the earth was made from the four basic elements—water, air, earth, and fire—and that all the celestial bodies, including space itself, were made from the fifth element, which he called the "Quintessence." The difference between the two is that the earth elements are continuously changing from one form into another; whereas the celestial element always remains unchanged and perfect. Aristotle rejected the Pythagorean concept of the universe and accepted that presented in the model of the "Spheres of Eudoxus." He also sensed that the earth was spherical and presented two evidences to prove it. The first was that the shape of the earth's shadow always appeared as an arc on the face of the moon during a lunar eclipse. This evidence was not accepted by some of the philosophers, because they reasoned that a cylindrical earth pointed toward the moon during an eclipse would also produce an arc on the moon's face. Although this was a possibility, Aristotle rejected it because a cylindrical earth would have to be fixed in its orientation in space to always produce an arc shadow. The second evidence was that the entire star sphere appeared to be displaced as the observer moved north or south on the earth's surface. An observer at a particular latitude could observe that the north pole star was at a certain height above the horizon and that when the observer moved to the north, the pole star would appear to move higher above the horizon. But when the observer moved to the south, the pole star appeared to move closer to the horizon. He reasoned that this could happen only on a spherical earth. He also believed that the earth was located in the center of the universe and that its distance was greater from the sun than from the moon. According to Aristotle, this had to be true because during a total solar eclipse, the moon completely obliterated the sun.

1.10 THE ALEXANDRIAN MUSEUM

During its later period Greek astronomy was centered in Alexandria, Egypt, which became the true center of western culture under the rule of several Greek Ptolemies. Many of the scholars of this period were members of the great school called the Alexandrian Museum. This school, with its famous library and observatory, reached its greatest heights in astronomy from 300 to 200 B.C. with such members as Aristarchus, Eratosthenes, and Hipparchus.

Aristarchus (about 300–250 B.C.) proposed the heliocentric theory of the universe, according to which the sun and the stars were considered to be fixed bodies, with the sun located in the center of the universe and the stars on the outer sphere. The earth and the planets revolved around the sun in circular orbits. The star sphere was at a tremendous distance from the earth, so great that as the earth revolved around the sun, it was impossible to observe any apparent motion in the stars. This amazingly accurate theory of the universe was proposed during the third century B.C. and was ignored by the scholars until the fifteenth century A.D.

Eratosthenes (about 276–194 B.C.), a Greek geographer and the third head of the Alexandrian Museum, was the first person to measure the circumference of the earth. He accomplished this feat by an ingenious method based on simple logic and a sound principle of geometry. On June 21, the first day of summer (summer solstice, Chapter 6.2), Eratosthenes observed in the town of

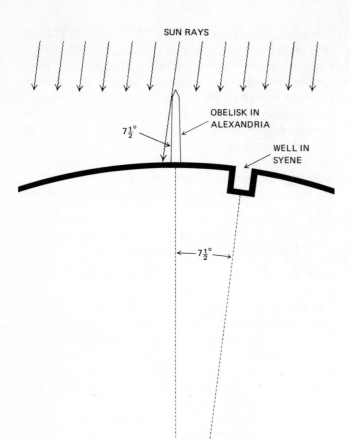

SUN RAYS

OBELISK IN
ALEXANDRIA

$7\frac{1}{2}°$

WELL IN
SYENE

$7\frac{1}{2}°$

EARTH'S
CENTER

Fig. 1.7 Eratosthenes' method of determining the circumference of the earth. The shadow angle produced by the obelisk at Alexandria is about 7−1/2°. The angle at the center of the earth is also 7−1/2° because when two parallel lines are cut by a straight line, the corresponding angles are equal. The distance between the two cities is about 5000 stadia. Since the shadow angle is about 1/48 of 360°, the distance between the two cities is 1/48 of the earth's circumference. Therefore, 48 times 5000 produces the circumference of the earth.

Syene, Egypt (the modern city of Aswân) that the noon sun appeared to be directly overhead, because its rays completely illuminated the entire floor of a deep, dry well (Fig. 1.7). On the same date in Alexandria, 5000 stadia to the north of Syene, the noon sun was not directly overhead, because objects in that city were casting shadows. He knew that the sun's distance from the earth was great; therefore, he reasoned correctly, the sun's rays reach the earth along parallel lines. He then measured the angle between an obelisk and its shadow and reasoned that its value of about $7\frac{1}{2}°$ was $\frac{1}{48}$ of a complete circle of 360° and equal to the angle at the earth's center which is subtended by the distance between Syene and Alexandria. Therefore, this distance was equal to $\frac{1}{48}$ of the earth's circumference. Multiplying the distance between the two cities by 48 produced the correct value within one percent of the earth's circumference. The error was introduced by three factors: the two cities do not lie on a north-south line; Syene is not exactly on the Tropic of Cancer, which means that

By permission of Johnny Hart and Field Enterprises, Inc.

the sun is not directly overhead on the first day of summer; and the *stadium*, the unit of distance that Eratosthenes used, was a rounded number which was determined by runners. Nevertheless, the measurement of the earth's circumference stands as a tremendous monument and triumph of logic and reason.

Hipparchus, who was born in Nicaea about 175 B.C., probably was the greatest astronomer of antiquity. He is credited with the development of the eccentrics and epicycles that were used in several models of the universe to reproduce the apparent motions of the celestial bodies. He accurately determined the length of the seasons, and from this he developed a chart which gave the position of the sun on the ecliptic for each day of the year. He compared the position of the important stars of his day with those recorded by astronomers during the preceding 150 years and made the startling discovery that the earth's axis is not fixed in space but precesses gradually (Chapter 6.3). With this discovery, he recognized the importance of old astronomical re-

cords and proceeded to compile an accurate catalog of the positions of nearly 1000 stars to be used by future astronomers. His work was justified when later astronomers, while using his catalog, made several important discoveries.

1.11 THE PTOLEMAIC SYSTEM

The last of the great Greek astronomers was Claudius Ptolemy, who lived in Alexandria about A.D. 150. His greatest contribution to astronomy was his famous book *Almagest*, in which he summarized the astronomical theories of his day and presented formally for the first time the earth-centered concept of the universe. This

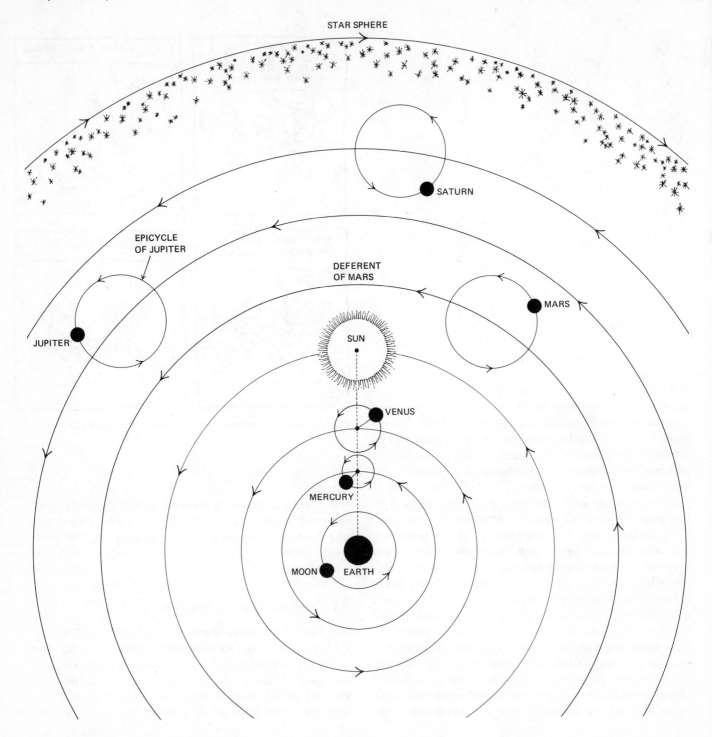

STAR SPHERE

SATURN

EPICYCLE
OF JUPITER

DEFERENT
OF MARS

MARS

JUPITER

SUN

VENUS

MERCURY

MOON   EARTH

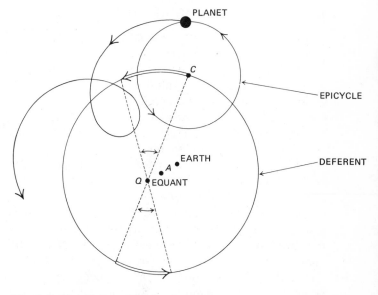

PLANET

C

EPICYCLE

EARTH
A
Q EQUANT

DEFERENT

Fig. 1.8 The Ptolemaic system of the universe. Each planet moves in an epicycle whose center revolves around the earth. The centers of the epicycles for Mercury and Venus are fixed in line with the sun and the earth, since these two bodies were always seen close to the sun.

Fig. 1.9 The Ptolemaic epicyclic system

concept is known as the Ptolemaic system. Since it did not originate with Ptolemy, he gave full credit to Hipparchus for the theoretical and observational information which served as the foundation for the theory—the idea that the earth is a sphere—and for providing the eccentric and epicycle theories.

According to the Ptolemaic system each planet moved in a circle (epicycle), the center of which moved around a stationary earth located in the center of the universe (Fig. 1.8). Since Mercury and Venus were always seen near the sun, Ptolemy placed the centers of their epicycles on a line between the earth and the sun, where they remained as the sun moved in its deferent. In developing this system, Ptolemy reasoned that if these bodies moved in circular orbits around the earth, an observer would always see them moving in one direction; this would not agree with the observed phenomenon because at times the planets appeared to move in the opposite direction. Therefore, to "save the phenomena," that is, to show geometrically the observed motions of the planets, Ptolemy had each planet move along the circumference of a small circle (epicycle) whose center (C) moved along the circumference of a larger circle (deferent) with its center at (A) (Fig. 1.9). The center of the epicycle moved at a uniform speed

around point (Q), called the equant, which was located on the opposite side of the deferent's center from the earth. The epicycle produced the retrograde motion and also accounted for minor observable variations in a planet's motion. Retrograde motion was produced when the planet was inside the deferent.

Ptolemy never claimed that his cosmological model described the actual conditions. It simply reproduced geometrically the observed motions of the celestial bodies and provided the means by which their positions could be easily predicted for any particular time. For over fourteen centuries, the *Almagest* was accepted as the prime source for knowledge of the theories of Greek astronomy and was used as the basis for all astronomical work. When the sun-centered theory was proposed by Copernicus in the sixteenth century, many astronomers continued to use the Ptolemaic system to predict the positions and motions of the planets because its intricate system of epicycles provided them with more accurate values.

1.12 ANCIENT MEXICAN ASTRONOMY

It is interesting to note that a great civilization flourished in Mexico in the western hemisphere and developed an extensive and most interesting astronomical knowledge. Although from our present information, this ancient civilization of Mexico exerted no influence on the development of astronomy because of its isolated geographical position, its astronomical achievements were so important that they deserve mention.

Evidence of the astronomical work pursued by the ancient Mexicans comes in the form of carvings on fragmentary rock slabs. From these we learn that they recognized star groupings which they associated with animals and objects in their religion. They also recognized the daily changing path of the sun in the sky and the apparent motion of the star sphere about the north celestial pole. Their main interest in the heavenly bodies appears to have centered on the sun, moon, and the planets, especially Venus and Mars.

The ancient Mexicans also developed several elaborate calendars. The one which they used for agricultural purposes had 365 days, and every fourth year had 366 days. The calendar which they used for astronomical purposes was most complex because it was based on the synodic periods of the moon and the planets.

1.13 MEDIEVAL ASTRONOMY

Let us take a brief look at the period between the introduction of the Ptolemaic system about A.D. 150 and the Copernican system in 1543. The Huns started their westward movement during the third century because of the great pressure that was applied from the East by the Chinese and the Mongols. As the Huns moved slowly westward during the next 200 years, they conquered and destroyed everything in their path. Their sacking of Rome in A.D. 455 marked the beginning of the slow decline of the Roman empire and the beginning of the rise of the Byzantine empire, which had been established by the Greek emperor Constantine when he moved the capital of the Roman empire to Constantinople. In 1453,

the Byzantine empire collapsed when the Turks captured Constantinople.

During the period from A.D. 400 to 1453 (which is known as the medieval period, or the Middle Ages), the acquisition of knowledge declined steadily because of the hostility that existed between the pagans and the Christians. Since the great schools in Greece and the Alexandrian Museum were pagan, they and their students were greatly resented by the newly converted Christians. In their enthusiasm for orthodoxy, these Christians destroyed many of the pagan institutions, such as the great library at Serapis, and burned many books which represented the heritage of Greek knowledge and culture.

With the medieval period in Europe, astronomy went into a state of dormancy. During these years, the Arabs became the trustees of Greek astronomical thought; many Greek treatises, the most important being Ptolemy's *Almagest*, were translated into Arabic. The Arabs invented our present, simplified number system and introduced the algebraic approach to the solution of scientific problems as opposed to the geometric approach of the Greeks. Arab science began to filter back into Europe through Spain in the tenth century.

REVIEW

1. Explain how primitive man established the cycle of the seasons.

2. Was there any astronomical significance attached in the building of the Egyptian pyramids? Explain.

3. What were the important precepts of astrology? What was the role of astrology in the development of astronomy?

4. For what purpose was astronomical knowledge used in the early cultures?

5. What was Thales' belief about the nature of the universe?

6. Who were the three greatest astronomers of the Pythagorean school of ancient Greece? Explain the theory which they developed to account for the motions of the heavenly bodies.

7. What was the significance of the "ecliptic," "zodiac," and "constellations" to the ancient Greeks?

8. Cite several reasons why the ancient Greek astronomers believed that the shape of the earth was spherical.

9. List the principal differences the ancients recognized between the planets and the stars.

10. If you were told that the earth is stationary in space and that the sun revolves around it, what one fact could you cite to prove that the statement is incorrect?

11. How did Aristotle defend his arguments against the heliocentric universe? Where did he err in his approach?

12. How did the early Greeks come to the conclusion that the sun moves about one degree to the east with respect to the stars every day?

13. Hipparchus is considered by many to be the greatest astronomer of the pre-Christian era. What were his major contributions to astronomy which gained him this acclaim?

14. What is meant by the retrograde motion of a planet? How did Ptolemy explain this phenomenon?

15. If the twelve zodiacal constellations are each 30° in length and the sun is just entering the constellation of Aries, in what constellation will the sun be in 50 days?

16. Explain how the ancients established the length of the year by observing the length of the shadow cast by a vertical stick and the shifting of the position at which the sun appeared to set.

2
Copernicus
to Einstein

Toward the end of the medieval period, there was an awakening in the pursuit of knowledge throughout Europe because an atmosphere was developing in which scholars were free to think without religious or political interference or control. This was a slow process which had developed from the failure of the crusades and the subsequent challenge to classical orthodoxy, from the translation of Arabic and Greek books into Latin, and from the founding and growth of secular universities. Modern astronomy had its birth during the sixteenth century when scholars began to think, question, and challenge the classical doctrines and principles of Aristotelian science.

It was in the early part of the sixteenth century that Nicolaus Copernicus proposed his heliocentric concept of the universe. Although this concept was essentially medieval, it served as the catalyst that began the movement away from Greek rationalism. His concept put a crack into the long sacrosanct Ptolemaic system. The rationalistic approach of the Greeks regarded mathematics and logic as the source of all knowledge and employed abstract reasoning in developing conceptual systems from simple observational material. For centuries, people believed that the earth-centered world (Ptolemaic system), the product of Greek science, was the only conceivable one, and this view was supported by the Church. The introduction of the heliocentric system shook the complacency of medieval dogma. Although the methods used by Copernicus were not revolutionary, they did infuse a new spirit and excitement into the developing science of astronomy.

2.1 THE COPERNICAN SYSTEM

Nicolaus Copernicus was born in Thorn, Poland in 1473. He was brought up by a wealthy uncle whose sole desire was to have him pursue an ecclesiastical career. Copernicus studied secular and ecclesiastical law and received a doctor's degree in canon law. While at the University of Cracow, his interest in mathematics and astronomy was kindled. When he attended the Universities of Bologna, Padua, and Ferrara in Italy, he studied and mastered Greek, read practically all the works of the Greek astronomers, and kept up with the theoretical and observational aspects of astronomy. From these pursuits, he gained the incentive to simplify the complicated Ptolemaic system.

Copernicus' greatest contribution to astronomy was his development of the heliocentric concept of the universe in which all planets, including the earth, revolved around the sun. Although this concept appeared in his book *On the Revolution of the Celestial Bodies* in 1543, the year of his death, his ideas on cosmology were already well known, since a letter written to a friend had been copied and widely circulated among interested people. About the end of the nineteenth century, two published copies of this letter, known as *The Commentariolus*, appeared which allowed scientists to reconstruct the original work. In this letter, Copernicus wrote that all the ancient concepts of the universe, which employed spheres and eccentric circles to explain the motions of the celestial bodies, failed to show the conditions as they existed. His system was simpler and closer to reality, for it was based on the assumptions that the earth rotates daily about its axis; that all celestial bodies have different centers; that the earth's center is not the center of the universe, but simply the center of the earth's and the moon's orbit; that all celestial bodies appear to revolve around the sun, which is at or near the center of the universe; and that a body closer to the sun travels at a greater orbital velocity than one farther away.

Ptolemy assumed that the sky revolved around a stationary earth because he believed that if the earth rotated about its axis it would be torn apart by the force produced by this motion. Copernicus disagreed with this conclusion because, he reasoned, if it were true, then the sky, which is a much larger body than the earth, should have been torn apart many years ago; he therefore concluded that it is the earth rather than the sky that rotates.

In spite of Copernicus' radical cosmological ideas, the Ptolemaic influence on him was great—to the extent that he conceded the celestial bodies as moving in epicycles. Copernicus' system and the Ptolemaic were identical except for two major differences: (1) Copernicus interchanged the positions of the sun and the earth and discarded the equant point; and (2) in order to account for the variations in the orbits of the celestial bodies and to approach reality more closely, he assumed that the planets move in thirty-four epicycles—seven for Mercury, five for Venus, three for Earth, five each for Mars, Jupiter, and Saturn, and four for the Moon.

2.2 THE RETROGRADE MOTION OF THE PLANETS

Ptolemy observed that constellations which appeared on the western and eastern horizons at the same time, reappeared later on the horizon in opposite directions. From this he concluded that the earth is at the center of the universe. Copernicus disagreed with this conclusion and assumed without proof that the earth revolves around the sun. This concept was first proposed by Aristarchus in the third century B.C. (Chapter 1.10).

Copernicus presented an esthetically simple explanation for the apparent looping of the planets in their motion through the sky. The actual motional direction of all planets around the sun, he reasoned, is always forward. When seen from the earth, they normally appear to move in an easterly direction in relation to the stars, a phenomenon called direct motion; however, they periodically appear to reverse their direction and to move westerly, that is, in retrograde motion. His explanation for retrograde motion was based on the planet's motion relative to the earth's and on the assumption that bodies closer to the sun travel at greater orbital velocities. For example, the earth, which is closer to the sun than Mars,

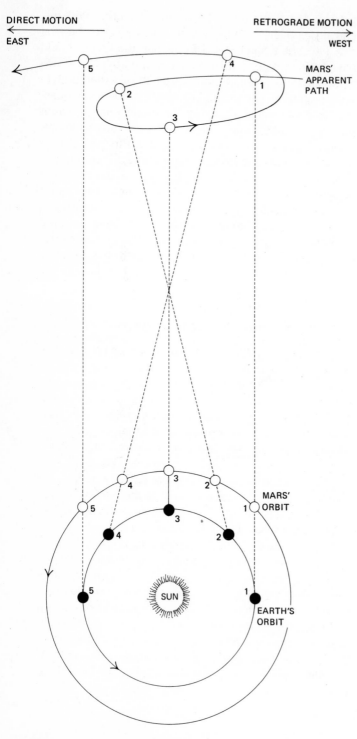

DIRECT MOTION ⟶

← EAST

RETROGRADE MOTION ⟶

WEST →

MARS'
APPARENT
PATH

MARS'
ORBIT

SUN

EARTH'S
ORBIT

Fig. 2.1 Retrograde motion of Mars. As the earth overtakes, passes, and moves away from Mars, Mars appears to slow down, stop, retrograde, stop, and resume its direct motion in relation to the stars in the background.

takes one year to complete one revolution around the sun, while Mars takes nearly two years.

In Fig. 2.1, the inner circle represents the earth's orbit; the outer circle, Mars' orbit; and the looped line, the apparent path of Mars as seen from the earth against the background of the stars. Periodically, the earth overtakes Mars, which appears to remain stationary. As the earth passes, Mars appears to move in a retrograde motion, and as the earth moves away Mars appears to stop again, then move in a direct motion. By assuming that the sun is at the center of the universe and the planets, including the earth, revolve around it, Copernicus was able to explain what had been a mystery to the ancient Greeks, the looping of the planets.

2.3 GIORDANO BRUNO

It was most unfortunate that the great work of Copernicus, *On the Revolution of the Celestial Bodies*, was too difficult for the average person to read and understand and was published at a time when its acceptance was almost impossible. One of Copernicus' champions was Giordano Bruno, a philosopher of great intellect, who firmly believed in the Copernican concept and extended it to include some of our present-day concepts of the universe. His mission in life appeared to be the presentation and defense of the Copernican system as well as his own cosmological ideas. He accomplished his mission by lecturing extensively and thus influencing many people throughout Europe.

By intuition and logical deduction, Bruno rejected the concept of a universe with a center. The universe, he felt, is an immense, limitless space in which all the celestial bodies move freely. He also considered the possibility that life inferior or superior to that on earth existed on these and other bodies. He maintained that the planets are cold bodies similar to the earth and that they shine by reflected sunlight. The stars, on the contrary, are very hot bodies and are visible because they give off their own light. The sun, which is but another star, is not located on the firmament, but is much closer to the earth than are the other stars. Also, the stars are at different and enormous distances from the earth—an idea which, for the first time, extended the concept of the universe beyond the star sphere to infinity. These ideas developed by Bruno were truly prophetic. For expressing them, the Inquisition found him guilty of heresy and burned him at the stake in Rome in 1600. Before he died, he said, "The time will come when all will see what I have seen."

2.4 TYCHO BRAHE

In 1546, three years after the death of Copernicus, Tycho Brahe was born. Of noble birth and in line to inherit wealth and property, he was brought up by a wealthy but childless uncle, although his parents were living. His uncle enrolled him in the Universities of Copenhagen and Leipzig where his education centered on languages and law. While Brahe was at the University of Copenhagen, a predicted solar eclipse occurred which changed the course of his life. He became intensely interested in mathematics and astronomy and devoted most of his time to acquiring as much knowledge as possible in these areas. His scientific pursuits were conducted without the permission of his uncle, who regarded such activities as hobbies for people of noble birth.

With the death of his uncle, Brahe was able to pursue his astronomical work without any interference. He built his first observatory in Augsburg, Germany and had skilled artisans construct the largest and finest instruments of his day—a quadrant to measure the altitude of celestial bodies and a sextant to measure the angle between the bodies. These were the same instruments used by the Greeks except that his measuring scales were more refined and accurate. With these instruments Brahe observed and measured the position of a brilliant object which appeared in the constellation of Cassiopeia the Queen on the evening of November 11, 1572. Since the object was clearly visible in the daytime and its position was accurately measurable, Brahe was able to prove that it was a new star. It is known today as "Tycho's star"; in actuality it is not a new star, but a supernova (Chapter 13.6).

King Frederick II of Denmark was so impressed with Brahe and his accomplishments that he invited him to teach mathematics and astronomy at the University of Copenhagen and later to be his court mathematician. Frederik presented Brahe with the island of Hven off the coast of Denmark, near Copenhagen, and provided him with money to build an observatory and an annual income to maintain it. On Hven, Brahe built Uraniborg, "The Castle of the Heavens," the finest observatory in the world. It was truly a castle fit for a king. Its elaborate facilities included an observatory with the most accurate instruments of his day, a machine shop, a laboratory for making glass, living quarters for himself, assistants, servants, and guests, and a jail. At Uraniborg Brahe spent fifteen years of his life, observing and measuring the positions of the celestial bodies. He used his fabulous equatorial armillary to measure with great accuracy the angles between the stars and to establish the first new star catalog since Hipparchus. He also secured the most extensive and accurate data on the motions and positions of the planets prior to the invention of the telescope. Brahe also calculated the error due to refraction of light by the earth's atmosphere and determined that the equinoxes annually precess about 51 seconds (Chapter 6.3). In 1577 Brahe observed the great comet and made it the subject of one of his books in which he proved that since the comet was much farther from the earth than the moon, it was therefore an astronomical rather than a meteorological phenomenon.

Brahe ruled Hven with a firm, harsh hand which was often quite ruthless. He made many enemies so that when Frederik II died, he was forced to abandon Urani-borg and leave Denmark. In 1599 he arrived in Prague at the invitation of his new patron, Emperor Rudolph II, to serve as his court mathematician. Two years after his arrival, Brahe died.

2.5 THE TYCHONIC SYSTEM OF THE UNIVERSE

Throughout his life, Brahe strongly believed that man's home, the earth, is at the center of the universe and that all bodies revolve around it. He could not accept the Copernican system, for he was never able to observe the parallax in any star, that is, its apparent motion in relation to the other stars in the background. In his attempt to make the Copernican system more compatible with his beliefs, Brahe devised a simple solution which preserved his own beliefs and still explained the looping of the planets (Fig. 2.2). The Tychonic system was a combination of the Ptolemaic and Copernican systems. At the center of the universe was the earth; the sun revolved around the earth, and the planets revolved around the sun. To account for the irregular motions of the planets, Brahe reasoned that the orbits of Mercury and Venus were very small, with radii less than the distance between the earth and the sun. The orbits of Mars, Jupiter, and Saturn, on the other hand, were very large, with radii greater than the distance between the earth and the sun.

2.6 JOHANNES KEPLER

Johannes Kepler was born on December 27, 1571, in Weil Der Stadt, Germany. His ambition was to become a Lutheran pastor; however, while attending the University of Tubingen, he came under the influence of Father Michael Mastlin, a professor of mathematics and astronomy, who provided him with the interest and motivation to abandon theology and pursue the study of astronomy. Mastlin taught that the Ptolemaic system was correct, but Kepler disagreed with him and assumed that the Copernican system was correct.

Later, when Kepler was teaching mathematics and astronomy at the boys' school at Graz, he recalled that Euclid's last book demonstrated that only five regular

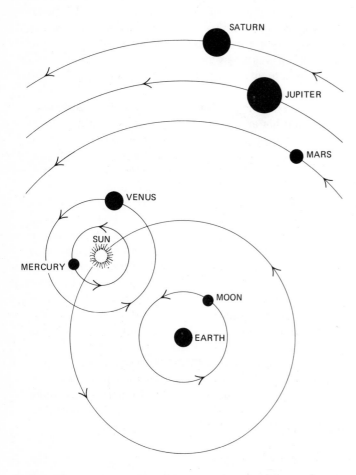

Fig. 2.2 The Tychonic system, a combination of the Ptolemaic and Copernican systems. The moon and the sun revolve around the earth; Mercury, Venus, Mars, Jupiter, and Saturn revolve around the sun.

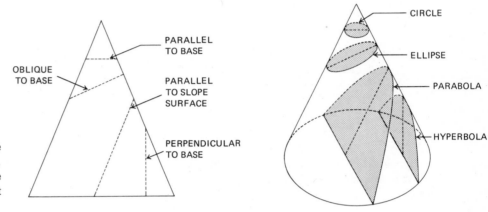

Fig. 2.3 Conic sections, the curves (circle, ellipse, parabola, and hyperbola) formed by the intersection of a plane and a right circular cone

shapes are possible—the cube, tetrahedron, octohedron, dodecahedron, and icosahedron. Kepler reasoned that if these shapes should fit between the spheres of the planets, then their relative distances from the sun could be easily calculated. The shape that fits between the spheres of two planets would establish the orbital limit of the inner planet. Thus, the orbital limit for Jupiter is established by the cube; for Mars, the tetrahedron; for Earth, the dodecahedron; for Venus, the icosahedron; and for Mercury, the octohedron. Kepler's findings were published in his first book, *Mysterium Cosmographicum.* Brahe was so impressed with the book's contents that he invited Kepler to join him in his work in Prague. In 1600, the year before Brahe's death, Kepler joined Brahe in Prague, and both worked on the *Rudolphian Tables*, which were completed and published in 1627. Based on the Copernican system and Kepler's three laws of planetary motion, these tables listed the orbital positions of the planets. The meeting of Brahe and

Kepler was of tremendous importance to astronomy; when Brahe died in 1601, he bequeathed his valuable cache of planetary data to Kepler, material which provided the foundation for Kepler's laws of planetary motion and ushered in the age of modern astronomy.

2.7 CONIC SECTIONS

Before we discuss Kepler's laws of planetary motion, let us take a look at the properties of conic sections—curves formed by the intersection of a plane and a right circular cone (Fig. 2.3). A plane parallel to the cone's base produces the intersection of a circle. If the intersection is a closed curve, a plane oblique to the cone's base produces an ellipse. A plane parallel to the slope surface of the cone produces a parabola, or a curve which is open at one end. A plane perpendicular to the cone's base produces another open-end curve, called a hyperbola.

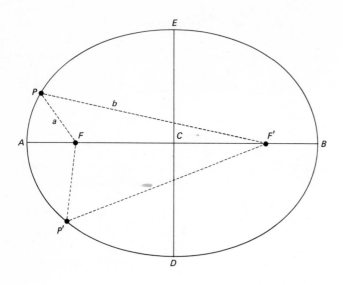

Fig. 2.4 The elements of an ellipse: major axis (*AB*), minor axis (*DE*), center of ellipse (*C*), and foci (*F* and *F'*). The sum of the distances of any point *P* on the ellipse to the two foci is always constant (*a* + *b* is constant). The eccentricity of the ellipse is *FF'/AB*.

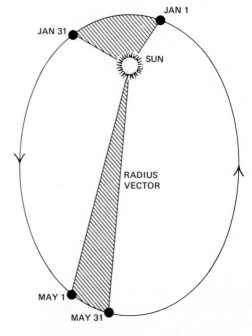

Fig. 2.6 The law of areas. The radius vector of a planet sweeps equal areas in space in equal intervals of time.

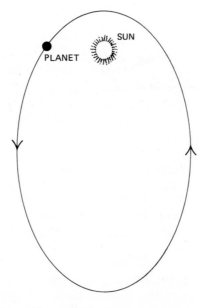

Fig. 2.5 The law of ellipses. The orbit of a planet is an ellipse with the sun at one of the foci.

The elements of an ellipse are the major axis, minor axis, center, and foci (Fig. 2.4). The maximum diameter (*AB*) is the major axis, the minimum diameter (*DE*) is the minor axis, the intersection of the two diameters (*C*) is the center, and the foci are the two fixed points (*F* and *F'*), located on the major axis. An important property of an ellipse is that from any point (*P*) on the ellipse, the sum of its distances to the foci (*a* + *b*) is constant. The shape of an ellipse is determined by the distance between the foci. As this distance increases, the shape of the ellipse becomes more elongated. When the foci coincide with the center, the curve is a circle. The eccentricity of a curve is defined as the ratio of the distance between the foci and the major axis—zero for a circle, one for a parabola, between zero and one for an ellipse, and greater than one for a hyperbola.

2.8 KEPLER'S LAWS OF PLANETARY MOTION

After more than five years of tedious work with Brahe's observational data on the positions of Mars, Kepler concluded that since the observational data could apply only to an elliptical orbit, the orbits of all planets are elliptical. It also became apparent to him that the orbital velocity of Mars is variable, that is, faster when nearest the sun. He therefore concluded that the orbital velocity of a planet depends on its distance from the sun.

In 1609 Kepler published his two basic laws of planetary motion in his book *Commentaries on the Motions of Mars*. The first law, known as the law of ellipses, states that the orbit of a planet is an ellipse with the sun at one of the foci (Fig. 2.5). The second law, known as the law of areas, states that the radius vector, the straight line which joins the sun and the planet, sweeps equal areas in space in equal intervals of time. This means that as the planet moves in its orbit, the area produced by its radius vector is proportional to the time. In Fig. 2.6, the time intervals and the areas are equal; therefore, the orbital velocity of the planet is greatest when it is nearest the sun.

Kepler's third law of planetary motion was published in his book *The Harmony of the World*. He believed that a divine harmonic relationship existed between the minimum and maximum velocities of the planets, which he demonstrated by a mathematical relationship between the planet's period of revolution and its distance from the sun. He assumed that the earth's period of revolution is one year; therefore, the periods for all the planets are 0.24, 0.62, 1.00, 1.88, 11.86, and 29.46. He assumed that the earth's distance from the sun is one unit; therefore, the distances for all the planets are 0.39, 0.72, 1.00, 1.52, 5.20, and 9.54. By squaring the period and cubing the distance, Kepler established his third law, the harmonic law, which states that the square of the sidereal period of a planet is directly proportional to the cube of its mean distance from the sun.

The sidereal period is the true period of revolution about the sun with respect to a fixed star or as seen by a hypothetical observer on the sun. The harmonic law is expressed by the formula

$$P^2 = ka^3,$$

where (*P*) is the sidereal period in years, (*a*) is the mean distance from the sun in astronomical units, and (*k*) is the constant of variation whose value varies with the type of unit used. Since the earth's mean distance from the sun is one astronomical unit and its sidereal period is one year, when a planet's period and distance are compared to the earth's, the proportion is reduced to the simple relationship of

$$P^2 = a^3.$$

A planet's sidereal period, or distance from the sun, may be determined from this relationship. For example, what is the sidereal period of a planet when its mean distance is four astronomical units?

$$P^2 = a^3$$
$$P^2 = (4)^3 = 64$$
$$P = 8 \text{ years.}$$

Kepler's third law is empirical because its distance and periods were obtained by proportion rather than by actual measurements. The complete relationship and proof were developed later by Newton (Chapter 2.15).

2.9 GALILEO GALILEI

Galileo Galilei was born in Pisa, Italy, on February 15, 1564. At the age of 16, he enrolled at the University of Pisa to obtain a medical degree. He left the university without a degree because his primary interest was in mathematics. About six years later, he returned to the University of Pisa as a professor of mathematics; at the age of 28, he was appointed professor of mathematics at the University of Padua, where he remained for the next 18 years.

In 1610 Galileo published his book *Sidereus Nuncius*, in which he reported the important astronomical observations and discoveries that he had made with the use of his new telescopes. He was the first man to observe the surface features of a celestial body. He saw the mountains, valleys, and craters on the moon's surface and calculated from the length of the shadows they cast that its mountains were much higher than those on the earth. He observed the "rings" around Saturn as two small fixed disks on either side of the planet because, unfortunately, his telescope was not able to resolve them. He was amazed to discover the presence of many dim stars within the Milky Way and to realize that the light from these stars produced the Milky Way. When he observed the image of the sun projected on a white paper, he recognized that the sunspots varied in number and location over a period of time. He also recognized that the sunspots move across the sun's image, disappear behind its limb, and then reappear from behind the other limb. From this observation he concluded that the sun rotates about its axis. His discoveries of the four satellites revolving around Jupiter, which revealed the presence of a miniature solar system in the universe, and the phases of Venus, which could happen only if the planet revolves around the sun, convinced him beyond the shadow of a doubt that the Copernican model of the universe was correct. Prior to these observations, Galileo had been an advocate of the Ptolemaic system.

In 1632 Galileo published *Dialogue Concerning The Two Chief World Systems*, a book in which he presented the Ptolemaic and the Copernican systems as hypotheses. The book was published under the auspices of the Catholic Church. Moreover, the material was given the form of a dialogue among three people, one of whom represented Galileo's own views on cosmology. In spite of these precautions, the book brought him into direct conflict with the Catholic Church and almost immediately after its publication, the Sacred Congregation of the Index placed the book on the forbidden list. It was kept there until 1835.

Galileo was tried under the Inquisition, found guilty of heresy, and prohibited from doing anything further in astronomy. Under the circumstances, the sentence was relatively light. He was not imprisoned but was allowed to return to his villa near Florence. Moreover, he was allowed to continue his scientific studies. In 1636 the results of his labor appeared in the book entitled *Discourse and Mathematical Demonstrations Concerning Two New Sciences*, in which he defined velocity, uniform and accelerated motions in terms of his own experimental evidence, and refuted the Aristotelian mechanics by demonstrating experimentally that it failed to explain the observable phenomena. To acquire this knowledge, Galileo developed and used the quantitative experimental method, one of his major contributions to science.

Galileo's heresy trial raised many interesting questions. His troubles appear to have been caused by his own actions. Pope Urban VIII was upset with Galileo's subterfuge in obtaining permission to publish his treatise from the Florentine inquisitor after he had been requested to make certain changes. The Pope, it was also rumored, felt that Simplicius, the bumbling character Galileo created to espouse the Ptolemaic system, was a caricature of himself. Even with these considerations in mind, the basic question remains: does a society have the right to restrict the free flow of ideas? Such restrictions in the field of science can set back progress of knowledge for years.

2.10 ISAAC NEWTON

Isaac Newton was born on a farm at Woolsthorpe, near Grantham, England, on December 25, 1642, the year of Galileo's death. His mother wanted him to become a farmer, but his ability in mathematics and mechanics gave him the opportunity to attend Trinity College, where he received his bachelor of arts degree and was elected a fellow of the college. When the Great Plague of 1665 closed Trinity College, Newton was forced to return to his farm for two years, a move which proved the most productive of his life. It was during this period that he developed the binomial theorem, invented the calculus, and laid the foundation for his discoveries in light and optics.

At the age of 26, Newton was appointed the Lucasian Professor of Mathematics at Trinity College, and a year later, in 1668, he invented the reflecting telescope. Although this was a remarkable instrument, it produced a faint image with colored streaks in it. In his unsuccessful attempt to solve this problem, he discovered the spectrum of light (Chapter 3.3). In 1672, when Newton was appointed a fellow to the Royal Society, he read a paper explaining the construction of the reflecting telescope and the work that he had completed on light and optics. The resulting controversy over its contents caused Newton to lose his interest in science, which was revived several years later and resulted in his monumental *Principia*, in which he organized the research he had performed and recorded over a period of 20 years on the motions of bodies.

To understand the motions of the celestial bodies, we must consider how motion is produced, maintained, and changed. Newton's treatment of motion appeared in the *Principia*, which was published in 1687. In formulating his three laws of motion and the universal law of gravitation, Newton took into account Kepler's three laws of planetary motion, Galileo's law of inertia (which states that a body at rest will remain at rest unless it is acted upon by an external force), and Galileo's idea that all bodies fall at the same rate regardless of size.

To understand motion, we must first define the following basic concepts. The volume of a body is a measure of the physical space that it occupies, and the mass is the amount of matter it contains. The mass of a body remains constant whether it is on the earth, in space, or on the moon and can be changed only by adding matter to it or subtracting matter from it. The amount of mass contained in a given volume is the density of the body and is expressed as mass per unit volume.

Every material body has the fundamental property of resisting a change in its state of motion, that is, a body at rest resists being set in motion, and a body in motion resists being stopped. Although inertia is usually used as a synonym for momentum, it is also identified with mass —the extent to which a body has inertia is the extent to which the body has mass; therefore, the mass of a body can be measured by its inertia.

The most important characteristic of a moving body is its speed, the ratio of distance to time, which may be expressed as average, constant, or instantaneous. Average speed is the ratio of the total distance to the total time. Constant speed is the ratio of equal distances to equal intervals of time. Instantaneous speed is speed at any instant of time, such as that recorded by the speedometer of an automobile. The velocity of a body is not its speed, but rather speed in a given direction. One-thousand miles per hour (1600 km) represents the speed of a body, whereas 1000 miles per hour in a southeasterly direction represents its velocity. Any change in the velocity, e.g., when a body stops or starts, increases or decreases its speed, or changes its direction, is called acceleration and is expressed in miles (or kilometers) per hour per second.

2.11 NEWTON'S FIRST LAW OF MOTION

The basic property of a material body to resist any change in its state of motion (if it is at rest, it remains so indefinitely; if it is in motion, it continues in motion in one direction at uniform velocity unless a force alters its state of motion) was formulated by Newton in his first law of motion. This law, known as the law of inertia, states that "every body tends to remain at rest or in motion with uniform velocity in a straight line unless it is acted upon by an external force." Since mass is inertia, an increase in a body's mass produces an increase in its inertia. For example, an empty, stationary truck requires a certain force to start it moving; however, when the truck is loaded and its mass and inertia have been increased, more force is required to change its state of rest.

2.12 NEWTON'S SECOND LAW OF MOTION

The second law of motion, known as the law of force and acceleration, states that "if a force acts upon a body, the body accelerates in the direction of the force." For example, a space ship which is moving at a uniform speed will accelerate when one of its rocket engines is ignited. Since acceleration has been defined as an increase or decrease in speed or a change in the direction of motion, a force can be defined as anything that accelerates a body. The degree of acceleration depends on the mass of the body and the force applied. When the force is increased, the acceleration is increased; when the mass is increased, the acceleration is decreased. Therefore, acceleration of a body varies directly as the force applied and inversely as the mass of the body. Force is expressed as the product of the mass of the body and its acceleration: force = mass × acceleration.

2.13 NEWTON'S THIRD LAW OF MOTION

Although the first two laws of motion involve only the force that acts on a single body, in actual practice the force involves the interaction of two bodies. Newton's third law of motion, known as the law of reacting forces, states that "for every force that acts on a body, there is a second force equal in magnitude but opposite in direction that acts on another body." The acting force is exerted by the first body on the second body, and the reacting force is exerted by the second body on the first. Although these forces are equal in magnitude, they are opposite in direction and can never neutralize each other because they act on two different bodies. A well-known example of action and reaction occurs when a man steps from a small boat to a dock. The force that he exerts on the boat (acting force) causes the boat to move away from the dock. The boat exerts a force equal in magnitude and opposite in direction (reacting force) on the man, causing him to move toward the dock.

From Newton's laws of motion, we derive the concept of momentum. A body's momentum is a measure of its inertia and is expressed as the product of the body's mass and velocity: momentum = mass × velocity.

By permission of Johnny Hart and Field Enterprises, Inc.

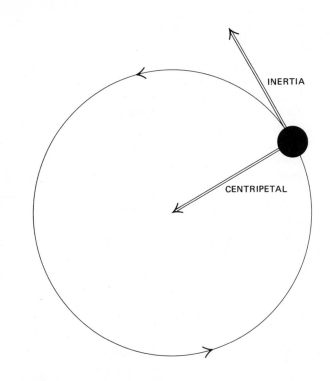

INERTIA

CENTRIPETAL

Fig. 2.7 A body in circular motion. Inertia moves a body in a straight line. Centripetal force acts toward the center, producing the acceleration which moves the body in circular motion.

2.15 NEWTON'S UNIVERSAL LAW OF GRAVITATION

Through ingenious geometrical proofs, Newton deducted from Kepler's three laws of planetary motion and the centripetal force formula a great deal more information about the forces which act on the planets. From Kepler's laws, he deduced that an attractive force exists between the sun and a planet which acts entirely in the plane of the planet's orbit and along the straight line which connects the two bodies. This force is proportional to the product of their masses and inversely proportional to the square of the distance between their centers. Although Newton's inquiry was limited to the solar system, he concluded that this force is universal. Therefore, he made his famous generalization that every mass attracts every other mass by a force which he called gravity. He stated this generalization formally in his universal law of gravitation: "Every particle in the universe attracts every other particle with a force that is directly proportional to the product of the masses of the two particles and inversely proportional to the square of the distance between them." He expressed this relationship by the formula

$$F = G(Mm)/d^2,$$

where F is the gravitational force between the two bodies, G is the gravitational constant, M and m are the masses of the two bodies, and d is the distance between their centers.

2.14 CIRCULAR MOTION

If a body moves in a circular path at constant speed, it must continuously accelerate toward the center of the circular path. The force that produces this acceleration is centripetal and acts toward the center of the path (Fig. 2.7). When the centripetal force is removed, the body tends to move in a straight line tangent to its circular path because of its inertia. This is illustrated when water flys off tangent from a rotating wheel.

For the sun and a planet, the centripetal force is the net force between the two bodies. Determined independently by both the Dutch physicist Christian Huygens and Isaac Newton, centripetal force is expressed by the formula

$$F = (MV^2)/R.$$

The centripetal force varies directly as the product of the mass and the square of the velocity and inversely as the radius of the circular path.

In confirming Kepler's third law of planetary motion,

$$P^2 = ka^3,$$

Newton restated it more precisely to include the masses of the bodies. For example, the product of the total mass of two mutually revolving bodies, such as the planet Mars and its satellite, Deimos, and their period of revolution is proportional to the cube of the mean distance between them. He expressed this relationship by the formula

$$(M + m)P^2 = Ka^3,$$

where $(M + m)$ represents the total mass of Mars and its satellite, a is the satellite's distance from Mars, P is the satellite's sidereal period, and K is the constant. When Mars is compared to the earth, and its satellite's distance and sidereal period are expressed in terms of the moon's mean distance from the earth and its sidereal period, the mass of Mars can be determined in terms of the earth's mass (Chapter 8.2). This is possible when we assume that the mass of a body is considerably greater than that of its satellite.

2.16 WEIGHT

Although they are two different things, mass and weight are often confused. The terms can, however, be used interchangeably without introducing a serious error as long as the body to which they refer remains on the earth. However, when the body leaves the earth, the terms cannot be used interchangeably. The weight of a body is a measure of the force of gravity exerted by the earth on the body. According to Newton's second law of motion, when a force F is exerted on a body of mass m, the body will accelerate according to the relationship $F = ma$. When a body of mass m falls freely on the earth with a constant accleration of g (32 feet, or 9.75 meters, per sec^2), the force exerted by gravity on the body is its weight and may be expressed by the relationship $W = mg$. Since this force decreases as the distance from the center of the earth increases, the weight of a body decreases as its distance from the center of the earth increases.

2.17 EINSTEIN'S THEORY OF RELATIVITY

Until the twentieth century, it was believed that Newton's laws of motion and gravitation applied to all natural phenomena. In Newtonian mechanics, the universe was considered to be permeated with an invisible medium through which the celestial bodies moved, and the immovable space was used as a fixed reference. This medium was also used in the propagation of light, and it was called the luminiferous ether. The ether was accepted as a fact even though it was impossible to prove or disprove its existence in space. It is interesting to note that the nineteenth century Scottish physicist James C. Maxwell, who philosophically accepted the existence of a substance in space because he could not get himself to accept the fact that there could be waves without a medium, formulated his electromagnetic theory without any reference to the ether (Chapter 3.1).

In 1887 A. Michelson and E. Morely conducted a very simple experiment to discover if a medium existed. Their specific problem was to determine whether the earth was at rest or moving in space. If a medium existed, there would be a recordable difference in the velocity of light moving toward the earth and away from it. This difference would be equal to the velocity of the earth in space. To accomplish this, they accepted that the velocity of light is 186,284 miles per second (299,787 km/second), and that the earth's orbital velocity is 20 miles per second (32 km). Then, they reasoned that light which travels in the same direction as the earth would have a velocity of 186,264 miles per second (299,755 km/second); in the opposite directions its velocity would be 186,304 miles per second (299,819 km/second). To detect these small differences, they constructed an instrument which they called the interferometer.

The results of their experiment were astounding. No apparent motion of the earth through space was discernible. Although the experiment has been repeated many times, no one has been able to detect the presence of a medium in space. Many explanations for the negative results of the Michelson-Morley experiment have been presented in an attempt to preserve the existence of the ether. According to one such explanation, when a body

Plate 6 (left) The earth as seen by the Apollo 10 astronauts at a distance of one-quarter million miles. The west coast of North America is clearly visible through a break in the cloud cover which appears to obscure the rest of the earth's land masses. (NASA photograph)

Plate 7 (above) The rising earth as seen by the Apollo 8 astronauts about 5° above the lunar horizon. The earth is 240,000 miles away, and its sunset terminator appears to bisect Africa. (NASA photograph)

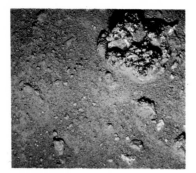 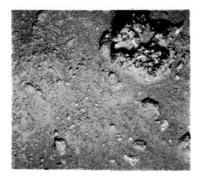

These stereo photographs were intended to be viewed through a stereo comparator, which re-creates the original depth of the subject. To achieve this three-dimensional effect, view the stereo pair through two identical low-power magnifying lenses spaced about 2¾ inches apart.

Plate 8 (top) An Apollo 12 stereo photograph of a lunar rock taken at a distance of nine inches. Image scale is one-half actual size, and details are as small as 40 microns. (NASA photograph)

Plate 9 (bottom) An Apollo 11 stereo photograph of a three-inch square clump of undisturbed lunar surface powder shows in fine detail many small pieces of different colors and small, shiny, spherical particles. (NASA photograph)

Plate 10 (right) Oblique view of the lunar far side photographed from Apollo 11. The large crater is the 50-mile diameter International Astronomical Union #308. The lunar far side appears to be more rugged, with fewer and smaller maria. (NASA photograph)

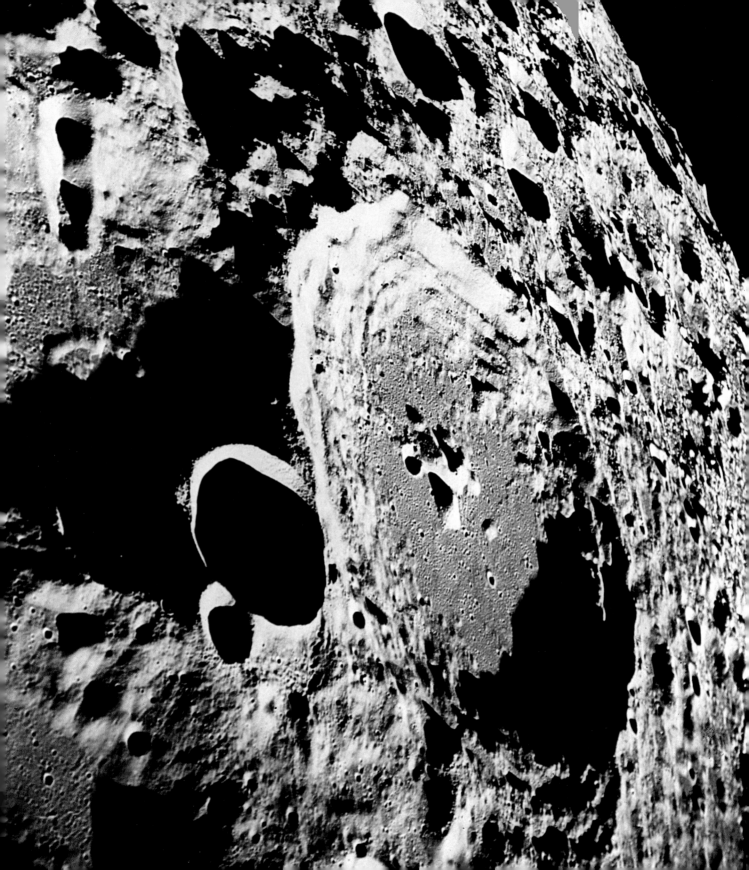

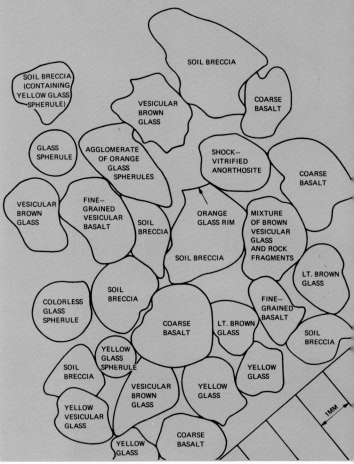

SOIL BRECCIA
(CONTAINING
YELLOW GLASS
SPHERULE)

SOIL BRECCIA

VESICULAR
BROWN
GLASS

COARSE
BASALT

GLASS
SPHERULE

AGGLOMERATE
OF ORANGE
GLASS
SPHERULES

SHOCK—
VITRIFIED
ANORTHOSITE

COARSE
BASALT

VESICULAR
BROWN
GLASS

FINE—
GRAINED
VESICULAR
BASALT

SOIL
BRECCIA

ORANGE
GLASS RIM

MIXTURE
OF BROWN
VESICULAR
GLASS
AND ROCK
FRAGMENTS

SOIL BRECCIA

LT. BROWN
GLASS

COLORLESS
GLASS
SPHERULE

SOIL
BRECCIA

COARSE
BASALT

LT. BROWN
GLASS

FINE—
GRAINED
BASALT

SOIL
BRECCIA

SOIL
BRECCIA

YELLOW
GLASS
SPHERULE

VESICULAR
BROWN
GLASS

YELLOW
GLASS

YELLOW
GLASS

1MM

YELLOW
VESICULAR
GLASS

YELLOW
GLASS

COARSE
BASALT

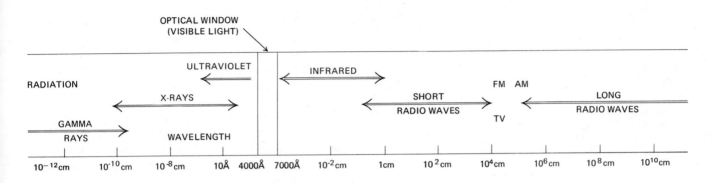

Fig. 3.2 The electromagnetic spectrum. The wavelength of visible light determines its color—4000Å is violet, and 7000Å is red.

length and frequency, and the energy of a photon is inversely proportional to its wavelength, then energy of a photon of visible light in the violet range is greater than in the red range because of its shorter wavelength.

3.2 THE INVERSE SQUARE LAW

Intuitively, one can easily recognize that the amount of light received by an object decreases as its distance from the light source is increased (Fig. 3.3). This important property in the propagation of light is indicated by the inverse square law, which states that the amount of light decreases as the square of the distance. For example, when a telescope receives a certain amount of light from a light source which is one unit distance away, it receives only $\frac{1}{4}$ the amount of light when the distance is doubled, $\frac{1}{9}$ when the distance is tripled, and $\frac{1}{16}$ when quadrupled.

3.3 THE PROPERTIES OF LIGHT

The properties of light that are basic in the design and construction of astronomical instruments are reflection, refraction, and dispersion.

Objects become visible when light from them is reflected to our eyes. When a ray of light strikes a rough surface it is reflected in all directions, and when it strikes

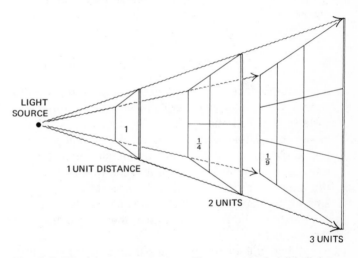

Fig. 3.3 The inverse square law. The amount of visible light that passes through a unit area decreases with the square of its distance from the light source.

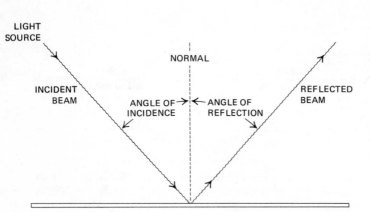

Fig. 3.4 Reflection of light. When light is reflected from a smooth surface, the angle of incidence equals the angle of reflection of light, and both beams lie in the same plane with the normal.

a smooth surface it is reflected in a single direction. As shown in Fig. 3.4, the perpendicular to the reflecting surface is called the normal. The angle between the incoming ray (incident beam) and the normal is called the angle of incidence, and the angle between the reflected ray (reflected beam) and the normal is called the angle of reflection. When light is reflected from a smooth surface, the angle of incidence equals the angle of reflection, and both beams lie in the same plane with the normal.

When a light beam passes from one medium into another of different density, it is refracted (bent). The refraction is toward the normal when the second medium is more dense than the first, and away from the normal when the second medium is less dense than the first. As shown in Fig. 3.5, a light beam which passes from air into glass is refracted toward the normal because the glass is the denser medium; when it passes from glass to air, it is refracted away from the normal. Another way of stating this property is that when a light

beam passes from one medium into another of different density, the angle it makes with the normal is always less in the medium of the higher density.

When Newton invented the reflecting telescope, colored streaks were observed in the images formed by it. In his attempt to eliminate them, he observed that when visible light passes from one medium into another, such as air into glass, it disperses into its component colors (wavelengths)—red, orange, yellow, green, blue, and violet; he concluded, therefore, that color is a basic property of light.

Visible light is a mixture of the wavelengths in the visible range of the electromagnetic spectrum. In a vacuum, their velocities are uniform, while in a medium, they are different. Therefore, when a beam of visible light passes through a material substance, it is dispersed into its component wavelengths. When it passes through a prism, as shown in Fig. 3.6, its component wave-

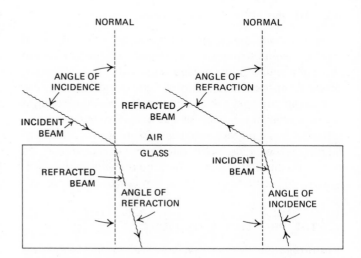

Fig. 3.5 Refraction of light. When a light beam passes from one medium into another of different density, the angle that it makes with the normal is always less in the medium of the higher density.

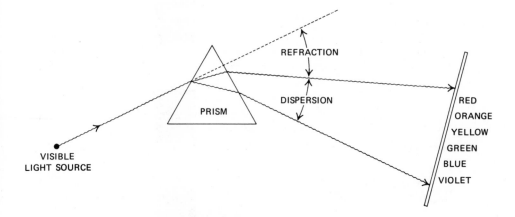

Fig. 3.6 The spectrum. When a beam of visible light passes through a prism, its component wavelengths are refracted differently. When the dispersed light beam is focused on a screen, it produces the colors of the different wavelengths.

lengths are refracted differently so that when the beam emerges from the prism, it is dispersed in a fan-shaped beam; when focused on a screen, the colors of the different wavelengths are arranged in the order of their frequencies from red to violet. This display of colors is called the spectrum. Spectroscopy, the study and analysis of spectra, provides very important data about the celestial bodies—their chemical composition, temperature, pressure, radial velocity, and rotation.

3.4 SPECTRA

With the invention of the spectrograph (Chapter 4.16), it was learned that spectra differ in their general appearance. They could be a continuous band of different colors (continuous spectrum), a series of bright-colored lines (discontinuous, or bright-line, spectrum), or a continuous spectrum with fine, dark lines superimposed on it (absorption spectrum).

The continuous spectrum (Plate 1[1]), which shows that all visible wavelengths are present, is produced by an incandescent body under high pressure. The electrons in the atoms are continuously interacting with one another to produce the blending of the colors of all wavelengths.

The bright-line spectrum (Plate 2), which shows only a few bright lines, is produced by a rarefied gas under low pressure. Since the atoms are relatively far apart and the electrons are free to move in their usual orbits, its spectrum displays their discrete characteristic lines.

The absorption spectrum (Plate 3), is produced when light from a continuous-spectrum source passes through a cooler gas that is under low pressure. The continuous spectrum is produced by the light source, and the dark lines are produced by the energy absorbed from

---

[1]Color plates 1–14 appear following p. 32.

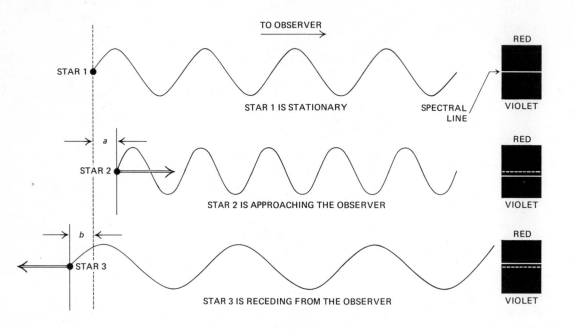

Fig. 3.7 The Doppler effect. When a star is stationary, its light waves reach the observer at normal frequency. When the star is approaching the observer, the wavelength is decreased because during the emission of one wavelength, the star has moved the distance *a*. Since the wavelength has been decreased, the spectral line shifts toward the violet. When the star is receding from the observer, the wavelength is increased because during the emission of one wavelength, the star has moved the distance *b* away from the observer. Since the wavelength has been increased, the spectral line shifts toward the red.

the light source by the cooler gas. Each dark line occupies the exact position of the bright-line spectrum which would be produced if the cooler gas alone was heated to incandescence and emitted its own radiation.

3.5 THE DOPPLER EFFECT

Christian Doppler, the Austrian physicist, demonstrated in 1842 that the frequency of sound increases as its source approaches the observer and decreases as it recedes. As it approaches and passes an observer, the rise and fall of the pitch of a locomotive's whistle is evidence of this phenomenon, which is called the Doppler effect. This occurs when the source of the sound, the observer, or both are in motion.

The Doppler effect also applies to light. In Fig. 3.7, the observer is stationary in all three views; the star is stationary in the top view, approaching the observer in the middle view, and receding from the observer in the bottom view. When the star is stationary, its light waves reach the observer at normal frequency. As the star approaches the observer, the wavelengths are shortened and the frequency is increased, that is, more waves reach the observer in a given interval of time. This effect is indicated by a shift of the spectral lines toward the violet end of the spectrum. The reverse is true when the star is moving away from the observer—the wavelengths are increased, the frequency decreased, and the effect indicated by a shift of the spectral lines toward the red end of the spectrum. Both the shift of the spectral lines and the rate at which the body is approaching, receding, or rotating about its axis can be established by photographing on the same plate and comparing the spectrum of the body with the spectrum of vaporized iron whose spectral lines have been accurately measured.

3.6 THE BLACK BODY

A radiating body would eventually deplete its energy and reach a temperature of absolute zero if it were unable to absorb energy from outside sources. Actually, in the surrounding region there are hotter bodies that are radiating energy as well as cooler bodies that are absorbing energy; therefore, a body will absorb energy if it is cooler than the surrounding region and will radiate energy if it is hotter. All bodies are radiators as well as absorbers, and a good radiator is also a good absorber. The so-called black body absorbs all the radiation that falls on its surface. Although there is no such body, a familiar approximation is a cavity hollowed out of a piece of charcoal. Since stars radiate energy in all wavelengths and behave almost like black bodies, a quantitative analysis of a black body can furnish important information about the stars' emission and absorption of radiation.

3.7 THE ENERGY DISTRIBUTION CHART

When heated, a black body emits energy in all wavelengths. The distribution of its energy at any particular temperature can be indicated by a smooth, solid curve on an energy distribution chart, where energy is plotted against wavelength. In Fig. 3.8, the relative intensity of the energy emitted over the entire electromagnetic radiation range is shown for three temperatures. The

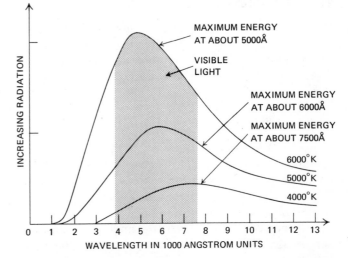

Fig. 3.8 The energy distribution chart of a perfect radiator (black body) shows energy emitted at three different temperatures. An increase in temperature increases the total radiation (represented by the area under the curve) and shifts the wavelength of maximum radiation (represented by the peak of the curve) toward the shorter wavelengths. The area under the curve represents the total energy emitted by a black body every second from one square centimeter of its surface.

maximum height of a curve represents the wavelength at which maximum energy is radiated. A black body at a temperature of 6000°K radiates its maximum energy at about 5000Å. When the temperature is increased, the energy emitted is increased in all wavelengths, and the maximum energy occurs progressively at the shorter wavelengths. This principle is illustrated by a burning log. At a low temperature, the log's general color is reddish because its maximum energy is emitted in the long red wavelengths. As the temperature increases, the log's general color changes progressively through orange, yellow, and finally bluish as the maximum energy emitted at each higher temperature shifts toward the shorter wavelengths.

3.8 THE RADIATION LAWS

The wavelength of the maximum energy radiated by a black body at a given temperature is the wavelength of the maximum height of the curve on the distribution chart. This value can also be obtained from the relationship

$$\lambda_{max} = 0.2897/T,$$

known as Wien's law, where (λ) is the wavelength in centimeters and (T) is the absolute temperature. This relationship was determined when it was recognized that the wavelength of maximum energy is inversely proportional to its absolute temperature.

Using Wien's law, we can determine the maximum surface temperature of the sun by observing the wavelength at which it emits its maximum energy. The sun's radiation is observed with a spectrograph, and its maximum radiation is measured with a radiometer (Chapter 4.13). Since the maximum energy is emitted at about 4700Å, we substitute this value in Wien's formula to determine the sun's maximum surface temperature.

$$1\text{Å} = 10^{-8} \text{ cm}$$

$$3700\text{Å} = 4.7 \times 10^{-5} \text{ cm}$$

$$\lambda_{max} = 0.2897/T$$

$$T = 0.2897/\lambda_{max}$$

$$= 0.2897/(4.7 \times 10^{-5})$$

$$= 6164°\text{K}.$$

The total energy that a black body emits every second from one square centimeter of its surface is represented by the area under the curve on the energy distribution chart. This value can also be determined from the relationship

$$E = \sigma T^4,$$

which is known as Stefan's law, where (E) is the total energy at a given temperature, (T) is the absolute temperature, and (σ) is Stefan's constant. In this relationship, the total energy emitted is proportional to the fourth power of the absolute temperature. A body with a temperature of 1000°K radiates a certain amount of energy every second from one square centimeter of its surface. When the temperature is doubled to 2000°K, the energy emitted is increased 16 times, and when the temperature is tripled to 3000°K, its energy is increased 81 times. Using Stefan's law, we can determine the maximum surface temperature of the sun by substituting the total energy which it emits from one square centimeter of its surface in one second.

A star's radius, in terms of the sun's radius, can also be determined from Stefan's law. In the following example, the subscripts ⊙ and * are used to designate the sun and star which have been observed and the following data recorded: the surface temperature of the sun, $T_{\odot}$, is 6000°K, the surface temperature of the star, T_{*}, is 3000°K, and the star's luminosity, L_{*}, is 400 times brighter than the sun's, $L_{\odot}$.

The total energy emitted every second from one square centimeter of the star's surface is obtained from Stefan's law

$$E_{*} = \sigma T_{*}^4.$$

When this value is multiplied by the star's surface area, $4\pi r_{*}^2$, its luminosity, L_{*}, is obtained. By comparing the star's luminosity with that of the sun, $L_{\odot}$, the star's radius, in terms of the sun's radius is obtained. The following procedure is presented as an illustration of a situation which at first appears to be complicated, yet with a little thought given to it, becomes quite simple. Its solution is based on simple proportion.

$$\frac{(\sigma T_{*}^4)(4\pi r_{*}^2)}{(\sigma T_{\odot}^4)(4\pi r_{\odot}^2)} = \frac{L_{*}}{L_{\odot}}, \qquad \frac{(T_{*}^4)(r_{*}^2)}{(T_{\odot}^4)(r_{\odot}^2)} = \frac{L_{*}}{L_{\odot}}$$

$$\frac{r_{*}^2}{r_{\odot}^2} = \frac{L_{*}(T_{\odot}^4)}{L_{\odot}(T_{*}^4)}, \qquad \frac{r_{*}}{r_{\odot}} = \frac{\sqrt{L_{*}}(T_{\odot}^2)}{\sqrt{L_{\odot}}(T_{*}^2)}.$$

Since the ratio $T_{\odot}^2/T_{*}^2$ is 4, and the ratio $\sqrt{L_{*}}/\sqrt{L_{\odot}}$ is $\sqrt{400}$, when these values are substituted in the preceding equation, we produce the ratio

$$r^*/r_\odot = 4(\sqrt{400}) = 80.$$

This means that the radius of the star is 80 times greater than the radius of the sun.

The energy emitted every second from one square centimeter of the black body's surface at a particular temperature and wavelength is represented by the ordinate to the curve on the energy distribution chart. This value can also be determined from a somewhat complicated relationship derived by the German physicist Max Planck, which is known as Planck's law.

3.9 THE STRUCTURE OF THE ATOM

To understand the process of the emission and absorption of light by celestial bodies, we must first understand the structure and behavior of the atom. About 450 B.C., the Greek philosopher Democritus proposed that matter consists of discrete particles—an idea that was rejected by both Plato and Aristotle. Centuries later, Newton and many other scientists accepted Democritus' idea solely on the basis of intuition. In 1808 the idea became well established on experimental data when the English scientist John Dalton proposed the atomic theory. The present modern theory of the structure of the atom was given in 1911 by the English scientist Lewis Rutherford. His atomic model consisted of a small, extremely concentrated nucleus of positively charged particles which were surrounded by a relatively large, tenuous cloud of negatively charged electrons (Fig. 3.9).

A study of the spectrum of the simplest atom, hydrogen, has revealed the important fact that its spectral lines are distributed in definite and regular patterns which are called spectral series. The first series was discovered by J. Balmer, a Swiss high school mathematics teacher, who recognized the regularity of the hydrogen spectral lines in the visible range of the spectrum. The Balmer series is shown in Fig. 3.10. The line with the longest wavelength and strongest intensity is designated hydrogen-alpha, Hα, with a wavelength of

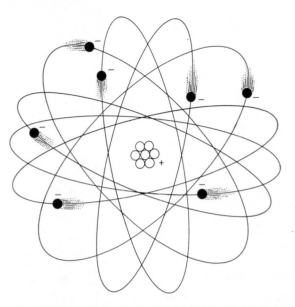

Fig. 3.9 The Rutherford model of the atom—a small, extremely concentrated nucleus of positively charged particles surrounded by a large, tenuous cloud of negatively charged electrons

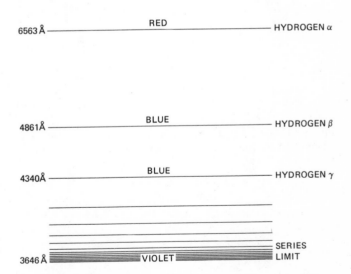

Fig. 3.10 The Balmer series of hydrogen. The spectral lines are in the visible region of the spectrum and are closer as the wavelengths become shorter.

41

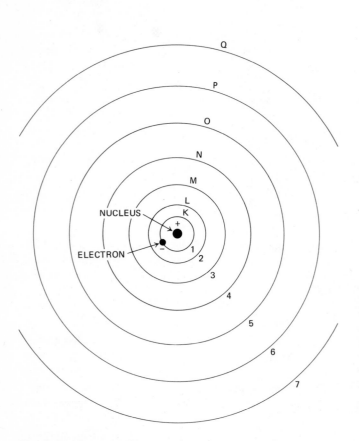

Fig. 3.11 The main energy levels in the model of an atom are designated by the quantum numbers 1–7 or by the letters K–Q

6563Å. As the wavelengths decrease, the lines appear less intense and closer together. The limit of the series has a wavelength of about 3646Å.

In 1913 the Danish physicist Niels Bohr presented his famous model of the hydrogen atom and a theoretical interpretation of its spectrum based on the concept of the quantum. The model consisted of one proton in the nucleus with one electron orbiting around it. Many developments since this model was presented reveal that the model and Bohr's interpretation do not adequately describe the structure or the behavior of the atom; however, it represented a great step forward in the development and understanding of the atom and quantum mechanics. Some of Bohr's concepts still serve as a link between the classical physics, which is based on the laws postulated by Newton, and the quantum physics, which is based on the laws governing the motions of extremely small bodies.

An explanation for the emission spectrum of hydrogen is provided in quantum physics. Atoms exist only with discrete energy levels, each characterized by a definite amount of energy. These levels are considered to be concentric spherical shells that are centered around the nucleus (Fig. 3.11). They represent the region in space where the electrons in each level are most frequently found. The main energy levels are designated from the nucleus outward, by the quantum numbers 1 through 7 or by the latters K through Q. The maximum number of electrons that can exist in each main energy level is determined by the formula

$$2n^2,$$

where n is the quantum number of the energy level. This means that the first level can hold only 2 electrons; the second level, 8; the third level, 18; and so on. Normally, the electrons fill the lower energy level to its maximum capacity before they enter the next higher level; however, there can never be more than eight electrons in the outermost level. Therefore, the main energy level may have as many as four sublevels, and the sublevel may be further divided into orbitals of two electrons each.

3.10 THE PARTS OF THE ATOM

The atom is the smallest particle into which a chemical element can be divided and still retain its chemical identity. An atom consists of three basic elementary particles: protons, neutrons, and electrons. The electron, with a mass of 9.1055×10^{-28} grams, is the least massive and is negatively charged. The proton is 1836.57 times more massive than the electron and is positively charged. The neutron has about the same mass as the proton, but is electrically neutral.

The atom has a negatively charged cloud of electrons (whose numbers range from 1 in the hydrogen atom to 103 in the Lawrencium atom) that revolve around a dense and positively charged nucleus. The nucleus consists of one proton in the hydrogen atom to a combination of protons and neutrons in the heavier atoms. The protons and neutrons are held together by a strong attraction, called the nuclear force. The electrons are held in shells, or orbits, by an electrostatic force which exists between the positively charged protons and the negatively charged electrons—a force that varies inversely as the square of the distance between the particles. The number of protons in the nucleus determines the atomic number of the atom, which is 1 for hydrogen, 2 for helium, and 92 for uranium. The mass of the atom is its atomic weight. Since almost all of the atoms have atomic weights that are fractional decimals and most of their mass is in the nucleus, the atomic weight is rounded off to a whole number to establish the mass number of the atom.

An atom with the same atomic number but with a different mass, that is, with a different number of neutrons, is called an isotope. A hydrogen atom with one proton and one neutron in its nucleus has a mass number of 2, is an isotope of the normal hydrogen atom, and is called deuterium. A hydrogen atom with one proton and two neutrons has a mass number of 3, is also an isotope of hydrogen, and is called tritium. The symbolic representation of deuterium is $_1H^2$. The subscript 1 indicates that there is one proton in the nucleus. The superscript 2 indicates that there is one neutron in the nucleus; this is determined by subtracting the subscript from the superscript.

3.11 EMISSION AND ABSORPTION

When the normal hydrogen atom is unexcited, the electron occupies the atom's lowest first energy level, which is the one next to the nucleus. In this condition, the electron is in the ground state and is stable. When the electron absorbs a discrete amount of energy, it becomes excited and moves to the next higher energy level. When it has absorbed a sufficient amount of energy to pass through all of the atom's permissible energy levels and escape from the atom, it is said to be ionized, and the nucleus in this condition is called an ion. Excitation can also be produced by the collision of one particle with another, causing part of their kinetic energy to be absorbed by the atom.

An atom always seeks its lowest energy level; therefore, it remains in the excited state for only a very brief period of time—less than one hundred-millionth of a second—before it returns to the ground state. As an electron moves from one energy level to the next lower level, it emits a photon of energy of definite wavelength. If (e) represents the energy of the atom in the excited state and (e') represents the energy at the next lower level, the electron emits energy equal to $(e - e')$ as it moves from the higher to the lower level. The movement of an electron to either a higher or a lower energy level is called a transition.

According to the present theory of the structure of the atom, a distinctive wave pattern with properties that can be expressed mathematically is associated with each energy level. A transition from a higher to a lower level is a transformation from one wave pattern to another and produces a spectral line. For the hydrogen atom (Fig. 3.12), all transitions from any energy level to the ground state produce a series of spectral lines in the ultraviolet region of the spectrum, which is called the Lyman series. All transitions from any higher level to the second energy level produce a series of spectral lines in the visible region of the spectrum, which is

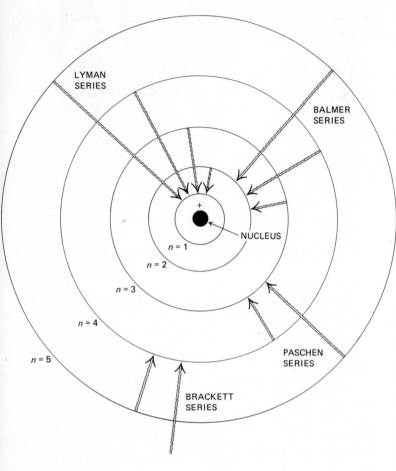

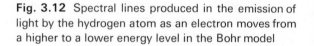

Fig. 3.12 Spectral lines produced in the emission of light by the hydrogen atom as an electron moves from a higher to a lower energy level in the Bohr model

of 4861Å and a blue color. A transition from the fifth to the second energy level produces the third line, which is called the hydrogen-gamma, with a wavelength of 4340Å and a blue color. Although there are many more lines in the Balmer series, as well as in the other series, only the first few are considered because the spectral lines produced by transitions from the outer energy levels are progressively closer together and are thus more difficult to isolate. These transitions explain how and why an emission spectrum is produced.

Before we explain how the absorption spectrum is produced, let us quickly review the excitation of the atom. We know that when light from a source which produces a continuous spectrum is allowed to pass through a cooler, low-pressure gas, it produces an absorption spectrum. The light source which produces the continuous spectrum emits photons in all wavelengths; therefore, when the light passes through the cooler, low-pressure gas, these photons bombard the atoms of the gas and are absorbed by their electrons. The energy of the photons appears in the electrons as increased energy, which causes them to make an upward transition. The electrons remain at the higher levels for about one hundred-millionth of a second, then fall back to their ground state. In the downward transition, they emit energy in the form of photons, which may or may not be

called the Balmer series. All transitions from any higher level to the third energy level produce the Paschen series, and those to the fourth energy level produce the Brackett series.

Since the Balmer series of spectral lines is in the visible region of the spectrum, it will be analyzed more thoroughly. A transition from the third to the second energy level produces the first line in the series, which is called the hydrogen-alpha, with a wavelength of 6563Å and a red color. A transition from the fourth to the second energy level produces the second line, which is called the hydrogen-beta, with a wavelength

of the same wavelength as those that were absorbed. If the transition was made directly to the ground, they are the same; if the transition was made in steps—in one or more energy levels at a time, or cascading—the wavelengths are different.

The absorption spectrum is produced in the following manner. When the cooler, low-pressure gas is not present, the beam from the light source will pass completely through the spectrograph and be recorded as a continuous spectrum. When the gas is present, its atoms will absorb the energy from the light beam, produce an upward transition, followed by a downward transition in which the gas atoms re-emit energy. Since the energy is re-emitted in all directions, very little of it will pass through the spectrograph; therefore, an absorption spectrum will be produced—a continuous spectrum with those wavelengths that did not pass through the spectrograph recorded as dark lines.

REVIEW

1. List the contributions made by Newton, Fresnel, Huygens, Maxwell, Hertz, and Einstein in the development of the theories of light.

2. The light from a point source is allowed to pass through an opening of one square unit area placed at one unit distance from the source. How large an area will it cover when the distance is tripled? What law applies in this situation?

3. State the law of refraction. Give a practical illustration of this law.

4. Arrange the following in order of decreasing wavelength: x-rays, visible yellow, ultraviolet, visible violet, infrared, and gamma rays.

5. What are the three types of spectra and how is each produced?

6. What information about the light source can be deduced from its spectrum? Explain your answer.

7. Define light. Cite several ways in which light behaves in a wave-like motion. What is the approximate wavelength of red light? What wavelength (color) is refracted the least as it passes through a prism? Cite several ways in which light behaves in a corpuscular manner.

8. What is meant by the Doppler effect as it applies to light? What information about the light source can be deduced from the Doppler effect? Give examples.

9. What is a perfect radiator? Is there such an object? Why is a perfect radiator called a "black body"? What important information can be obtained from a quantitative analysis of a black body?

10. Explain how the maximum surface temperature of the sun can be obtained from the energy distribution chart and from Wien's law.

11. What information can be obtained from the relationship known as Stefan's law?

12. State Planck's law. Explain how the value derived from this relationship can be obtained from the energy distribution chart.

13. Explain what is meant by "wavelength," "frequency," and the speed of a wave.

14. Compare and contrast the atom as proposed by Democritus and Rutherford.

15. List the basic particles that compose the nuclei of atoms. What are their characteristics? How do nuclei differ? What is the term given to two or more elements whose atoms have the same atomic number but different atomic mass? Discuss the stability of the nuclei of such atoms.

16. Explain what takes place when an atom: (a) absorbs and (b) emits radiation. Why do atoms emit light in definite wavelengths?

17. Explain what is meant by: (a) normal, (b) neutral, (c) excited and, (d) ionized atoms.

18. Compare the terms "quantum" and "photon."

19. Explain how the absorption spectrum is produced.

4
The Tools of
the Astronomer

Astronomy is not simply a body of theories that has come into existence fully grown like Athena from the head of Zeus. Astronomy is closely associated with technology. The invention of a new instrument or the improvement of an old one has often produced a tremendous impact on the development of astronomy. The Ptolemaic system was seriously challenged when Galileo, using the newly invented telescope, discovered four of Jupiter's satellites and realized that they were bodies that did not revolve around the earth. The use of the photographic plate in astronomical research allowed astronomers to observe objects that were not visible through a telescope. The invention of the radio telescope greatly extended the astronomical horizons because it was not affected by atmospheric conditions and it permitted the detection and measurement of the radiation of stars emitting energy in the radio frequency. The radio telescope also made it possible to analyze the structure of our own and other galaxies and to change our concept of the universe.

4.1 EARLY INSTRUMENTS

One of the most important and frequently used instruments which originated in antiquity was the astrolabe— a simple device consisting of a metallic disk whose outer edge was divided into 360° with a pointer which rotated about the disk's center. When the astrolabe was held vertically, the height of a celestial body above the horizon was measured; when it was held horizontally, the position of a celestial body was determined. The astrolabe was also used to tell time by observing the direction of a shadow cast by an object. Other early astronomical

46

instruments were the wall quadrant for measuring the angle of a celestial body as it crossed the observer's meridian, the armillary sphere for determining the co-ordinates of a celestial body, and the sundial (Plate 4) and water clock for determining time.

4.2 ELEMENTS OF THE TELESCOPE

The telescope, which was invented in 1608 by the Dutch lens grinder Hans Lippershey, is the astronomer's basic tool. It serves the deceptively simple function of resolving celestial objects and bringing new and more distant ones into view. The telescope has either a lens or a mirror (called the objective) whose purpose is to collect the light from an object and form its image (Fig. 4.1). This is accomplished by allowing the light to pass through the lens or to be reflected by the surface of the mirror. Where the light is brought to a focus and the image is formed is called the focal point. Its distance from the center of the lens or the surface of the mirror is the focal length. The ratio of the focal length to the diameter of the objective is called the focal ratio, or the f-ratio. A 10-inch, f-9 telescope has an objective with a diameter of 10 inches and a focal length of 90 inches. For refracting telescopes (lenses), the f-ratio is about 15, and for reflecting telescopes (mirrors) it is about 6. The f-ratio of the 200-inch Hale telescope is 3.3, and its focal length is about 660 inches. The image formed at the focal point is examined with an eyepiece, which is simply a magnifying glass of short focal length.

4.3 PROPERTIES OF THE IMAGE

The image that is formed by a telescope has three important properties—size, brightness, and resolution. The size of the image depends on the focal length of the objective—it increases as the focal length increases. A 10-inch, f-5 telescope whose focal length is 50 inches forms a smaller image than a 10-inch, f-8 telescope whose focal length is 80 inches.

The amount of light collected by a telescope is called its light-gathering power and is proportional to the area, the square of the radius, or the square of the diam-

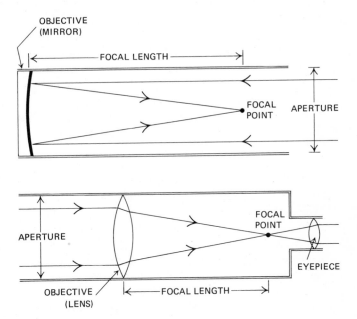

Fig. 4.1 The elements of the telescope

eter of the objective. The light-gathering power of a 2-inch telescope is 4; for a 4-inch telescope, it is 16. Therefore, when the diameter of the objective is doubled, the light-gathering power is increased four times. For a point source of light, such as a star, the brightness of its image depends on the amount of light collected by the objective. As the size of the objective is increased, the image becomes brighter, and more of the dimmer stars become visible. For an object which appears as a disk, such as the moon, the brightness of its image varies inversely as the square of the focal length of the telescope. Two telescopes with objectives of the same diameter collect the same amount of light, regardless of their focal lengths. If the focal length of one telescope is twice that of the other, it will form an image whose linear dimension and area are twice and four times as large, respectively, as the image formed by the other telescope. Since both telescopes receive the same amount of light, the brightness of one square unit of surface of the image formed by the telescope with the longer focal length is one-fourth as great as the brightness of one square unit of the image formed by the telescope with the shorter focal length.

A telescope does not reproduce the geometrical shape of a star; it simply produces an image called a diffraction pattern, which consists of a bright central spot containing about 85% of the total light surrounded by faint concentric rings. The size of the diffraction pattern depends on the diameter of the objective and the wavelength of the light and has no relation to the brightness of the star. The ability of a telescope to separate the angular distance between two stars so that two distinct diffraction patterns are visible is called the resolving power of the telescope. If the telescope cannot resolve this angular distance, the two stars will appear as a single image of two overlapping patterns. The resolving power increases as the size of the diffraction patterns decrease. This is accomplished by using a telescope with a larger objective. The resolving power is expressed in simplified form by the relationship

$$d = 4.56/a,$$

where (d) is the smallest angle in seconds of arc between two stars, and (a) is the diameter of the objective in inches. A 10-inch telescope can resolve two stars that are 0.456 seconds apart, while the 200-inch Hale telescope can resolve two stars that are 0.023 seconds apart. These are theoretical values. Actually, these values are lower because of limitations imposed by the structure of the eye and atmospheric disturbances.

4.4 ABERRATIONS OF THE TELESCOPE

A lens or a mirror, both spherical, have imperfections (aberrations) which make it impossible for them to produce a perfect image. These imperfections are called spherical and chromatic aberration. Spherical aberration results when light is brought to a focus at a greater distance in front of either the lens or the mirror when it

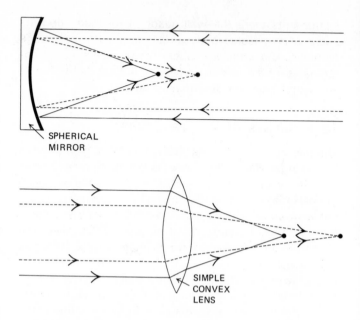

Fig. 4.2 Spherical aberration. A spherical mirror and a simple convex lens do not bring parallel rays of light to a focus at a single point.

passes near its axis rather than near its periphery (Fig. 4.2). This effect, which is greater for a mirror than for a lens, can be corrected in a lens by using a second lens with a different index of refraction, thereby canceling the error produced by the first lens. Spherical aberration in a mirror can be eliminated by changing its spherical surface to a parabola.

Chromatic aberration results when visible light passes through a lens, the short wavelengths are refracted more, and are focused closer to the lens than the long wavelengths (Fig. 4.3). Before a lens is corrected, its purpose must be established so that only those wavelengths affected are corrected. For visual observation, the lens is corrected for the yellow and green wavelengths because these are more sensitive to the eyes. For photographic work, the blue and violet wavelengths are corrected because most photographic plates are

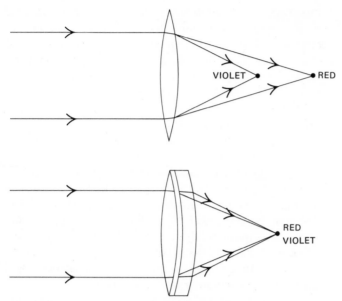

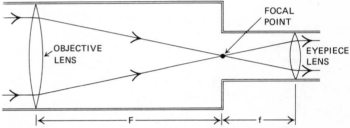

Fig. 4.3 Chromatic aberration. A simple convex lens brings blue and red light rays to a different focus. Two lenses of different index of refraction bring the two rays to a single focal point.

Fig. 4.4 The refracting telescope. For visual use, the eyepiece is used to refract the light into parallel rays. For photographic work, the photographic plate is placed at the focal point.

sensitive to these wavelengths. The corrections are accomplished by placing a second lens of different index of refraction close to the convex lens. The two lenses bring the two colors to a common focal point. Chromatic aberration can also be reduced by increasing the focal length of the lens; however, this is expensive because it increases the size and weight of the telescope mount.

4.5 TELESCOPES

The two general types of optical telescopes in use today are refractors and reflectors. In both types, the objective which produces the image is a fixed part of the telescope and cannot be changed without changing the instrument completely. In a refractor, the objective is a lens; in a reflector, a mirror. The eyepiece, which is a magnifying lens of short focal length, is easily interchangeable.

4.6 REFRACTING TELESCOPES

The essential features of a refracting telescope are two lenses separated by a distance equal to the sum of their focal lengths (Fig. 4.4). The larger lens serves as the objective and the smaller as the eyepiece of the telescope. The fixed objective collects the light from an object which it receives in parallel rays, focuses it, and forms its image at the focal point. The moveable eyepiece receives the light from the focal point, magnifies it, and transmits it to the eye in parallel rays.

4.7 REFLECTING TELESCOPES

The objective of a reflecting telescope is a paraboloidal mirror, which reflects the parallel rays of light it collects from an object and focuses them at the focal point where

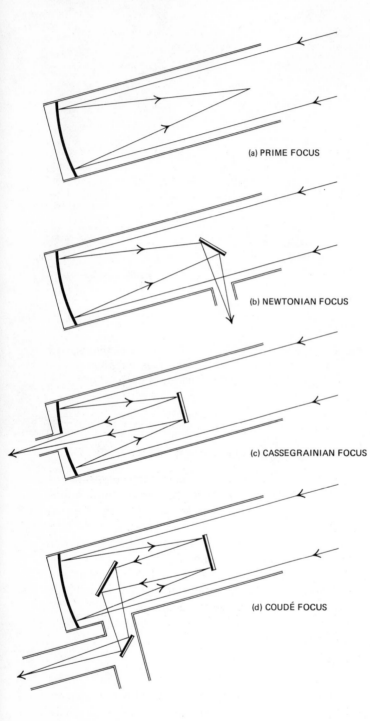

(a) PRIME FOCUS

(b) NEWTONIAN FOCUS

(c) CASSEGRAINIAN FOCUS

(d) COUDÉ FOCUS

Fig. 4.5 Reflector-type telescopes

the image is formed. When the diameter of the objective is very large, as in the 200-inch Hale telescope, the observer and the photographic equipment may be located at the focal point (Fig. 4.5a). This sytem, seldom used for visual observation but used extensively in photography and spectroscopy, is called the prime focus.

The Newtonian focus, invented by Newton, is the most popular system for visual observation, especially in the smaller telescopes (Fig. 4.5b). It consists of a secondary flat mirror located in the axis of the telescope at an angle of 45°, which diverts the light rays to the side of the tube. The image is formed and observed through an eyepiece located on the side of the tube. The diagonal, which consists of three rods, supports the secondary mirror to the tube and blocks out about 10 percent of the incoming light. This slight loss is more than compensated for by making the focal point and the eyepiece accessible to the observer.

Another paraboloidal mirror system, called the Cassegrainian focus, uses a secondary hyperbolic mirror located in the axis of the telescope at 90° (Fig. 4.5c). The secondary mirror diverts the light rays back through a hole in the objective and forms the image behind the objective where it can be observed visually or photographed. The Cassegrainian focus produces a better-balanced instrument than does the Newtonian focus (because the focal point is located at the lower end of the telescope), a larger image, and better magnification (because its focal length is nearly three times longer than the Newtonian focus). Its disadvantages are smaller field of view, field curvature, astigmatism, and weaker image contrast (caused by light falling on the image).

A fourth paraboloidal mirror system, the Coudé focus, uses a secondary hyperbolic mirror similar to that in a Cassegrainian focus and a flat mirror located between the objective and the secondary mirror, which diverts the light down through a hole in the polar axis of the telescope to a stationary observation station (Fig. 4.5d). Since the secondary mirror and the image rotate with the telescope, a dove prism is used to maintain the image in a fixed position by rotating the image in the opposite direction. As a fixed-focus system, the Coudé telescope is used for spectroscopic analysis with large and complicated auxiliary equipment.

Fig. 4.6 The 200-inch Hale telescope, as seen from the east, is pointing to zenith. (Photograph from the Hale Observatories)

4.8 THE 200-INCH HALE TELESCOPE

The 200-inch Hale telescope at Palomar Observatory in southern California is one of the technological wonders of our century. Its objective is a hyperboloidal mirror, 200 inches in diameter, 24 inches in thickness at the edge, and about 29,000 pounds (13,000 kilograms) in weight. The construction of this giant telescope, which was conceived in 1928 by the American astronomer George Ellery Hale, required many years of painstaking work. The major problem was in casting the disk; the technical problems that had to be overcome were staggering. Two years and over half a million dollars were lost at the outset in an attempt to cast the disk out of quartz. After several setbacks, a perfect disk using Pyrex was cast in 1934. Seven hours were required to cast, ten months to cool, and eleven years to polish the disk. The Hale telescope was completed and placed in operation in 1949 (Fig. 4.6).

Fig. 4.7 This view of the 200-inch Hale telescope shows the observer in the prime-focus case and the reflecting surface of the 200-inch mirror. (Photograph from the Hale Observatories)

This telescope was the first one to use a diameter large enough to permit a cage to be placed at the prime focus for the observer and auxiliary equipment. The amount of the incoming light intercepted by the cage is no more than that intercepted by the secondary mirror of the Newtonian focus. The cage is six feet in diameter and is divided into two sections—the upper section provides working area for the observer, while the lower section houses the photoelectric equipment, spectrograph for low dispersions, and the secondary mirrors for the Coudé and the Cassegrainian focus systems. Most of the photographic work is done at the primary focus (Fig. 4.7).

4.9   THE 236-INCH SOVIET TELESCOPE

The world's largest optical telescope, the 236-inch Soviet reflector located near the village of Zelenchukskaya in the Caucasus mountains northwest of Tiflis, will soon be in operation. The mirror, which is nearly 20 feet in diameter, is housed in an 82-foot tube. The prime-focus cage is located at the upper end of the tube, and two observation stations are on each side of the tube's horizontal axis.

Because of its tremendous size and weight—the telescope weighs 850 metric tons (771,000 kg) and the moving parts weigh 700 metric tons (635,000 kg)—its mounting is altazimuth, which permits the telescope to be rotated easily about a vertical axis for altitude and about a horizontal axis for azimuth. This mounting has three advantages: the horizontal axis always remains horizontal for all observations; the loading conditions remain the same for all azimuth positions; and the mirror-support system is simpler than the equatorially mounted telescope. It has two disadvantages: in tracking a star, the azimuth and altitude speeds are nonuniform, and the field of view must be adjusted for rotation. To compensate for these disadvantages, a complicated digital computer is used. The design and construction of this telescope are major accomplishments for the Soviet Union, and when the telescope becomes operational it will be one of the world's great astronomical research tools.

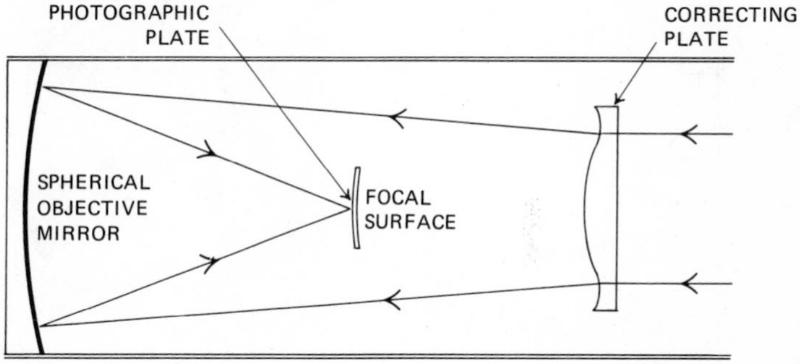

Fig. 4.8 The optical elements of the 48-inch Schmidt telescope at Mount Palomar Observatory

4.10 THE SCHMIDT TELESCOPE

In 1932 Bernhard Schmidt, an optician at the Hamburg Observatory, invented a lens-mirror system which permitted the use of a concave spherical mirror as the objective of a telescope. He accomplished this by placing at the center of curvature of the objective a thin aspherical lens, which provided the necessary correction for the spherical aberration of the objective (Fig. 4.8). Even though the correcting lens was difficult and expensive to produce, its use was justified because it permitted the photographing of a large field of view which was relatively free from aberrations. The optical system's short focal length and the placement of the photographic plate along a curved surface produce an image that is nearly perfect in its entire field of view. With such features, the Schmidt telescope is used almost exclusively for photographing large areas of the sky. The size of the Schmidt telescope is determined by the diameter of the correcting lens, which is two-thirds of the objective. The largest Schmidt telescope, at Palomar, has a 48-inch correcting lens and a 72-inch objective (Fig. 4.9).

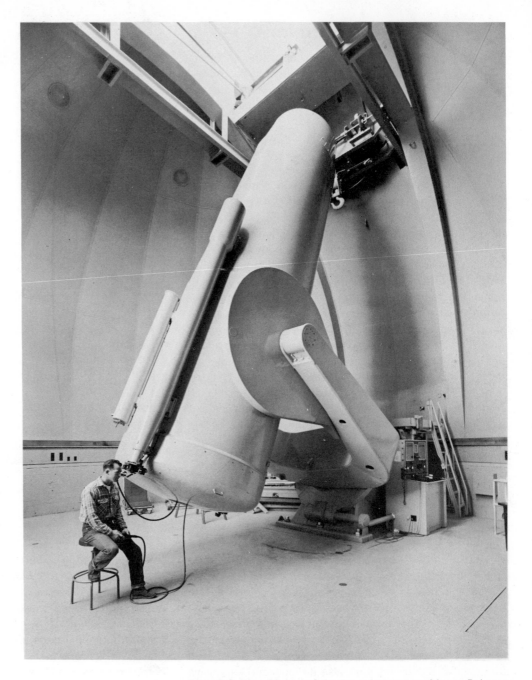

Fig. 4.9 The 48-inch Schmidt telescope at Mount Palomar Observatory. (Photograph from the Hale Observatories)

Fig. 4.10 An equatorial telescope mounting. The polar axis supports the declination axis and the hour circle. The declination axis supports the telescope tube and the declination circle.

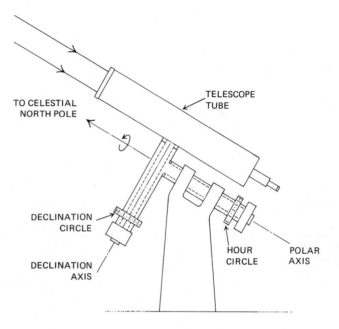

4.11 TELESCOPE MOUNTINGS

Most telescopes are supported by an equatorial mount, which rotates the instrument about its polar axis, which is parallel to the earth's axis (Fig. 4.10), thus permitting the telescope to follow a celestial body in its daily motion across the sky. The polar axis is inclined to the horizontal by an angle equal to the latitude of the observer and is directed toward the north celestial pole star, Polaris. Attached and at right angles to the polar axis is the declination axis. The telescope tube is mounted at right angles to the declination axis and rotates about it. The telescope can be pointed to any celestial body by rotating the tube around the declination axis. By simply rotating the telescope about its polar axis at the proper uniform rate, the telescope will follow the body's daily motion.

4.12 THE MAGNIFICATION OF THE TELESCOPE

Magnification is defined as the number of times the diameter of a body is increased when seen through a telescope rather than with the unaided eye. Magnification depends on the brightness of the body and the steadiness of the atmospheric air. An increase in the brightness permits an increase in the magnification, whereas an increase in the unsteadiness of the atmospheric air does not permit an increase in the magnification because when the body is magnified, the air disturbance will also be magnified, producing a blurred image.

The magnifying power of a telescope is determined by the ratio of the focal length of the objective to the focal length of the eyepiece. It is expressed by the relationship

$M = F/f,$

where (M) is the magnification, (F) is the focal length of the objective, and (f) is the focal length of the eyepiece. If the focal length of the objective is 10 feet and the focal length of the eyepiece is $\frac{1}{2}$ inch, the magnifying power of the telescope is

$$M = \frac{10 \, (12)}{\frac{1}{2}} = 240.$$

Since the objective and its focal length are fixed in a telescope, the magnification of the image can be changed only by using eypieces of different focal lengths. However, the magnifying power of a telescope cannot be increased effectively beyond a certain limit even under the best observational conditions. This limit is about 50 times per inch of the objective's diameter. An 8-inch telescope, which is a typical size for student use, has a maximum effective magnification of about 400.

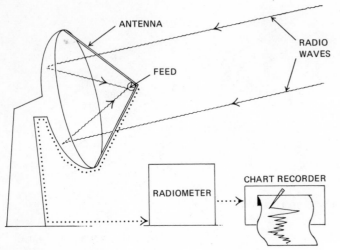

Fig. 4.11 The elements of a radio telescope

4.13 RADIO TELESCOPES

Although celestial bodies emit radiation in all wavelengths, most of the radiation does not reach the earth; it is either absorbed or prevented from reaching the earth by the molecules in the atmosphere. Prior to 1931, the optical telescope limited man's view of the universe to the visible wavelengths of the electromagnetic spectrum; however, in 1931, Karl Jansky at Bell Telephone Laboratories accidently discovered radio waves coming from the region of the Milky Way. He realized that they were being emitted by celestial bodies because their sources moved westward at the same daily rate as the stars. This discovery opened up the new branch of astronomy called radio astronomy (Chapter 13). The construction of the radio telescope greatly extended man's astronomical horizons. It opened up a new "window" in the electromagnetic spectrum which permitted the use of a small portion of the radio region for the radio observations of stars and galaxies. Most of the radio observations are made in the range from 1-centimeter to 15-meter wavelengths.

The principle of the radio telescope is based on several properties of radio waves: radio waves can penetrate the earth's atmosphere; they are not affected by the weather elements; they can be refracted and reflected in the same manner as light waves; and they can be amplified by electronic techniques. The essential features of a radio telescope are the antenna and the receiver (radiometer). In Fig. 4.11, the antenna collects and concentrates the radio energy at its focus, where it is picked up by a "feed" which conveys it to the radiometer where the energy is measured and its value recorded. The radiometer is a specially constructed receiver which eliminates the noise of a regular receiver by using special circuitry. This is necessary because the internal noise of a regular receiver is far greater than the signal created by the radio energy.

The resolving power of a radio telescope is its ability to separate the angular distance between two radio sources. This ability varies directly with the wavelength of the radio energy and inversely with the diameter of the antenna dish, which is similar to the resolving power of an optical telescope. Since the wavelengths of radio radiation are considerably greater than the wavelengths of visible light, the resolving power of a paraboloidal

Fig. 4.12 An extended view of the Mills Cross radio antenna at the Molonglo Radio Observatory, operated by the University of Sydney. (Photograph courtesy Bernard Y. Mills)

radio telescope is much less effective than the optical telescope of the same diameter, that is, the radio telescope is less effective in distinguishing details. To offset the moderate angular resolving power of a single radio telescope, the radio interferometer was developed. It is simply two or more antennae connected to a single radiometer. The antennae may be placed several miles apart, as are the two California Institute of Technology 90-foot steerable reflectors at Owens Valley, California, which establishes a long-baseline interferometer, or several thousand miles apart, thus establishing a world-wide network (Plate 5).

The antenna known as the Mills Cross (Fig. 4.12), which was built in 1953, increases the resolving power of a radio telescope at a low cost. This is accomplished by two beams with a common physical and electrical center. The product of these beams, the intersection of a north-south beam with an east-west beam, produces a pencil beam of high resolving power at a low cost. This means that more stars are detectable within a given pattern. However, the Mills Cross also has several important disadvantages: difficulty in changing the beam

position, limited frequency, and narrow band width.

These disadvantages are not present in a steerable radio antenna telescope. An excellent example of a steerable antenna is the 250-foot paraboloidal reflector at the Jodrell Bank Experimental Station at the University of Manchester, England. By being mounted on a double circular rail track, 350 feet in diameter, it can be easily pointed to any position in the sky. The instrument, designed for both radio and radar research, uses a wide range of frequencies and band widths. The world's largest fully steerable radio telescope is the new Bonn 328-foot at the Max Planck Institute for Radio Astronomy, Bonn, West Germany (Fig. 4.13). It is altazimuth-mounted on a circular track that is only 210 feet in diameter. The reflector dish has a very short focal length of about 100 feet and will operate down to a wavelength of 1.2 centimeters.

Another interesting radio telescope is the stationary, spherical antenna located at the Arecibo Ionospheric Observatory, near the port of Arecibo, Puerto Rico which is operated by Cornell University (Fig. 4.14). This instrument fills a natural bowl which is over 1000 feet (300

Fig. 4.13 The 100-meter, fully steerable radio telescope near Bonn. (Photograph from the German Information Center)

Fig. 4.14 The great radio-radar telescope at the National Astronomy and Ionosphere Center in Arecibo, Puerto Rico. The feed system is suspended at the focus by cables from the three towers. (The National Astronomy and Ionosphere Center is a national research center operated by Cornell University under contract with the National Science Foundation.)

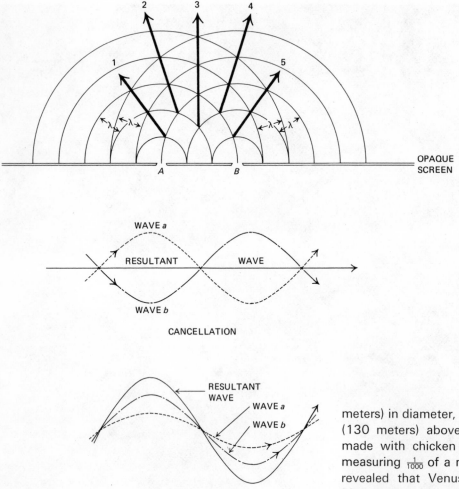

WAVE a

RESULTANT WAVE

WAVE b

CANCELLATION

RESULTANT WAVE

WAVE a

WAVE b

AMPLIFICATION

Fig. 4.15 The principle of the interferometer. Light from a single source passes through pinholes (A and B) in an opaque screen. Amplification results along lines 1, 2, 3, 4, and 5 when the crests of two waves meet and produce bright fringes. Cancellation results between these lines when the troughs of the two waves meet and produce dark fringes.

meters) in diameter, and its antenna is located 435 feet (130 meters) above the ground. The reflector dish is made with chicken wire, yet it receives radio signals measuring $\frac{1}{1000}$ of a millionth of a watt. This instrument revealed that Venus' rotation is clockwise and that Mercury's period of rotation is about 57 days.

4.14 THE STELLAR INTERFEROMETER

Although scientists have developed new and exciting auxiliary instruments such as the image tube, which increases the effective light-gathering power of a telescope, and the laser beam, which permits the distance to a celestial body to be measured with great precision, a few basic auxiliaries will be presented to show how a star's angular diameter and brightness can be measured and how light emitted by bodies is observed and analyzed.

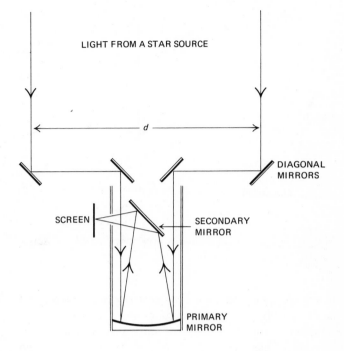

LIGHT FROM A STAR SOURCE

DIAGONAL MIRRORS

SCREEN

SECONDARY MIRROR

PRIMARY MIRROR

Fig. 4.16 The stellar interferometer. The four small mirrors are mounted on a steel beam; the inside ones are fixed, and the outside ones are moveable.

The stellar interferometer, which was invented by the American physicist A. A. Michelson, is used to measure the angular diameter of stars. Its operation is based on the property of light called interference. As Fig. 4.15 illustrates, an amplification in the wave is produced when the crest of one wave meets the crest of another wave or when the trough of one wave meets the trough of another wave. When the crest of one wave meets the trough of another wave, they cancel each other. This property is also illustrated in Fig. 4.15. When parallel light passes through two pinholes, the light which emerges from each pinhole moves outward in spherical waves as though the light source were at each pinhole. Along lines 1, 2, and 3, the crests of the two waves meet, producing amplification which is visible as bright regions; between these lines, the troughs and the crests meet and produce cancellation which is visible as dark regions.

Basically, the interferometer consists of a steel beam with a movable mirror at each end. As shown in Fig. 4.16, the light from a single star falls on the surface of the two movable mirrors and is directed on the screen into two diffraction patterns—one overlapping the other. The image appears as a fringe pattern of alternating bright and dark parallel bands. To obtain the angular diameter of the star, the two movable mirrors are moved until the fringe pattern disappears. The distance between the mirrors is related to the angular diameter of the star.

4.15 THE PHOTOELECTRIC PHOTOMETER

The photoelectric photometer is used to measure the brightness of a body to an accuracy of several thousands of a magnitude. Its operation is based on the principle of the photoelectric effect, which states that when light falls on a light-sensitive surface, photoelectrons are emitted in proportion to the intensity of the light. When the frequency of the light and the accelerating potential, i.e., the voltage between the emitting and collecting surfaces, are both held constant, the photoelectric current is a linear function of the intensity of the light. The flow of current is measured by a microammeter and is a measure of the body's brightness.

When the intensity of the light is extremely weak or the required measurement is most sensitive, a photoelectric cell (photomultiplier tube), in which there are several light-sensitive surfaces, is used. When light from a celestial body falls on the first surface, one or more

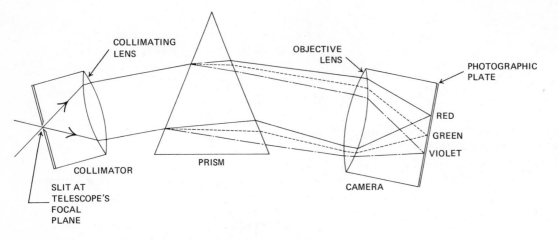

Fig. 4.17 The optical elements and principles of a spectrograph

electrons are emitted and accelerated toward the second surface, where more electrons are emitted. This is repeated on each successive surface until a sufficient number of electrons have been emitted to be amplified by an electronic amplifier and counted by an electronic counter.

4.16 THE SPECTROGRAPH

The spectrograph, one of the most important instruments of astronomical research, permits the observation and analysis of the light emitted by a celestial body. Its basic function is to identify the wavelengths, intensities, and characteristics of the light emitted. From this information, the astronomer can derive the physical characteristics and behavior of the celestial body.

The essential features of the spectrograph are a narrow slit, collimator, prism, and camera (Fig. 4.17). The light rays from a celestial body converge at the focal point of the instrument where the narrow slit is located. They pass through the slit, diverge, then pass through the collimator lens, and emerge in parallel rays. When the rays pass through the prism, each wavelength is deviated by a different angle to produce the different colors in the spectrum. When the spectrum is photographed, the instrument is called a spectrograph.

A diffraction grating can be used in place of the prism to produce the spectrum. It consists of a flat surface that is ruled by thousands of very fine, parallel, and equidistant lines which disperse the light beam into the spectrum by either refraction or reflection. In the transmission grating the surface is transparent and the light is refracted, while in the reflection grating the surface is opaque and the light is reflected. The lines in both gratings can be either ruled in the surface or formed by alternating clear and opaque strips.

Both the prism and the diffraction grating are widely used in spectroscopic work; however, they differ considerably in the spectra that they produce. In a prism, the red wavelengths are deviated the least and the violet the most, whereas the opposite is true in a diffraction grating. This means that the spectrum produced by the grating is the reverse of that produced by the prism. The dispersion of the light beam is greater toward the violet end of the spectrum produced by a prism, which means that the grating disperses the wavelengths more uniformly than the prism. Also, the angle of deviation of any wavelength can be accurately determined from the line spacing of a grating and can be approximated from the type of material used in the construction of a prism.

A spectrograph is designed so that the spectrum of a known source (comparison spectrum) can be placed on

travel through the interior of the earth. The primary waves are fast, longitudinal waves, similar to sound waves, which travel through both solid and liquid materials. The secondary waves, which travel only through solid materials, are slow, transverse waves that are similar to light waves (Fig. 5.3).

Since the velocity of these waves increases with an increase in the density of the earth's material, the elapsed time for a wave to travel from its source to a station on the earth's surface provides the key in estimating the density and structure of the earth's interior. The average density of the earth is 5.5 grams per cubic centimeter, and the average density of the material at or near the earth's surface is 2.7 grams per cubic centimeter, a fact which indicates that the interior is considerably denser than the surface.

The solid part of the earth consists of three main layers of material: the crust, mantle, and core. The crust is the outer, most familiar layer; the mantle is below the crust; and the core is the layer at the earth's center. The crust is not uniform in either thickness or composition. The thickness varies from about 3 miles, or 5 km (under the ocean bottoms) to over 30 miles, or 48 km (below the mountainous parts of continents). An analysis of the composition of the crust reveals that most of the elements are in scarce supply. The approximate composition of the most abundant elements are: 46.6% oxygen, 27.7% silicon, 8.1% aluminum, 5.0% iron, 3.6% calcium, 2.8% sodium, 2.6% potassium, and 2.1% magnesium.

The mantle extends to a depth of about 1800 miles (2900 km) and consists of the basic silicates that are rich in magnesium and iron. Seismographic studies indicate that the core is divided into two parts, the outer and the inner. The outer core has a depth of slightly over 1000 miles (1600 km), and the inner core has a depth of slightly less than 1000 miles. Direct information about the composition of the core is not available; however, scientists believe that the outer core consists of nickel-iron in the liquid state, because the secondary waves do not pass through this layer, and that the inner core consists of nickel-iron in the solid state.

From the study of the temperatures that have been recorded in deep mine shafts and wells, geologists

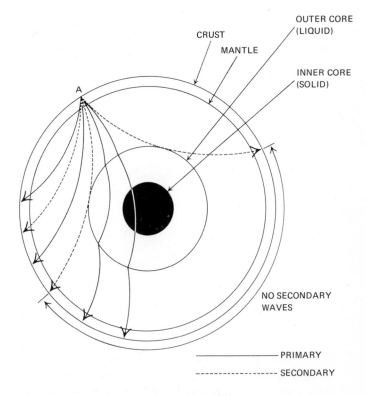

Fig. 5.3 The interior structure of the earth. The paths of the primary and secondary waves through the earth.

have estimated that the temperature of the crust near the earth's surface increases at the rate of about 1°F for each 50 feet of depth; however, it is not known whether this rate continues to the earth's core. Since the heat in the inner core escapes through the outer core, the mantle, and the crust, and since the rate of conductivity of the earth's material is low, the inner core must cool at a relatively slow rate. Calculations indicate that only about 15% of the heat in the earth's crust comes from the inner core. The remaining 85% comes from the decay of the unstable radioactive elements in the earth's crust.

Radioactive material can also be used to establish the earth's age. These elements decay at a constant and uniform rate which is expressed as the element's half-

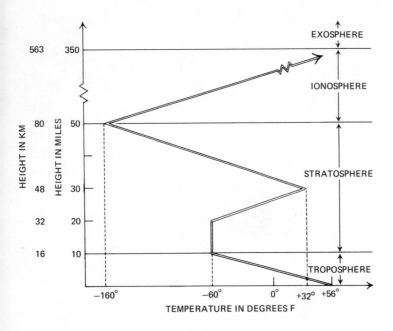

EXOSPHERE

IONOSPHERE

STRATOSPHERE

TROPOSPHERE

HEIGHT IN KM

HEIGHT IN MILES

563 350

80 50

48 30

32 20

16 10

−160°   −60°   0° +32° +56°

TEMPERATURE IN DEGREES F

Fig. 5.4 The vertical distribution of the earth's atmosphere

The atmosphere is a mixture of gases (78% nitrogen, 21% oxygen, and 1% water vapor, carbon dioxide, and the inert gases) and man-made pollutants (sulphur dioxide, nitrous oxide, and ammonia). Although at the present time these pollutants have not affected the composition of the atmosphere, they have begun to affect the ecology, man's health, and possibly his very existence. Many projects have been initiated by scientists to determine how these pollutants are affecting man's environment. One interesting project, "Project Astra," was launched by the astronomer Paul W. Hodge and his associates at the University of Washington to study the changes produced in the earth's atmosphere by pollutants. They compared the brightness of the zenith stars recorded at the Mount Wilson Observatory during a 50-year period and discovered that there has been a dimming of about 0.3 magnitude in the ultraviolet light and 0.1 in the visible light.

The atmosphere's density decreases rapidly with an increase in altitude. Calculations indicate that about 50% of the atmosphere's total mass is located within three miles above the earth's surface. The data obtained by the artificial satellites Vanguard 1 (1958) and Explorer 9 (1961) clearly show that the density at any given altitude varies considerably from day to day as the result of solar activity (Chapter 10).

The atmosphere is composed of four important layers: the troposphere, the stratosphere, the ionosphere, and the exosphere. Figure 5.4 shows that the troposphere, which is closest to the earth's surface, has a depth that varies from 5 miles (8 km) at the poles to 10 miles (16 km) at the equator. It contains over three-fourths of the atmosphere's total mass and the meteorological elements such as water vapor, dust, smoke, clouds, and winds. The temperature of the troposphere

life—the time it takes half of its atoms to decay. Uranium 238 has a half-life of 4.5 billion years, which means that in this period of time one-half of its atoms will decay. Since this is a continuing process, one-half of the remaining atoms will decay during each successive 4.5 billion year period. By comparing the present amounts of radioactive elements to the decay products found in the surface rocks, one can obtain a fairly accurate estimate of the earth's age. The age of the oldest earth rocks has been estimated to be between 3 and 4 billion years, and the age of the earth at about 4.6 billion years.

5.5 THE ATMOSPHERE OF THE EARTH

The earth's atmosphere is a complex, invisible, and vital shell which completely encircles the earth. It protects man from the deadly ultraviolet radiation of the sun and helps to maintain a fairly uniform temperature on the earth by means of the "greenhouse effect" (Chapter 5.8). Although the atmosphere is vital to the existence of life on the earth, it is a nuisance to the astronomer, because it seriously hampers his viewing of the celestial bodies.

Fig. 5.5 The effect of atmospheric refraction on viewing is maximum at the horizon and minimum at the zenith, causing celestial bodies to appear higher above the horizon than they actually are

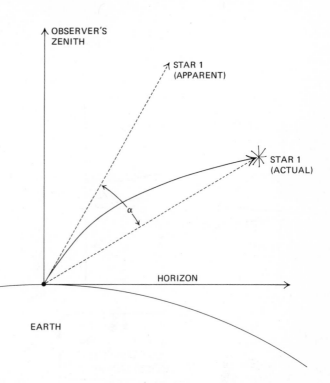

decreases at a uniform rate from about 56°F (13°C) at the earth's surface to about −60°F (−51°C) at the top of the layer.

Above the troposphere is the stratosphere, which has a depth of 40 miles (64 km) and extends to 50 miles (80 km) above the earth's surface. The meteorological elements are missing in this layer, and the air currents are horizontal rather than vertical as in the troposphere. The temperature in the stratosphere remains constant for the first 10 miles (16 km), gradually increases to +32°F (0°C) at 30 miles (48 km), then gradually decreases to a minimum temperature of −160°F (−107°C) at 50 miles (80 km). This increase in temperature at the lower levels of the stratosphere is due to the absorption of the ultraviolet radiation near the 3000 Å wavelength by the molecular oxygen O_2. The molecular oxygen is dissociated into atomic oxygen O, which recombines with unaffected molecular oxygen to form ozone, O_3 (oxygen molecules composed of three atoms).

Above the stratosphere and extending to about 350 miles (563 km) above the earth's surface is the ionosphere, so named because many of the gas molecules have been broken up into atoms, ions, and electrons by intense ultraviolet radiation and high-speed particles. The ionized particles appear in layers at different heights based on the solar radiation that produced the ionization. These layers reflect radio wavelengths longer than 18 miles (28 km), therefore making long-range radio transmission possible. The burning of meteoroids and the display of auroras occur in the ionosphere.

Even though the density of the atmosphere at the upper level of the ionosphere is extremely tenuous, the atmosphere extends beyond the ionosphere, where it gradually thins out to practically nothing. This outer layer is called the exosphere.

5.6 ATMOSPHERIC REFRACTION

The presence of an atmosphere around the earth produces several astronomical effects through the processes of refraction, diffusion, and absorption.

The density of the earth's atmosphere decreases with an increase in elevation, so that it is maximum at sea level and (theoretically) approaches zero at an elevation of about 550 miles (885 km). For simplicity, the earth's atmosphere is assumed to be stratified in layers of decreasing densities. When a beam of light from a star passes through the atmosphere obliquely, the increasing atmospheric density causes it to be progressively refracted by a greater amount as it approaches the earth's surface. When the light beam reaches the observer, its direction is more vertical than when it first entered the earth's atmosphere (Fig. 5.5). Refraction is maximum for a body that is at or near the horizon and zero when a body is directly overhead. When a body is near the horizon, its light will pass through a greater depth of atmosphere and will be refracted at a greater angle; when a body is directly overhead, its light will pass through the atmosphere normal to each atmospheric layer and will not be refracted.

Atmospheric refraction produces some interesting astronomical effects. One such effect is the apparent elevation of the position of a celestial body—the body appears to be higher above the horizon than it actually is. Another effect is the apparent rising and setting of a celestial body—it appears to rise earlier and set later than it would otherwise. The "twinkling" of a star can also be explained by atmospheric refraction. As the light beam from a star passes through the atmosphere, it encounters air of different densities, each refracting the beam by a different amount and in a different direction so that when it reaches the observer, the light beam appears unsteady and produces the twinkling effect of the star. A final interesting effect of atmospheric refraction is the flattening of a celestial body when it appears at or near the horizon. This phenomenon is produced by the unequal refraction of the light from the lower and upper limbs (edges) of the body. The light from the lower limb is refracted more than that from the upper limb because it is closer to the horizon and passes through a greater depth of atmosphere.

Many people erroneously believe that the apparent increase in the size of the moon at or near the horizon is caused by atmospheric refraction. Actually, when the moon appears near the horizon, its distance from the earth is about one earth-radius farther away than when it is observed higher in the sky; therefore, its actual size is smaller and is further reduced by atmospheric refraction. In spite of these two facts, the moon appears to be noticeably larger when it is near the horizon than at a higher altitude. The explanation for the apparent increase in the size of the moon is provided by psychologists who have presented the theory that it is an optical illusion. When the moon is observed near the horizon, it is compared to the earth's surface features visible on the horizon, which causes the moon's image to appear larger. When the moon is observed high in the sky, it appears smaller because it is seen by itself.

By permission of Johnny Hart and Field Enterprises, Inc.

5.7 ATMOSPHERIC DIFFUSION

The air molecules and the extremely small solid particles in the atmosphere diffuse (scatter) the shorter wavelengths of visible light more effectively than longer wavelengths. Diffusion occurs when the light interacts with the individual air molecules and solid particles. In the encounters, the light beam is deflected in random directions by the interfering substances.

Atmospheric diffusion produces the reddening of the rising and setting sun and the blue sky. The sun on the horizon appears redder than the noon-day sun, because the direct light beam to the observer passes through a greater depth of atmosphere and more of the blue light is diffused. Actually, the direct beam of light does not contain any more red light—it simply has less blue light; therefore, it appears redder. Since sunlight is diffused innumerable times by the molecules in the atmosphere, it becomes progressively bluer as the distance from the direct light beam increases and causes the sky to appear blue. If the earth had no atmosphere, the daytime sky would appear black, and the stars and planets would be clearly visible. Normally, the stars and planets are not visible in the daytime, because diffused sunlight is much brighter than starlight or the reflected light on the planets.

5.8 ATMOSPHERIC ABSORPTION

When solar radiation passes through the earth's atmosphere, the atmospheric elements absorb light and produce their own characteristic absorption lines and bands in the spectra of celestial bodies. These absorption lines are called telluric lines. For example, molecular oxygen absorbs light in the red part of the spectrum and produces the A red band (oxygen line at 7600Å) and the B red band (oxygen line at 6867Å). Water vapor and carbon dioxide absorb light in the infrared part of the spectrum. Telluric lines can be easily identified; they are not as broad as the solar lines, show no Doppler effect, and increase in intensity at sunset.

Between 10 and 30 miles (16 and 48 km) above the earth's surface, the molecules in the earth's atmosphere "absorb" the sun's ultraviolet radiation by converting the molecular oxygen into atomic oxygen and then recombining to form triatomic oxygen (ozone). This process of atmospheric absorption protects man from the sun's deadly ultraviolet radiation. The atmosphere also "absorbs" the small meteoroids that pass through it. As these bodies move through the atmosphere, they are heated to incandescence by friction with the air molecules, so that they are completely consumed before they reach the earth's surface. The atmosphere also prevents the energy that the earth receives from the sun from escaping into space and reradiates it in the form of infrared radiation. Since water vapor and carbon dioxide in the atmosphere are opaque to infrared radiation, they prevent this form of energy from escaping into space. This "greenhouse effect" helps the earth's atmosphere maintain a fairly even temperature.

5.9 THE EARTH'S MAGNETIC FIELD

The earth's magnetic properties were known to the Chinese as early as 1300 B.C. For centuries man has used these properties to set and maintain his course at sea. When a magnetized needle that is free to rotate in a horizontal plane is placed in the earth's magnetic field, it will orient itself parallel to the magnetic lines of force. Therefore, its orientation indicates the direction of the force at that particular point on the earth's surface. The points where the needle is parallel to the earth's surface mark the magnetic equator, and the two points where the needle is perpendicular to the earth's surface mark the north and south magnetic poles. The north magnetic pole N is located in the Hudson Bay area of Canada, and the south magnetic pole S is located in Victoria Land, Antarctica. The two poles are not at diametrically opposite points on the earth's surface, nor are they fixed. The magnetic pole axis misses the earth's center by about 600 miles (966 km).

The actual cause of the movement of the magnetic poles is not known; nor is the nature of the magnetic field that is inside the earth. Scientists believe that the field is induced by an electric current that flows within the earth's core and is associated with the rotation of the

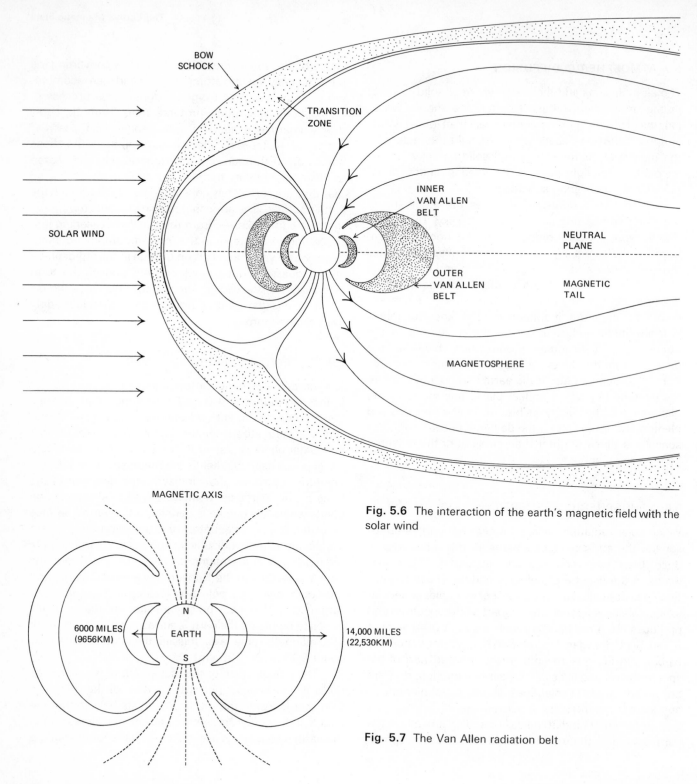

BOW
SCHOCK

TRANSITION
ZONE

INNER
VAN ALLEN
BELT

SOLAR WIND

NEUTRAL
PLANE

OUTER
VAN ALLEN
BELT

MAGNETIC
TAIL

MAGNETOSPHERE

Fig. 5.6 The interaction of the earth's magnetic field with the solar wind

MAGNETIC AXIS

6000 MILES
(9656KM)

14,000 MILES
(22,530KM)

N

EARTH

S

Fig. 5.7 The Van Allen radiation belt

earth. The strength of the magnetic field at the magnetic poles is double that at the magnetic equator. Its overall strength is relatively weak when compared to the sun with many sunspots or to certain stars. These bodies possess magnetic fields whose strength is thousands of times greater than the earth's.

Scientific research with orbiting satellites and space probes by the United States and the Soviet Union have shown that the earth's magnetic field is not symmetrical. The sun is continuously emitting streams of ionized gas that move in all directions into space at speeds of about 350 miles (563 km) per second. This gas is known as the "solar wind," or "plasma," and consists of about 95% hydrogen and 5% helium atoms that are very hot, tenuous, and whose outer electrons have been stripped to form ions. The solar wind, which contains its own magnetic field, is compressed and confined within a region known as the magnetosphere as it interacts with the earth's magnetic field. The interacting boundary between the magnetosphere and the solar wind is known as the magnetosheath (Fig. 5.6).

The shape of the earth's magnetic field is altered considerably by its interaction with the solar wind. The side facing the sun is compressed into an elliptical shape whose outer limit is about 50,000 miles (80,465 km) from the earth's center. The side away from the sun is extended into the shape of a comet-like tail whose diameter and length are each about 160,000 miles (257,488 km)—more than half the distance to the moon. The presence of the tail was revealed in 1961 from measurements taken by the artificial satellite Explorer 10. The field within the tail is divided into two regions by a neutral plane that is parallel to the magnetic equator. North of the neutral plane, the magnetic field is directed toward the sun; south of the plane, it is directed away from the sun.

5.10 THE VAN ALLEN RADIATION BELT

The artificial satellite Explorer 1, which was launched on January 31, 1958, revealed that the earth is completely surrounded by a belt of high-energy charged particles. The belt is named after the American scientist, James Van Allen, physicist at the State University of Iowa, who devised the radiation-detecting procedure on Explorer 1 which made the discovery of its presence possible.

Figure 5.7 shows the structure of the Van Allen radiation belt. The signals from Explorer 1 revealed that the belt is "doughnut-shaped" and consists of charged atomic particles, mostly protons and electrons, that are trapped by the earth's magnetic field in two concentrated regions. The maximum proton intensity is centered in the inner region in the plane of the earth's magnetic equator, at about 6000 miles (9656 km) from the earth's center; the lesser maximum intensity is centered in the outer region, at nearly 14,000 miles (22,530 km) from the earth's center. The inner region has a diameter of about 3000 miles (4828 km), and the outer region has a diameter of about 5000 miles (8047 km). All these values vary considerably with time and solar activity. The outer region may extend to a distance of about 36,000 miles (57,935 km) from the earth's center. Within these two regions the charged particles bounce against one another at great speeds as they move from one pole to the other.

5.11 THE ROTATION OF THE EARTH

The idea that the earth rotates about its axis had its roots in antiquity. Cicero wrote that some of the philosophers of his period believed that all the celestial bodies, except the earth, are fixed in space and that the motions of the other bodies are produced by the earth's rotation. Others believed that this theory was nonsensical. One of these was Ptolemy, who reasoned that if the earth rotates, the force of its rotational speed would tear the earth apart and scatter the bits into space; therefore, the earth had to be stationary and located in the center of the universe. Initially, Copernicus was in complete agreement with Ptolemy's conclusion. Still, he continued to search for the reason behind a theory which gives the sun a pre-eminent position in the universe. His search ended when he accepted the earlier Greek concept that the sun had to be in the center of the universe because, as the main source of life and energy on the earth, it is the most important body in the universe.

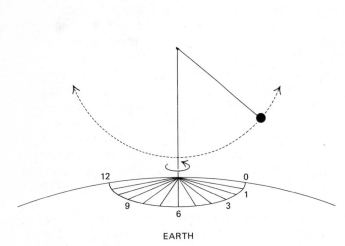

Fig. 5.8 The Foucault pendulum at the north pole of the earth. Its apparent period of rotation is 24 hours.

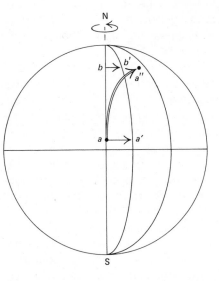

Fig. 5.10 The Coriolis effect. In the northern hemisphere, a body (*a*) moving northward is deflected to the right.

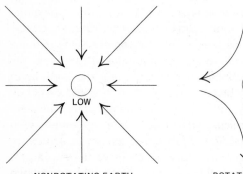

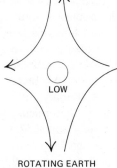

Fig. 5.9 The deflection of air and water currents by a rotating body

Fig. 5.11 Elements of the earth's orbit

Although it is impossible to sense that the earth rotates about its axis, two pieces of evidence can be presented to indicate that this motion exists: the action of the Foucault pendulum and the deflection of air and water currents.

5.12 THE FOUCAULT PENDULUM

In 1851 the French physicist Jean Foucault performed an experiment which established the fact that the earth rotates about its axis. When he suspended a 62-pound brass sphere from the dome of the Pantheon in Paris by means of a 219-foot wire and then set the pendulum oscillating back and forth in a north-south direction, he observed that the direction of oscillation appeared to move slowly around the Pantheon rotunda in a clockwise direction. Since it is impossible for a pendulum to change its plane of oscillation—the only force which acts on it is gravity—he concluded that the apparent change was due to the rotation of the earth which caused the Pantheon to move in a counterclockwise direction. As shown in Fig. 5.8, the experiment is more obvious when the pendulum is located at the north pole, because the apparent period of the earth's rotation is equal to its actual period of 24 hours. At the equator, the apparent period of the earth's rotation is infinity, because there is no apparent change in the direction of oscillation. If the pendulum is oscillating in a north-south direction, it will always move perpendicular to the equator and therefore show no apparent change in its direction of oscillation. Between the poles and the equator, the apparent period of rotation will vary from 24 hours at the poles to infinity at the equator.

5.13 THE DEFLECTION OF AIR AND WATER CURRENTS

A second proof that the earth rotates is the deflection of air and water currents. As shown in Fig. 5.9, the currents on a stationary earth converge radially toward the low-pressure area, whereas on a rotating earth they move in a counterclockwise direction in the northern hemisphere and clockwise in the southern. As the currents move from the equator to the poles, they are deflected to the right in the northern hemisphere and to the left in the southern. This is accomplished in the following manner. All objects on the earth's surface rotate around the earth's axis once every 24 hours at different speeds, depending on their location. If two objects are located on the same north-south line in the northern hemisphere, the one which is closer to the equator travels at a faster speed. If the two objects (a) and (b) (Fig. 5.10) are to complete one rotation in 24 hours, object (a), which is closer to the equator, must move faster because it has a greater distance to travel. Therefore, in a given interval of time, objects (a) and (b) have moved to positions (a') and (b'), respectively. If object (a) moves to the north, it retains its higher eastward speed; therefore, at the end of this interval of time at the higher latitude, it will be in position (a''), ahead and to the east of position (b'). Consequently, as object (a) moves northward in a given interval of time, it will be deflected to the right. This is known as the Coriolis effect.

5.14 THE REVOLUTION OF THE EARTH

The earth revolves eastward around the sun in an elliptical orbit once every year. As shown in Fig. 5.11, the sun is located at one of the ellipse's foci; therefore, its distance from the earth varies during the year. The earth is at perihelion, or nearest point to the sun, about January 3 and at aphelion, or farthest point from the sun, about July 3. The earth's mean distance from the sun, which is half the length of the major axis, is 92,900,000 miles (149,500,000 km).

Although we accept the fact that the earth revolves around the sun, there are many who would find it difficult to present evidence of its motion. Three important proofs can be given: the parallactic motion of the stars, the variation in the radial velocities of the stars, and the aberration of starlight.

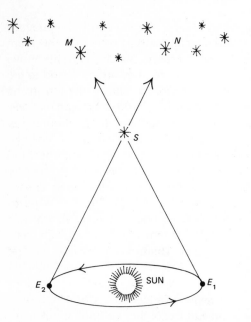

Fig. 5.12 The parallactic motion of the stars. As the earth revolves around the sun, the nearer star *S* appears to oscillate annually from *M* to *N* with respect to the more distant stars.

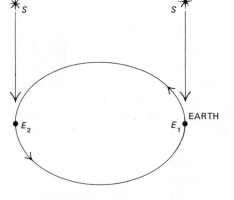

Fig. 5.13 Effects of the earth's revolution on the radial velocities of stars. The radial velocity of a star is greater when the earth is moving toward the star (as in position E_1 and lesser when moving away (as in position E_2).

5.15 THE PARALLACTIC MOTION OF THE STARS

The parallactic motion of a star, which is its apparent motion with respect to the more distant stars, is one evidence that the earth revolves around the sun. When the earth is in position (E_1) (Fig. 5.12), the star (*S*) is observed to be in line with the more distant star (*M*). Six months later when the earth is in position (E_2), star (*S*) is observed to be in line with the more distant star (*N*); twelve months later when the earth has returned to position (E_1), star (*S*) is observed to be in line with star (*M*). In one year, as the earth completes one turn around the sun, star (*S*) has appeared to have made one complete cycle in the sky. Its path is a straight line when the star is located in the plane of the ecliptic, a small circle when it is at 90° from the plane of the ecliptic, and an ellipse when it is between these two extremes.

5.16 THE VARIATION IN THE RADIAL VELOCITY OF A STAR

Evidence that the earth revolves around the sun can also be determined by observing a star's radial velocity, that is, its velocity toward or away from the observer. If a star were observed from a stationary earth, its radial velocity would appear to remain constant. Since the earth does revolve around the sun, however, the radial velocity of a star varies with different earth-orbital positions. In Fig. 5.13, star (*S*) is moving toward the earth; therefore, its radial velocity is greater when it is observed from E_1 than from E_2 because from the first position, the earth is moving toward the star, whereas from the second position, it is moving away from the star. This difference in the star's radial velocity is evidence that the earth revolves around the sun.

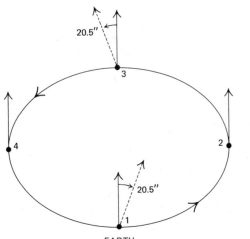

Fig. 5.14 The aberration of starlight. There is no aberration when the earth is moving toward the star (2) or away from the star (4). Maximum aberration of 20.5″ occurs when the earth is moving at right angles to the star, as in positions (1) and (3).

the raindrops are falling vertically, they will appear to move in a vertical direction downward on the window of a stationary automobile. When the automobile is moving forward, the raindrops appear to move in a slanting direction to the rear, and the degree of slant is determined by the speed of both the automobile and the falling raindrops.

A similar effect occurs with starlight reaching the earth. A telescope mounted on the earth is moving forward at the earth's orbital velocity, and the starlight is moving toward the earth at the speed of light. In Fig. 5.14, the solid line represents the true direction of the starlight, and the dotted line represents its apparent direction. When the earth is in position 1 and moving to the right, the telescope must be pointed forward along the dotted line if the star is to be seen. In this position, the angle of displacement is maximum at 20.5 seconds. When the earth is in position 3 and moving to the left, the angle of displacement is again maximum and in the direction in which the earth is moving. In position 2, the earth is moving toward the star; in position 4, it is moving away from the star. Therefore, in these two positions the displacement is zero. This means that as the earth revolves around the sun, the star appears to move in an orbit 20.5 seconds around the true direction of the star.

The radial velocity of a star is determined from the Doppler effect in the star's spectrum. The star is approaching the earth when the spectral lines are displaced toward the violet end of the spectrum and is receding from the earth when the displacement is toward the red end of the spectrum.

5.17 THE ABERRATION OF STARLIGHT

The aberration of starlight was first announced in 1727 (the year of Newton's death) by James Bradley, the Astronomer Royal at the Greenwich Observatory. The aberration of starlight, which is the apparent displacement of a star in the direction of the earth's motion, can be illustrated by observing the motion of raindrops on the side window of an automobile. On a calm day, when

5.18 TWILIGHT

The instant when the sun's upper limb disappears below the horizon is called sunset. Even though the sun is below the horizon after sunset, the earth still receives some of its light by refraction, reflection, and diffusion, and this light is visible above the western horizon.

Astronomical twilight is defined as the interval of time between sunset and when the sun's center is 18° below the horizon. This value represents the maximum angle at which light can be refracted by the earth's atmosphere. Civil twilight is defined as the interval of time between sunset and when the sun's center is 6° below the horizon. This value was selected arbitrarily, because when the sun is in this position, it is believed that the amount of light which the earth receives is insufficient

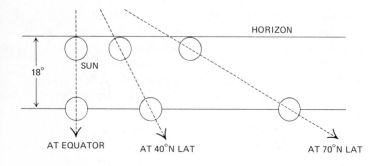

Fig. 5.15 The duration of twilight at different latitudes. As the latitude increases, the duration of twilight increases because the sun's path becomes more inclined to the horizon.

for the continuation of ordinary outdoor activities. The duration of twilight, as shown in Fig. 5.15, varies with the latitude—it depends on the time required for the sun to travel the 18° below the horizon. The sun's path with respect to the horizon also varies with the latitude. At the equator, the sun sets vertically with the horizon; as the latitude increases, the angle becomes more oblique. The duration of twilight at the equator is about one hour, whereas in the northern midlatitudes, it is several hours.

REVIEW

1. List several evidences to show that the earth's shape is spherical.

2. Define the oblateness of the earth's spheroid. What is its value?

3. Describe a method that is used to measure the earth's mass. What is the approximate value for the earth's mass?

4. Discuss the probable structure of the earth's interior. How was information about the structure of the earth's core obtained?

5. What is meant by the half-life of a radio element? Explain how a fairly accurate estimate of the earth's age can be determined.

6. Describe the vertical distribution of the earth's atmosphere as to its composition, density, temperature, and physical phenomena that occur.

7. What is the most abundant element in the earth? What is the most abundant element in the earth's atmosphere?

8. What is atmospheric refraction? Describe some of the interesting effects produced by atmospheric refraction.

9. Explain why the planets and stars are not normally visible in the daytime sky.

10. What are the "telluric lines"? How can they be identified from the absorption lines produced by celestial bodies?

11. Describe the earth's magnetic field in terms of size, shape, composition, intensity, and variations.

12. Describe the structure and composition of the Van Allen radiation belt.

13. Describe and explain the changes in the shape and color of the setting sun.

14. Give three observable proofs that the earth both rotates and revolves.

15. At what time of the year at your own latitude will the longest period of twilight occur? Use a diagram to explain your answer. Explain by means of a diagram why the duration of twilight decreases with a decrease in latitude.

16. Since the earth rotates in a counterclockwise direction, explain why the stars appear to move in the opposite direction.

6
The Earth—
A Celestial Body

When the earth is considered as a celestial body, many terrestrial occurrences, such as the cycle of the seasons, the precessional motion of the earth's axis, the phenomenon of time, and the motions and positions of the celestial bodies, are more easily understood. The facts we must keep in mind are that the earth is a nearly spherical body hurtling through space at a speed of about $18\frac{1}{2}$ miles per second, revolving around the sun in an elliptical orbit, and rotating about its axis.

6.1 THE ORIENTATION OF THE EARTH IN SPACE

As the earth revolves around the sun, an observer sees the sun revolving around the earth in an easterly direction, which is an apparent motion. The sun's path in the sky is called the ecliptic. The earth maintains its equator at an angle of $23\frac{1}{2}°$ to the plane of its orbit (the plane of the ecliptic), which means that the earth's axis of rotation is maintained at an angle of inclination of $23\frac{1}{2}°$ from the perpendicular to the plane of the ecliptic. When the north end of the earth's axis is extended, it intersects the celestial sphere to within one degree of the north pole star, Polaris. The angle that Polaris makes with the horizon can be used to determine the latitude of the observer. For example, when the observer is at latitude 40° north, Polaris is observed at an angle of 40° above the horizon. At this latitude (Fig. 6.1) the celestial bodies appear to move along diurnal circles (circles parallel to the celestial equator) that are inclined 50° to the horizon. Stars that are located within 40° of Polaris will never set. These are called circumpolar stars and are always above the horizon.

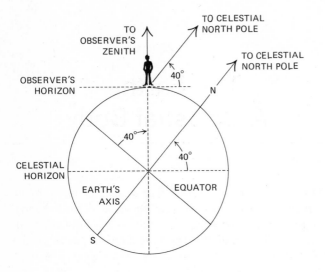

Fig. 6.1 The latitude of the observer is equal to the angle of the celestial north pole above the observer's horizon. For an observer at latitude 40°, any star within 40° of the celestial north pole is a circumpolar star and never sets.

When the observer is at latitude 90° north (north pole), Polaris is observed at an angle of 90° above the horizon, that is, directly overhead at the observer's zenith. At this latitude, the stars appear to move along diurnal circles parallel to the horizon. This means that the stars neither rise nor set; thus, at this latitude the observer is able to see half of the star sphere during one year.

When the observer is at latitude 0° (equator), Polaris is observed on the horizon. At this latitude, the stars appear to move along diurnal circles that are perpendicular to the horizon, which means that they appear to rise vertically on the eastern horizon and set vertically on the western horizon.

6.2 THE SEASONS

Many people have the fallacious belief that the seasons are caused by the earth's distance from the sun—the earth is closer to the sun in summer than in winter. Actually, the earth is nearest the sun in the winter (about January 3) and farthest from the sun in the summer (about July 3). During the year its distance from the sun varies by about 3 million miles (4,827,900 km), and this difference produces a temperature change on the earth's surface of about two degrees. Therefore, a change in the

earth's distance from the sun does not produce a change in the earth's seasons. The two factors that produce the earth's seasons are the inclination of the earth's equator to the plane of the ecliptic and the revolution of the earth around the sun.

The orientation of the earth in space is such that its axis always points toward the north pole star (Polaris), and its equator always maintains an angel of $23\frac{1}{2}°$ with the orbital plane which is the plane of the ecliptic (Fig. 6.2). However, as the earth revolves around the sun, the inclination of the earth's equator to the sun gradually moves from $23\frac{1}{2}°$ below to $23\frac{1}{2}°$ above the plane of the ecliptic during a one-year period. On June 21, the first day of summer, the earth is inclined toward the sun, the earth's equator is $23\frac{1}{2}°$ below the plane of the ecliptic, and the sun appears directly overhead to an observer at $23\frac{1}{2}°$ north latitude. This parallel of latitude on the earth's surface is called the Tropic of Cancer and marks the farthest point north of the equator that the sun reaches. Six months later, on December 21, the first day of winter, the earth's axis is inclined away from the sun, the earth's equator is $23\frac{1}{2}°$ above the plane of the ecliptic, and the sun appears directly overhead to an observer at $23\frac{1}{2}°$ south latitude. This parallel of latitude on the earth's surface is called the Tropic of Capricorn and marks the farthest point south of the equator that the sun reaches. On March 21, the first day of spring, and on September 21, the first day of autumn, the earth's axis points neither toward nor away from the sun, and the sun appears at the intersection of the equator and the ecliptic.

Since the plane of the earth's orbit coincides with the plane of the ecliptic, the latter is inclined $23\frac{1}{2}°$ to the plane of the celestial equator (Fig. 6.3), and the celestial equator coincides with the terrestrial equator. On the first day of summer the sun appears $23\frac{1}{2}°$ above the celestial equator and occupies a point on the ecliptic called the summer solstice. On the first day of winter, the sun appears $23\frac{1}{2}°$ below the celestial equator and occupies a point on the ecliptic called the winter solstice. The intersection of the ecliptic and the celestial equator as the sun is moving from below to above the equator is called the vernal equinox. The sun is in this position on March 21, the first day of spring. Six months later, when the sun is moving from above to below the equator, it crosses the celestial equator at the point called the autumnal equinox. The sun is in this position on September 21, the first day of autumn. Because of leap years, the dates at which the sun reaches the summer and winter solstices and the vernal and autumnal equinoxes vary slightly from one year to the next.

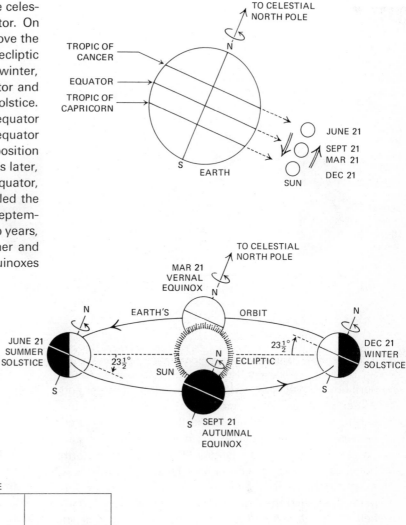

Fig. 6.2 Orientation of the earth's axis in space. The earth maintains its equator at an angle of 23–1/2° to the plane of ecliptic. The north pole of the earth's axis of rotation points to the north celestial pole, which is within one degree of Polaris.

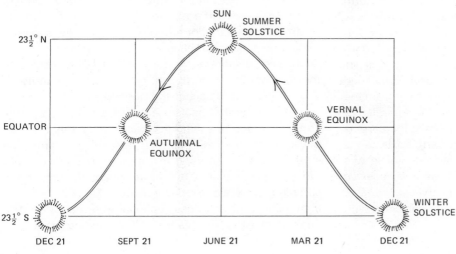

Fig. 6.3 As the earth revolves around the sun, the sun appears to move annually from 23–1/2° below the celestial equator (winter solstice) to 23–1/2° above the celestial equator (summer solstice), and back to 23–1/2° below.

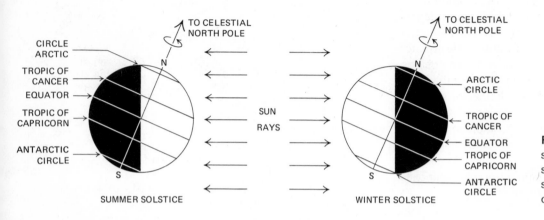

CIRCLE ARCTIC
TROPIC OF CANCER
EQUATOR
TROPIC OF CAPRICORN
ANTARCTIC CIRCLE

TO CELESTIAL NORTH POLE

N

S

SUN RAYS

SUMMER SOLSTICE

TO CELESTIAL NORTH POLE

N

ARCTIC CIRCLE
TROPIC OF CANCER
EQUATOR
TROPIC OF CAPRICORN
ANTARCTIC CIRCLE

S

WINTER SOLSTICE

Fig. 6.4 In the northern hemisphere the longest day and shortest night occur at summer solstice. At winter solstice, the opposite occurs.

Figure 6.4 shows the earth-sun relationship in the northern hemisphere when the sun is at summer and winter solstices. At summer solstice, one-half of the earth's surface, including the north pole, is illuminated because the earth's polar axis is inclined toward the sun. The earth's surface from latitude $66\frac{1}{2}°$ north to the north pole has the sun above the horizon for 24 hours each day, a condition called the midnight sun. The $66\frac{1}{2}°$ north parallel is called the Arctic circle. At winter solstice, one-half of the earth's surface, including the south pole, is illuminated because the earth's solar axis is inclined away from the sun. The midnight sun is visible from the south pole to $66\frac{1}{2}°$ south latitude. The $66\frac{1}{2}°$ parallel of latitude is called the Antarctic circle. When the earth is at the vernal or autumnal equinox, the earth's axis points neither toward nor away from the sun; on these two dates, therefore, the entire earth's surface receives exactly twelve hours of daylight and twelve hours of darkness because the sun's diurnal path coincides with the celestial equator.

Figure 6.5 shows the sun's daily path on these four important dates for an observer in San Francisco, which is located approximately half way between the northern and southern borders of the United States on about the 38th parallel of latitude north. At winter solstice, the sun rises in the southeast, reaches a height of about $28\frac{1}{2}°$ above the horizon at noon, and sets in the southwest. At vernal or autumnal equinox, the sun rises directly in the east, reaches a height of about 52° at noon, and sets directly in the west. At summer solstice, the sun rises in the northeast, reaches a height of about $75\frac{1}{2}°$ at noon, and sets in the northwest.

The amount of heat received by a given area of the earth's surface (insolation) varies throughout the year because the direction in which the sun's rays strike the earth's surface also vary. In summer the sun's rays are more perpendicular, whereas in winter they strike the surface more obliquely. As shown in Fig. 6.6, a ray of light with a given cross-sectional area has a definite amount of heat. As this ray of light strikes the earth's

Fig. 6.5 The sun's daily path in the city of San Francisco at winter solstice (*a*), summer solstice (*b*), and vernal and autumnal equinoxes (*c*)

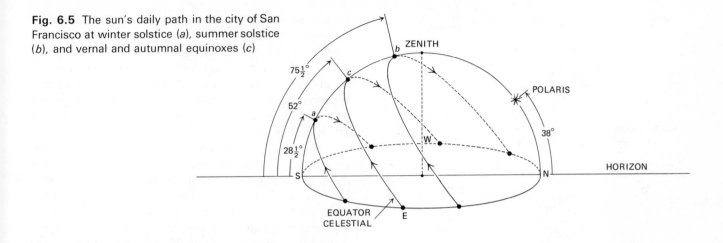

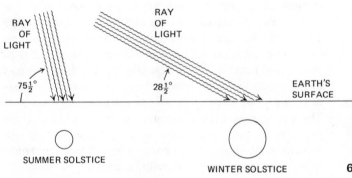

SUMMER SOLSTICE

WINTER SOLSTICE

Fig. 6.6 At summer solstice in San Francisco, the sun is at its highest position above the horizon, and maximum energy is deposited on a unit area of the earth's surface in one minute. At winter solstice the sun is low, and the same amount of energy is deposited over a larger area.

6.3 THE PRECESSION OF THE EARTH

The ancient Greeks observed that the planets move within a band in the sky about 18° in width with the ecliptic, the apparent path of the sun, as its center-line. They divided this band into 12 equal segments, each 30° in length, with each segment named for the constellation which lies within it. The Greeks called the band the "Zodiac" because many of the constellations represented animals. About 2000 B.C., the vernal equinox was located in the constellation of Aries the Ram. During the period that Christ lived, the vernal equinox had moved into the constellation of Pisces the Fishes. It is interesting to note that the early symbol of Christ was the fish and that the period was known as the Piscean Age. Today, the vernal

surface at San Francisco at summer solstice, its heat will be deposited over a given area of its surface. At winter solstice, a similar ray of light with the same amount of heat strikes the earth's surface more obliquely and deposits the heat over almost twice the surface area; therefore, the temperature of a unit area on the earth's surface will be subsequently lower in winter.

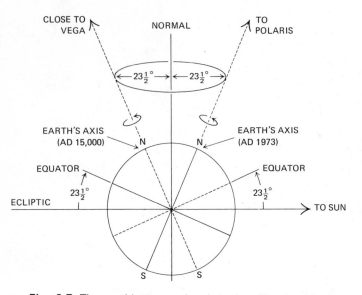

Fig. 6.7 The earth's precessional motion. The earth's axis completes one revolution about a line that is perpendicular to the plane of the ecliptic in about 26,000 years.

by the gravitational attraction of the sun and moon for the earth. The sun's gravitational force tends to pull the earth's equatorial bulge toward the plane of the ecliptic, and the moon's gravitational force tends to pull the earth's bulge toward the plane of the moon's orbit. Since the moon's gravitational attraction for the earth is greater and more differential than the sun's, only the moon's effect on the earth will be illustrated.

The earth as a rotating body acts like a gyroscope and resists the moon's efforts to move the bulge to the plane of the moon's orbit. The earth's equator maintains its angle of $23\frac{1}{2}°$ to the plane of the ecliptic, and the earth's axis moves in a direction opposite to the earth's rotation, describing a circle of $23\frac{1}{2}°$ radius about the ecliptic pole, which is a point 90° from the ecliptic plane. When the earth is observed from above its north pole, the precessional motion is clockwise. This motion is similar to that of a spinning top, whose axis of rotation is inclined toward the vertical. At the present time, the earth's axis points toward the star Polaris. Nearly 4000 years ago, the earth's axis pointed toward the star Thuban in the constellation of Draco the Dragon. About 12,000 years from now, it will be pointing toward the star Vega in the constellation of Lyra the Harp. As the earth precesses, the equinoxes slide westward along the ecliptic. The precession of the equinoxes does not affect the seasons or their sequence. It simply causes a given season to occur when the earth is in a different position in its orbit around the sun with respect to the stars.

6.4 THE TERRESTRIAL SPHERE

An understanding of the relationship that exists between the earth and the celestial bodies is essential for traveling by land, water, or air, for establishing the position of the celestial bodies in relation to the observer's position on the earth, and for understanding the phenomenon of time. To determine the observer's position on the earth's surface, we first assume that the earth is a sphere and that a coordinate system (grid) based on the earth's axis of rotation (Fig. 6.8) is established. This axis is an excellent, convenient, and natural reference. Its ends are designated as the north and south poles of the grid. The

equinox is in the constellation of Pisces and is moving toward the constellation of Aquarius the Water Carrier. This westward movement of the equinoxes is called the precession of the equinoxes. The equinoxes slide westward along the ecliptic at the rate of about 50.2 seconds each year and will complete one circle in the sky in about 26,000 years.

Although the vernal equinox is still in the constellation of Pisces and is moving toward the constellation of Aquarius, some people believe that the Age of Aquarius has already started. The misunderstanding appears to stem from the fact that the early astrologers had assigned only 24,000 years for the period of the earth's precession, or 2000 years for each age.

The precession of the equinoxes is produced by the earth's third principal motion, called precession, which is defined as the slow circular motion of the earth's axis about a line that is perpendicular to the plane of the ecliptic (Fig. 6.7). This motion is caused

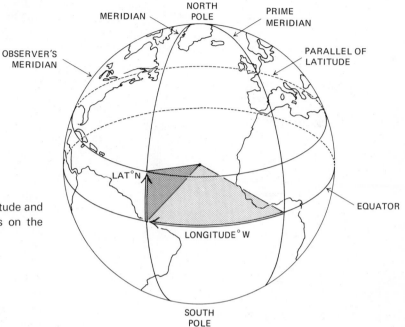

NORTH
POLE

MERIDIAN

PRIME
MERIDIAN

OBSERVER'S
MERIDIAN

PARALLEL OF
LATITUDE

LAT°N

EQUATOR

LONGITUDE°W

SOUTH
POLE

Fig. 6.8 The terrestrial sphere. The coordinates latitude and longitude are used to locate the position of places on the earth's surface.

great circle (formed by a plane passed through the center of the sphere) that is half way between the poles is the equator. The great circles which pass through both poles and intersect the equator at right angles are meridians. The meridian which passes through the Greenwich Observatory, England is the reference meridian, or zero meridian. The meridian which passes through the observer's position (represented by a circle in Fig. 6.8) is the observer's meridian. The small circles (formed by a plane that does not pass through the center of the sphere) that are parallel to the equator are latitude circles.

The observer's position on the earth's surface is determined by two coordinates, longitude and latitude. Longitude is the angle measured from the reference meridian, east or west along the equator, to the meridian which passes through the place. It varies from 0° to 180° east or west. Latitude is the angle measured from the equator, north or south along a meridian, to the latitude circle which passes through the place. It varies from 0°

to 90° north or south. Since the earth is an oblate spheroid, the length of one degree of latitude at the poles is about 0.7 statute miles (1.13 km) longer than at the equator. At the poles it is about 69.4 statute miles (111.69 km), while at the equator it is about 68.7 statute miles (110.56 km).

The longitude and latitude of a position vary over a period of years. The variation is produced by the movement of the land with respect to the earth's axis of rotation and involves the complex movement of the poles along two paths that are almost circular. One is slightly less than 10 feet, while the other varies from 10 to 20 feet (3.05 to 6.10 meters) in diameter. The period of motion along the first circle is about one year and is believed to be caused by the seasonal shifting of the earth's masses; the period along the second circle is about 14 months and is believed to be caused by a natural oscillation due to the earth's mass not being symmetrical about its axis of rotation.

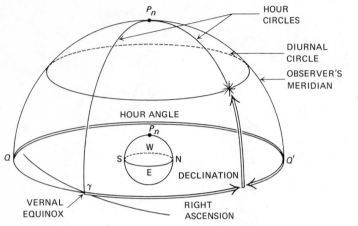

Fig. 6.9 The celestial sphere. The coordinates right ascension or hour angle and declination are used to locate the position of celestial bodies in the sky.

The position of a celestial body on the celestial sphere is determined by the coordinates right ascension and declination or by the coordinates hour angle and declination, which are analogous to longitude and latitude on the terrestrial sphere. Right ascension is the angle measured from the hour circle which passes through the vernal equinox (the imaginary intersection of the celestial equator and the ecliptic) eastward along the celestial equator to the hour circle which passes through the body. This angle varies from 0° to 360°. Declination is the angle measured from the celestial equator, north or south along an hour circle, to the diurnal circle which passes through the body. This angle varies from 0° to 90° north or south. The hour angle is measured from the upper branch of the observer's celestial meridian, westward along the equator, to the hour circle which passes through the body. The upper branch is the half of the observer's meridian that includes the zenith, the point directly above the observer.

6.5 THE CELESTIAL SPHERE

A casual observer watching the evening sky has the distinct feeling the he is at the center of an immense sphere (celestial sphere) which appears to rotate slowly around him. This concept, which the ancient Greeks believed to be true, is a useful device for understanding the apparent motion of the celestial bodies, the orientation of these bodies in relation to the observer, and the determination of time.

The celestial sphere is hollow and of infinite radius. The earth is at its center, and the celestial bodies appear to be attached to its inner surface. The celestial sphere's grid is an extension of the terrestrial grid and is called the equator system (Fig. 6.9). The extension of the earth's axis to the celestial sphere is the celestial axis, and its ends mark the north and south celestial poles. The projection of the earth's equator is the celestial equator and the earth's meridians are hour circles. The observer's celestial meridian, which is represented by a circle in Fig. 6.9, is the projection of the observer's terrestrial meridian. The projection of a latitude circle is a diurnal circle and represents the daily apparent path of a celestial body.

6.6 THE HORIZON SYSTEM

The position of a celestial body can also be located on a grid (horizon system) which is based on the observer's horizon and zenith point (Fig. 6.10). The axis which passes through the observer and the center of the earth, when extended to the celestial sphere, marks the zenith (located directly above the observer) and the nadir (directly below the observer). The great circle on the celestial sphere whose points are 90° from the zenith is the observer's horizon, and the great circles which pass through the zenith and nadir and intersect the horizon at

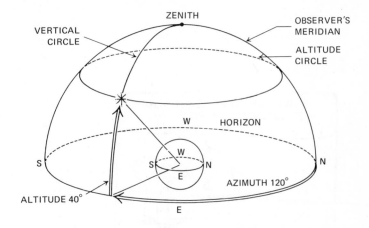

Fig. 6.10 The horizon system. The coordinates altitude and azimuth are used to locate the position of celestial bodies in the sky.

right angles are vertical circles. The small circles that are parallel to the horizon are altitude circles.

The two coordinates that determine the position of a body in the horizon system are azimuth and altitude. Azimuth is the angle measured from the north point on the horizon clockwise along the horizon to the vertical circle which passes through the body. The angle varies from 0° to 360°. Altitude is the angle measured from the horizon north along a vertical circle to the altitude circle which passes through the body.

6.7 ARC AND TIME UNITS

The circumference of a circle is divided into 360 equal units (degrees). The degree is subdivided into 60 equal units (minutes), and the minute is subdivided into 60 equal units (seconds). A portion of the circumference is usually expressed as an angle or as an arc, because an angle of 12° 17′ 23″ subtends, or corresponds, to an arc of the same value.

Astronomical angles are often expressed as units of time. On the first day of spring the sun follows a path in the sky which coincides with the celestial equator. During that 24-hour period, the sun travels along 360 degrees of arc. Therefore, in one hour the sun travels 15°; in four minutes, it travels 1°; and in one minute, it travels four seconds.

Arc Units	Time Units
15 degrees	= 1 hour, or 60 minutes
1 degree	= 4 minutes
1 minute	= 4 seconds

6.8 TIME

Alice sighed wearily, "I think you might do something better with the time," she said, "than wasting it in asking riddles that have no answers."

"If you knew Time as well as I do," said the Hatter, "you wouldn't talk about wasting it. Its him."

"I don't know what you mean," said Alice.

"Of course you don't!" the Hatter said, tossing his head contemptuously. "I dare say you never even spoke to Time!"

Lewis Carroll, *Alice in Wonderland*

Time is one of the most disquieting concepts the human mind has ever pondered. Men can measure time, they can go into great detail in describing it (my apologies to the Hatter), and yet they cannot define time—they cannot give time an objective denotation. With this fundamental limitation in mind, some of the basic descriptive facts about time and some of the complexities which lie below the surface will be presented. One should not lose sight of the fact that "time" is simply a word which convenience has given to a number of different phenomena. There is subjective time, historical time, religious time, and scientific time. Yet all these different phenomena come under the rubric "time." Although the

By permission of Johnny Hart and Field Enterprises, Inc.

purpose of this text does not permit going into all the labyrinths of time, some of its aspects which deal directly with astronomy will be presented.

Time is a phenomenon with which we come into contact every day of our lives. Like early man, we are aware of the diurnal alternation between day and night. As modern men, we continually consult our watches (the demigods of industrial society) to be certain that unlike the white rabbit, we are not in danger of losing our heads by being late. Time is embodied in the very language that we use to communicate with one another; the tenses of verbs in English break up the world into the past, present, and future and incorporate subtle distinctions in progressive tenses. We see time which is lineal and cyclical working in nature. Days become nights; the year passes through the four seasons and then repeats the process; waves beat upon the shore in what appears to be the rhythm of eternity. Although the waves seem to be eternal, the shoreline is slowly eroded away. Man's life is a definite linear transition: birth, growth, and death. All these phenomena are aspects of time's presence in the world.

From the average man's perspective, time is a normal part of his life. Without time, a three-minute poached egg would almost be an impossibility. Yet time is a frightening question because it is a force that devours man. Wise men have realized that happiness and love are vulnerable to time. Moreover, deep reflection on time brings the realization that there are things in the universe that are beyond man's ability to comprehend. Man must finally accept his own inadequacies and realize that he is not as all-powerful as he believes. Alfred N. Whitehead, a profound philosopher and physicist, said that "it is impossible to meditate on time and the mysteries of the creative passage of nature without an overwhelming emotion at the limitations of human intelligence."[1]

6.9 SOME VIEWS OF TIME

The Greek philosopher Heraclitus (fl. 500 B.C.) believed that change is the sole reality of the universe. His

[1]Alfred N. Whitehead, *Concept of Nature*, Cambridge: Cambridge University Press, 1920, p. 73.

conception of the flux is embodied in the dictum that "you never step twice into the same river: for fresh waters are ever flowing in upon you."[2] He further explained that if things were stationary, time would not exist and there would be nothing in the universe. The universe exhibited a state of being only because it was continuously changing. Time was a continuous movement of things. The symbol of Heraclitus' world was fire, which he saw as a continuous process of becoming.

The Greek philosopher Parmenides (fl. 540 B.C.) took the diametrically opposite point of view: only things which are permanent can be real. Thus, fire, in order to exist, must be a complete entity rather than a process of becoming. Change and time are unreal and do not exist.

Plato accepted both conclusions, but he relegated Heraclitus' theory of becoming to the temporal world. Plato translated Parmenides' theory of being into his own theory of Ideas, or Forms; these Forms are the eternal foundation upon which the ephemeral world of time and matter is built.

Christianity, an excellent example of linear time, sees itself as a historical religion—the events upon which it is based are considered real. Thus, Christ, although God incarnate, is considered to be a historical personage who lived and died on earth. He is seen as the catalyst that set in motion a running down of time, a process beginning in Genesis and ending in the Bible's final book, Revelations, ". . . and there should be time no longer" (Revelations 10:6). Christians see history as moving inexorably toward that day in the future when Christ will reappear. They believe that at that instant, time will cease forever, and only the pure beauty of eternity will remain. Thus, time is linear, bringing the world ever closer to the millenium.

John Locke (1632–1704), the British empiricist, was not concerned with the basic nature of time. He believed that all human knowledge comes from the senses. Thus, man's notion of time is a product of experience. He rejected the theory (developed later by Kant) that ideas precede experiences. He said that as a metaphor for human knowledge, the human mind is a blank sheet upon which experience is imprinted, thus providing man with ideas. Time is a complex idea created in the mind by combining the simple ideas of succession (the movement of ideas in the mind) and duration (the distance between the ideas). Thus, time is merely a mental construction.

Isaac Newton (1642–1727), the British philosopher and scientist, gave us two views of time:

absolute, true, and mathematical time, of itself, and from its own nature, flows equably without relation to anything external, and by another name is called duration: relative, apparent, and common time, is some sensible and external (whether accurate or unequable) measure of duration by means of motion, which is commonly used instead of true time; such as an hour, a day, a month, a year.[3]

Thus, time is both absolute and relative. The time which man experiences directly, "common time," is only a meager approximation of absolute, or mathematical, time. Absolute time exists in a state above the physical universe; it has many characteristics of the Platonic form. Newton's view of time was generally accepted until Einstein brought time back into the physical world and made it the fourth dimension in his model of the universe.

6.10 TIMEKEEPERS

Although accurate records are not available, we can imagine what early man's attempts were to understand the apparent motion of the celestial bodies and to measure the flow of time. The apparent motion of the sun and the moon presented two natural and simple means of measuring time. The recurring astronomical phenomenon of the rising sun was the interval of time defined by early man as the day. The interval of time between two consecutive new moons was defined as the lunar month. The interval of time called the year, or the seasons, was determined by the apparent position of the rising sun.

---

[2]Quoted from John Burnet's *Early Greek Philosophy*, New York: Harper & Row, fragment 41.

[3]*Sir Isaac Newton's Mathematical Principles of Natural Philosophy and the System of the World (Principia)*, trans. by Andrew Motte, revised by Florian Cajori, Berkeley: University of California Press, 1934, 1962, p. 6.

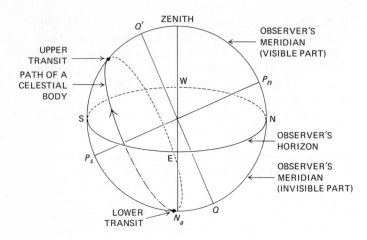

Fig. 6.11 The upper and lower transits of a celestial body in its daily path in the sky. When a body crosses the visible part of the observer's meridian, it is called upper transit. When a body crosses the observer's meridian below the horizon, it is called lower transit.

In the summer, it appeared to rise in the northeast. With each passing day, its rising position shifted slowly to the south so that by winter, it appeared to rise in the southeast. Then, its rising position shifted slowly to the north until it appeared to rise once again in the northeast in the summer.

One of the earliest devices used in determining the sun's position and the length of the year was the shadow clock, or "gnomon," developed by the Egyptians. In its simplest form it was just a straight stick placed vertically in the ground. The length of the stick's shadow indicated the season. The longest shadow occurred in the winter when the noon sun's position was low in the sky, and the shortest shadow occurred in the summer when the noon sun's position was high in the sky. The counting of the sunrises during the interval of time between two consecutive appearances of the shortest shadow established the number of days in the year.

Since the "gnomon" could be used only during the day when the sun was visible, the water clock (clepsydrae), which could be used both day and night, was developed in Egypt about 1500 B.C. It operated on the principle of water entering or leaving a container at a regular rate of flow. In the middle of the seventeenth century, the Dutch physicist Christian Huygens invented the pendulum, which revolutionized the manufacture of timekeepers and made all previous methods and devices obsolete. With the invention of the pendulum and the discovery by Galileo that its period of oscillation is independent of its amplitude, the construction of a pendulum-operated clock was made possible. The pendulum clock and the electric clock, which was invented later, permitted the passing of time to be recorded by measuring the short intervals of time which result from the apparent motions of the celestial bodies.

6.11 SIDEREAL TIME

Figure 6.11 shows that when a body crosses the visible part of the observer's celestial meridian (upper branch), it is called an upper transit; when it crosses the part below the horizon (lower branch), it is called a lower transit. The interval of time between two successive upper transits by a celestial body is defined as one day. When the body is the sun, it is called a solar day; the moon, a lunar day; and a star, a sidereal day. Solar and lunar days commence at lower transit, whereas sidereal days commence at upper transit.

Since the position of the vernal equinox is fixed (for all practical purposes) with respect to the stars, it can be

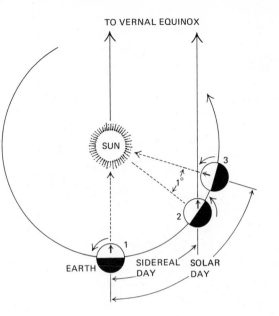

TO VERNAL EQUINOX

SUN

EARTH

SIDEREAL DAY

SOLAR DAY

Fig. 6.12 The duration of time for the earth to complete one rotation with respect to the vernal equinox or a star is a sideral day. A sideral day is approximately 3 minutes 56 seconds shorter than a solar day, the time in which the earth completes one rotation with respect to the sun.

used to determine sidereal time. When the vernal equinox is at upper transit, both the sidereal time and the hour angle of the vernal equinox are zero hours.

The sidereal day is approximately 3 minutes 56 seconds shorter than the solar day. This difference can be easily recognized in Fig. 6.12. When the earth has revolved around the sun from position 1 to 2, it has completed one rotation with respect to the vernal equinox and one sidereal day. Before the earth can complete one rotation with respect to the sun and one solar day, it must rotate about one more degree at the end of the sidereal day. To accomplish this, the earth must move in its orbit around the sun approximately 3 minutes 56 seconds. Since the sidereal day is about four minutes shorter than the solar day, the stars appear to rise and set about four minutes earlier each day by solar time; thus, at any given time each evening, the star sphere appears to have moved slightly to the west.

6.12 APPARENT SOLAR TIME

Time measured by the actual sun is called apparent solar time. The apparent solar day begins at midnight, when the sun is at lower transit. The interval of time between midnight and noon (when the sun is at upper

transit) is designated A.M., which means "before the meridian," and the interval of time between noon and midnight is designated P.M., which means "past the meridian." Apparent solar time is variable for two important reasons: (1) according to Kepler's second law of motion, the earth's orbital motion is faster when the earth is closer to the sun, and (2) since the sun appears to move along the ecliptic rather than the celestial equator, it also moves either northward or southward as it moves eastward.

6.13 MEAN SOLAR TIME

Since the actual sun is not a uniform timekeeper, a fictitious sun was invented to move along the celestial equator at a uniform rate equal to the average rate of the actual sun's motion along the ecliptic. The time kept by the fictitious sun is called mean solar time. The difference between mean solar time and apparent solar time at any instant is called the equation of time. This difference is never more than $16\frac{1}{2}$ minutes and is tabulated

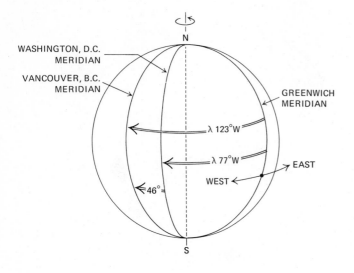

Fig. 6.13 Local time is determined by the observer's celestial meridian. The difference in the local time at two places is equal to the difference of their longitudes.

for every day of the year in the *American Ephemeris (Nautical Almanac)*. The equation of time is designated (+) when the apparent time is faster, and (−) when it is slower than the mean time. About four times each year, the apparent and mean solar times are equal, and then the equation of time is zero.

6.14 LOCAL TIME

When the observer's celestial meridian is used as the reference to determine time, it is called local time. By international agreement, the local mean solar time at the meridian which passes through the Greenwich Observatory at Greenwich, England is called universal time. Astronomical and navigational data are usually recorded in this time. Since the earth's rotational motion is to the east, the sun appears to move across the sky to the west; therefore, local times at places to the east of the observer are always later. For example, the local time at Vancouver, British Columbia is earlier than at Washington, D.C., and the time at both places is earlier than at Greenwich, England because the sun passes over the eastern meridians first. In Fig. 6.13 the difference in the local time at two places is equal to the difference of their longitudes.

When the longitude of both places and the local time at one place are known, the local time at the other place can be determined by adding the difference of the longitudes to the known local time (if the other place is to the east) and subtracting the difference (if it is to the west). When the local mean time at Vancouver (longitude 123°W) is 7 hours 43 minutes, the local mean time at Washington (longitude 77°W) is determined by adding the difference of their longitudes, which is 46°. Since 1° of arc equals 4 minutes of time, 46° is equivalent to 3 hours 4 minutes, which is the difference in time between Vancouver and Washington. Therefore, the local time at Washington is 10 hours 47 minutes.

6.15 STANDARD TIME

Today, if each community in the United States kept its own local mean time, as was the case nearly 80 years ago, the situation would be chaotic, and only places on the same meridian would have the same time. To avoid this situation, a world-wide system of time zones was established by dividing the earth into 24 zones of 15° widths (Fig. 6.14). The time for all places in each zone is established by the zone's central meridian, which is designated as the standard meridian. The longitudes of the standard meridians are increments of 15 degrees, starting with the standard meridian which passes through the Greenwich Observatory (longitude 0°). The standard meridians to the west of Greenwich are designated positive; those to the east, negative.

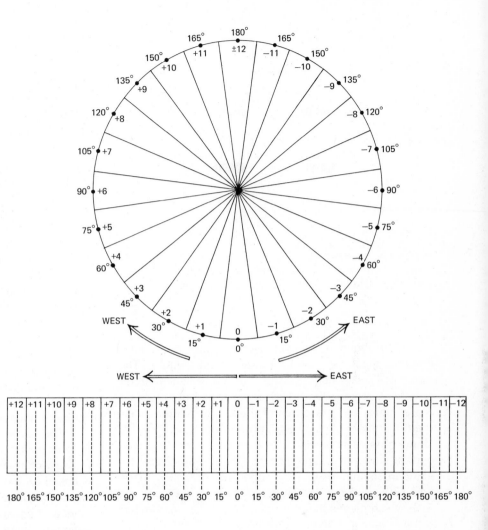

Fig. 6.14 Diagram of the earth's time zones as viewed from above the north pole. The degrees indicate the longitudes of the standard meridians of the zones from the Greenwich meridian. The inside numbers indicate the corrections in hours applied to universal time to obtain the standard time of the zones.

The zone in which a place is located can be determined by dividing its longitude by 15. Chicago, with a longitude of 88° west, is in zone +6. This designation makes it simple to convert the observer's standard time to universal time by simply applying the zone number with its appropriate sign. The +6 designation means that the time in that zone is 6 hours earlier than universal time. An easy rule to remember is that "when the longitude is west, Greenwich is best, and when the longitude is east, Greenwich is least." "Best" implies later time, and "least" is earlier time. What is the universal time when the standard time is 10:32 A.M. at longitude 79° 42′ west? The standard meridian for longitude 79° 42′ west is 75°, and its zone designation is +5.

Standard time	10:32
Zone number	+ 5:00
Universal time	15:32, or 3:32 P.M.

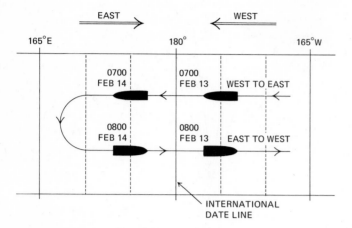

Fig. 6.15 The international date line. When the date line is crossed from west to east, the date is moved one day ahead. When the date line is crossed from east to west, the date is moved one day back.

Zone boundaries over water areas are regular, whereas those over land areas are most irregular. This difference was instituted for the convenience of the people in regional and local areas. There are places in the established time zones of the United States where the time differs by one hour from the standard time. The United States is divided into four time zones: eastern, central, mountain, and pacific. The longitudes of the standard meridians of each zone are: 75°, 90°, 105°, and 120°. The zone designations are: +5, +6, +7, and +8, which means that their standard times are from 5 to 8 hours earlier than universal time.

6.16 INTERNATIONAL DATE LINE

As an observer travels westward, he sets his watch back one hour for each 15° of longitude, because time is always later to the east; therefore, during a 24-hour period, he would lose 24 hours, and time would appear to be standing still. This, however, is impossible; therefore, by international agreement the date is changed when the observer crosses the international date line, which generally runs along the 180° longitude meridian, except for the land areas where it moves to the west

around the Aleutian Islands and to the east around Siberia. In Fig. 6.15, when the international date line is crossed from west to east, the date is moved one day ahead, and when it is crossed from east to west, it is moved back one day. Phineas Fogg, in *Around the World in 80 Days*, must have been eternally grateful to the man who devised this correction!

6.17 THE EARLY HISTORY OF CALENDARS

The earth's rotation, the apparent motion of the sun, and the apparent motion of the moon serve as the foundation for determining time; however, all attempts to combine these motions into a single system for determining time and establishing a calendar have always led to complications. The fact that the time units of the day, month, and year are not integral multiples of one another has prevented the establishment of a system based on any one motion to keep in step with the other two. If the earth rotated an exact number of times for each revolution made around the sun or if the earth rotated an exact number of times for each revolution of the moon around the earth, there would be considerably less difficulty in developing an accurate calendar.

The earliest known calendar used by most of the ancient people was the lunar calendar, which is still used by the Mohammedans. Of the simplest type, this calendar is based on the observation that the "new moon" occurs regularly about every $29\frac{1}{2}$ days. The lunar year has 354 days and consists of 12 months. Odd months have 30 days, and even months have 29 days.

The Egyptians were the first to develop and use a solar calendar based on the annual apparent motion of the sun and the recurring cycle of the seasons. At first, there were 360 days in the year, but this was later revised to 365 days. This calendar had 12 months of 30 days each, except for the last month, which had 35 days. Later, the Egyptians established the length of the year as $365\frac{1}{4}$ days; however, nothing was done about it until 238 B.C., when Ptolemy Evergetes I introduced the leap year, i.e., every fourth year had 366 instead of 365 days.

The ancient Jewish 12-month lunisolar calendar, a complex compromise of the lunar and solar calendars, is still in use today. Although it was adopted in the third century A.D., it had its roots in antiquity. It is probably the only calendar in which the counting of years started not from any particular event in their history, but from the day of creation, which the Jews established as having occurred in the fall of 3761 B.C., according to our present calendar.

In the Jewish calendar, each month is based on the motion of the moon around the earth, that is, $29\frac{1}{2}$ days. This makes the lunar year of 12 months about 11 days shorter than the solar year. Since three lunar years are about 33 days shorter than three solar years, every third lunar year has 13 lunar months instead of 12. This correction was inadequate, because there are $1091\frac{1}{2}$ days in 37 lunar months and $1095\frac{3}{4}$ days in 36 solar months, which means that there are about four days less in three lunar years than there are in three solar years. To correct this discrepancy, the 19-year period was established in which 19 solar years contain 6939.60 days, while 19 lunar years (12 years of 12 months each and 7 years of 13 months each) contain 6939.69 days.

The ancient Roman calendar was first a lunar type of 10 months and later a lunisolar type of 12 months. The passing of the years was counted from the legendary date of the founding of the city of Rome. The year was designated by the symbol A.U.C., the first letters of the Latin phrase *ab urbe condita*, which means the "year of the city." Since the Roman calendar was partly lunar, it was necessary to periodically add days to it so that the religious holidays could be observed at the proper time. This task, the prerogative of the priest, was so poorly administered and abused that the calendar soon fell out of step with the occurrence of natural events—the first day of spring was occurring in December rather than in March.

6.18 THE JULIAN CALENDAR

The history of the calendar is a record of compromises and reforms. The first great reform was made on the Roman calendar in 46 B.C. by Julius Caesar on the advice and recommendation of the Greek astronomer Sosigenes of Alexandria. Julius Caesar decreed that the year 46 B.C., which became known as the "year of confusion,"

would have 445 rather than 354 days. This was done to correct the nearly 90-day difference that existed between the calendar and the occurrence of the seasons. Caesar also decreed that the new calendar would commence on the first day of the new moon following the winter solstice in the year 45 B.C. In the new calendar, 31 days were assigned to the odd months, which were considered to be lucky, and 30 days to the even months, which were considered to be unlucky. February, however, was assigned 29 days because it was the "month of the dead." The Egyptian leap year was also added to the calendar. The new calendar is known as the Julian calendar, named in honor of Julius Caesar who instituted its reforms. Julius Caesar also changed the name of the seventh month, Quintilis, to July, in honor of himself.

Minor changes were made in the Julian calendar in 8 B.C. by Augustus Caesar. He changed the eighth month, Sextilis, to August, in honor of himself, and made the month 31 days long by taking one day from February. This change produced three consecutive months of 31 days each, which was considered unlucky; to rectify this, September and November were changed to 30 days, October and December to 31 days.

Another minor reform was made in the Julian calendar in the early part of the fourth century A.D. by the Greek emperor Constantine, who introduced the so-called Christian, seven-day week into the calendar by decree and made it legal throughout the Roman empire. Some scholars believe that the Christian seven-day week originated with the Babylonians rather than with the early Christians and that it was adopted by the Jews during their captivity. It is also believed that the Sabbath was adopted by the Jews from the Babylonian Sabbatu.

6.19 THE GREGORIAN CALENDAR

Even though the Julian calendar eliminated much of the confusion in the Roman lunisolar calendar, it was far from perfect. By 1582 the Julian calendar had accumulated an error of 10 days so that the first day of spring occurred on March 11 instead of March 21. To correct this error, which made the Julian year slightly longer than the tropical year, the second great reform on the Julian calendar was made in 1582. Authorized by the

Council of Trent and instituted by Pope Gregory XIII, 10 days were dropped from the calendar, and a unique rule, suggested by the Vatican librarian, Aloysuis Giglio, was adopted to keep the calendar closer in step with the length of the tropical year. All years divisible by 4 were designated leap years, except century years not divisible by 400, starting with the year 1700. This rule eliminated three days every 400 years, and this new calendar is known as the Gregorian calendar.

Unfortunately, since the Gregorian calendar was instituted by a Catholic pope shortly after the Reformation, many princes who had become Protestants would not accept the papal bull directing them to use the new calendar. The Catholic world adopted it in 1582, and the first Protestant country adopted it in 1700. The last four adoptions occurred in the twentieth century: China in 1912, Turkey in 1917, Soviet Russia in 1918, and Greece in 1923. Despite the fact that the Gregorian calendar is a great improvement over the Julian calendar, the Greek and the Russian Orthodox churches still use the Julian calendar.

6.20 PROPOSED CALENDAR REFORMS

Some people consider the Gregorian calendar to be imperfect because during a period of 1000 years, the date of the first day of spring will change by one day. This error is negligible for all practical purposes and can be easily corrected; however, these people have proposed further reforms to the calendar. The three most interesting of the proposed reforms are the 13-month calendar, the World calendar, and the Jubilee calendar.

In the 13-month calendar, a new month, "Sol," is placed between June and July. The year has 364 days, and each month has exactly four weeks of 28 days. The 365th day, which is placed at the end of the year, is considered an extra day and not part of a week. The 366th day is placed at the end of every fourth year, which is a leap year. It, too, is considered an extra day. The important feature of the 13-month calendar is that all the months are identical; therefore, only a one-month calendar would be required.

The World calendar year is divided into four equal quarters of 91 days. Each quarter is divided into three

months of 31, 30, and 30 days, respectively. Since the year has 364 days, the extra day is placed at the end of the year, and the 366th day is placed at the end of June in the leap year. The important feature of this calendar is that any given date will fall on the same weekday every year.

Many people oppose the adoption of these new calendars on the ground that they violate the Christian seven-day week. The basic major calendar reforms in the past have been astronomically inspired, whereas the proposed calendars are based on a change in the traditional, seven-day week. The Jubilee calendar was proposed by several religious groups in an attempt to preserve the seven-day week. A most interesting and unique calendar, it contains 12 months and 52 weeks. Every fifth year, except those divisible by 400 or ending in 25 or 75, is a leap year of 53 weeks.

6.21 THE JULIAN-DAY CALENDAR

Many attempts have been made to determine from the Bible and other sources the exact date of creation. Medieval Jewish scholars established the date as 3761 B.C. In A.D. 1650 James Ussher, an Anglican archbishop, placed the date of creation at 4004 B.C. The oldest date of creation, 5508 B.C., was established by Greek Orthodox theologians.

In 1585 Julius Scaliger proposed a calendar according to which days are numbered consecutively from noon, universal time, January 1, 4713 B.C., the date of creation he had established. This is a very practical calendar because it has no weeks, months, or years. To obtain the interval of time between any two events or to determine the time of an event requires a simple addition or subtraction of two numbers. The day on which the event occurred is called the Julian day. This calendar is used by astronomers in predicting the date of the occurrence of a celestial event and the times of maxima and minima in the period of variable stars. The Julian-day numbers for each year are tabulated in the *American Ephemeris and Nautical Almanac* and the *Handbook of the Royal Astronomical Society of Canada*. The Julian day for January 1, 1973, for example, is designated as 2,441, 684 J.D.

REVIEW

1. Describe the orientation of the earth's axis in space. What is the effect on the position of the celestial north pole (Polaris) as an observer moves (a) northward, (b) eastward?

2. Explain the location of the vernal equinox, autumnal equinox, summer solstice, and winter solstice on the ecliptic with respect to the celestial equator.

3. As viewed from the earth, what is the direction of the sun's apparent motion? Explain.

4. Discuss the validity of the statement that since summer in the northern hemisphere is warmer than winter, the sun is closer to the earth at that time.

5. Explain what seasonal variations would result if the earth's axis were (a) perpendicular to its orbital plane, and (b) parallel to its orbital plane.

6. What is the precession of the equinoxes? What causes this motion? What is its period?

7. Suppose that the observer is at the equator. (a) Where is his zenith point located? (b) Where is the north celestial pole located? (c) Describe the daily motion of the celestial bodies.

8. What coordinates are used to locate a star on the horizon system? How can it be located on the equator system?

9. What are the altitude and azimuth of the west point of the horizon?

10. What are the names of the following elements of the terrestrial sphere when they are projected to the celestial sphere: equator, meridian, and a small circle parallel to the equator.

11. What is meant by a circumpolar star? What is the minimum declination for a circumpolar star at your latitude?

12. What are the right ascension and declination of the (a) vernal equinox, (b) autumnal equinox, (c) summer solstice, and (d) winter solstice?

13. Convert 2 hours 18 minutes to arc units. Convert 79° 30′ to time units.

14. Define a sidereal and a solar day. What is the difference between these two time intervals? Which is longer? Why? How does this difference affect the time that the stars rise on successive days as based on solar time?

15. What timekeepers are used to determine apparent solar time and mean solar time? What is the equation of time? How is it used?

16. What is the difference in the local civil time between two places whose difference in longitude is 75°?

17. In what time zone do you live? What is the longitude of its central meridian? What is the difference between your standard time and local civil time?

18. Are the time zones spaced uniformly on the earth's surface? Explain.

19. What is universal time? Who uses it? Why?

20. Why was the international date line established? A ship moving in an easterly direction crosses the international date line at 2:30 A.M. standard time on February 13. What will be the time and date when the ship has crossed the line?

21. When was the Julian calendar introduced? Explain the reforms that were made to establish the Julian calendar. Who instituted these reforms?

22. On what calendar were the Gregorian reforms made? Why? What were these reforms? How did the people react to the Gregorian calendar? Why?

23. Will there be a need to reform the Gregorian calendar? What is your reaction to the 13-month calendar and the World calendar that have been proposed? Should they be adopted? Why?

24. Explain the principle on which the Julian-day calendar is based. What is the Julian day for an event that will occur on November 19, 1973?

7

The Moon—Earth's
Nearest Neighbor

After the sun, the moon is the most conspicuous object in the sky. At a mean distance of 238,857 miles (384,393 km), it is earth's nearest neighbor and only natural satellite. Before the invention of the telescope, man saw the moon as a beautiful and mysterious silvery sphere patched with irregular dark areas. Most of the pictures of the moon drawn in manuscripts and executed on stained-glass windows by medieval man depicted the dark areas as the outline of a human face. After the invention of the telescope, Galileo sketched rather crudely the surface features of the moon from telescopic observations and presented them with a complete description in his book *Sidereus Nuncius*. He named the dark areas maria, believing them to be seas, and recognized the light areas as irregular land forms.

7.1 TRUE MOTIONS

The two true motions of the moon are revolution and rotation. When the sun is used as a reference point, the moon revolves around the earth in an elliptical orbit in about $29\frac{1}{2}$ days. This is called a synodic month and is the interval of time from one full moon to the next. When a star is used as a reference point, the moon completes one revolution around the earth in about $27\frac{1}{3}$ days. This interval of time is called a sidereal month. The difference between these two periods is approximately two days (Fig. 7.1).

As the earth revolves around the sun and the moon revolves around the earth during a synodic month, the moon continuously changes its position with respect to the sun and follows a wave-like path around the sun

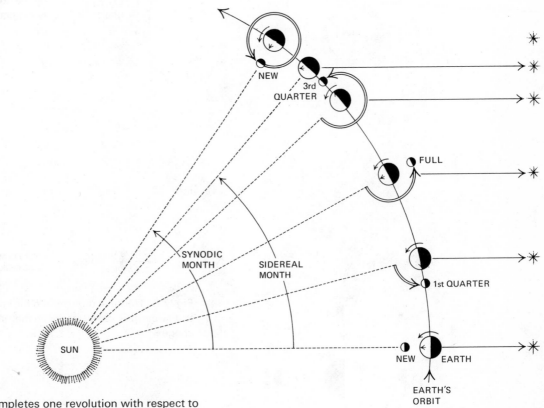

Fig. 7.1 The moon completes one revolution with respect to the stars in $27\frac{1}{3}$ days, the sidereal month. One revolution with respect to the sun is $29\frac{1}{2}$ days, the synodic month.

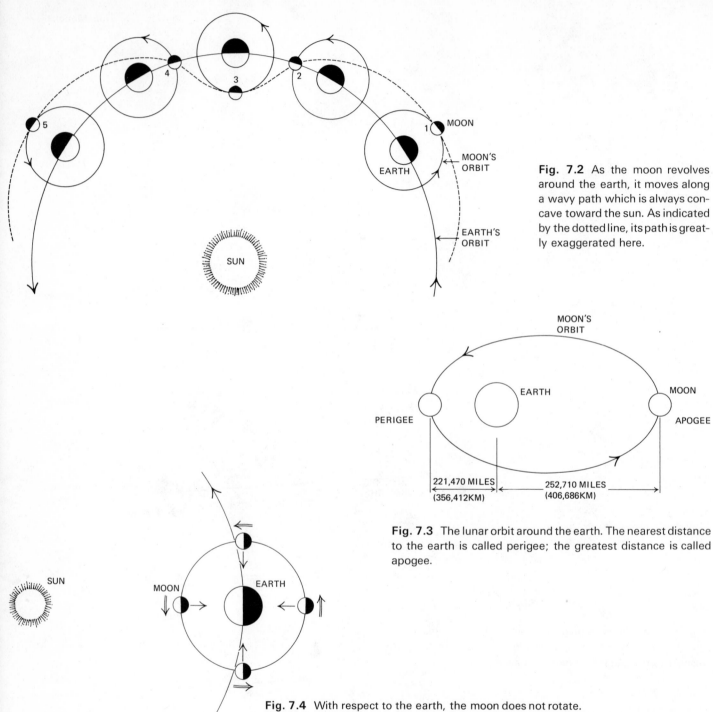

Fig. 7.2 As the moon revolves around the earth, it moves along a wavy path which is always concave toward the sun. As indicated by the dotted line, its path is greatly exaggerated here.

Fig. 7.3 The lunar orbit around the earth. The nearest distance to the earth is called perigee; the greatest distance is called apogee.

Fig. 7.4 With respect to the earth, the moon does not rotate. With respect to the sun, the moon completes one rotation in $29\frac{1}{2}$ days.

(Fig. 7.2). Since the sun's distance from the earth is nearly 400 times greater than the moon's, the moon's path is considerably flatter than that shown in the figure. Also, the gravitational force exerted on the moon by the sun is more than twice that exerted by the earth; therefore, the moon's greatest acceleration is always in the direction of the sun, which causes the moon's path to be concave toward the sun.

The moon's orbit is inclined to the ecliptic at a mean angle of 5°09'. This angle varies about 24 minutes because of the moon's perturbations. The moon's equator is inclined about $6\frac{1}{2}°$ to its orbital plane. The point in the moon's orbit that is closest to the earth is called perigee, and the point farthest from the earth is called apogee (Fig. 7.3). The perigee distance is about 221, 470 miles (356,412 km), and the apogee distance is about 252,710 miles (406,686 km).

As the moon revolves around the earth, it rotates about its axis; its period of rotation is equal to its period of revolution. Therefore, the moon always presents the same face to the earth and does not appear to rotate (Fig. 7.4); with respect to the sun, the moon does rotate.

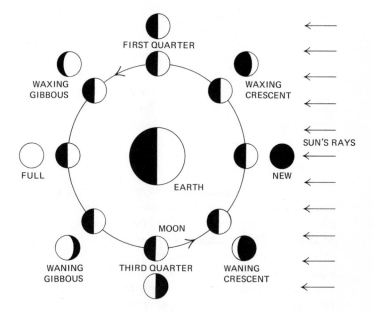

Fig. 7.5 Phases of the moon. The outer figures show the phases of the moon as seen from the earth.

7.2 APPARENT MOTIONS

The moon appears to rise daily in the east, move across the sky, and set in the west. This daily apparent westward motion is caused by the rotation of the earth about its axis. Every day the moon and the sun appear to travel eastward with respect to the stars—the moon at the rate of about 13°, and the sun at the rate of about 1°. Therefore, since the moon's travel eastward is faster than the sun's by about 12° each day, it circles the sun once every $29\frac{1}{2}$ days.

7.3 PHASES

The daily apparent eastward motion of the moon produces changes in the shape of its illuminated disk. These changes are called the phases of the moon. When the moon is between the earth and the sun, its disk is dark and its phase is new. The new moon rises and sets with the sun. For the next $7\frac{1}{2}$ days, the moon's phase is a waxing crescent (Fig. 7.5) and is seen rising higher in the western sky each day after sunset. When the moon has traveled about one-fourth of its path around the earth and is about 90° east of the sun, it is in the first-quarter phase, and one-half of its disk appears illuminated. The first-quarter moon rises at noon and sets at midnight. During the second $7\frac{1}{2}$-day period, the phase is a waxing gibbous, and the moon rises between noon and sunset and sets between midnight and sunrise. When the moon has traveled one-half of its path around the earth and is about 180° from the sun—on the opposite side of the earth—it is in the full phase, and the entire disk appears illuminated. The full moon rises at sunset and sets at sunrise. During the last half of the cycle, the phases change from full, to waning gibbous, to third-quarter, to waning crescent, and back to new. A

summary for the time of the rising and setting of the phases of the moon follows.

Phases	Rises	Sets
New	Sunrise	Sunset
First-quarter	Noon	Midnight
Full	Sunset	Sunrise
Third-quarter	Midnight	Noon

7.4 THE HARVEST MOON

The moon's apparent eastward motion produces an average daily delay of about 51 minutes in the time of moonrise and moonset. In the middle latitudes of the northern hemisphere in September, a minimum delay of about 10 minutes occurs when the sun is at or near the autumnal equinox. The full moon that appears at this time is called the harvest moon because it rises shortly after the sun has set, thus permitting the farmer to extend his working day.

A graphic explanation of the harvest moon is shown in Fig. 7.6. In September at sunset, when the sun is at or near the autumnal equinox, the harvest moon is at or near the vernal equinox and is rising on the eastern horizon directly opposite the sun. At this time of the year, the ecliptic is below the celestial equator and makes a minimum angle with the horizon. Since the moon's orbital plane is inclined only 5° 09' to the plane of the ecliptic, we will assume for simplicity that both coincide and that the moon moves in the plane of the ecliptic. On the following evening at sunset, the moon is in position 2, having traveled 13° eastward along the ecliptic. Due to the earth's rotation, the moon's daily motion is along lines parallel to the celestial equator; therefore, since the length of this path to the horizon is considerably less than 13°, the harvest moon appears to rise much earlier than the average 51-minute delay.

A similar situation occurs during the next several days as the moon travels to positions 3 and 4. In October, the situation has changed only slightly; the angle that the ecliptic makes with the horizon has increased by a small amount so that the full moon, or hunter's moon, rises later than the harvest moon, but still much earlier than the average 51-minute delay. In March, the situation is reversed. The autumnal equinox is on the eastern horizon and the ecliptic, which is above

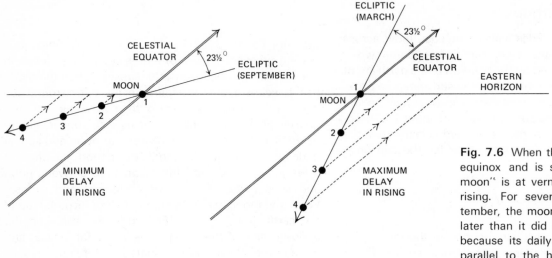

Fig. 7.6 When the sun is at autumnal equinox and is setting, the "harvest moon" is at vernal equinox (1) and is rising. For several evenings in September, the moon rises a few minutes later than it did the previous evening because its daily path is more nearly parallel to the horizon. The greatest delay in the rising of the moon occurs in March, when its path makes the greatest angle with the horizon.

the celestial equator, makes a maximum angle with the horizon; therefore, the full moon rises later than the average 51-minute delay.

7.5 LIBRATIONS

Although we can see only 50% of the moon's surface at any one time, during each lunar month we are able to see 9% more of its surface because of slight changes in its orientation toward the earth. These changes, called librations, are latitudinal, longitudinal, and diurnal.

Latitudinal libration occurs because the moon's equator is inclined about $6\frac{1}{2}°$ to the plane of its orbit, permitting the observer to see a few degrees beyond the moon's north pole during the first two weeks of the lunar month and a few degrees beyond the south pole during the last two weeks.

Since the moon's rotational motion is uniform whereas its orbital motion is variable, the moon is displaced slightly eastward and then slightly westward during each lunar month. This variation, which is called longitudinal libration, permits the observer to see a few degrees beyond in longitude at each edge of the moon.

Diurnal libration results from the earth's rotational motion and from the fact that the moon is observed from the earth's surface rather than from its center. The rotation of the earth permits the moon to be observed from two widely separated positions during a 12-hour period and enables the observer to see about 1° around both edges of the moon—western edge at moonrise and eastern edge at moonset.

7.6 ATMOSPHERE

The moon shines by reflected sunlight; therefore, its spectrum is a dim replica of the sun's spectrum. From this we can conclude that the moon does not have an atmosphere. If one did exist, it could be detected spectroscopically by the presence of absorption bands produced when sunlight passes through the moon's atmosphere twice before reaching the observer on the earth. Without an atmosphere, none of the weather elements that exist on the earth would be found on the moon, and the daytime lunar sky would appear black, with the celestial bodies clearly visible.

There are also other evidences that the moon lacks an atmosphere. The moon's illuminated surface has always been clearly visible telescopically, and clouds have never been observed on the moon. Also, when the moon passes in front of a star (occultation), the star disappears and reappears abruptly at the moon's edge rather than gradually, as it would if the moon had an atmosphere. Another evidence is that no twilight zone is visible on the moon; no sunlight is scattered into the dark portion next to the illuminated side of the moon.

In spite of these land-based evidences that the moon lacks an atmosphere, a mass spectrometer on the Apollo 15 flight found evidences that the moon has a very thin atmosphere. The instrument detected small isolated areas of argon and neon as it orbited the moon. It also detected carbon dioxide at one point on the moon's terminator, and scientists believe that it might have come from a fissure near the terminator. Finally, the temperature range is quite extreme between the illuminated and the dark portions of the moon. When the sun is directly overhead (lunar noon), the lunar surface temperature is about $+270°F$ ($132°C$); at lunar midnight, it is about $-270°F$ ($-168°C$). This range of about $540°F$ ($300°C$) indicates that the moon either lacks an atmosphere or has an extremely thin one.

7.7 DISTANCE FROM THE EARTH

The moon's distance from the earth can be determined by several methods. The triangulation method involves the solution of a triangle. This method has been simplified by photographing the moon from two positions on the earth's surface at the same instant when it is on the observer's horizon so as to produce two similar right triangles (Fig. 7.7). When the photographs are compared, they show that the center of the moon's disk has moved in relation to the stars an angular distance of (P); therefore, the two angles at the moon in the two right triangles are each equal to ($P/2$). In practice, the angle ($P/2$) is called the moon's horizontal equatorial parallax and is defined as the angle which subtends the earth's radius.

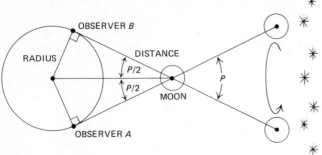

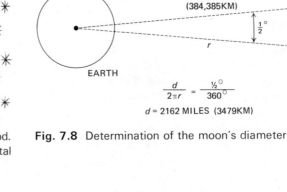

$$\frac{d}{2\pi r} = \frac{\frac{1}{2}^{\circ}}{360^{\circ}}$$

$$d = 2162 \text{ MILES } (3479 \text{KM})$$

Fig. 7.7 The moon's distance by the triangulation method. The solution of the right triangle involves the moon's horizontal equatorial parallax (*P/2*) and the radius of the earth.

Fig. 7.8 Determination of the moon's diameter

The moon's parallax is not constant because the moon's distance from the earth is variable; therefore, its average parallax is nearly 1° (57′02.62″). The moon's distance from the earth can be calculated by solving the right triangle when the moon's parallax and the earth's radius are known. The moon's mean distance is 238,857 miles (384,393 km).

Another method for measuring the moon's distance from the earth is to use the optical laser radar. This device consists of a short ruby rod in which atoms are stimulated to a high-energy level by intense lamp radiation. When the laser "fires," it emits an intense beam of coherent light, that is, light of definite wavelength which travels at great distances with practically no dispersion. The optical radar has been perfected so that the laser beam of light can be directed to a cluster of 300 silica reflector cubes mounted on a square frame which the Apollo 15 astronauts left on the moon. By measuring the time between sending and receiving the signal, the moon's distance can be determined to an accuracy of about six feet.

7.8 LINEAR DIAMETER

The moon's linear diameter can be determined from the moon's angular diameter of 31.09′ (approximately $\frac{1}{2}$°) at its mean distance from the earth (238,857 miles, or 384,393 km). In Fig. 7.8, a circle is drawn with the

earth's center as its center and a radius equal to the moon's mean distance from the earth. The observer is assumed to be located at the earth's center. Since the angular diameter of the moon is very small, the linear diameter (*d*) is assumed to be equal to the angular diameter ($\frac{1}{2}$°). Therefore, the linear diameter is in the same ratio to the complete circle ($2\pi r$) as the angular diameter is to 360°. Solving for (*d*) in the proportion

$$d/2\pi r = \tfrac{1}{2}/360$$

gives us the moon's diameter—about 2162 miles (3479 km).

7.9 MASS

The moon's diameter of 2162 miles (3479 km), which is over one-fourth the size of the earth's diameter, makes it the largest satellite in the solar system in comparison to the size of the planet around which it revolves. The earth-moon system, which is often called the "double planet" system, is unique in the solar system because of the moon's relatively large size in comparison to the earth and its nearness to that body (Fig. 7.9).

An astronaut in the vicinity of Venus would see the earth as a brilliant, bluish body and the moon as a beautiful, yellowish body about the same brightness as the planet Jupiter. He would also observe that the

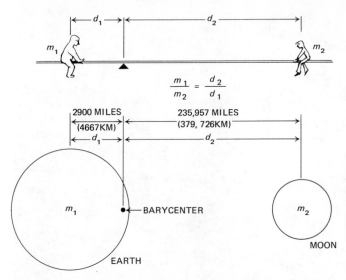

$$\frac{m_1}{m_2} = \frac{d_2}{d_1}$$

Fig. 7.9 The location of the barycenter of the earth-moon system and the determination of the moon's mass

moon slowly oscillates from one side of the earth to the other through an angular distance of approximately $\frac{1°}{2}$, which is the apparent diameter of the full moon. Therefore, the earth and the moon would appear to him as two planets always seen close together.

Although the moon appears to revolve around the earth as the earth revolves around the sun, the earth and moon actually revolve around their common center of mass, which is also their common center of gravity. This center of mass is called the barycenter and moves around the sun in an elliptical orbit. The barycenter lies on the line which joins the centers of the two bodies, and its distance from each body is inversely proportional to the mass of the body. The distance is determined by the formula

$$m_1/m_2 = d_2/d_1,$$

where m_1 is the earth's mass, d_1 is the earth's distance from the barycenter, m_2 is the moon's mass, and d_2 is the moon's distance from the barycenter. A similar situation exists when a large and small boy sit on a seesaw. If the seesaw is balanced, the large boy is seated closer to the fulcrum (pivot) than is the small boy.

The location of the barycenter was established when the sun was observed to oscillate in its motion on the ecliptic. During the first half of the lunar month, the earth in its orbit is slightly ahead of the barycenter, which causes the sun to appear on the ecliptic slightly to the east of its expected position. During the last half of the lunar month, the earth is slightly behind the barycenter, which causes the sun to appear on the ecliptic slightly to the west of its expected position. This means that during the first half of the lunar month, the earth is farther inside the orbital path of the barycenter, and during the last half it is farther outside. The sun's oscillation indicates that the barycenter is located about 2900 miles (4667 km) from the earth's center, which places it within the earth.

When the values for the earth's and moon's distances are substituted in the formula

$$m_1/m_2 = d_2/d_1,$$

the ratio of the earth's mass to the moon's mass (m_1/m_2) equals $\frac{1}{81}$ that of the earth's mass. Thus, the moon's mass is equivalent to 8.1×10^{19} tons. The moon's low mass produces a force of gravity that is one-sixth that of the earth's. This means that an astronaut who weighs 180 pounds weighs only 30 pounds on the moon.

The moon's density (mass per unit volume) is 3.34 grams per cubic centimeter. An analysis of the lunar rocks that were returned by the Apollo 11 and 12 astronauts revealed that the anorthosites have a density of 2.85 grams per cubic centimeter, and the basalts have a density of 3.3 grams per cubic centimeter. There is no close genetic relationship between these two types of rocks from the lunar seas. Since there is an amazing agreement between the chemical composition of the anorthosites and the samples analyzed by Surveyor 7 from the highlands north of the crater Tycho Brahe, there is the possibility that the anorthosites recovered at Mare Tranquillitatis might have come originally from the highlands. Also, concentrations of large, dense material (Mascons) which lie beneath the moon's surface were discovered and observed in serveral mare basins by Lunar Orbiter 5 and Apollo 8 as they circled the moon. The discovery was made when the spacecrafts un-

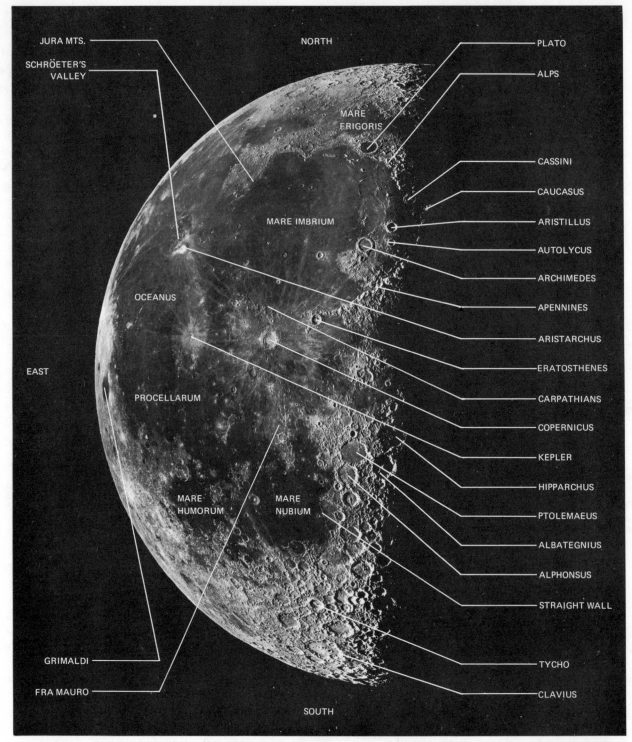

JURA MTS.

SCHRÖETER'S
VALLEY

NORTH

PLATO

ALPS

MARE
FRIGORIS

CASSINI

CAUCASUS

ARISTILLUS

AUTOLYCUS

MARE IMBRIUM

ARCHIMEDES

APENNINES

OCEANUS

ARISTARCHUS

ERATOSTHENES

CARPATHIANS

EAST

COPERNICUS

PROCELLARUM

KEPLER

HIPPARCHUS

PTOLEMAEUS

MARE
HUMORUM

MARE
NUBIUM

ALBATEGNIUS

ALPHONSUS

STRAIGHT WALL

GRIMALDI

TYCHO

FRA MAURO

CLAVIUS

SOUTH

Fig. 7.10(a) Third-quarter moon as seen by the unaided eye. (NASA photograph)

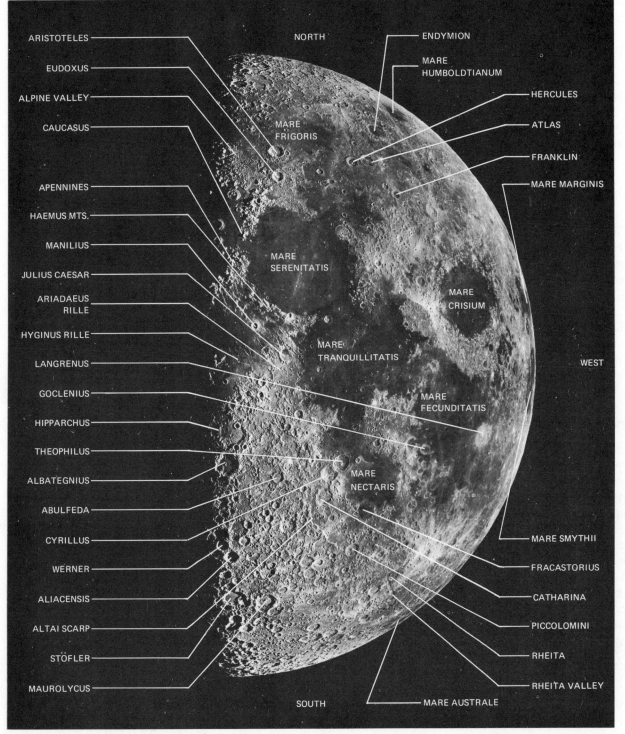

ARISTOTELES

EUDOXUS

ALPINE VALLEY

CAUCASUS

APENNINES

HAEMUS MTS.

MANILIUS

JULIUS CAESAR

ARIADAEUS RILLE

HYGINUS RILLE

LANGRENUS

GOCLENIUS

HIPPARCHUS

THEOPHILUS

ALBATEGNIUS

ABULFEDA

CYRILLUS

WERNER

ALIACENSIS

ALTAI SCARP

STÖFLER

MAUROLYCUS

NORTH

ENDYMION

MARE HUMBOLDTIANUM

HERCULES

ATLAS

FRANKLIN

MARE MARGINIS

MARE FRIGORIS

MARE SERENITATIS

MARE CRISIUM

MARE TRANQUILLITATIS

WEST

MARE FECUNDITATIS

MARE NECTARIS

MARE SMYTHII

FRACASTORIUS

CATHARINA

PICCOLOMINI

RHEITA

RHEITA VALLEY

SOUTH

MARE AUSTRALE

Fig. 7.10(b) First-quarter moon as seen by the unaided eye. (NASA photograph)

expectedly increased their speeds as they passed over these concentrations. The increase in speed was caused by an increase in the lunar gravity due to the concentration of dense material. This raises the possibility that the moon's density might not be uniform; therefore, samples from different regions must be recovered and analyzed before this question can be resolved.

7.10 THE TELESCOPIC VIEW OF THE MOON

Telescopic views of the first- and third-quarter moons are shown in Fig. 7.10. They give a general overview of the important surface features of the moon and the landing sites of the Apollo flights. When the moon is seen through a telescope, its image is inverted and reversed— north is at the bottom, with the moon's western limb visible at first-quarter and its eastern limb visible at third-quarter. Note that the surface features are the sharpest at the terminator (the line of demarcation between the illuminated and dark portions), which is often called the sunrise line.

7.11 EXPLORATION OF THE MOON

For many years prior to the Apollo mission, the moon had been the subject of observations and study by both professional and amateur astronomers. During this period a great deal of knowledge about the moon had been accumulated; knowledge of the lunar structure and its physical characteristics was derived indirectly from the studies of the lunar spectra, radar penetrations of its surface, analysis of supposed meteorites and tektites from its surface, high-resolution photographs taken by the Orbiter and Ranger spacecrafts, and experiments conducted by Lunar Surveyor.

Over 8% of the moon's surface visible from the earth was photographed by the Lunar Orbiters (Figs. 7.11, 7.12, 7.13). From these high-resolution photographs, surface features to eight feet across were resolved, and three general terrain characteristics were established: the flat broad areas, rolling hills with slopes less than 10°, and irregular hills with slopes greater than

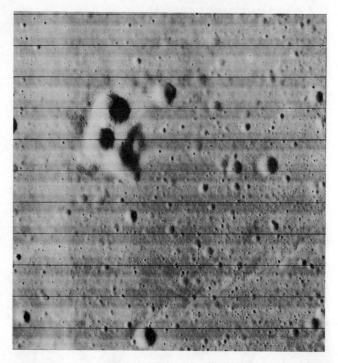

Fig. 7.11 Lunar Orbiter 2 photograph of an area 10 square miles in the Sea of Tranquility. The Orbiter was 30 miles above the lunar surface when it took this photograph. (NASA photograph)

10°. The flat areas are the dark areas of the lunar "seas," and the rolling and irregular hills are the light areas of the highlands. Dispersed over the entire lunar surface are thousands of craters that appear to be randomly clustered. Most of the craters are located in the flat areas and rolling hills, and only a relatively few craters are in the irregular hills.

The exploration of the moon took on a new dimension on July 20, 1969 when two astronauts from the Apollo 11 flight landed on the moon. The moon could now be studied at first hand, and direct confirmation of earlier observations could be obtained. By 1972, three

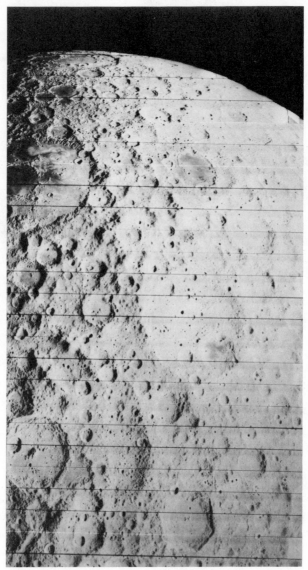

Fig. 7.13 Lunar Orbiter 2 photograph of a large, heavily cratered area of the moon. The lunar equator is at the top, and the south pole is at the bottom of the photograph. The smallest surface visible is about 20 miles across. (NASA photograph)

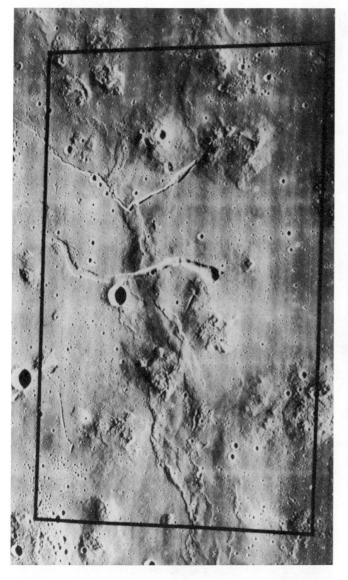

Fig. 7.12 Lunar Orbiter 5 photograph of the Marius Hills taken from 69 miles above the lunar surface. Surface features as small as eight feet in diameter are clearly visible. (NASA photograph)

Fig. 7.14 Apollo 15 astronaut David R. Scott on the moon in August 1971. Close-up view of the lunar module "Falcon," lunar soil, and bootprints. Looking southeast, one can see the Apennine Front in the left background at a distance of about 3 miles and the Hadley Delta in the right background about 2.5 miles above the plain. (NASA photograph)

more moon landings had been made. On November 19, 1969, the second landing took place during the Apollo 12 flight, a landing of greater scientific significance than the Apollo 11 flight because the astronauts left instruments on the moon's surface to detect the presence of an atmosphere, ionosphere, dust, and solar wind.

The Apollo 11 and 12 flights were made to establish and perfect landing techniques. Systematic exploration of the different types of lunar terrain for clues to the origin and evolution of the moon began with the Apollo 14 flight. Apollo 14 astronauts landed near Fra Mauro Crater. They explored the North Boulder Field and the rugged terrain almost up to the rim of Cone Crater. The Apollo 15 astronauts landed at the Hadley/Apennine

site and explored the Hadley rille and the slope of the Apennine mountains (Fig. 7.14). The rocks they brought back from this area are expected to reveal more scientific information than all the rocks from the three previous landings. The discoveries and knowledge gained from these four landings will be presented in the following sections.

7.12 LUNAR MARIA

The important surface features of the moon are the maria, mountains, craters, rays, and rilles. Of these, the most conspicuous are the maria—the dark, grayish areas that cover about one-half of the moon's visible

Fig. 7.15 The northern portion of Oceanus Procellarum is at the top of this Lunar Orbiter 3 photograph. The largest crater in the background is Galilei—about 10 miles in diameter, 1 mile deep, and with rims about 1000 feet above the outside terrain. The Cavalerius Hills are in the foreground. (NASA photograph)

disk and less than one-third of the moon's total surface area. Most of the maria are located in the northern hemisphere of the visible surface from the earth and are interconnected. The one notable exception is Mare Crisium, which is completely surrounded by rough terrain.

The maria are nearly circular, although when seen near the moon's limb, they appear quite elliptical. They have relatively smooth, undulating surfaces that are pockmarked with craters, mountains, hills, ridges, depressions, rays, and rilles. The largest of the dark areas is Oceanus Procellarum with an area of nearly 900,000 square miles, or 1,448,370 square kilometers (Fig. 7.15). The next in size, Mare Imbrium (about 700 miles, or 1127 km, across and an area of over 300,000 square miles, or 482,790 square kilometers) is one of the most interesting because it is almost completely encircled by a series of great mountain ranges: Carpathians, Apennines, Caucasus, and the Alps. It also contains examples of each of the important lunar surface features.

Several theories have been proposed to explain the origin of the maria. Most astronomers believe that they were created by the impact of gigantic meteorites. Others believe that they were created by great lava outpourings from the moon's molten interior. Mare Imbrium is believed to have been created by the impact of a tremendous meteorite, and its ejected material is believed to have covered the Fra Mauro Crater region.

Fig. 7.16 This photograph shows the texture of the surface at the southern part of Mare Tranquillitatis and Apollo 11 astronaut Neil Armstrong's clear and well-defined footprint in the lunar soil. (NASA photograph)

When the Apollo 11 astronauts landed on the southern part of Mare Tranquillitatis, they found the texture of the lunar surface to be very porous, sticky, and compressible (Fig. 7.16). The material adhered to the soles and sides of their boots in layers, like graphite. An analysis of the soil indicated that it consists of a layer of fragmented material, a physical mixture of loose, unconsolidated basaltic rocks, breccias, glasses, and iron meteoric fragments which vary in size from extremely fine particles to objects about three feet in length (Plates 8 and 9).

The Apollo 12 astronauts found the surface of Oceanus Procellarum somewhat different than that of Mare Tranquillitatis—it is much finer and dustier. Just walking stirred up enough dust to hinder visibility. The Apollo 11 astronauts' footprints were depressed fairly uniformly to about an eighth of an inch in Mare Tranquillitatis, whereas those of the Apollo 12 astronauts were at times depressed by as much as three inches. At Oceanus Procellarum, the very fine lunar dust seemed to adhere to everything as though it was electrostatically charged.

The Apollo 12 astronauts observed that the color of the lunar surface changed with the angle of the sun from very dark brown, similar to a freshly plowed field, to dull gray. The soil in some areas was so soft and fine that walking was very difficult, whereas in other areas it was so coarse and firm that walking was quite easy.

When the Apollo 14 astronauts landed in the Fra Mauro Crater region located about 630 miles (1014 km) south of the crater Copernicus, they described the region as rolling highland, pockmarked with small shallow craters, ridges, and rocks. The terrain is so rolling that not a single level area was visible, and even when standing next to a large-size crater, the astronauts had difficulty recognizing it. The albedo (reflecting power) of the highland is greater than the dark areas on which Apollo 11 and 12 astronauts landed. The ridges were observed to be radially aligned to the center of Mare Imbrium.

7.13 LUNAR MOUNTAINS

Most of the moon's great mountain ranges are located in its northern hemisphere. An interesting series of mountain ranges, which almost completely encircle Mare Imbrium, is shown in Fig. 7.17. The Carpathians are located on the southern border, the Apennines and the Caucasus on the western border, and the Alps on the

Fig. 7.17 In this telescopic view of Mare Imbrium, north is at the bottom. At the upper right are the Carpathians; upper left, the Apennines; lower center, the Alps; and lower right, the Jura mountains. The large crater near the top is Copernicus; that in the Apennines is Eratosthenes; the large one in Mare Imbrium is Archimedes; and the dark crater in the Alps is Plato. (Photograph from the Hale Observatories)

Fig. 7.18 The Apennine Mountains are in the background, with Mount Hadley to the left. The layering of Mount Hadley is clearly visible. Note the boulder in the foreground. (NASA photograph)

northern border. The eastern border of Mare Imbrium opens into Oceanus Procellarum. Its present appearance might have been the result of a gigantic meteoric impact which obliterated the mountain range in the east and increased the height of the ranges to the west. These four mountain ranges appear to slope abruptly on the side facing Mare Imbrium and to slope gradually away from Mare Imbrium on the opposite side.

Lunar mountains appear more rugged than those on the earth because of the absence of water and the weather elements which produce the drainage and erosion features that are typical of terrestrial mountains. The Apollo 15 astronauts reported that the Apennines appeared to be smooth and rounded, with many rough cratered places. The highest peak in the Apennines is about 18,000 feet (5490 meters) above its base, but the highest peak on the moon (located on the southern limb) rises to almost 30,000 feet (9150 meters) above its base (Fig. 7.18).

7.14 LUNAR CRATERS

A lunar crater is a nearly circular object with a floor at a lower level than the outside terrain and is ringed by mountains. From this description, a better name for a lunar crater would be a ring mountain. Thousands of

Fig. 7.19 The crater Tycho Brahe is believed to have been created by a giant meteor impact which ejected the tektites and glasses that are found on the earth. (NASA photograph)

craters appear on all parts of the lunar surface, with the greatest number appearing in the southern hemisphere around the south pole and on the far side of the moon.

Lunar craters range in size from small pitholes several feet in diameter to great craters such as Clavius with a diameter of about 146 miles (235 km). As Apollo 15 was orbiting the moon, astronaut Worden estimated the walls of the Gagarin Crater, located on the far side of the moon, to be about four miles high, making it the deepest crater that has been discovered. Generally, the inside walls of the craters are steeper than the outside, and their floors are level. Near the center of the floor, there is frequently an isolated mountain mass or a group of mountains, and smaller craters are sprinkled on the floor, inner and outer slopes, and on the rim.

In 1967 Lunar Orbiter 5 took a remarkable photograph of the crater Tycho Brahe from about 135 miles (217 km) above the moon's surface (Fig. 7.19). This crater, located near the south pole of the moon in the rugged highlands, is nearly circular and has a diameter of about 32 miles (52 km). The crater appears to be relatively young, because the material that was ejected when the crater was formed lies on the surface of the outside terrain, and the texture of the ejected material is very similar to that on the crater's floor. Old craters, such as Copernicus (Fig. 7.20), are recognized by the

Fig. 7.20 This Lunar Orbiter 2 photograph of the crater Copernicus was taken about 28 miles above the lunar surface and 9150 miles south of Copernicus. The crater is 60 miles in diameter and 2 miles deep. The floor of the crater is shown in fine detail. The mountains clearly visible on the floor rise about 1000 feet and are covered with rubble. The rounded knolls in the foreground were formed by the debris from Copernicus when it was formed after a tremendous explosion from the impact of a giant meteorite. (NASA photograph)

Fig. 7.21 The Apollo 12 Lunar Module, seen in the background, landed in the Ocean of Storms within 600 feet of Surveyor 3, which is in the foreground. Dimpled craters are visible on the floor of the Ocean of Storms. (NASA photograph)

presence of landslides, rockfalls, and terraces. The terraces are formed by the material in the rim and wall of the crater slumping to the floor.

Photographs taken by Rangers 7 and 8 revealed a new lunar surface feature, found in abundance on the maria and on the floors of the craters Alphonsus and Ptolemaeus. They were appropriately named "dimple craters," because they appear as shallow depressions in the general terrain. It is believed that they were caused by the collapse of the surface material from internal forces. The dimple craters are clearly visible on the floor of the Ocean of Storms around the spacecraft Surveyor 3, which rests on the slope of a small crater (Fig. 7.21).

Most of the lunar craters are believed to be the result of meteoric impacts, although some of the smaller craters appear to be of volcanic origin. A few of the older

and larger craters, which are called walled plains, appear to have been caused by the collapse of portions of the moon's surface. Astronaut Worden observed that a large area of the west wall of the large, young crater Tsiolkovsky is covered with material from a tremendous rockslide. He also observed that the crater's central peak is layered to a considerable length. Geologists believe this indicates that the moon accreted during its early period by laying one layer of material upon another.

7.15 LUNAR RAYS

The surface features that are unique to the moon are the bright rays that appear to radiate from only a few of the large craters such as Tycho Brahe, Copernicus, Kepler, and Aristarchus. These rays, clearly visible when the

Fig. 7.22 This excellent photograph of Schröeter's Valley, a sinuous rille, was taken by the Apollo 15 astronauts. The head of the valley, which starts to the right of the bright crater Aristarchus, is called the Cobra Head. This rille meanders downward to the Ocean of Storms. (NASA photograph)

moon is full, range from 5 to 10 miles (8 to 16 km) in width and extend up to about 1500 miles (2414 km) in length, without interruption or deflection across mountains, valleys, maria, and craters. The rays from Tycho appear to radiate as spokes from the hub of a wheel, whereas those from Copernicus appear to intertwine with one another. The origin of these rays is probably dust particles and small pieces of debris which have been ejected at great speeds from primary craters when they were formed by meteoric impacts.

7.16 LUNAR RILLES

Lunar rilles, which at this time are an enigma, appear as narrow cracks or valleys about one-half mile (.8 km) in width and up to about 300 miles (483 km) in length.

They appear to be of uniform width, with a taper, and are continuous. Many of them are nearly straight, but some are quite sinuous and strongly resemble meandering terrestrial rivers. They start in the highlands around craters and meander down to the plains of the maria. One such sinuous rille is Schröeter's Valley, as shown in Fig. 7.22, which appears like a great river meandering down and to the right. Its apparent origin is near a crater located in the highland to the right and near the beautifully bright crater of Aristarchus. Harold C. Urey and others have suggested that rilles are former riverbeds; others have suggested that they are dust flows, collapsed lava ditches, or tensile cracks.

While the Apollo 8 astronauts were orbiting the moon in 1968, they photographed the crater Goclenius (41 miles, or 66 km in width), which is located on the edge

of Mare Fecunditatis. This photograph (Fig. 7.23) clearly shows the system of rilles that criss-cross the floor of Goclenius. One rather broad, shallow rille appears to traverse the entire length of the crater's floor, over the crater's west wall, and then move out into the plain.

When the Apollo 15 astronauts explored the mile-wide, 1200-foot deep Hadley rille canyon, they reported evidence of the layering of rock on one side of the canyon (Fig. 7.24). This formation suggests that the rille may have been the path of several hot lava flows occurring at different times. The material that the astronauts brought back from the rille is thought to be bedrock.

7.17 THE FAR SIDE OF THE MOON

On October 4, 1959, the U.S.S.R. Luna 3, an automatic planetary station, took the first photographs of the far side of the moon from 34,500 feet (10,523 meters) above the moon's center. Although these photographs are not of high resolution, the larger lunar surface features are recognizable. Since then, the U.S.S.R. and the U.S. have photographed the far side of the moon with a resolution equal to the side facing the earth. Both hemispheres of the moon have identical surface features; however, the far side appears to be more rugged and contain fewer and smaller maria (Plate 10).

Fig. 7.23 A beautiful pattern of rilles is clearly visible on the floor of the large crater Goclenius, which lies on the edge of Mare Fecunditatis. One long, straight, wide, and shallow rille appears to stretch across the floor and over the crater's west wall. From left to right the three craters in linear alignment are: Magelhaens A, Magelhaens, and Guttenberg D, all of which show evidences of meteoric impacts. (NASA photograph)

Fig. 7.24 Astronaut Scott and the Lunar Rover are at the edge of Hadley Rille on Hadley Delta. (NASA photograph)

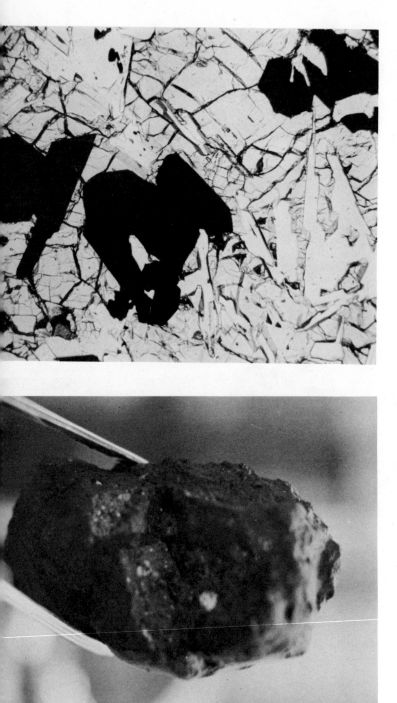

Fig. 7.25 This thin section of lunar basalt shows a continuous grading from very fine to coarse crystals, which may indicate that the basalts were cooled from lava flows. The black crystals are ilmenite, the white ones are calcic plagioclase feldspar, and the gray ones are pyroxene. (Photograph courtesy John A. Wood, Smithsonian Astrophysical Observatory)

7.18 THE LUNAR ROCK SAMPLES

On July 24, 1969, the Apollo 11 astronauts brought back from Mare Tranquillitatis the first lunar rock and soil samples; for the first time in history man could make direct studies of the structure and physical characteristics of the moon. The moon samples analyzed were classified into four important categories: basaltic crystalline rocks, soil breccias, glasses, and anorthosites. The basaltic crystalline rocks appear to be of igneous origin, range from fine to coarse-grain, and are unusually rich in titanium, scandium, zirconium, and hafnium, which are rare in terrestrial igneous rocks (Fig. 7.25). They also have free metallic iron, which is rarely present in terrestrial rocks, and have densities of about 3.3 grams per cubic centimeter. Their very dark color is due to the presence of very fine grains of ilmenite (Plate 11). The average age of the basalts is 3.7 billion years; however, the age of one of the basaltic rocks was found to be about 4.4 billion years, which indicates that it may have come from another area of the moon and that the age of different areas of the moon varies.

The soil breccias (Fig. 7.26) are similar to the igneous rock, yet distinctive for their richness in nickel, zinc,

Fig. 7.26 A close-up view of one of the breccia returned by the Apollo 12 astronauts. These rocks were common in the Apollo 11 samples, but rare in the Apollo 12 collection. (NASA photograph)

copper, silver, and gold. Large amounts of rare gases have been found in the breccias, indicating that they were probably part of the solar wind before they were eventually trapped in the lunar soil.

The presence of glasses in the soil and rocks from Mare Tranquillitatis came as a complete surprise to scientists (Plate 12). The glasses are very small and show a wide variety of forms, colors, and chemical properties. They are spherical and angular in shape, with highly lustrous brown, yellow, and clear colors. The glasses are believed to have been produced when large meteorites hitting the moon's surface vaporized the surface rocks on contact and created gases which condensed and solidified into the glasses. The glasses are the most abundant constituent (about 50%) of the lunar fines (dust) on Mare Tranquillitatis. The question has been raised as to whether these glasses are peculiar to this one area of the moon or whether they exist over the entire lunar surface.

The color, composition, and density of the anorthosites (Plate 13) are very different from the basalts and the breccias, for they are either light gray or white, granular in texture, rich in aluminum and calcium, and low in titanium (Fig. 7.27). Their most abundant mineral is calcic plagioclase. The anorthosites show evidences of having suffered severe shock—their composition is similar to the material ejected from the crater Tycho, which was analyzed by Surveyor 7, suggesting that the anorthosites are out of place on Mare Tranquillitatis, having been thrown to the mare by a meteoric impact occurring in the highlands.

The Apollo 12 astronauts found many rocks on the surface of Oceanus Procellarum that were so soft that they crumbled very easily when picked up. They also saw rocks of an odd glassy-green color, one of which was

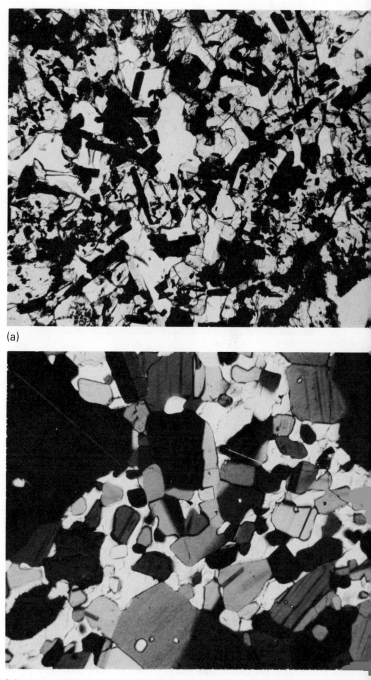

(a)

(b)

Fig. 7.27 The crystalline structure of anorthositic gabbro shows anorthositic crystals embedded in gabbroic melt with olivine crystals. (Photograph courtesy John A. Wood, Smithsonian Astrophysical Observatory)

Fig. 7.28 A close-up view of an interesting boulder near the rim of the Cone crater, with an apparent contrast in color and structure between the top and bottom of the boulder. (NASA photograph)

covered with many ¾-inch pits that were glass-lined. When the Apollo 14 astronauts approached the Cone crater, they saw a large boulder field with boulders up to five feet in diameter. The largest boulders had smooth surfaces with angular edges where pieces of the boulder had broken off (Fig. 7.28).

The age of the moon appears to be equal to that of the earth. This conclusion was reached from an analysis of a rock (83 grams) returned by the Apollo 12 astronauts from Oceanus Procellarum. The rock contained a higher percentage of uranium, thorium, and potassium, which made it about twenty times more radioactive than any other lunar sample previously studied. It has been dated at 4.6 billion years, thus making it the oldest rock recovered from the lunar surface and the oldest rock ever seen by man. Its age was determined by measuring the amount of strontium 87 and rubidium 87 present in the rock. Strontium 87 is produced from the radioactive decay of rubidium 87, and the abundance ratio of these two isotopes is an indication of the time that has elapsed since the rock was formed. It is believed that the rock must have come from either the highlands, which are older than the maria, or deep below the surface of the lunar maria. Scientists believe that the oldest rock is not an isolated phenomenon but indicates that at least a part of the lunar surface is as old as the earth.

Other rocks from the Apollo 11 and 12 flights have ages that range from 3.3 to 3.7 billion years; dust samples have ages up to 4.4 billion years. The analysis of these younger rocks indicates that they were crystallized from igneous liquid. Since the solar system is approximately 4.6 billion years old, the oldest lunar rock dates to almost the same time as the solar system.

Most of the Apollo 14 samples from the Fra Mauro region were found to be fragmental, with evidences of pronounced shock effects. Their composition is definitely different from that of the basaltic rocks returned from the maria. This indicates that the rocks are probably ejected material. The moon rocks returned by the Apollo 15 astronauts contained a most interesting sample, called "Genesis rock," which was picked up at Spur Crater. It has been described as a small, crystalline rock whose age is believed to be about 4.6 billion years, which probably places it back to the birth of the moon. When moon rocks returned by Apollo 11, 12, and 14 astronauts were pulverized and fed to plants, plant growth in some species was retarded, whereas in others it was accelerated. This pulverized material also appeared to kill microorganisms such as bacteria and virus. These two factors about the moon rocks still remain unknown. Further studies will be conducted using the Apollo 15 and 16 moon rocks.

Moon rocks returned by Apollo 11, 12, and 14 astronauts show no sign of life. The soil and rock material injected into mice produced no toxic effects and no bacteriological growth. None of the complex carbon compounds that are necessary for life on the earth have been identified in any of the rock samples; however, all the elements necessary for life have been identified,

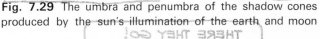

Fig. 7.29 The umbra and penumbra of the shadow cones produced by the sun's illumination of the earth and moon

including the most important element, carbon. The presence of carbon leaves open the possibility that life may exist on the moon.

7.19 ORIGIN OF THE MOON

Although many theories have been proposed to explain the origin of the moon, the basic question of how it originated still remains unanswered. Did the combination of the earth's rapid rotation and the sun's gravitational force cause the plastic earth to extend into the shape of an unsymmetrical dumbbell and to eventually separate into two unequal spheres, with the smaller one becoming the moon? Was the moon created at the same time and from the same condensate as the sun and the earth? Or, during a close encounter was the moon captured by the earth and become its satellite? The best that can be said at this time is that the search for the answers to the origin of the moon continues. The rock samples from the highlands returned by the Apollo 15 astronauts may provide a record of the early history of the moon, which may in turn give us the clue to its origin

and possibly to the origin of the earth and the solar system as well.

7.20 ECLIPSES

Eclipses are one of the most beautiful and awe-inspiring spectacles of nature. Primitive man regarded them as evil omens, and their appearance always struck terror in his mind. The earliest recorded eclipse was seen by the Chinese in 2137 B.C.

Since the earth and the moon are opaque bodies and are illuminated by the sun, they cast conical shadows which can be illustrated (Fig. 7.29) by drawing external and internal tangents to the sun and the body. The external tangents ABC and DEC produce the shadow cone BCE in which the sunlight is completely cut off. This region is called the umbra. The internal tangents AEG and DBF produce the region FBCEG around the umbra in which the sunlight is partially cut off. This region is called the penumbra. The length of the earth's umbra is about 860,000 miles (1,383,998 km), and the moon's umbra is about 232,000 miles (373,358 km).

Eclipses occur when the sun, earth, and the new or full moon are approximately in line and lie in the same plane. Since the moon's orbital plane is inclined to the earth's orbital plane, the new or full moon is either above or below the earth's orbital plane; therefore, an eclipse cannot occur. However, periodically these three bodies do lie in approximately the same plane because the orientation of the moon's orbit is not fixed in space. The moon's orbit moves eastward in the moon's orbital plane and completes one rotation every 8.85 years. Also, the line of nodes moves westward in the plane of the ecliptic and completes one rotation every 18.6 years. The line of nodes is the straight line which connects the ascending node (point where the moon crosses the ecliptic from south to north) to the descending node (point where the moon crosses the ecliptic from north to south). These motions are caused by the moon's perturbations, which are produced by the sun's unequal attraction for the earth and moon and by the earth's equatorial bulge. In Fig. 7.30, (n) represents the ascending node and (n') the descending node. When the moon is at or near either the ascending or descending node and the line of nodes points toward the sun, a solar eclipse will occur when the moon is new; a lunar eclipse when the moon is full.

7.21 MECHANICS OF A LUNAR ECLIPSE

On the mean cross-sectional (end-on) view of the earth's shadow cone (Fig. 7.31), the dark area is the umbra and the light area the penumbra. When the full moon passes through the earth's shadow cone and completely misses the umbra, the moon appears to darken and redden slightly—a phenomenon called an appulse; when only part of the moon passes through the umbra, it is called a partial eclipse; and when the entire moon passes through the umbra, it is called a total eclipse. The longest total lunar eclipse occurs when the moon passes through the center of the umbra.

The six important points of contact in the sequence of events of a total lunar eclipse are: first contact, when the moon enters the penumbra (beginning of the penumbral phase); second contact, when the moon enters the umbra (end of the penumbral phase and the begin-

By permission of Johnny Hart and Field Enterprises, Inc.

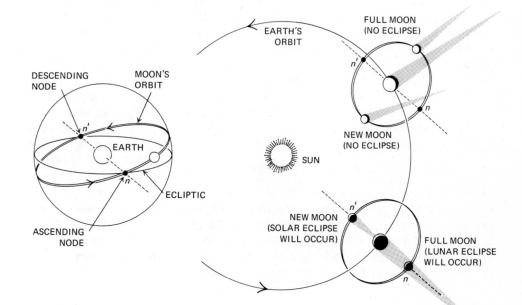

Fig. 7.30 Solar and lunar eclipses occur when the sun is at or near the ascending or descending node and the line of nodes points toward the sun

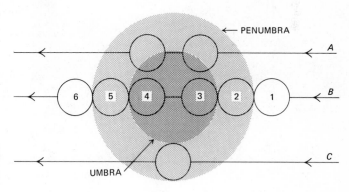

Fig. 7.31 Cross-sectional view of the earth's shadow cone (umbra and penumbra), showing the moon's paths for a partial eclipse (*A*), central total eclipse (*B*), and penumbral eclipse (*C*)

ning of the darkening of the moon); third contact, when the moon is completely within the umbra (beginning of totality, the total phase of the eclipse); fourth contact, when the moon emerges from the umbra; fifth contact, when the moon leaves the umbra and once again begins the penumbral phase; and sixth contact, when the moon leaves the penumbra (end of the eclipse). During the penumbral phase, the full moon appears to darken and redden slightly, and during the total phase, which lasts for about two hours, it is not completely obscurred, but appears as a dull-reddish disk.

7.22 MECHANICS OF A SOLAR ECLIPSE

Since the moon's distance from the earth varies from about 221,000 to 252,000 miles (355,655 to 405,543 km) and the length of the moon's umbra is about 232,000 miles (373,358 km), the moon's umbra spot on the earth's surface varies from zero to a maximum of about 167 miles (269 km) in diameter. It is maximum when the

moon is at perigee and the earth is at aphelion (Fig. 7.32). Since the moon revolves around the earth from west to east, its shadow cone appears to move in the same direction across the earth's surface. When an observer is in the path of the moon's umbra, a total eclipse will be visible, and when he is in the moon's penumbra, a partial eclipse will be visible.

When the sun and moon are at their mean distances from the earth, the moon's umbra spot fails to reach the earth's surface, and an annular eclipse occurs (Fig. 7.33). Since in this position the apparent diameter of the moon is smaller than the sun's, an observer located within the extension of the moon's umbra will observe the annular eclipse as a dark disk (new moon) surrounded by a brilliant annular ring. The ring is the light that comes from the edge of the sun and appears less white than the sun's disk. An observer within the region of the penumbra will observe a partial eclipse. The annular ring is maximum when the moon is at apogee and the earth is at perihelion.

Fig. 7.32 To observe a total solar eclipse, the observer must be in the moon's umbra spot on the earth's surface, which varies from zero to about 167 miles. A partial solar eclipse will be observed when the observer is in the penumbral circle.

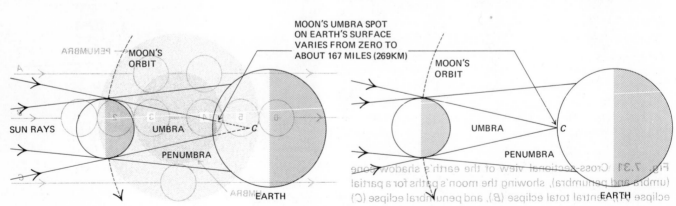

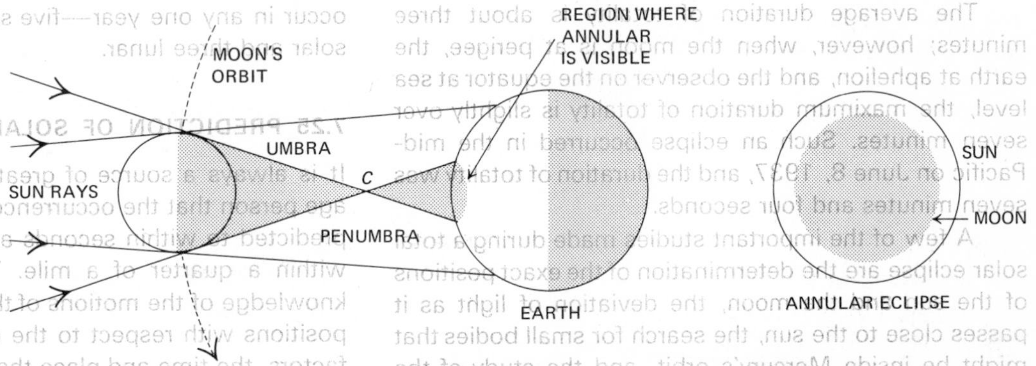

Fig. 7.33 When the moon's umbra does not reach the earth's surface, an annular eclipse is produced, because the moon's apparent diameter is smaller than the sun's

7.23 TOTAL SOLAR ECLIPSE

The spectacular phenomenon of a total solar eclipse commences when the moon makes contact with the west edge of the sun. As the moon moves slowly across the face of the sun, the sun's visible disk diminishes, and its diffused light becomes less intense. During a total solar eclipse, unusual reddish tones appear on the earth's landscape because the light comes from the sun's limb, where it is less blue.

Before totality, the sun appears as a very thin crescent of light, and as the light filters through the foliage of the trees and plants, beautiful crescent-shaped images appear on the ground. Also, peculiar shadows appear to move over the landscape in ripples and wave-like motions, and animals and plants behave as they do at sunset. The crescent of light soon becomes a series of irregular bright spots of light around the moon's limb, "Baily's Beads," with the beautiful "diamond ring" effect (Plate 14). They are caused by the sunlight's passing through the irregularities of the terrain on the moon's limb. At totality, as shown in Fig. 7.34, the beads disappear, and the corona, the sun's outer atmosphere, appears. During totality there is a noticeable darkening effect on the earth, a drop of several degrees in the earth's temperature, and the appearance of the planets and brightest stars. As the moon continues to move eastward, it slowly uncovers the sun.

Fig. 7.34 The solar corona near sunspot maximum, photographed during a total eclipse. (Photograph from the Hale Observatories)

The average duration of totality is about three minutes; however, when the moon is at perigee, the earth at aphelion, and the observer on the equator at sea level, the maximum duration of totality is slightly over seven minutes. Such an eclipse occurred in the mid-Pacific on June 8, 1937, and the duration of totality was seven minutes and four seconds.

A few of the important studies made during a total solar eclipse are the determination of the exact positions of the sun and the moon, the deviation of light as it passes close to the sun, the search for small bodies that might be inside Mercury's orbit, and the study of the sun's atmosphere and surface features.

7.24 ECLIPSE LIMITS AND SEASONS

When the full moon is near a node, the line of nodes points toward the sun, and the moon appears to be tangent to the sun; this point, the solar eclipse limit, marks the extent from either side of the node in which a solar eclipse is possible. This angular distance is variable, because the apparent diameter of the moon changes with its distance from the earth. When the maximum and minimum apparent diameters of the sun and moon are used, the solar eclipse limits range from $15°21'$ to $18°31'$.

When the full moon is near a node, the line of nodes points toward the sun, and the moon appears to be tangent to the earth's umbra; this point, the lunar eclipse limit, marks the extent from either side of the node in which a lunar eclipse is possible. When the maximum and minimum apparent diameters of the moon and the umbra of the earth's shadow are used, the lunar eclipse limits range from $9°30'$ to $12°\ 15'$.

The time during which the sun or the earth's umbra is within the eclipse limit is called the eclipse season. Since the lunar eclipse limit is about 24 days and the moon-phase interval is about $29\frac{1}{2}$ days, it is possible for a year to pass without a single lunar eclipse because the moon will not be full during the eclipse season. Since the solar eclipse limit is about 31 days and two eclipse seasons occur every year, only two solar eclipses can occur in any one year. A maximum of seven eclipses can occur in any one year—five solar and two lunar or four solar and three lunar.

7.25 PREDICTION OF SOLAR ECLIPSES

It is always a source of great amazement to the average person that the occurrence of a solar eclipse can be predicted to within seconds and its path determined to within a quarter of a mile. This requires a thorough knowledge of the motions of the sun and moon and their positions with respect to the earth's center. With these factors, the time and place that an eclipse will occur can be determined.

In predicting an eclipse, the cycle of the "saros," an interval of 18 years $11\frac{1}{3}$ days, or $6585\frac{1}{3}$ days, is used. The saros, which was well known to the ancient Chaldeans, represents an interval of time that is very nearly evenly divisible by the lunar synodic month of $29\frac{1}{2}$ days and by the eclipse year of 346.6 days. This means that the saros contains about 223 synodic months and about 19 eclipse years; when an eclipse occurs, another one will follow in $6585\frac{1}{3}$ days because in 19 eclipse years the sun will return to the same node, and in 223 synodic months the moon will again be in the new phase.

7.26 THEORETICAL TIDES

The earth, as part of the earth-moon system, experiences tides that are produced on its surface by the gravitational force of the sun and the moon. Although the sun's force is greater than the moon's, its effect on all parts of the earth is about the same because of its great distance from the earth. The moon's gravitational force is considerably less; however, its tide-raising influence on the earth is slightly greater than the sun's because of its nearness to the earth. The moon's gravitational force is inversely proportional to the square of its distance from the earth. This means that the moon's gravitational force is differential, that is, greater for those parts that are closer to the moon.

For simplicity in determining the tide-raising force at any point on the earth's surface, we will assume that the sun's influence is negligible, the moon is stationary, and the earth is covered with a uniform layer of water. In Fig. 7.35, the moon's gravitational force at any point depends on that point's distance from the moon. It is greatest at point (A), less at point (B), and least at point (C). These conditions are represented in a relative manner by vectors (a), (b), and (c). If we accept the earth's center as the reference point, the tide-raising force at any point on the earth's surface can be defined as the difference between the force exerted at the surface point and at the earth's center. Therefore, the tide-raising force at point (A) is ($a - b$); at point (D), ($d - b$); at point (E), ($e - b$); and at point (C), ($c - b$). Subtracting one vector quantity from another is equivalent to adding the negative of the vector (direction reversed) (Fig. 7.36).

If the moon is stationary and the rotating earth is completely covered with water, a point on its surface would experience two high and two low tides approximately every 24 hours. At any particular time, the earth experiences two high tides—one at the point nearest the moon (A) and the other on the opposite side of the earth (C)—and two low tides at right angles to the highs (F and G). Point (A) will experience the higher of the two tides because of its nearness to the moon.

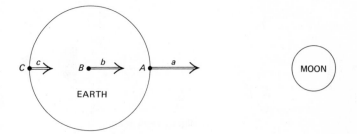

Fig. 7.35 The moon's gravitational force at any point on the earth's surface depends on its distance from the moon. The vectors (a, b, and c) indicate the relative magnitude and direction of the force.

Fig. 7.36 The tide-raising force at any point on the earth's surface is the difference between the force exerted by the moon at the surface point and at the earth's center

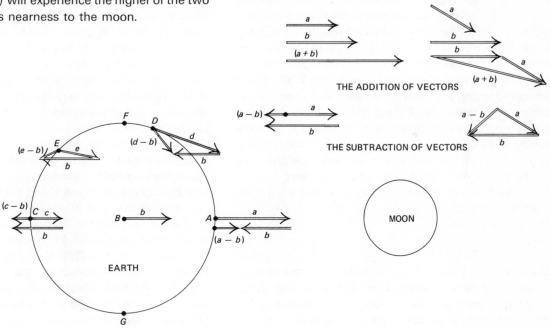

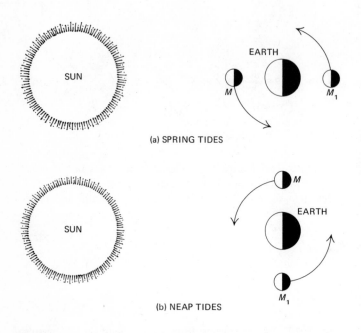

(a) SPRING TIDES

(b) NEAP TIDES

Fig. 7.37 The highest high tides (spring tides) occur when the moon is in the new (M) and full (M_1) phases. The lowest low tides (neap tides) occur when the moon is in the first- and third-quarter phases.

In our discussion of tides, we ignored the sun's effect. Even though it is considerably less than the moon's, it does produce noticeable effects in the size of the tides. When the moon is in line with the sun and the earth (syzygy), the tide-raising forces of the sun and moon combine to produce tides that are higher than any high tide produced during that month (Fig. 7.37). These are called spring tides and occur twice each month when the moon is in the new and full phases. When the moon forms a right angle with the sun and the earth, the tide-raising force of the sun reduces the moon's effect to produce tides that are lower than any low tide produced during the month. These are called neap tides and occur twice each month when the moon is in the first- and third-quarter phases.

7.27 ACTUAL TIDES

So far, the tides which have been discussed would occur under ideal and theoretical conditions. Under actual conditions, there are several factors that affect the tides. Since the earth's surface is about 71% water, the first factor that affects the tides is the location of the land areas. Tides move in a westerly direction; therefore, the tides on the east coast of continents are higher than those on the west coast. The second factor affecting tides is the shape and slope of the ocean floor off the land areas. Gradual slopes and narrow ravines produce higher tides. The third factor is the shape and slope of the coastline. Higher tides are produced in funnel-shaped, gradually sloping bays than along straight, steep shore lines.

The range of the tide varies considerably over different parts of the earth. Tides are almost negligible at the eastern end of the Mediterranean Sea. They average less than one inch in the Great Lakes and slightly over one foot in the Gulf of Mexico. In New York harbor, they are about 2.5 feet (.76 meters). The highest tides in the world occur in Bay of Fundy in Nova Scotia, where they average 65 feet (20 meters) every day. The Bay of Fundy is ideally situated for the occurrence of these exceptionally high tides; it is on the east coast of the North American continent, its bay is V- shaped, and its continental shelf is channel-shaped and sloping.

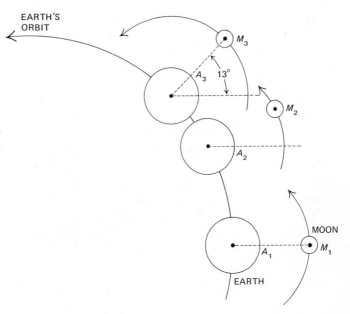

Fig. 7.38 The tides for any point on the earth's surface occur approximately 50 minutes later each day because during a 24-hour period, the moon has moved in its orbit about 13°

The fourth factor affecting tides is the revolution of the earth around the sun and the moon around the earth. In Fig. 7.38, point (A_1) on the earth's surface is experiencing a high tide because it is in line with the moon. Twenty-four hours later, the earth is in position 2 in its orbit around the sun and has completed one rotation so that the point is in position (A_2). During this approximate 24-hour period, the moon has moved in its orbit around the earth to position (M_2). Before the point can experience another high tide, the earth must rotate through an angle of about 13°, when it will be in line with the moon as in position (A_3). This angle is equivalent to about 50 minutes of time; therefore, for any particular point on the earth's surface, the tides will occur approximately 50 minutes later every day, that is, every 24 hours 50 minutes. Although the tides are fairly constant at a particular place, they quite often differ considerably from those at an adjacent place. The times and special effects for the tides at any particular place, known as the "establishment of the port," are tabulated in the tide tables published by the *United States Coast and Geodetic Survey*.

REVIEW

1. Explain why the moon always keeps the same side toward the earth. Does the moon rotate with respect to the sun?

2. What is the direction of the moon's rotational motion? In what direction does the moon revolve around the earth? What apparent motion of the moon in the sky is produced by each of these two motions? Explain.

3. The moon is first visible at about 3:00 P.M. Where is it located in the sky and what is its approximate phase?

4. Describe the position of the crescent-shaped moon in relation to the horizon in the (a) spring and (b) fall. Explain why its orientation changes.

5. What is meant by a harvest moon? When is it visible? What causes it?

6. What are the moon's librations and what are the causes?

7. Compare the density of the moon with that of the earth.

8. What are lunar "mascons" and how were they discovered?

9. Compare lunar mountains with those on the earth.

10. What are the characteristics of lunar craters? What are "dimple craters"? Discuss the origin of craters.

11. Discuss the differences in the composition and characteristics of the maria visited by the astronauts.

12. Compare the physical characteristics of the lunar rays and rilles.

13. Discuss what the analysis of the lunar rock samples has revealed about the structure and composition of the lunar surface.

14. Discuss the age of the moon.

15. Discuss the unique experimental advantages a scientist on the moon would enjoy.

16. What is the proper way for an amateur to eliminate the possibility of eye injury when viewing a solar eclipse? How is this accomplished when a telescope is used?

17. What are the descending and ascending nodes of the moon? Are they fixed in space with reference to the stars? Explain.

18. Under what conditions will a lunar and solar eclipse occur?

19. Explain why a total lunar eclipse lasts longer than a total solar eclipse. What are the durations of totality?

20. In what direction does the shadow of the earth move across the moon's face during a lunar eclipse?

21. What is meant by the "lunar eclipse limit"? What are its values? What two factors are used to determine this limit?

22. Explain what the "saros" is and how it is used in predicting eclipses.

23. Prove or disprove the statement that the moon and the sun have about the same effect in producing tides on the earth.

24. What are spring and neap tides? When do they occur?

25. Discuss the four factors that affect the actual tides.

8
The Solar System

The solar system consists of the sun, nine planets, thirty-two natural satellites, thousands of asteroids and comets, and interplanetary material.

8.1 THE SUN

The sun, a large gaseous sphere 864,400 miles (1,391,079 km) in diameter, is about one-third of a million times more massive than the earth and contains over 99% of the total mass of the solar system. By virtue of its enormous mass, it exerts a gravitational force that keeps the members of its family together. The sun is a typical star—typical because it is average in size and brightness, and a star because it shines by its own light. It derives its energy from the nuclear reactions that take place in the core, producing temperatures of about 11,000,000°K and surface temperatures of about 5750°K. (Chapter 10 deals specifically with the sun.)

8.2 THE PLANETS

There are nine known planets in the solar system. Six of them—Mercury, Venus, Earth, Mars, Jupiter, and Saturn—were known to the ancients. The three most distant planets—Uranus, Neptune, and Pluto—were discovered after the telescope had been invented in 1609. The planets are relatively cold and are visible only by reflected sunlight. Their diameters range from about 3032 miles (4879.40 km) for Mercury to about 88,640 miles (142,648 km) for Jupiter. All planets except Venus rotate from west to east. Jupiter has the shortest period of rotation (9 hours 55 minutes) and Venus the longest (243 days).

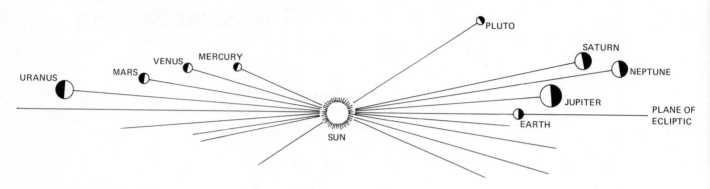

Fig. 8.1 The inclination of planetary orbits to the plane of the ecliptic ranges from 17° for Pluto to 46′ for Uranus

a. Classification

Planets may be classified according to the relationship between their respective orbital positions and that of the earth. If their orbits lie inside the earth's, as do those of Mercury and Venus, they are called inferior planets, and if they lie outside the earth's, as do those of Mars, Jupiter, Saturn, Uranus, Neptune, and Pluto, they are called superior planets. Planets may also be classified according to their physical characteristics. If they resemble the earth (small size, high density, low escape velocity, relatively long rotational period, and few satellites), they are called terrestrial planets. If they resemble the giant planet Jupiter (large size, low density, high escape velocity, short rotational period, large equatorial bulge, dense atmosphere, and several satellites), they are called giant, or Jovian, planets. In this classification system, Pluto remains an enigma. Although its known physical characteristics place it in the terrestrial group, several of its characteristics are still not accurately known, and therefore it cannot be classified.

b. Orbits

Using the north pole of the earth as a point of orientation, we can say that the planets revolve around the sun in a counterclockwise direction—west to east. Their mean distances from the sun range from about 36 million miles (57,934,800 km) for Mercury to nearly 4 billion miles (6,437,200,000 km) for Pluto. The orbital velocities of the planets range from about 30 miles (48 km) per second for Mercury to 3 miles (5 km) per second for Pluto.

The orbits of all the planets lie very close to the plane of the ecliptic (Fig. 8.1). Pluto's orbit, at 17° 09′, has the greatest angle of inclination to the ecliptic. Although all planetary orbits are elliptical, most of them are almost circular. Their eccentricities range from 0.007 for Venus, which is the most circular, to 0.249 for Pluto, which is the most eccentric, and all are less than 0.1, except for Mercury and Pluto. Mercury has the shortest period of revolution (about 88 days), and Pluto has the longest (about 248 years).

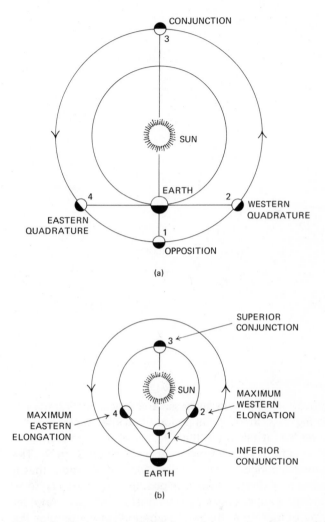

Fig. 8.2 Planetary configurations: (a) superior planets; (b) inferior planets

c. Configurations

To locate the positions of a planet in its orbit with respect to the earth and the sun, special positions, called configurations, have been established (Fig. 8.2). For an inferior planet, the following configurations occur: (1) inferior conjunction, when the planet passes between the sun and the earth; (2) maximum western elongation, when the planet is leading the sun (west) so that its elongation (angle between the sun, earth, and planet) is maximum; (3) superior conjunction, when the planet is on the opposite side of the sun from the earth; and (4) maximum eastern elongation, when the planet is following the sun (east) and the elongation is maximum. For a superior planet, the following configurations occur: (1) opposition, when the planet is on the opposite side of the earth from the sun; (2) western quadrature, when the planet is to the west of the sun and forms a 90° angle with the earth and sun; (3) conjunction, when the planet is on the opposite side of the sun from the earth; and (4) eastern quadrature, when the planet is to the east of the sun and forms a 90° angle with the earth and sun.

d. Sidereal and Synodic Periods

There is a difference between a planet's true and apparent periods of revolution around the sun. The true, or sidereal, period is the interval of time the planet takes to complete one revolution with respect to a star as seen by a hypothetical observer on the sun. The apparent, or synodic, period is the interval of time the planet takes to

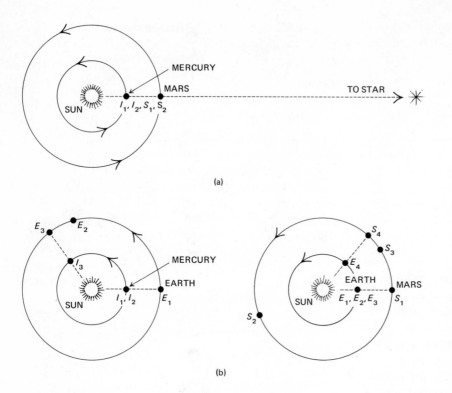

(a)

(b)

Fig. 8.3 The (a) sidereal and (b) synodic periods of planets. The sidereal period of a superior (S_1 to S_2) and an inferior (I_1 to I_2) planet is the interval of time for the planet to make one complete revolution around the sun with respect to a star. The synodic period of an inferior planet (Mercury) is the interval of time for both the earth and Mercury to move from position 1 to position 3. The synodic period of a superior planet (Mars) is the interval of time for both the earth and Mars to move from position 1 to position 4.

move between two successive identical configurations. In Fig. 8.3, the sidereal period of an inferior planet is the time that it takes the body to travel from position I_1 to I_2, and for a superior planet, from position S_1 to S_2. The synodic period of an inferior planet is the time that it takes the body to travel from position I_1, through I_2, to I_3, and for a superior planet, from position S_1 to S_4. Another way of looking at the synodic period is to determine the time required for the faster-moving planet to gain one lap on the slower-moving planet.

The relationship between the sidereal and synodic periods of a planet can be expressed by the formulas

$$1/S = 1 + 1/P$$

for an inferior planet and

$$1/S = 1 - 1/P$$

for a superior planet, where (S) is the planet's sidereal period and (P) is its synodic period, both expressed in years. When one of the planet's periods is known, the other can be determined from these formulas. For example, if the sidereal period of a superior planet is four years, its synodic period is:

$$1/S = 1 - 1/P$$

$$1/P = 1 - 1/S$$

$$1/P = 1 - 1/4 = 3/4$$

$$\therefore P = 4/3, \text{ or } 1\ 1/3 \text{ years.}$$

e. Masses

There is a difference in the oblateness of the terrestrial and giant planets. The difference between the polar and equatorial diameters for the earth is about 27 miles (43.45 km) in 8000 miles (12,874 km), and about 5500 miles (8851 km) in 88,000 miles (141,618 km) for Jupiter. The oblateness of the giant planets results from their rapid rate of rotation, which means that much of the planet's mass is concentrated in a small core with an average density of 4.5 grams per cubic centimeter, whereas the outer layers have a very low density. It has been assumed that since a marked difference exists in the physical characteristics of the terrestrial and giant planets, a marked difference in their internal structure must also exist. The mean densities of Saturn and Jupiter, 0.71 and 1.4 grams per cubic centimeter, respectively, are so low in comparison to the earth's mean density of 5.5 grams per cubic centimeter that a large portion of their material must be either solidified hydrogen, the least dense solid, or solidified helium. If the material were solidified helium, the planets' densities would be considerably higher; therefore, it has been concluded that a large portion of the material in Jupiter and Saturn must be solidified hydrogen.

The most accurate method for determining the mass of a planet is to observe its gravitational reaction to one of its satellites. This information is applied to Kepler's third law of planetary motion, which Newton expressed as

$$(M + m)P^2 = ka^3,$$

where $(M + m)$ represents the total mass of the planet and its satellite in terms of the earth's mass, (a) is the satellite's distance from the planet in terms of the moon's distance from the earth, (P) is the satellite's sidereal period in sidereal lunar months, and (k) is the constant. For example, determine the mass of Mars when its satellite Deimos has a sidereal period of 1.262 days and a mean distance of 14,600 miles (23,496 km) from Mars' center. The solution: Deimos' period in sidereal months is 1.262/27.3, or 0.0463. Deimos' distance from Mars in terms of the moon's distance from the earth is 14,600/238,000, or 0.0613.

$$(M + m) = a^3/P^2$$

$$= (0.0613)^3/(0.0463)^2$$

$$= 0.108 \text{ earth masses.}$$

This means that Mars has a mass 0.108 times that of the earth. Jupiter, the most massive planet, is 318 times greater than the earth, and Mercury, the least massive, is 0.01 times that of the earth.

f. Temperatures

A planet's surface temperature depends on the amount of solar radiation that falls on one square unit of its surface and the amount that it absorbs. The amount of solar radiation that reaches a planet depends on its distance from the sun, and the amount that it absorbs depends on the physical characteristics of its surface. For Mercury, with an albedo of 6% (which means that its surface absorbs 94% of the radiation that falls on it and reflects and reradiates 6%), the surface temperature is about 640°F (338°C). This is not a thermometer temperature such as is obtained on the earth, but is the heat reflected, or reradiated, by the planet. The surface temperature of the planets ranges from about 800°F (427°C) for Venus to −400°F (−240°C) for Pluto.

g. Atmospheres

An atmosphere around a planet may be indicated by its high albedo or the presence of a twilight zone. A dense atmosphere and opaque clouds around a planet reflect more sunlight than a planet's solid surface. The dense atmosphere of Venus reflects about 74% of the sunlight it receives. The presence of a twilight zone on a planet, or a halo around it, indicates the presence of an atmosphere, because both phenomena are produced by the reflection and diffusion of sunlight by the molecules in the atmosphere. Both the gradual occultation of a star by a planet, that is, the gradual obscuration of a star when the planet passes between it and the earth, and the appearance of absorption lines in the planet's spectrum further indicate the presence of an atmosphere.

Whether or not a planet is able to retain an atmosphere depends on its escape velocity and the velocity of the molecules in its atmosphere. A planet's escape velocity, the velocity required for a molecule to escape the planet's gravitational force, depends on the planet's size and mass. Mercury, whose size and mass are small, has a weak gravitational force and a low escape velocity; Jupiter, whose size and mass are great, has a strong gravitational force and a high escape velocity.

The velocity of the molecules depends on their temperatures. Since the radiation a planet receives from the sun is inversely proportional to the square of its distance from the sun, the temperature of the molecules in the atmospheres of planets closer to the sun is much higher than for those farther away. Therefore, molecules with velocities greater than the planet's escape velocity will escape from the gravitational force of the planet, so that eventually the planet will lose its atmosphere.

Since the velocity of the atmospheric molecules around all the giant planets is below the escape velocity, they still have dense atmospheres. The terrestrial planets, which are smaller, have lower escape velocities and are closer to the sun; therefore, their atmospheric molecules have higher velocities. Under such conditions, the terrestrial planets have been able to hold the heavier elements in their atmospheres, whereas the lighter elements have been able to escape into space. The exception may be Mercury which, because of its small size and mass and high surface temperature, might have lost its atmosphere completely. However, recent studies indicate that the planet may have a tenuous atmosphere (Chapter 8.7).

8.3 SATELLITES

The 32 known satellites in the solar system are bodies that revolve around the planets. Most of them revolve in the same direction as their planets, in orbital planes that lie very close to the planets' equatorial planes. Three of the planets—Mercury, Venus, and Pluto—have no known satellites. Jupiter has the largest number, 12; Saturn has 10 (its latest, Janus, was discovered in 1967); Uranus has 5; Neptune and Mars have 2; and Earth has 1. Six of the satellites are as large or larger than the earth's moon. The two largest are Jupiter's Callisto and Ganymede—each with a diameter of about 3200 miles (5150 km). The smallest is Mars' Deimos, with a diameter of about 8 miles (13 km). Titan, Saturn's largest satellite, is believed to be the only one with an atmosphere.

8.4 ASTEROIDS

The thousands of small, irregular, slightly elongated, barren rocks which revolve around the sun in elliptical orbits are called asteroids. Their orbital eccentricities and inclinations are quite varied. Most of their orbits lie between those of Mars and Jupiter. Some extend beyond Jupiter's orbit, whereas others come within the orbit of Venus. The largest asteroid (Ceres), with a diameter of about 480 miles (772 km), is not large enough to be resolved into a visible disk by a telescope. Vesta, with a diameter of about 240 miles (386 km), is the only one that is visible to the unaided eye. The total mass of the asteroids has been estimated at less than 1% of the earth's. Asteroids are discussed further in Chapter 9.

8.5 METEOROIDS

In addition to the asteroids, there are a great many extremely small bodies (meteoroids), too small to be observed with a telescope, which revolve around the sun. When these bodies leave their orbits and pass through the earth's atmosphere, they are heated by the friction which they encounter as they collide with the molecules in the atmosphere. As the heat increases, they vaporize, become luminous, and are visible from the earth. When a meteoroid becomes visible, it is called a meteor, or a shooting star. It has been estimated that over 200 million meteors appear in the sky during a 24-hour period over the entire earth. On a clear, moonless night, an observer can see about six meteors every hour. (For further discussion, see Chapter 9).

8.6 COMETS

A comet consists of a swarm of meteoritic material embedded in ice with frozen gases of ammonia and methane, and this basic part of a comet is called the nucleus. Comets revolve around the sun in very eccentric orbits so that they are visible only from several days to several months. Many of them are visible only through a telescope or appear as hazy spots of light to the unaided eye. When they are near the sun, comets consist of three

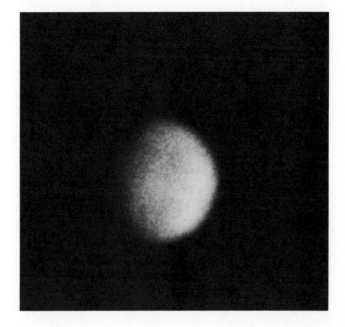

Fig. 8.4 Surface markings of Mercury, 13 July 1969, 1310 U.T., Red Light. (Photograph from New Mexico State University Observatory)

parts: a small nucleus, a coma of gas which surrounds the nucleus, and a tail of gaseous material. The diameter of an average head, which consists of the nucleus and coma, is 55,000 miles (88,512 km), and the diameter of an average tail is 85 million miles, or 136,790,500 km (see Chapter 9).

8.7 MERCURY

As an object as bright as the star Sirius, the planet Mercury was well known to many of the ancient people. Because of its rapid motion with respect to the stars, the ancient Greeks associated this celestial body with the swift messenger of the gods, Mercury. Since Mercury is the planet nearest the sun, it appears to oscillate about the sun to a maximum angular distance of about 28°. When Mercury is to the west of the sun, it appears in the morning before sunrise; when it is to the east of the sun, it is seen in the evening and sets after the sun. The ancient Greeks, who believed they were seeing two separate bodies, called the morning star "Mercury" and the evening star "Apollo."

Mercury's nearness to the sun hampers observation with the unaided eye when the planet is high in the sky; therefore, the best time to view it is just before sunrise or just after sunset. Since the planet is very bright, it can be viewed telescopically when it is high above the horizon, where atmospheric interference to viewing is greatly reduced. Even under these conditions, only a few of the many photographs taken of Mercury show any of its surface markings. One excellent photograph of Mercury taken through the 24-inch telescope at New Mexico State University is shown in Fig. 8.4.

a. Orbit

Mercury revolves around the sun in an elliptical orbit at a mean distance of 36 million miles (58 million km). Its orbit is inclined about 7° to the plane of the ecliptic. At perihelion it is about 29 million miles (47 million km), and at aphelion it is about 44 million miles (71 million km). With this difference of 15 million miles (24,139,500 km), its eccentricity is about 0.206. As the fastest planet in the solar system, it has a mean orbital velocity of about 30 miles (48 km) per second. Its sidereal period of about 88 days and its synodic period of about 116 days are the shortest of any planet. Since its orbit is inside the earth's, its phases are similar to those of the moon, although its apparent size changes considerably more than does the moon. At inferior conjunction its apparent diameter is about three times greater than at superior conjunction.

When Mercury is at inferior conjunction and at either of the nodes, it transits the sun's disk. This is a telescopic phenomenon which is observed as a small black spot, about $\frac{1}{160}$ the sun's diameter, moving across the sun's face for about eight hours. The next two transits will occur on the mornings of November 10, 1973 and November 13, 1986. The 1973 transit will be almost across the sun's center. The astronomical importance of these transits is that the event can be timed most accurately, and from these times our knowledge of Mercury's orbit and motions can be improved.

b. Physical Properties

Having a diameter of 3032 miles (4879 km), which is about 0.38 that of the earth, Mercury is the smallest planet in the solar system. Since Mercury has no known satellites and produces very small perturbations on the orbit of Venus, its mass has been determined by observing the perturbations it produces on the orbit of the asteroid Eros as the latter passes close to the planet. The best value is about 5% of the earth's mass. Using this uncertain value, its density (mass per unit volume) is estimated to be 5.2 grams per cubic centimeter, which is slightly less than that of the earth.

c. Rotation

For many years astronomers believed that Mercury's period of rotation was synchronous with its period of revolution (88 days). While using the 1000-foot radio reflector at Arecibo, Puerto Rico, in 1965, Gordon H. Pettengil and Robert B. Dyce (radio astronomers from Cornell University) found that Mercury's period of rotation is about 59 days. Subsequent radar measurements indicated that the planet's rotational period is 58.65 days, approximately two-thirds of the planet's orbital period of 88 days. This means that the planet rotates three times in two revolutions around the sun. The planet rotates in a counterclockwise direction, with its axis of rotation nearly perpendicular to its orbital plane.

d. Atmosphere

Until recently it was believed that Mercury is without an atmosphere. As the nearest planet to the sun, its surface temperature is extremely high; therefore, the velocities of the atmospheric molecules (if an atmosphere exists) would be correspondingly high. Also, because of its small size and mass, its gravitational force and escape velocity are low. Microwave measurements have indicated that Mercury's surface has a low conductivity (its albedo is 6%), similar to the moon's, and that its surface is physically similar to the moon's. These findings—high surface temperature, high atmospheric molecule velocities, and low escape velocity—support the belief that Mercury would have lost its atmosphere millions of years ago.

During the past few years, however, radio astronomers have recorded the measurements of thermal radiation from Mercury at 3.4-mm and 19-mm wavelengths during all of its phases. These microwave measurements indicate that the average temperature of the face of the planet at full phase is about 700°F (371°C), and at first quarter, about 350°F (177°C). The first-quarter phase temperature is rather high, indicating that a portion of the radiation must come from the dark side of the planet. This may mean that Mercury has a very tenuous atmosphere. The high first-quarter phase temperature readings are probably caused by the heating of the tenuous atmosphere by surface radiation or by radioactive material below the planet's surface. Recently, scientists have noticed what they suspect are the spectral lines of carbon dioxide in the planet's atmosphere.

Some observers have seen a haze around the planet which they believe is caused by the glowing of the atmospheric gases. Since Mercury receives almost 10 times more solar radiation per unit area than the moon, it is believed that the tremendous amount of ultraviolet energy in the solar radiation produces the luminescence that appears as haze around the planet.

8.8 VENUS

The planet Venus, which was named after the Roman goddess of love and beauty, is one of the most beautiful objects in the sky. It is third only to the sun and moon in brightness, and when its position is known, it is clearly visible in the daytime sky.

The Babylonians first recorded the appearance of Venus nearly 4000 years ago. As an inferior planet, it appears to oscillate about the sun and is never seen more

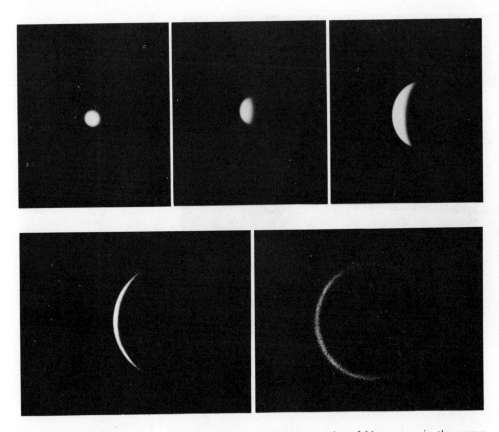

Fig. 8.5 These five photographs of Venus are in the same scale and show that in the full phase Venus appears smaller because it is farther from the earth; the crescent phase it appears because it is nearer the earth. (Lowell Observatory photograph)

than 48° on either side of it. This confused the ancients, who believed that they were two separate stars—a "morning star" rising just before sunrise and an "evening star" setting just after sunset. The ancient Greeks called the morning star "Lucifer" and the evening star "Hesperus." About 500 B.C., the Greek philosopher Pythagoras recognized that the two "stars" were actually the same body.

a. Telescopic View

Galileo was the first to observe Venus telescopically. When he noted that it displayed phases similar to those of the moon and that it changed its apparent size over a continuously recurring cycle (Fig. 8.5), he was convinced that Venus revolves around the sun. Thus, he realized that the sun is the center of revolution for all the planets and that the Copernican model of the universe is correct.

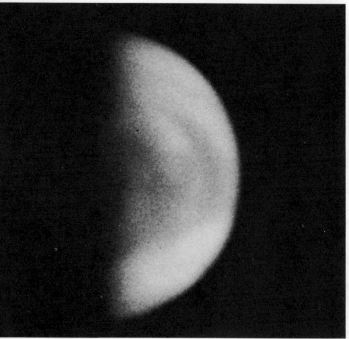

Fig. 8.6 Cloud structure of Venus in ultraviolet light, 24 May 1967, 0132 U.T. (Photograph from New Mexico State University Observatory)

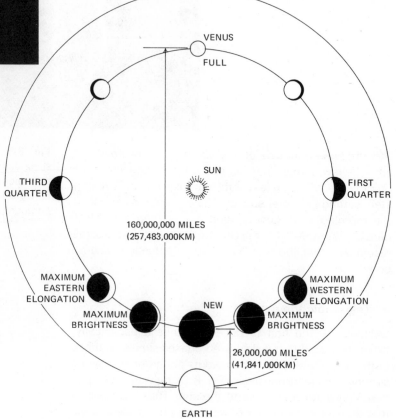

Fig. 8.7 The phases of Venus, its average maximum and minimum distance from the earth, and its relative apparent size as seen from the earth

Even under the most favorable viewing conditions, the telescopic view of Venus is almost featureless and unimpressive. The few observable features consist of small differences in color contrast as shown in the unusual photograph taken at the New Mexico State University (Fig. 8.6). Quite often the cusps appear brighter than the rest of the crescent, and a narrow strip along its entire limb appears brighter when the planet is in the crescent phase. There is also a darkening effect of the illuminated edge of the terminator (the line of demarcation between the illuminated and dark portions of the face of Venus).

b. Orbit

At a mean distance of 67 million miles (108 million km), Venus revolves around the sun in an elliptical orbit that is the most nearly circular of any planet's. The difference between its aphelion and perihelion distances is only 1.25 million miles (2 million km), which gives its orbit an eccentricity of 0.007, the lowest of any planet's. As shown in Fig. 8.7, Venus is the closest planet to the earth when at inferior conjunction, a distance of 26 million miles (42 million km). At superior conjunction, it is nearly 160 million miles (257 million km) from the earth. This great difference in its distance from the earth produces a large variation in its apparent size. At superior conjunction, its apparent diameter is about 10″ and at inferior conjunction, about 64″ (Fig. 8.8).

The orbital plane of Venus is inclined 3° 24′ to the plane of the ecliptic. At an orbital speed of about 22 miles (35 km) per second, its sidereal and synodic periods are about 225 and 584 days, respectively.

The transit of the sun's disk by Venus is a rare phenomenon and is visible to the unaided eye. It occurs when Venus is at inferior conjunction and close to one of the nodes. The last two transits occurred in 1874 and 1882, and the next two will occur on June 8, 2004 and on June 6, 2012.

c. Physical Properties

Venus is often called the earth's twin because of the similarity in the general physical properties of the two planets. The exact size of Venus is uncertain because

Fig. 8.8 Venus, photographed with the 200-inch telescope near inferior conjunction in the crescent phase, appears over six times greater in size than when at superior conjunction in the full phase. (Photograph from the Hale Observatories)

dense clouds completely shroud the planet. A diameter of about 7600 miles (12,200 km) was obtained from data which were based on visual, photographic, and photoelectric observations of the occultation of the star Regulus by Venus on July 7, 1959. This diameter is about 0.96 that of the earth's. Venus has an escape velocity of about 6.5 miles (10.46 km) per second as compared to about 7 for the earth.

d. The Mariner 2 Probe

On December 14, 1962, when Mariner 2 passed within 21,598 miles (34,758 km) of Venus, it radioed back to earth data which revealed more information about the planet than man had acquired since the beginning of recorded history. These data were the first ever recorded by man from the vicinity of another planet. As the spacecraft approached Venus, a change of course was required, which was based on the planet's mass. Since this produced the desired course, its mass was established at about 0.81 that of the earth's. This gives Venus a mean density of about 5.2 grams per cubic centimeter, which is about 0.91 that of the earth's.

The magnetometer on the spacecraft observed that the strength of the magnetic field at a distance of 21,598 miles (34,758 km) from Venus is comparable to that found in space between the earth and Venus. Therefore, it was concluded that at this distance no discernible magnetic field exists around Venus and that there is no radiation belt of trapped high-energy particles.

The dark areas visible in the atmosphere of Venus were observed at two different regions of the spectrum through the use of infrared and microwave radiometers. If they represent "breaks" in the clouds, they would be sharply defined in the infrared region, otherwise the readings on both radiometers would be close. However, the temperature readings from both radiometers were about the same, which indicated that the cloud cover is solid around the planet.

The scattering of the radar signals from the spacecraft confirmed the belief that Venus' surface is rough and similar to the moon's. The distortion of the clear, sharp radar signals reflected by the planet's surface

indicated that the planet is rotating slowly in a clockwise direction, which is opposite to the rotational motion of the other planets. The planet's period of rotation is 243 days, and its period of revolution is 225 days.

e. Venera 4 and Mariner 5

Two further explorations of cloud-shrouded Venus were made on October 18, 1967, when the U.S.S.R. spacecraft Venera 4 flew into the atmosphere of Venus and parachuted an instrument package through the Venusian atmosphere, and on October 19, 1967, when the U.S. spacecraft Mariner 5 passed within 6300 miles (10,139 km) from the planet's center.

Study of the data from the probes confirmed Mariner 2's findings that Venus has neither a radiation belt of charged particles nor a magnetic field. A bright hydrogen corona extending to a height of 13,000 miles, or 20,921 km, (with the first 1800 miles, or 2897 km, as bright as the earth's corona) was discovered around the planet. The data also produced unmistakable evidence of the interaction of the solar wind with the planet's ionosphere. The solar wind (plasma of very hot, tenuous, ionized gas particles within a magnetic field) moves around the ionosphere and forms a "bow shock" on the bright side of the planet and a cavity on the dark side. This phenomenon indicates that because of its slow penetration of the planet's ionosphere, most of the plasma fails to reach the planet's atmosphere.

Atmospheric samples analyzed directly by Venera 4 indicated a carbon dioxide (CO_2) abundance of about 90%, with traces of oxygen (O_2), carbon monoxide (CO), water (H_2O), and nitrogen (N). Hydrogen chloride (HCL) and hydrogen fluoride (HF) were found by ground-based interferometric observations. Mariner 5, using a radio technique to analyze the Venusian atmosphere, obtained a CO_2 abundance of about 80%. A Lyman-alpha airglow was observed in the upper atmosphere, which indicates the presence of atomic hydrogen (H) in amounts comparable to those found in the earth's upper atmosphere. Since the atomic hydrogen does not extend to the height found in the earth's atmosphere, the temperature of the Venusian atmosphere is considerably lower than the earth's at any given height. The weak ultraviolet night-glow, observed on the dark limb of the planet, is believed to be caused by either chemical reactions in the upper atmosphere or charged-particle discharges.

It is believed that the Venusian atmosphere contains more dust particles than are found in the earth's atmosphere. Clouds are created by either condensation of water vapor around hydroscopic nuclei or a mixing of dust particles. Since the presence of an adequate condensate on Venus has not been detected, the theory that the clouds might be formed by dust particles is being explored. The data from the probes indicate that the radio temperature is about 200°F (93°C) at the base of the clouds, about 45 miles (72 km) above the planet's surface; the tops of the clouds are about 15 miles (24 km) above the base.

The planet's temperature varies from −30°F (−34°C) at the center of the planet's disk to about −60°F (−51°C) at its edges. This temperature range and the fact that one sees through a deeper atmosphere at the center of the planet's disk than at its edges, explain the limb-darkening effect detected by the microwave radiometer on Mariner 2. The instrument package of Venera 4 measured the temperature of the Venusian atmosphere directly as it parachuted through it. The maximum temperature recorded was 536°F (280°C); however, it is believed that this is not the surface temperature—atmospheric pressure probably prevented the instrument from functioning all the way down to the surface.

The data indicate that the lower atmosphere of Venus is very hot and dry, with strong convective currents. The noon surface temperature is about 780°F (416°C), with a pressure of about 90 atmospheres; the midnight surface temperature is about −450°F (−268°C). Although the insolation of Venus is about twice that of the earth, it is not sufficient to account for the high surface temperature. The increase in temperature is probably due to the "greenhouse effect," i.e., as incoming solar radiation passes freely through the Venusian atmosphere, the reradiated energy in the infrared is absorbed by the carbon dioxide in the atmosphere and is thereby prevented from escaping out into space.

8.9 MARS

Mars, with its colorful history, is one of the most fascinating and intriguing planets in the solar system (Plate 15).[1] Since antiquity, its bright, reddish orange disk has inspired people to associate disaster, war, and death with the planet. The Greeks called it "Ares," which means disaster; the Chaldeans called it "Nergal," the god of the dead; and the Romans called it "Mars," their god of war.

The planet has played a very important role in the development of astronomical thought. Kepler deduced the three laws of planetary motion from the voluminous visual observations of Mars recorded by Tycho Brahe and from the planet's eccentric orbit. In 1877 the American astronomer Asaph Hall discovered the planet's two small satellites, and the Italian astronomer Giovanni Schiaparelli discovered the controversial Martian canals, seeing them as dark lines across the face of the planet.

The description of the canals as "a veritable cobweb" by De Vaucouleurs and the theory presented by Percival Lowell that they were constructed by a race of intelligent beings started the great dispute as to the nature of the canals and the speculation of the possibility of life existing on its surface. This dispute and speculation, which are still with us, have given Mars a mystery and a fascination not shared by any other planet. The speculation has been greatly increased by the many stories that have been written about Mars in books, magazines, and comics. These writings have had a tremendous hold on man's imagination, as witnessed by Orson Wells' dramatic radio presentation of the "Men from Mars" in 1938. In the form of a special news broadcast, this imaginary invasion of the United States by Martians was so realistic that many people panicked when they turned in on the program.

With the Mariner 4, 6, and 7 space probes and the 1971 Mariner Orbiter, our knowledge and understanding of the planet's physical characteristics and its biological conditions have increased significantly. There are still many unanswered questions about the planet, some of which will be forthcoming when the Viking spacecraft makes its landing on Mars in 1976.

---

[1] Plates 15–23 appear following p. 160.

a. Telescopic View

Telescopically, Mars appears as a bright, reddish orange disk, brighter than any planet except Venus. Even under the most favorable atmospheric conditions for viewing, the 200-inch Hale telescope cannot obtain high-resolution photographs of Mars. Photographs (Plate 16) show that three-fifths of the planet's visible surface appears reddish orange and represents the dry, desert areas; the remaining two-fifths appears darker and grayer and represents the controversial areas where some form of plant life may exist. The color of the desert areas appears to be uniform and constant, whereas the color of the darker areas appears to change with the seasons—from gray in winter to blue in summer.

The most conspicuous features are the brilliant white areas (polar caps) visible in the winter around the north and south poles. During the fall season in the northern hemisphere, the north polar cap begins to form under a heavy blanket of clouds. By midwinter, the white mantle has increased so that it extends almost half way to the equator. In the spring the cap begins to shrink, while at the same time the south polar cap begins to form. As the north polar cap continues to shrink, a dark band appears on its periphery. When the north polar cap has disappeared, the south polar cap has completely formed. The south polar cap is larger than the north polar cap and extends almost to the planet's equator. This indicates that the climatic conditions are more extreme in the southern hemisphere than in the northern.

The most controversial features on Mars' surface have been the "canals." The nature of these finely detailed features has been most difficult to determine; the most powerful telescopes have failed to resolve them, and viewing has been hampered by the earth's atmosphere. There are two widely separated points of view about these surface features. Some interpret them as long dark lines that stretch across the desert areas and join with the polar caps and the dark areas; others will not admit to ever seeing any such lines. This controversy probably has been resolved by the close-range photographs taken by Mariner 4 on July 14, 1965, which clearly show the "canals" as a series of small craterlets.

b. Physical Properties

Mars is often called the earth's poor relative because its general physical properties are similar but somewhat smaller than the earth's. Mars is an oblate spheroid with an equatorial diameter of 4225 miles (6799 km) and a polar diameter of 4193 miles (6748 km). These values, reported by French astronomer A. Dollfus at the Meudon Observatory, were based on radar and spacecraft experiments. The planet's mass is 0.11 that of the earth, and its mean density of 3.92 grams per cubic centimeter is about 0.71 that of the earth. These values give Mars a surface gravity of 0.38 that of the earth, which means that a 100-pound girl would weigh only 38 pounds (17.25 kg) on Mars. Mars' escape velocity of 3.1 miles (4.99 km) per second is about half of the earth's; its albedo is 0.15.

The Martian atmosphere is extremely thin—at its surface, it is comparable to what would be found around the earth at a height of about 20 miles (32 km). The thin atmosphere permits observation of the Martian surface features, which have enabled astronomers to measure the planet's period of rotation and the angle of inclination of its axis of rotation. Its rotational period is 24 hours 37 minutes 23 seconds, and its equator is inclined 24° 48' to its orbital plane. The north pole of its axis points toward the star Deneb in the constellation of Cygnus the Swan. The planet's axis of rotation precesses like the earth's, but at a much slower rate. Mars' precessional period is about 183,000 years.

The surface temperature of Mars varies considerably. When the planet is at perihelion, the highest noon temperature at the equator is 80°F (27°C); the lowest midnight temperature is −90°F (−68°C). The average temperature at the poles is 50° F (10° C) in the summer and −130°F (−90°C) in the winter. The temperature of the south polar cap in the winter reaches about −150°F (−101°C). The average temperature of the illuminated surface of Mars has been determined from infrared measurements to be −30°F (−34°C), and the average temperature of the planet's entire surface has been determined from thermal radio emission waves to be −60°F (−51°C). The thermal emission temperature is higher because the thermal radio emission waves come from just below the planet's surface.

With a thin atmosphere, a low atmospheric pressure, and a small gravitational field, clouds have been observed at heights of about eight miles above the planet's surface. They have been classified into three main types, according to the predominant color which they reflect— white, blue, and yellow. The white clouds, generally thick and brilliant, are seen as large, stationary masses over the winter polar cap and as large masses in motion at speeds of about 30 miles (48 km) per hour in the mid-latitudes. The white clouds have been compared to the earth's cirrus clouds.

Blue clouds are observed near the equator, either at sunrise or sunset, and near the poles in winter. At times it is difficult to differentiate between white and blue clouds because of a gradation in color that exists between them. The blue clouds are believed to be condensation nuclei that reflect blue and violet light.

The yellow clouds are seen infrequently, vary considerably in color and brightness, and are probably dust clouds. A. Dollfus believes that they consist of minute, highly absorbent particles that are suspended in the atmosphere for long periods of time. He bases his belief on the negative polarization of the clouds. These clouds have been observed to travel at speeds up to 75 miles (121 km) per hour. These speeds are sufficient to produce dust storms, and the planet's small gravitational field permits these dust particles to remain suspended in the atmosphere for long periods of time.

c. Orbit

Mars travels around the sun in a counterclockwise direction at a mean distance of about 141,690,000 miles (228,022,000 km). It has a rather eccentric elliptical orbit whose eccentricity is 0.093. Its perihelion distance

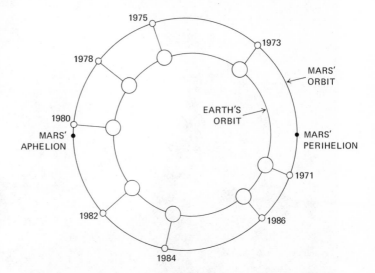

Fig. 8.9 The oppositions of Mars occur at intervals of about 780 days, Mars' synodic period. Favorable oppositions usually occur in either August or September at intervals of about 15 years, when Mars is at or near perihelion.

is 128,400,000 miles (206,634,120 km) and its aphelion distance is 154,900,000 miles (249,280,570 km)— a difference of about 26 million miles (42 million km). Its orbital path is inclined 1°51′ to the plane of the ecliptic. With a mean orbital speed of about 15 miles (24 km) per second, its sidereal period is about 687 days, and its synodic period is about 780 days, the longest of any planet. During its synodic period, Mars moves eastward with respect to the stars (direct motion) for 710 days and then moves westward (retrograde motion) for 70 days. It retrogrades as it approaches the earth at opposition, and at the same time it appears to increase its luminosity.

The most favorable time for viewing Mars occurs when the planet is close to opposition. Because of its orbital eccentricity, the opposition distance varies from the most favorable, at about 35 million miles (56 million km)—which occurred in 1971—to the least favorable, at 62.5 million miles (100.6 million km). The dates and distances of opposition are shown in Fig. 8.9. The most

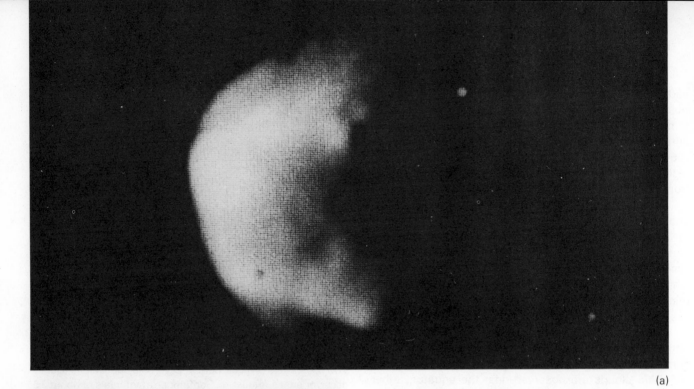

(a)

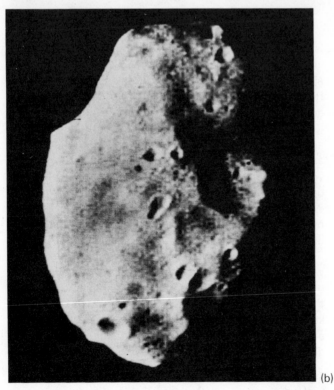

(b)

Fig. 8.10 Mars' satellites. (a) This is the first detailed photograph of Deimos, Mars' outermost satellite, taken by Mariner 9. Two large craters, about one mile across, are visible near the terminator which separates the dark and bright sides of the satellite. Deimos appears to be smoother than its companion satellite, Phobos. (b) This computer-enhanced photograph taken by Mariner 9 is the most detailed image of Phobos available to date. Photograph was taken 3444 miles from Mars. Many small craters, with one large crater at right center, are visible. The large number of craters suggests that Phobos is very old and possesses considerable structural strength. (NASA/JPL photographs)

Fig. 8.11 This photograph of northwestern Phaethontis on Mars was taken by Mariner 4 on 14 July 1965 at a slant range of 7600 miles. The sun was 29° above the Martian horizon. The craters range in diameter from 75 miles (for the one just discernible in the center of the photo) to 2.5 miles. The abundance of craters is similar to areas of the moon's surface. (NASA/JPL photograph)

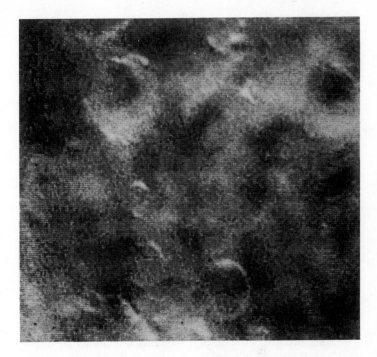

favorable oppositions occur in August or September, when the planet is near perihelion; the least favorable oppositions occur in February or March, when the planet is at aphelion. Unfortunately for observers in the northern hemisphere, the most favorable oppositions occur when Mars is in an unfavorable viewing position in the sky. At these times, the planet is almost 30° below the celestial equator, which means that the planet is seen low in the sky.

d. Satellites

Mars has two known satellites, which were discovered in 1877 (when Mars was in a most favorable opposition) by Asaph Hall, director of the U.S. Naval Observatory. He named them Phobos (fear) and Deimos (panic). Phobos (about 13 miles high and 16 miles long) is the inner satellite, and Deimos (about $7\frac{1}{2}$ miles high and $8\frac{1}{2}$ miles long) is the outer satellite (Fig. 8.10). The orbits of the satellites are almost circular and lie very close to the planet's equatorial plane. Phobos revolves around the planet at a distance of 5800 miles (9334 km) from the planet's center in 7 hours 39 minutes, and Deimos at a distance of 14,600 miles (23,496 km) in 30 hours 18 minutes. Phobos' period of revolution is unique in the solar system because it revolves around the planet in less time than it takes the planet to rotate, completing about three revolutions every day.

Although their presence was neither known nor suspected prior to their discovery in 1877, Kepler, in 1600, wrote a letter to Galileo in which he speculated on the possibility that Mars has two small moons re-

volving around it. In his imaginative *Micromegas*, Voltaire mentions the presence of these satellites. Also, Dean Jonathan Swift, a contemporary of Newton, wrote in his *Gulliver's Travels* (1726) that the Lilliputian astronomers had discovered two satellites revolving around the planet Mars. Their sizes and distances from the planet as given by Swift were remarkably close to their actual values.

8.10 MARINER 4, 6, 7, AND 9 PROBES

On July 14–15, 1965, U.S. Mariner 4 became the first spacecraft to successfully fly by Mars and complete its mission. It came within 6118 miles (9846 km) of the planet's surface and radioed back to earth 21 photographs of Mars' surface. The resolution of these photographs produced the amazing discovery that the planet has a moon-like surface of densely packed impact craters. In a single photograph of 150 miles square, or 241.4 km square (Fig. 8.11), over 70 craters ranging in size from

2.5 miles (4.02 km) to 75 miles (120.7 km) in diameter were observed. The rims of the craters have gentle slopes of less than 10° and rise only several hundred feet above the surrounding terrain. The craters' floors are several thousand feet below the surrounding terrain. The general appearance of the terrain is smooth, round, and eroded, with no sharp edges to cast shadows. There are no mountains or ocean basins in any of the photographs.

Mariner 4 photographs produced no evidence of the controversial Martian canals that were observed and reported by Giovanni Schiaparelli in 1877. Under adequate resolution and magnification, these "canals" were resolved into a series of chains and clusters of small, secondary craters. They appear to be very similar to the lunar rays resolved in the photographs taken by the Ranger spacecraft.

The atmospheric effects on the radio signals as Mariner 4 passed close to Mars indicate that the planet has an extremely thin atmosphere around it. The atmospheric pressure at its surface is about 1.5% of the earth's. This tenuous atmosphere explains the presence of the densely packed craters, because a dense atmosphere would shield the planet from many of the meteoritic impacts. Mariner 4 also revealed the presence of minute quantities of water vapor in the atmosphere; however, it left unanswered the question as to whether the water vapor is present throughout the atmosphere.

Water vapor in the Martian atmosphere was detected spectroscopically in 1963 by Munch, Kaplan, and Spinard when they observed the water-vapor lines in the spectra taken with the 100-inch Mount Wilson telescope. This was accomplished by obtaining the spectrum when Mars was receding from the earth at a high velocity so that the Doppler effect caused the Martian water-vapor lines to be separated from the stronger ones of the earth's atmosphere. The major component of the Martian atmosphere was found to be carbon dioxide. Mariner 4 also found that Mars has no radiation belt and a weak magnetic field, which indicates that Mars probably does not have a liquid core as does the earth.

On July 31, 1969, Mariner 6 came within 2100 miles (3380 km) of the planet's surface along an equatorial path, and on August 5, 1969, Mariner 7 came within 2000 miles (3219 km) of the planet's surface along an angular path over the south pole. The photographs from both probes have a resolution of about 900 feet (275 meters) and clearly show that except for the polar regions and areas where clouds appear temporarily, the planet's surface is usually visible.

Analysis of the photographs revealed new and interesting information about the atmospheric and surface features of Mars. When the "near-encounter" photographs were compared to those taken from the earth at the same time, the earth-bound photographs revealed the presence of the "blue haze" and its usual obscuration of the planet's dark features, whereas the Mariner photographs, even through red, green, and blue filters, failed to reveal the "blue haze." The dark features are clearly visible in the Mariner photographs through all the filters. There is no explanation for the "blue haze" and the "blue-clearing" phenomenon that appears in the earth-bound photographs. The possibility of the existence of atmospheric haze on Mars might be indicated by the amazing darkening of the southern limb of the planet around the polar region and by the daily variation in the brightness of several of the planet's large areas. Nix Olympica, Candor, and other regions appear to increase in brightness during the morning and afternoon each day. Photographs of the northern limb of the planet have produced evidence of scattering in the Martian atmosphere similar to that in the earth's atmosphere.

The Martian terrain, with its large number of craters, appears to be more moon-like than earth-like. From radar measurements, Dr. Gordon Pettengil has determined that the highest point on Mars is about 8 miles (13 km) above its lowest point; however, this difference in elevation is hardly noticeable because the terrain is very smooth, round, and gently sloping. The typical arid-region features of the earth, such as mountain ranges, dune fields, and techtonic activity (the folding and faulting of the earth), have not been identified in any of the Mariner photographs.

The Mariner 6 and 7 photographs reveal that Mars has three significantly different types of terrain—cratered, chaotic, and featureless. The dominant features of the

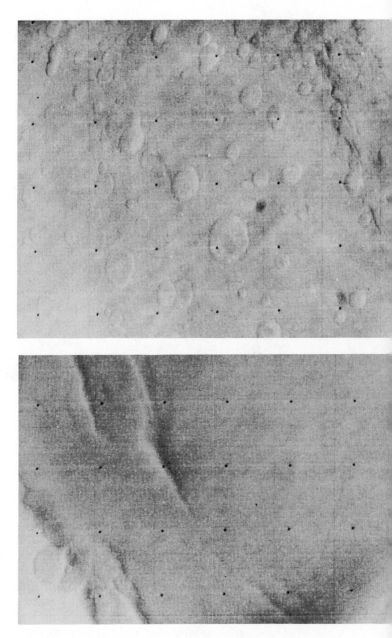

Fig. 8.12 Mariner 7 photograph of the Martian regions of Hellespontus and Hellas. This 450-by-600-mile area was photographed from 2500 miles. Almost the entire photograph is of the dark, cratered terrain of Hellespontus. At the upper right is the escarpment which forms the boundary of Hellespontus and the light, craterless terrain of Hellas. (NASA/JPL photograph)

cratered terrain (Fig. 8.12) are the craters which appear prominently in the southern hemisphere. Although they look like lunar craters, many of them show distinctive differences, which suggests that a different geological process might have produced them. The Martian craters generally appear to be much shallower and smoother than the lunar craters and show various degrees of preservation, suggesting that the weathering process is still taking place on Mars. The large craters appear to be old and to have very flat floors; the small craters are young with bowl-shaped floors like those on the moon. Some of their interior slopes are less than 10°, while others are more than 20°. There are fewer central mountain peaks on the floor of craters, an absence of secondary craters, and more of the "ghost" craters.

The chaotic terrain, which is relatively free of craters, has short ridges and depressions that are chaotically distributed over a region nearly three-quarters of a million square miles. This region, located between the dark areas of Aurorae Sinus and Margaritifer Sinus, has the appearance of a terrestrial landslide, although its area is much greater than any similar condition on earth.

The bright circular "desert" of Hellas (Fig. 8.13) is the largest featureless terrain that has been identified on Mars. Over its 1200-mile diameter floor not a single crater is visible in the Mariner 7 photograph, whose resolution is about 900 feet. This extensive featureless desert is unique on the planet. To the west of Hellas is the heavily cratered, dark area of Hellespontus. The region between Hellas and Hellespontus is also cratered.

Fig. 8.13 Mariner 7 photograph of the craterless plain of Hellas. The ridges in the escarpment at the border of Hellas and Hellespontus are clearly visible to the left. (NASA photograph)

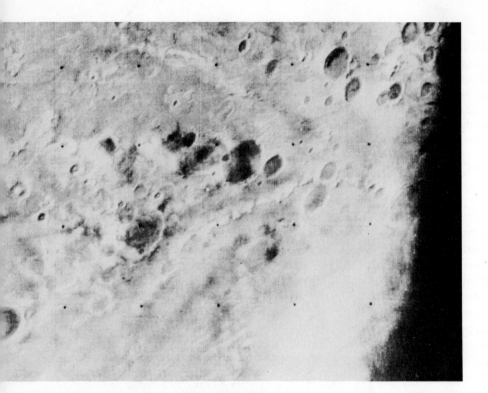

Fig. 8.14 This remarkable Mariner 7 photograph of Mars' south polar region shows craters of many sizes and forms, linera, and blotchy features unrelated to cratering. The south polar cap, which is seen to the right, may be either a layer of finely granulated dry ice a few feet deep or a one-inch layer of water ice. (NASA photograph)

There is no explanation as to why the terrain abruptly changes from cratered to featureless at the edge of Hellas; however, it has been suggested that the floor of Hellas consists of porous material which shifts easily with the Martian winds to fill any depressions that might be created by meteoric impact.

The most conspicuous features on the Martian surface are the brilliant, white caps which appear to form around the north and south poles during the winter months. No direct information is available on the composition and thickness of this "snow." The possibility that the polar caps are composed of ice has been rejected because the slow evaporation rate for water and the observed vapor density of the planet's atmosphere would make it impossible to move such large quantities of water vapor from one pole to the other in the observed period of time. Since CO_2 is the major component of the Martian atmosphere and since radio occultation measurement of its atmosphere indicates that the atmospheric conditions are suitable for the condensation of CO_2, the composition of the "snow" on the polar caps is assumed to be primarily frozen CO_2, with possible traces of frozen H_2O.

Mariner photographs of the south polar cap reveal that its north edge is sharp but irregular; the earth-bound photographs, on the other hand, have always shown the edge to be somewhat smooth (Fig. 8.14). This irregularity is believed to be caused by the direction in which the surface of the cap's edge slopes. Those surfaces that slope away from the pole probably evaporate the frozen CO_2 faster than those that slope toward the pole. The variation in the brightness of "snow" material suggests a variable thickness ranging from a very thin layer to several feet. The photographs reveal craters ranging in size from about .5 miles to 75 miles (.8 to 121 km) in diameter within and outside the south polar cap. The largest crater, which is circular, is near the center of the cap's edge, and its interior, near the center and on the west wall, appears to be grooved. The floors of the larger craters appear to be rather dark and their rims quite bright. A very definite dark area appears near the south limb of the south polar cap, which does not rotate with the planet, indicating that this dark area is probably a thin atmospheric haze.

The controversial "canals" and the "oases" that have been observed from the earth appear to have been resolved in the Mariner photographs. The Cantabras and Gehon canals appear as dark craters in linear alignment. The Juventae Fons oasis appears as a large, dark crater, and the Oxia Palus oasis appears as a cluster of small dark craters. With further exploration, probably all the canals and oases will be resolved into craters of different alignment, thus eliminating them as separate, distinctive surface features.

There has been no direct evidence from Mariner's observations to suggest the existence or nonexistence of life on Mars. This is understandable, because if life does exist on Mars, it would not be detectable in the Mariner photographs with a resolution of 900 feet (275 meters). If life does exist, it probably is in the form of microbes rather than plants or animals. Man may have an answer to this question when the Viking Lander spacecraft lands on Mars, scoops up some soil, and tests it for life.

When Mariner 9 went into orbit around Mars in November 1971, it marked the first time that man had placed a spacecraft in orbit around another planet. All previous missions were fly-bys, that is, the spacecrafts were in the vicinity of the planet for only a brief period of time. Mariner 9 is expected to remain in orbit for several years, with its closest approach being about 860 miles (1384 km). The basic objectives of its mission are to obtain data from 70% of Mars' surface for longer periods of time and to observe changes in the planet's atmosphere and surface.

Although a massive, severe dust storm enveloped the planet during the spacecraft's first two months in orbit, Mariner 9 has considerably increased man's knowledge of Mars. By means of special computer processing,

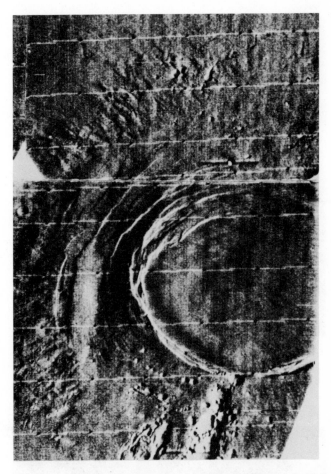

Fig. 8.15 The 70-mile diameter Martian crater near Nodud Gordii (the Gordian Knot) photographed by Mariner 9. (NASA/JPL photograph)

the photographs taken have revealed details of the Martian surface not seen before. Near Ascraeus Lacus in the Tharsis region, a crater complex was photographed which consists of several intersecting, shallow, crater-like depressions. The complex is about 25 miles (40 km) wide, and the main crater is about 13 miles (21 km) in diameter. A crater 70 miles (113 km) wide photographed near the Nodus Gordii (Gordian Knot) region of the Martian equator (Fig. 8.15) is probably a remnant of an extinct volcano. The several concentric fractures on

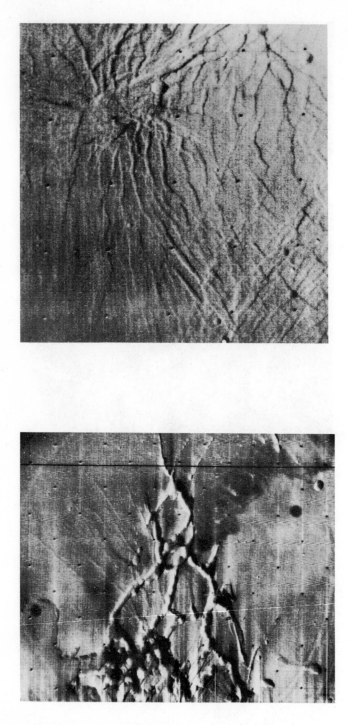

Fig. 8.16 The Phoenicis Lacus plateau with its mosaic-like faults, photographed by Mariner 9. (NASA/JPL photograph)

its western rim and the numerous rimless craterlets suggest that the crater may be a caldera, equal in size to the largest found on the earth or the moon.

During its 67th orbit, the spacecraft photographed the area of Phoenicis Lacus, a plateau about 3.5 miles (6 km) above the mean elevation of Mars, located just south of the Martian equator. This Martian view (Fig. 8.16) turned out to be unlike any other yet obtained. Even though the lower areas are still hidden from view by the dust storm, the photograph is most striking for its mosaic-like appearance. Relatively few craters are visible in this area, which indicates that the surface may be young and covered with volcanic deposits. The mosaic-like appearance may have been produced when the surface was broken by faults, which appear in the photograph to be about 1.5 miles wide.

The Martian canyonlands were photographed in Noctis Lacus, on the northern border of the Solis Lacus region. The canyons appear to be about 6 to 12 miles (10 to 19 km) wide, .5 to 1.25 miles (.8 to 2 km) deep, with smooth floors and walls that slope from 10 to 15 degrees. The canyon walls appear to be both curved and straight. The curved portions may be parts of incomplete craters, and the straight portions appear to be parallel to each other. The canyons are separated by flat-surfaced plateaus, or mesas. Their overall size is like that of the Grand Canyon. These observations suggest that the canyons are of structural origin and that the fluting of the walls is the result of erosion. Figure 8.17 shows an elaborate network of formidable canyons that appears to

Fig. 8.17 The Chandelier of Mars, an intricate network of great canyons that appear to hang like a chandelier from the Martian equator, photographed by Mariner 9. (NASA/JPL photograph)

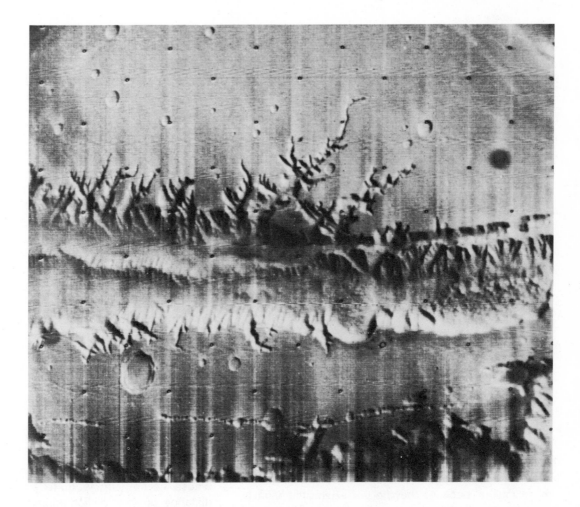

Fig. 8.18 Marina 9 photograph of a unique Martian land form consisting of tree-like canyons located in Tithonius Lacus, 300 miles south of the equator. (NASA/JPL photograph)

hang like a giant chandelier from the Martian equator. This photograph, which covers a 336-by-264 mile (541 by 425 km) area, provides dramatic evidence of the erosional processes at work on the volcanic plateaus of Noctis Lacus.

A unique land form was photographed in Tithonius Lacus, 300 miles (483 km) south of the Martian equator (Fig. 8.18). This system of canyons, which resemble terrestrial, tree-like tributaries, are closed depressions. It is believed that they evolved from subsidence along lines of weakness in the Martian crust and from deflation by the Martian winds.

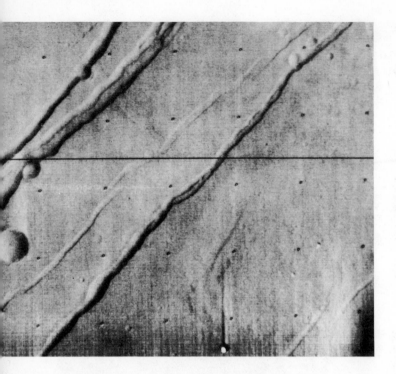

Fig. 8.19 The rilles of Mare Sirenum, photographed by Mariner 9. (NASA/JPL photograph)

8.11 JUPITER

a. Physical Properties

The fifth planet from the sun has been appropriately named after the ruler of the Greek gods, Jupiter. The planet deserves this title because next to the sun, it is the dominant body in the solar system (Fig. 8.20). It is the largest planet (88,640 miles, or 142,648 km in diameter, which is about 11 times larger than the earth), and the most massive (318 times greater than the earth and 2.5 times greater than all the other planets combined). Its mean density is 1.33 grams per cubic centimeter, which is about one-fourth that of the earth's and slightly less than the sun's. Its surface gravity is 2.64, which means that a 100-pound girl would weigh 264 pounds (119.75 kg) on Jupiter. Its velocity of escape is 37 miles (59.54 km) per second, which is the greatest of any planet.

b. Orbit

Jupiter revolves around the sun in an elliptical orbit whose eccentricity is quite small (0.05) at a mean distance of 484 million miles (779 million km). The orbit is inclined 1° 18′ to the plane of the ecliptic, and the planet's equator is inclined 3°07′ to its orbital plane. At an orbital speed of 8.1 miles (13.04 km) per second, Jupiter's sidereal period is 11.86 years, and its synodic period is 398.9 days.

c. Telescopic View

To the unaided eye, Jupiter appears as a bright yellowish object. When Jupiter is faintest, it is slightly fainter than the star Sirius; when Jupiter is at its brightest, it is almost twice as bright as the star. Next to Venus and Mars, it is the brightest planet.

Mariner 9 also photographed remarkable pits and hollows about 500 miles (805 km) from the Martian south pole and the first clear view of rilles in the Martian crust in Mare Sirenum. The small pits and hollows are about 1 to 2 miles (1.6 to 3.2 km) in diameter and are most unusual because they do not exhibit the usual interior terraces that are present in volcanic-collapse depressions. It has been suggested that these pits may have resulted from the thawing of large accumulations of ground ice or by wind action in loosely consolidated materials. The rilles of Mare Sirenum are more impressive than those on the moon because the cracks extend to over 1100 miles (1770 km), which is longer than any on the moon. Figure 8.19 shows that the rilles range up to one mile in width and appear to be parallel to one another. The widest rille, which appears in the upper left of the photograph, has a shallower rille located on its floor. The origin of the Martian rilles is believed to be similar to that of the lunar rilles—the stretching of the upper rock layers.

When Jupiter is seen through a telescope, it appears as a bright disk with prominent bands, or belt-markings, that run nearly parallel to the planet's equator. These markings have colors that range from orange to dull red and include an occasional green. The belts are currents in Jupiter's atmosphere similar to the wind systems found on the earth. They are moving, cloud-like formations that seem to maintain their general appearance and size, although their speed and the detail of their appearance show changes. The belts nearest the poles appear to be more stable in position, arrangement, and size than those nearest the equator.

One of Jupiter's most interesting atmospheric features appeared suddenly in August 1878 in the planet's south tropical zone at about 20° south of the equator. It was "The Great Red Spot," 30,000 miles (48,279 km) long and 8000 miles (12,874 km) wide, with its major axis parallel to the planet's equator (Plate 17). Jean D. Cassini, the first director of the Paris Observatory, first saw the spot and from its motion determined the planet's rotational period to be 9 hours 55 minutes. This was the first time that the rotational period of any planet had been determined. The planet's visible surface, however, does not rotate as a solid body. The equator rotates at 9 hours $50\frac{1}{2}$ minutes, while the temperate zones take about five minutes longer.

The spot has undergone many changes in color, brightness, and size. It appears to brighten, fade, then brighten again in irregular periods. It remains prominently bright for several years, then fades slowly until it is barely visible. The shape of the spot always appears elliptical, and its width remains fairly constant; however, its length has varied considerably over the years. At present it is pear-shaped, the interior is lighter than its edges, and dark areas appear at both ends. It also appears to drift in the planet's atmosphere at a variable rate—sometimes faster and other times slower than the planet's rotational rate. Elmer Reece and H. Gordon Solberg, Jr., at the New Mexico State University Observatory, have recently found from accurate measurements of the spot's position on photographic plates that its longitude changes along a complex sinusoidal oscillation curve during a period of about 88 days.

Fig. 8.20 Jupiter, 23 October 1964, 0858 U.T., Blue Light. (Photograph from New Mexico State University Observatory)

Recently, a new, bright circular spot (about 4000 miles in diameter) in the northern hemisphere of Jupiter was discovered photographically by Elmer Reece. Its rotation period of 9 hours 47 minutes 5 seconds is the shortest of any of the planet's markings. Because of its brightness when photographed in ultraviolet light, this new spot is believed to be located in the planet's upper atmosphere. This is the sixth disturbance that has occurred in this region—the first was in 1880.

d. Atmosphere

In 1932 Rupert Wildt made a spectroscopic discovery of ammonia (NH_3) and methane (CH_4) in Jupiter's atmosphere, with methane in more abundance. Also, a trace of hydrogen was discovered in the infrared region. In 1958 W. Demarcus concluded from theoretical studies that Jupiter's atmosphere contains about 78% hydrogen by weight. His model of Jupiter's structure consisted of a solidified gas core surrounded by an atmosphere of hydrogen. There has been no spectroscopic evidence of the existence of such a rich atmosphere of hydrogen around Jupiter.

On November 20, 1952, W. A. Baum and C. A. Code observed the occultation of a star by Jupiter, and from the rate at which it was dimmed, they determined the index of refraction of the planet's atmosphere. This involved the planet's apparent motion, its surface gravity, its gas temperature, and its molecular weight. The molecular weight was the only unknown factor; therefore, from the light curve they calculated its probable value at about 3.3. Since hydrogen has a molecular weight of 2.0, there must be a heavier gas present in the atmosphere. Since helium has a molecular weight of 4.0, they concluded that the planet's atmosphere is a mixture of hydrogen and helium. The determination of the abundance of hydrogen and helium in Jupiter's atmosphere has been a very difficult problem and as yet has not been resolved. Investigation suggests that Jupiter's composition is basically hydrogen and helium, very much like that of a star.

Since 1955 Jupiter has been emitting occasional bursts of radio noise at frequencies near 20 megacycles per second. Individual bursts are about one second in duration and occur in groups that last for about one hour. The bursts appear to be related to the position of the planet's satellite Io, to the planet's rotation, and to a particular alignment of Jupiter's magnetic field with the earth.

e. Satellites

Jupiter has 12 known satellites. Four are about equal to or larger than the moon, whereas the others are less than 100 miles (160.93 km) in diameter. The four largest— Io, Europa, Ganymede, and Callisto—were discovered in 1610 by Galileo and can easily be observed with an ordinary pair of binoculars. The mean values for their important physical characteristics are:

	Io	Europa	Ganymede	Callisto
Magnitude (apparent)	6	6	5	6
Diameter (miles)	2050	1800	3050	2900
Diameter (km)	(3299)	(2897)	(4908)	(4667)
Mass (moon's mass = 1)	1	.6	2	.6
Density (grams/cm^3)	3	3	2	.6
Sidereal period (days)	1.77	3.55	7.16	16.69

It is interesting to note that if the satellite Ganymede orbited the sun instead of Jupiter, it would be classified as a planet and its size would be comparable to Mercury's. With densities slightly less than that of the moon, the composition of Io and Europa could be similar to that of the moon, and Callisto's density of 0.6 could be similar to that of Jupiter.

E. E. Barnard discovered the fifth satellite visually in 1892. It is about 100 miles (161 km) in diameter and is located at a distance of about 112,500 miles (181,046 km) from the planet's center. At an orbital speed of 17 miles per second, the fastest of any satellite in the solar system, its sidereal period is about 12 hours. The last seven satellites, with diameters considerably less than 100 miles (161 km), were discovered photographically, and only five of them have been observed visually.

Jupiter's satellites may be classified according to the position of their orbits into the inner, middle, and outer groups. The orbits of the five satellites in the inner group are small, circular, and lie close to the planet's equator. The three satellites in the middle group have orbits that are eccentric and inclined about 30° to the planet's equator. The four satellites in the outer group have orbits with large eccentricities and inclinations, and all four move around Jupiter in a retrograde motion, that is, they revolve in a clockwise direction.

8.12 ROEMER'S EXPERIMENT IN THE SPEED OF LIGHT

In 1675 the Danish astronomer Olaus Roemer successfully conducted the first experiment to determine the speed of light by measuring the orbital periods of Jupiter's

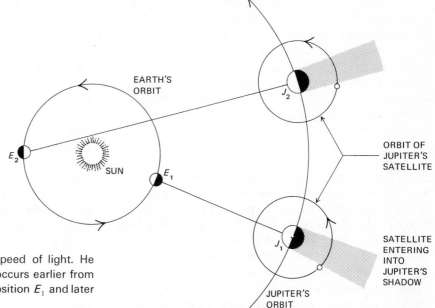

EARTH'S
ORBIT

SUN

E_2

E_1

J_2

J_1

ORBIT OF
JUPITER'S
SATELLITE

SATELLITE
ENTERING
INTO
JUPITER'S
SHADOW

JUPITER'S
ORBIT

Fig. 8.21 Roemer's experiment in the speed of light. He observed that the eclipse of the satellite occurs earlier from the predicted time when the earth is in position E_1 and later when in position E_2.

satellites. Roemer observed that the period was minimum when Jupiter is in opposition and maximum when in conjunction (Fig. 8.21). Since the orbital period of a satellite is constant, he concluded that the difference between the two periods is due to the time it takes light to travel the diameter of the earth's orbit. From this, he was able to show that the speed of light is finite. His value for the speed of light was slightly inaccurate because he used an inaccurate value for the diameter of the earth's orbit. With new techniques, determination of the speed of light has been improved so that its present speed in a vacuum is about 186,282 miles (299,783 km) per second.

8.13 SATURN

a. Physical Properties

Saturn, with an equatorial diameter of about 75,100 miles (120,858 km) and a polar diameter of about 67,800 miles (109,111 km), is the most oblate planet in the solar system. Its mass is 95 times that of the earth, and its mean density of 0.68 grams per cubic centimeter (which is about 0.71 that of water) is the lowest of any planet. With such a density, the planet could easily float in water. If the composition of Saturn is similar to Jupiter's (mostly hydrogen and helium), its smaller size would produce a smaller gravitational force; consequently, the gases would not be as compressed as they are in Jupiter. This would explain the planet's low density. Its surface gravity is 1.2 times that of the earth, and its escape velocity is 22 miles (35.4 km) per second.

Although white spots appear frequently in the equatorial region of the planet, they are too faint and short-lived to be used to determine the planet's rotational period. Spots are rarely seen near the polar regions. One was observed in 1960 in latitude 58°N, which gives the planet a rotational period at this latitude of 10 hours 40 minutes. In 1969 the first measurable spot was observed in the south polar region in latitude 57°S. It was about 4000 miles (6437 km) long and 5000 miles (8047 km) wide and gives the planet a rotational period of 10 hours $36\frac{1}{2}$ minutes.

Infrared measurements indicate that the planet's temperature is $-230°F$ ($-146°C$). The atmosphere of Saturn is similar to that of Jupiter, except that its spectrum shows stronger methane and weaker ammonia bands. Since Saturn's temperature is lower than Jupiter's, the ammonia freezes out of the atmosphere, settles to a lower level, and thus permits the viewing of the methane to a greater depth. No trace of hydrogen has been found in Saturn's atmosphere.

b. Orbit

Saturn, the outermost planet known in antiquity, revolves around the sun in an elliptical orbit whose eccentricity is 0.056 and at a mean distance of about 887 million miles (1.4 billion km). Its orbit is inclined $2\frac{1}{2}°$ to the plane of the ecliptic, and the planet's equator is inclined $26°45'$ to the plane of its orbit. In January 1974 the planet will be at perihelion, and when it is in opposition to the earth, it will be at its shortest distance to the earth. With an orbital speed of 6 miles (9.66 km) per second, the planet's sidereal period is $29\frac{1}{2}$ years, and its synodic period is 378 days.

c. The Ring System

Viewed from a telescope, Saturn is one of the most impressive objects in the sky, appearing as a large, yellowish disk with faintly defined markings that are parallel to the planet's equator. Surrounding the disk and concentric to it is a unique ring system that lies parallel to the planet's equator. In 1610, one year after the invention of the telescope, Galileo observed Saturn through his crude, homemade telescope. Since the instrument could not resolve the rings, he announced that he had observed two satellites revolving around the planet at a very close distance to its surface. In 1655 Christian Hygens gave the first correct explanation for the rings when he described them as thin, flat, concentric rings completely separate from the planet. This unique ring system (Plate 18) is the one feature that differentiates Saturn from the other planets and sets it in a class by itself. The system consists of three, concentric rings (known as A, B, and C, counting from the inside) whose outside diameter is about 171,000 miles (275,190 km) and whose thickness is less than 10 miles (16.09 km). The inner edge of the A ring, which is also known as the inner, or crepe, ring, is about 7000 miles (11,265 km) from the top of the planet's atmosphere and has a width of about 11,000 miles (17,702 km). The B ring, which is also known as the middle, or bright, ring, is about 16,000 miles (25,748 km) in width and is in juxtaposition with the A ring. Between the B ring and the C ring is a 2500-mile (4023.25 km) gap, which is called the Cassini division. The C ring, also known as the outer ring, is about 10,500 miles (16,898 km) in width. In 1969 the French astronomer Pierre Guerin discovered a fourth ring next to the A ring, which makes it the ring closest to the planet. Although it has been observed visually by other astronomers, as yet no one has been able to photograph it.

The ring system lies in the plane of the equator, which is inclined about $27°$ to the plane of the ecliptic. The planet and its ring system maintain a fixed orientation in space as they revolve around the sun; therefore, when seen from the earth, the shape of the ring system changes in a recurring cycle. As shown in Fig. 8.22 when the planet is in position 2 or 4, the ring system and the earth lie in the same plane; therefore, the rings are observed edgewise and appear as very thin, dark lines across the planet and as short, faint, thin lines on each side of the planet. When the planet is in position 3, the top of the ring system is visible; when in position 1, the bottom is visible. Since the sidereal period of the planet is $29\frac{1}{2}$ years, the ring system will pass through this cycle during this period of time.

The rings are not solid; their spectrum clearly shows large Doppler shifts, with the inner parts of the rings moving more rapidly than the outer parts, as shown in Fig. 8.23. If the rings were solid, the opposite effect would be observed. The rings were originally believed to be composed of small pieces of frozen water and ice-coated rocks that revolved around the planet in the same direction in which the planet rotated, but at different speeds. Observations of the infrared spectrum of Saturn's rings, made in 1969 by Kuiper, Cruikshank, and Fink at the University of Arizona, indicate that the rings are composed of frozen ammonia (NH_3). It is also believed that the particles are small and very cold; other-

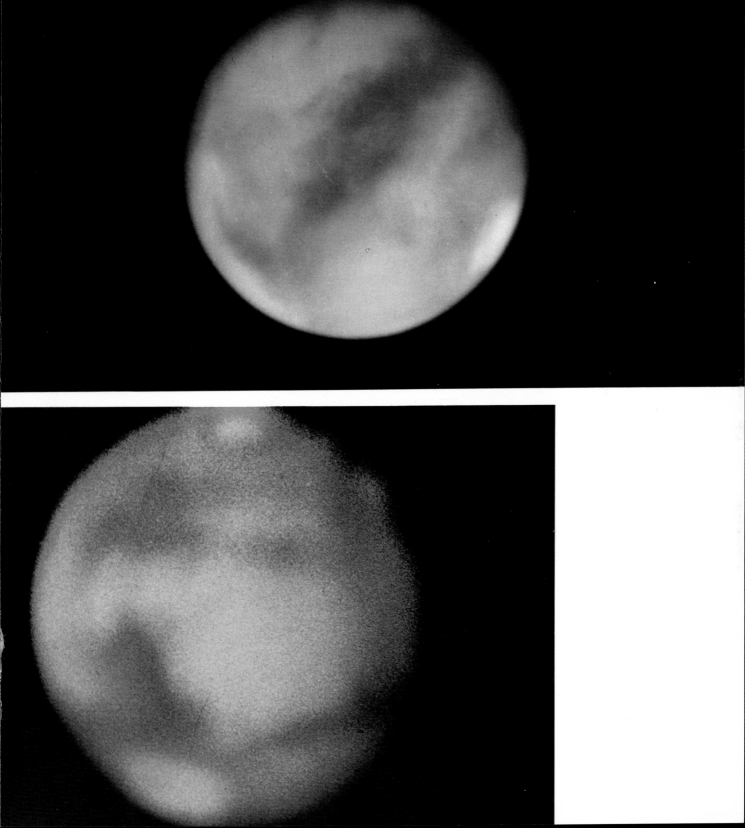

Plate 15 (preceding page, top) Sixty-inch photograph of the planet Mars, Earth's neighbor and the solar system's most intriguing member. (Photograph from the Hale Observatories)

Plate 16 (preceding page, bottom) Photograph of the planet Mars during its 1967 opposition, taken with the Catalina Observatory 61-inch telescope. The white spot at the top of the photograph is the north polar cap. The other white markings are either clouds or haze. (NASA photograph by the Lunar and Planetary Laboratory, University of Arizona)

Plate 17 (above) Jupiter's dark belts parallel to its equator. (The belt nearest the equator is the most conspicuous.) The belts display a wide range of colors — from dark brown to yellowish white. The famous ''Red Spot'' is clearly visible in the upper left. (Photograph from the Hale Observatories)

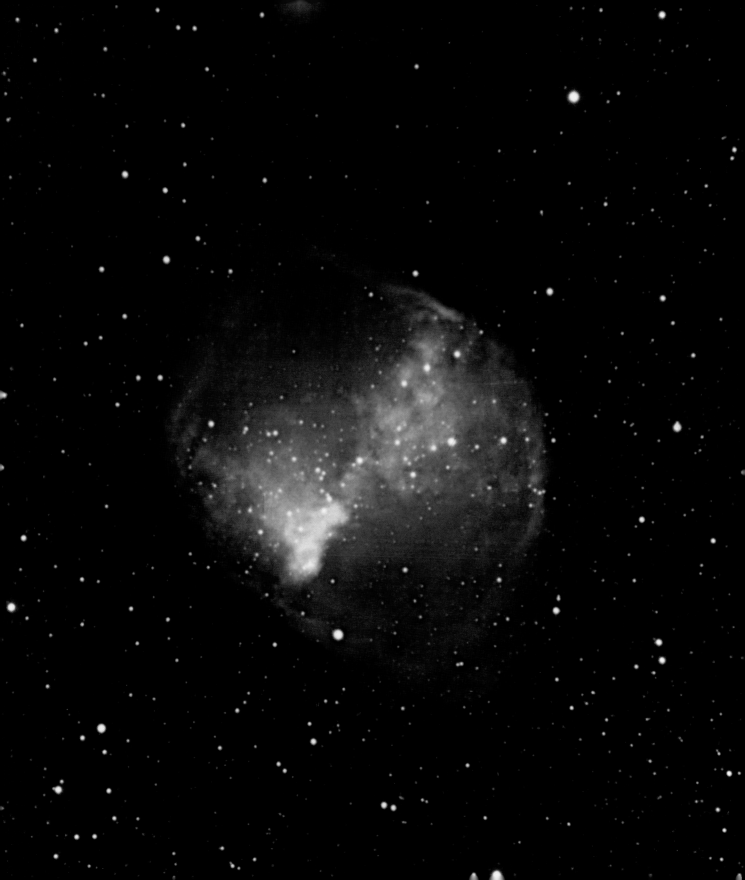

Plate 21 (preceding page, left) Planetary Nebula in Aquarius, NGC 7293, photographed with the 200-inch telescope. (Photograph from the Hale Observatories)

Plate 22 (preceding page, right) The Dumbbell Nebula in Vulpecula, a planetary nebula with a small, hot, blue star surrounded by a sphere of tenuous gas. Photographed with the 200-inch telescope. (Photograph from the Hale Observatories)

Plate 23 (above) The central region of the Great Nebula of Orion. The ultraviolet energy from the hot star embedded in the nebula makes the great cloud of interstellar dust and gas flouresce. (Photograph from the Hale Observatories)

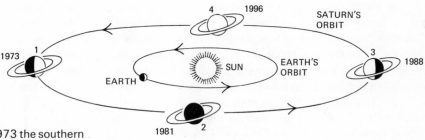

Fig. 8.22 The aspects of Saturn's rings. In 1973 the southern side of the rings will be visible. In 1981 the rings will be seen edgewise. In 1988 the northern side of the rings will be visible. In 1996 the rings will again be seen edgewise. These changes are caused by Saturn's revolving around the sun once every $29\frac{1}{2}$ years and by the plane of its rings being inclined 27° to the planet's orbital plane.

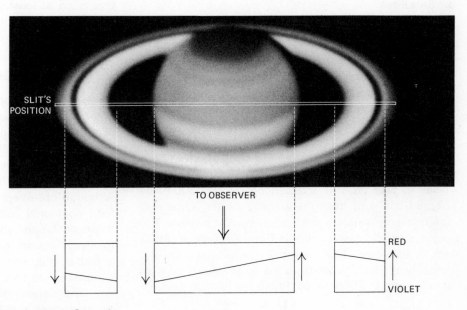

Fig 8.23 Placing the slit of a spectrograph across Saturn's sphere and rings provides proof that both are rotating and that the rings consist of small particles, because the spectral lines shift to the red when the bodies are receding and to the violet when approaching the observer. (Photograph from the Hale Observatories)

wise, their evaporation rate in space would be quite rapid.

A controversy still exists about the origin of the rings. Some believe that they represent the debris of a satellite that approached the planet too closely and was broken up by its gravitational force. Others believe that they represent the original material which failed to coalesce either with Saturn or into a satellite of the planet.

In 1850 E. A. Roche stated that the disruptive tidal force of a planet will exceed the cohesive gravitational force of a satellite of the same density as that of the planet within a distance of about 2.44 times the planet's radius. This is known as "Roche's limit." The outer edge of Saturn's ring system is 2.3 times the planet's radius, which is within the Roche limit; therefore, it is possible that a satellite approached the planet too closely and disintegrated. In the solar system only the rings of Saturn lie within the Roche limit.

d. Satellites

Saturn has ten known satellites which in many ways are similar to, but smaller than, those of Jupiter. Saturn's nearest satellite, located just outside its outer ring, is Janus, which was discovered on December 15, 1966 by Audouin Dollfus at the Meudon Observatory in France. Janus has a diameter of about 190 miles (306 km), follows a circular path at a distance of about 98,000 miles (157,711 km) from the planet's center, and has an orbital period of about 18 hours. The most distant satellite is Phoebe, 180 miles (290 km) in diameter, which revolves in 550 days at a distance of 7,700,000 miles (12,391,610 km) from the planet's center. Phoebe is Saturn's only satellite with a retrograde motion. The largest and brightest satellite is Titan, 2860 miles (4603 km) in diameter. Titan is rather unique because it is probably the only satellite in the solar system with an atmosphere; in 1944 Kuiper found methane in its spectrum.

8.14 URANUS

The discovery of the first planet since antiquity was made by William Herschel on March 13, 1781 while he was making a routine observation of the small stars in the vicinity of Gemini the Twins with his 7-inch reflecting telescope. In his report to the Royal Society, he announced that he had discovered a comet. About five months later, A. J. Lexell announced that Herschel's comet was actually a planet traveling in a nearly circular orbit around the sun. Herschel proposed the name Georgium Sidus for the new planet, in honor of King George the Third during whose reign the planet was discovered. This broke with tradition in the naming of planets and it was not received favorably. At the suggestion of J. E. Bode, tradition was followed by naming the planet Uranus, after the Greek deity who sprang from Chaos and became Heaven. The planet was appropriately named, because Uranus was the father of Saturn, who in turn was the father of Jupiter.

The visual brightness of Uranus is such that under the most favorable conditions on a clear, moonless evening it can be seen with the unaided eye as a very faint star. Nearly 100 years before its discovery, Uranus was seen at least 23 times by several observers and was recorded on charts as a star. The first such recording was made by Flamstead in 1690.

a. Telescopic View

Through a telescope the planet appears as a small, pale greenish disk because of the abundance of methane in its atmosphere (Fig. 8.24). The high-resolution photographs of Uranus taken in 1970 by the Princeton University Observatory Stratoscope II unmanned balloon show the planet to be slightly oblate with a darkened limb. Although observers have reported the presence of very faint equatorial belt markings on the planet similar to those of Jupiter and Saturn, the Stratoscope II failed to reveal any of them. It is possible that they do exist but that they are difficult to observe because their contrast might be even lower than Saturn's.

By observing the white spots that sometimes appear on its surface and by the occasional periodic variation in the total brightness of the planet, its period of rotation has been determined to be about 10 hours 49 minutes. This period of rotation, which is slightly slower than Jupiter's, is still fast enough to account for the planet's equatorial bulge of nearly 2500 miles (4023 km).

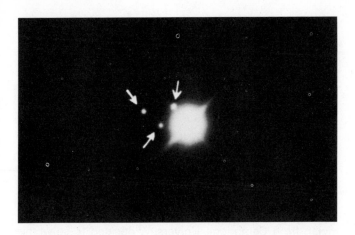

Fig. 8.24 Uranus with three of its satellites, photographed with the 120-inch telescope. (Lick Observatory photograph)

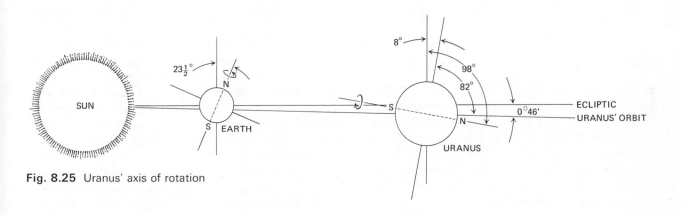

Fig. 8.25 Uranus' axis of rotation

b. Orbit

Uranus revolves around the sun at a mean distance of about 1,783,000,000 miles (2,869,381,900 km) in an elliptical orbit whose eccentricity is 0.047. The discovery of this planet almost doubled the known size of the solar system, since Uranus' distance is nearly twice that of Saturn's. The plane of the planet's orbit is inclined 0°46' to the plane of the ecliptic, which is the smallest angle of inclination of any planet. Its orbital speed is about 4.5 miles (7.25 km) per second; its sidereal period is 84 years, and its synodic period is 369 days.

A remarkable and unique feature of Uranus is that its equator is inclined 82° to the plane of its orbit. Since the planet's axis of rotation lies about 8° below its orbital plane, an observer oriented above the solar system and able to look down at the north pole of the earth would find that Uranus appears to rotate in a clockwise direction. Uranus lies on its side, and its axis of rotation points almost in the direction of the sun (Fig. 8.25); therefore, its seasons would be 42 years of summer and 42 years of winter. An observer at the poles would also observe 42 years of daylight and 42 years of darkness.

c. Physical Properties

Uranus has a mean diameter of about 30,000 miles (48,279 km) and a mass $14\frac{1}{2}$ times that of the earth. Its mean density of 1.3 grams per cubic centimeter is identical to Jupiter's. The planet has a surface gravity 1.08 times that of the earth and an escape velocity of about 14 miles (23 km) per second. The spectrum of Uranus shows very strong bands of methane and absorption lines of molecular hydrogen. Ammonia has not been detected in the spectrum of Uranus, although astronomers believe that the gas is present in its atmosphere. Uranus has a radiometric surface temperature of about $-300°F$ ($-185°C$), which would cause any ammonia to freeze and drop to a lower level in the atmosphere. Spectral observations of Uranus are probably limited to the top of the planet's atmosphere, where the ammonia would not be visible.

d. Satellites

Uranus has five known satellites—Ariel, Miranda, Oberon, Titania, and Umbriel. Their diameters range from about 150 miles, or 241 km (Miranda) to 600 miles, or 966 km (Titania). Their distances from the center of the planet range from 77,000 miles (123,916 km) for Miranda to 364,000 miles (585,785 km) for Oberon. Miranda has the shortest period of revolution, less than $1\frac{1}{2}$ days, while Oberon has the longest, with $13\frac{1}{2}$ days. All the satellites revolve around the planet in circular orbits that coincide with the equatorial plane of the planet. Since the equatorial plane of the planet is nearly perpendicular to its orbital plane, the satellites appear to move in an almost north and south direction.

8.15 NEPTUNE

The discovery of the planet Neptune was one of the most interesting achievements of mathematical astronomy. It was a tremendous triumph for the validity of Newton's laws of gravitation on which the calculations for the discovery were based. The existence of Neptune was detected by its gravitational effect on Uranus before the body was actually discovered. Neptune was discovered within 52 minutes of arc of its calculated predicted position.

Twenty years after the discovery of the planet Uranus, a difference between its observational and calculated positions appeared. Some astronomers believed that Newton's laws of gravitation did not apply to bodies at great distances from the sun and that therefore these laws could not be used to determine the elements of their orbits. Others believed that the perturbations of Uranus were caused by the gravitational force exerted by a body farther out in space.

John Couch Adams, a brilliant young mathematician from Cambridge University, decided to solve this unprecedented problem. His treatment of the problem was most systematic. First, he evaluated all the available observations pertaining to the problem; then he calculated the perturbations of Uranus that would be produced by the gravitational forces of Jupiter and Saturn, which he found to be insufficient to account for the observed perturbations. After he had discussed with others the possibility that Newton's laws did not apply to distant bodies, he concluded that they did apply and that the perturbations of Uranus were caused by the presence of a body farther out in space. By 1845 Adams had calculated the position of the unknown body, sent the information to Sir George Airy (the Astronomer Royal of England), and requested a search be made to locate it. Unfortunately, Airy believed that Newton's laws of gravitation had no effect on the perturbations of Uranus. Having very little faith in Adams' theoretical calculations, he devoted his time and effort in trying to prove that Newton's laws did not apply.

In 1845, while Adams was making his unsuccessful attempts to get Airy to search for the unknown body, the French astronomer and mathematician Urbain Leverrier began to work on the problem, unaware that Adams was also working on it. In 1846 Leverrier completed his calculations and sent the position of the unknown body to Johann Galle, the director of the Berlin Observatory. The same night that he received the information from Leverrier, Galle was able to locate and identify the planet.

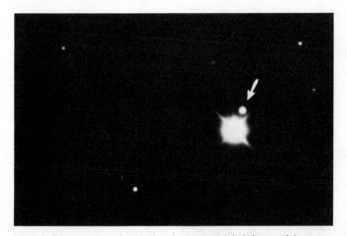

Fig. 8.26 Neptune and the larger and brighter of its two satellites, Triton, photographed with the 120-inch telescope. (Lick Observatory photograph)

Credit for the discovery of Neptune is shared by both Adams and Leverrier. Tradition was followed when the planet was named for Neptune, the ancient Greek god of the sea.

a. Telescopic Appearance and Orbit

When Neptune is seen through a telescope, it appears as a small, greenish disk with no conspicuous surface markings (Fig. 8.26). It has a small oblateness of about $\frac{1}{40}$. It revolves around the sun at a mean distance of 2,797,000,000 miles (4,501,212,100 km) in a very nearly circular orbit whose eccentricity is 0.009. Its orbit is inclined 1°47′ to the plane of the ecliptic, and its equator is inclined 29° to the plane of its orbit. At an orbital speed of 3.3 miles (5.3 km) per second, the planet's sidereal period is 164.8 years, and its synodic period is 367.5 days. Its period of rotation, about 15 hours 48 minutes, was determined from the Doppler shift in its spectrum.

b. Physical Properties

Since their size and other physical characteristics are similar, Neptune and Uranus are considered to be twins.

Neptune's mean diameter is about 28,000 miles, or 45,000 km (Uranus' is 30,000 miles, or 48,000 km), and its mass is 17.3 times that of the earth (Uranus' is 14.5 times that of the earth). It has a density of 2.2 grams per cubic centimeter (as compared to Uranus' 1.3 grams per cubic centimeter), a surface gravity 1.41 times that of the earth (Uranus' is 1.07 times that of the earth), and an escape velocity of about 14 miles (23 km) per second (that of Uranus' is 13.9 miles, or 22.4 km per second).

The planet's high albedo of 0.55 suggests that it is surrounded by a dense atmosphere. Its spectrum shows strong methane bands and molecular hydrogen absorption lines. It has a surface temperature of about −350°F (−212°C), and its internal structure is probably the same as that of the other giant planets.

c. Satellites

Neptune has two known satellites—Triton and Nereid. Triton is larger, brighter, and nearer than Nereid. Triton has a diameter of about 2240 miles (3605 km), which is slightly larger than the moon. It revolves around the sun in a retrograde motion at a distance of 220,000 miles (354,046 km) from the planet's center in a nearly circular orbit inclined about 40° to the plane of the planet's orbit. Its orbital period is 5 days 21 hours.

Nereid, which was discovered by Kuiper in 1949, has a diameter of about 200 miles (322 km), revolves around the planet in a direct motion, and has the most eccentric orbit of any satellite (0.75). At its nearest approach to the planet, Nereid is 730,000 miles (1,175,000 km) away; at its farthest, it is 7 million miles (11 million km) distant. Its orbital period is 359.9 days.

8.16 PLUTO

Two American astronomers, Percival Lowell and W. H. Pickering, predicted the existence of a planet beyond Neptune's orbit. Their predictions were based on the slight residual deviations between the predicted and observed motion of Uranus. Because Neptune had traveled only a short distance in its orbit since discovery,

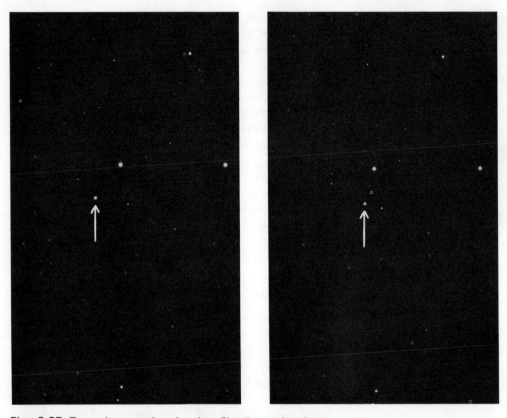

Fig. 8.27 Two photographs showing Pluto's motion in a period of 24 hours as recorded by the 200-inch telescope. (Photographs from the Hale Observatories)

there was no information available on its orbital perturbations. Independently, each astronomer calculated that in order to produce Uranus' observed perturbations, the unknown planet would have to be in the constellation of Gemini the Twins. The mass of the unknown planet was calculated by Lowell to be nearly $6\frac{2}{3}$ times that of the earth; Pickering calculated it as slightly less than that of the earth. Both undertook an intensive search of the sky to locate the unknown planet. It was a monumental task, because Gemini lies near the Milky Way, in which thousands of stars appear in a single photographic field of view. Both men were denied success; Lowell died in

1916. In 1919 Pickering photographed the area in which the planet was located, but failed to recognize it because of a flaw in the photographic plate and the appearance of a very bright star near the planet.

After Lowell's death, his associates at the Lowell Observatory continued the search with the new 13-inch astrographic telescope given to the observatory by Lowell's brother. On March 13, 1930, Clyde W. Tombaugh announced the discovery of the planet. He used the new blink comparator, a device which projects in rapid sequence on one screen two photographs taken several days apart of the same field of view. If the star images on both photographs are the same, an observer sees a series of flickering, identical photographs. If a body such as a planet appears in the photographs, its position in the two photographs will be different because of its apparent motion in relation to the stars; therefore, the observer sees a series of flickering photographs in which the planet appears to jump back and forth as the two photographs are alternated by the blink comparator. The unknown planet was located within 6° of Lowell's predicted position. It was named Pluto after the Greek god of the lower world, the world of the dead (Fig. 8.27).

a. Orbit

Pluto, which is the remotest of the known planets, revolves around the sun at a mean distance of 3,675,000,000 miles (5,914,000,000 km) in an elliptical orbit whose eccentricity of 0.249 is the largest of any planet. Its orbit is so eccentric that its perihelion distance of 2.8 billion miles (56 million km) within Neptune's orbit, there is no its aphelion distance is 4.5 billion miles (7.2 billion km). Although one point of Pluto's orbit lies nearly 35 million miles (56 million km) within Neptune's orbit, there is no chance of a collision, because Pluto's orbit has an inclination of 17°09′, which is the highest of any planet. At an orbital speed of 2.9 miles (4.7 km) per second, the planet's sidereal period is 248.4 years, and its synodic period is 367 days.

b. Physical Properties

Our knowledge of Pluto is incomplete and inconclusive because of the planet's great distance from the earth. Soon after its discovery, a very disturbing problem developed. Although Pluto was found to be moving very closely in its calculated orbit, its observed apparent size and brightness did not agree with Lowell's calculated values. The planet appeared much smaller and dimmer. The problem became more confused when Pluto's mass was estimated at $\frac{1}{10}$ that of the earth's—an estimate based on its observed size and dimness. Later, two pre-discovery observations of Neptune made by M. J. Lalande

in 1795 were used to determine Pluto's gravitational effect on Neptune's orbit. From these calculations, Pluto's mass was estimated to be equal to that of the earth. In 1950 Kuiper was able to observe Pluto in the 200-inch Hale telescope as a tiny disk with an angular diameter of about $\frac{1}{4}''$. This value corresponds to a linear diameter of about 3700 miles (5954 km), which is about half that of the earth, and with a volume that is one-tenth that of the earth. If the density of the earth and Pluto are the same, then the mass of Pluto is about one-tenth that of the earth.

Kuiper's value for Pluto's diameter has been supported by evidence obtained when Pluto passed close to a star on April 28–29, 1965, during a predicted possible occultation. Although the occultation failed to occur, several major North American observatories took a series of photographs showing Pluto passing south of the star. Ian Halliday and his colleagues at the Dominion Observatory, Ottawa, Canada established the minimum separation between Pluto and the star at 0.125 seconds of arc, making it possible for them to set the upper limit for Pluto's diameter at about 3600 miles (5800 km).

Based on recurring light variations measured with a photoelectric photometer, Pluto's rotational period is 6.39 days, longer than that of any of the giant planets. These light variations indicate that there might be two different types of surfaces on Pluto. The planet's surface temperature is probably near −400°F (−240°C). No gases have been observed in its spectrum, and there is no evidence that the planet has an atmosphere. The gases probably have either been frozen out or have escaped from the atmosphere. Pluto has no known satellites.

Pluto appears to be out of place in its position along with the giant planets. It is considerably smaller, less massive, and rotates slower. Its orbit has the greatest inclination and is the most eccentric of any planet. Pluto's present position in its orbit is such that its distance from the sun is decreasing rapidly; by 1979 Neptune will become the most distant planet in the solar system. All these facts have raised the possibility that Pluto was once Neptune's third satellite.

REVIEW

1. Name two ways in which planets may be classified. List the planets in both classifications.

2. What are the characteristics of planetary orbits?

3. What is the criteria for membership in the solar system?

4. What is meant by planetary configurations? Assuming that an observer is looking down on the north pole of the earth, list the configurations in proper order for an (a) inferior planet and (b) superior planet.

5. Explain the retrograde motion of planets. Do superior planets retrograde? Near what configuration do inferior planets retrograde?

6. Distinguish between a planet's sidereal and synodic periods.

7. Write the formula for the relationship between the sidereal and synodic periods for a superior planet. Determine the synodic period of Jupiter when its sidereal period is about 12 years.

8. Explain how the mass of a planet can be determined.

9. What factors determine whether a planet is able to retain its atmosphere?

10. Briefly state the differences between satellites, asteroids, and meteoroids.

11. Which one of the following planets can never appear at opposition: Venus, Mars, Jupiter, Saturn, and Neptune? Why?

12. Explain why Mercury and Venus show phases like those of the moon.

13. When is the best time for viewing Mercury? Why?

14. What is Mercury's rotational period? How was this determined? Is there anything about it that is unique?

15. Explain why the apparent diameter and brightness of Venus change. Who first observed this? Was it an important astronomical discovery? Why?

16. Explain the role that Mars has played in the development of astronomical thought.

17. When is the best time for viewing Mars? Why? How often does Mars appear in this favorable position?

18. Explain what is meant by the statement "Mercury is one of the hottest while at the same time it is one of the coldest planets."

19. Discuss the type of terrain on Mars revealed by the Mariner probes.

20. What are the two important factors which determine whether or not a planet has seasons? Compare the seasons on the earth with those on Mars.

21. List the possibilities that life on Mars exists. What observations have been made in the Mars probes to encourage or discourage the possibility?

22. What is unique about the satellites of Mars? What has Mariner 9 revealed about Phobos and Deimos?

23. Discuss the controversial "canals" on Mars.

24. Describe Jupiter's atmosphere. How does it compare with the other giant planets?

25. How can Jupiter's period of rotation be determined? How does it compare with the rotational period of the other planets?

26. Although Jupiter's four large satellites appear as stars (point source of light) through binoculars, what observational evidence can you use to show someone that they are really satellites?

27. Explain how Roemer was able to show that the speed of light is finite.

28. How many rings does Saturn have? How are they oriented? Describe their structure and composition. Discuss their origin.

29. Why are Uranus and Neptune called the twin planets?

30. What is unique about Saturn, other than its ring system?

31. What is unique about Uranus?

32. What were the events, beliefs, and reasoning that led to the discovery of Neptune?

33. What made Lowell institute a search for a planet beyond Neptune? When and how was Pluto discovered? How was it verified that it is a planet and not a star? Give reasons for the suggestion that Pluto might once have been a satellite of Neptune.

9
Asteroids, Comets, and Meteoroids

Although the sun, moon, and the planets are the most conspicuous and dominant bodies in the solar system, there are many thousands of minor bodies, called asteroids, comets, and meteoroids, which exist between the planets. Most of the asteroids (large rocks) are orbiting the sun between Mars and Jupiter and appear in large telescopes as points of light. Comets (swarms of frozen gas particles) appear as hazy, luminous clouds as they approach the sun in their solar orbit. Meteoroids (small particles of interplanetary matter orbiting the sun) appear as streaks of light as they pass through the earth's atmosphere.

9.1 THE DISCOVERY OF ASTEROIDS

In 1766 Johannes Titius, professor of mathematics at Wittenberg, developed an interesting and curious mathematical relationship which expressed rather closely the distances of the planets from the sun. This relationship, known as the Bode-Titius rule, was published in 1772 by Johann Bode, director of the Berlin Observatory. Developed from the series 0, 1, 2, 4, 8, 16, 32, 64, 128, 256, each term was multiplied by 3 to produce the new series 0, 3, 6, 12, 24, 48, 96, 192, 384, 768. Four was added to each term, then each sum was divided by 10, producing the final series 0.4, 0.7, 1.0, 1.6, 2.8, 5.2, 10.0, 19.6, 38.8, 77.2. Titius used this rather convoluted procedure so that the third number in the series, 1, represented earth's distance from the sun. The series of numbers represents the distances of the planets from the sun in astronomical units (1 a.u. equals about 93 million miles, the earth's distance from the sun). When these distances were compared with the actual distances (Table 9.1), their closeness made the Bode-Titius relationship most interesting.

Table 9.1 Planetary distances by Bode-Titius rule and actual measurements

Planet	Bode-Titius rule (a.u.)	Actual distance (a.u.)
Mercury	0.4	0.39
Venus	0.7	0.72
Earth	1.0	1.00
Mars	1.6	1.52
Missing planet	2.8	2.80
Jupiter	5.2	5.20
Saturn	10.0	9.54
Uranus	19.6	19.19
Neptune	38.8	30.08
Pluto	77.2	39.46

When William Herschel discovered the planet Uranus in 1781 and found its actual distance to be very close to that predicted by the Bode-Titius rule, many astronomers were convinced that the rule was valid and that a planet existed at a distance of 2.80 astronomical units.[1] To expedite its discovery, the zodiac was divided into 24 regions, and each region was assigned to an astronomer. One of these was the Italian Father Giuseppe Piazzi; however, on January 1, 1801, before he had received his assignment, he observed during a routine survey of the sky a star-like object in the constellation of Taurus, which he believed was a new comet. After sufficient data had been obtained and its orbit calculated, astronomers believed that the missing planet had been found. Piazzi named the body Ceres, after the protecting goddess of Sicily.

In 1802, slightly over one year after the discovery of Ceres, another star-like object, similar in appearance and close to Ceres, was discovered by Heinrich Olbers. He named the body Pallas. In 1804 a third object, named Juno, was discovered, and in 1807 a fourth object was discovered, which was named Vesta. With these four discoveries, it became apparent that several small objects rather than one large planet exist at the mean distance of 2.80 astronomical units from the sun. Since these objects are small and have orbital paths around the sun, they are called planetoids (minor planets), and since they appear as star-like objects in a telescope, they are called asteroids (little stars). As a result of these discoveries, the "planet" Ceres was demoted to the status of another asteroid.

During the nineteenth century, over 300 asteroids were discovered. In 1891 the discovery rate increased tremendously when Max Wolf at Heidelberg introduced the camera as part of the discovery technique. The simple and efficient photographic method involves a long photographic exposure of an area in the sky. On the photographic plate, the stars appear as points of light; the asteroid as a streak. Several hundred asteroids have been discovered by this method.

A newly discovered asteroid is assigned a number only after it has been observed in at least two oppositions and its orbital elements have been computed. In many instances, these later sightings are extremely difficult because the asteroid's orbit has been greatly altered by the gravitational effects of the earth, moon, and the near planets.[2]

---

[1]The Bode-Titius rule is no longer seen as a law because of the discrepancies between Neptune's and Pluto's actual distances and those predicted by the rule. It is recognized today as simply a convenient, empirical rule-of-thumb.

[2]One astronomer had an even more difficult time getting his asteroid authenticated. His asteroid was the one on which Saint Exupéry's little prince lived: "This asteroid has only once been seen through the telescope. That was by a Turkish astronomer, in 1909. On making his discovery, the astronomer had presented it to the International Astronomical Congress, in a great demonstration. But he was in Turkish costume, and so nobody would believe what he said. Grown-ups are like that . . . Fortunately, however for the reputation of Asteroid B-612, a Turkish dictator made a law that his subjects, under pain of death, should change to European costume. So in 1920, the astronomer gave his demonstration all over again, dressed with impressive style and elegance. And this time everybody accepted his report." Antoine de Saint Exupéry, *The Little Prince*, tr. Katherine Woods. New York: Harcourt, Brace, and World, 1943, p. 15.

9.2 PHYSICAL CHARACTERISTICS

Even though the observed asteroids have diameters that range from about 1 mile (1.6 km) to 480 miles (772 km), it is believed that there are many more smaller ones with diameters the size of pebbles. The four largest and brightest asteroids are Ceres (480 miles, or 772 km), Pallas (300 miles, or 483 km), Vesta (240 miles, or 386 km), and Juno (120 miles, or 193 km). Their albedoes range from 0.06 for Ceres to 0.26 for Vesta and Pallas. Since Ceres' albedo is almost the same as that of the moon, its surface characteristics might be similar to the moon's. Reflective studies of Vesta indicate that its surface is covered with some kind of dust, probably formed by extreme temperature changes, meteoric impacts, or high radiation exposure. The brightness of the larger asteroids appears to be steady, whereas the smaller ones show a continuous variation. This indicates that the larger ones may be almost spherical and that the smaller ones may be block-shaped with angular faces. When the asteroid Eros came within 14 million miles (23 million km) of the earth in 1931, observations revealed that it is an elongated object about 17 miles (27 km) in length, about 4 miles (6 km) in width, and rotates about its short diameter in $5\frac{1}{4}$ hours (the period of rotation of the asteroids range from about 2 to 18 hours). Eros also exhibited variations in brightness (2 maxima and 2 minima), indicating that as it rotates, it presents different surfaces to the earth.

There is no definite information on the exact mass of any of the asteroids. Even though there are many thousands and most are very small in size, their total mass is believed to be considerably less than that of the moon. It has been estimated that the four largest asteroids contain more than half of the total mass of all the asteroids.

9.3 ORBITAL CHARACTERISTICS

The orbits of most of the asteroids lie between the orbits of Mars and Jupiter. A few have their perihelion within Mars' orbit, and still fewer have it within the earth's orbit. The orbital motion of all the asteroids is direct, that is, they move from west to east in the same direc-

Fig. 9.1 The asteroid Icarus, photographed in 1949 with the 48-inch Schmidt telescope, appears as a streak of light moving at about 20 miles per second. (Photograph from the Hale Observatories)

tion as the planets. Most of their orbits, which lie close to the plane of the ecliptic, have a mean angle of inclination of $9\frac{1}{2}°$ (some 30 of them have angles greater than 25°), a mean value of eccentricity of 0.15, and a mean orbital period of five years. In comparison to the planetary orbits, the asteroid orbits are more highly inclined to the ecliptic and slightly more eccentric.

9.4 UNUSUAL ASTEROIDS

Asteroid 1566 Icarus, discovered in 1949 by Walter Baade at Mount Palomar Observatory, has the smallest orbit (1.08 a. u.) (Fig. 9.1). It is the only planetary body, other than meteors and comets, that passes within the orbit of Mercury; at perihelion it is inside Mercury's orbit, and at aphelion it is outside of Mars' orbit. In 1968 it passed within 4 million miles (6 million km) of the earth. Icarus is nearly spherical, less than one mile in diameter, and has a surface that is quite jagged. From its periodic light variations, its rotational period is about $2\frac{1}{4}$ hours. Hidalgo, which has the largest orbit (5.79 a. u.), is close to the orbit of Mars when at perihelion and close to the orbit of Saturn when at aphelion. When Hermes was discovered in 1937, it became the nearest planetary body to the earth, with an approach of less than 1 million miles (1,609,000 km).

9.5 DISTRIBUTION OF THE ASTEROIDS

The asteroids are not uniformly distributed between the orbits of Mars and Jupiter. Gaps exist in regions whose periods are simple fractions of Jupiter's orbital period of 12 years, such as one-third, two-fifths, one-half, and so on. An explanation for these gaps was presented in 1866 when Daniel Kirkwood said that when an asteroid drifts close to these regions, Jupiter's gravitational force perturbs and prevents the asteroid from moving into the region. A new theory, proposed by Y. Hagihara to explain these narrow regions, which are called the Kirkwood gaps, is that the interaction of the asteroids themselves, in resonance, forces them out of these orbits.

9.6 THE TROJAN ASTEROIDS

In 1772 the French mathematician Joseph Lagrange proved that the position in Jupiter's orbit either 60° ahead or behind the planet is gravitationally stable. A body which occupies either position thus forms an equilateral triangle with Jupiter and the sun. It always remains in this position as it revolves around the sun, because the gravitational effects of the sun and Jupiter on it are in equilibrium. It came as no surprise, therefore, when an asteroid discovered in 1906 was found to revolve around the sun in the same orbital path and 60° ahead of the planet Jupiter. By 1959 14 asteroids had been discovered—9 in a group 60° ahead of Jupiter and 5 in a group 60° behind Jupiter (Fig. 9.2). These asteroids are called the Trojans after the Homeric heroes;

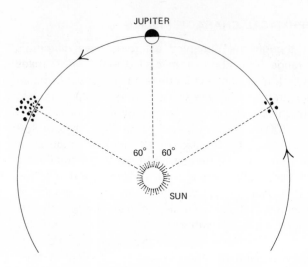

Fig. 9.2 The Trojan asteroids

the largest, Hector, named after the greatest warrior of Troy, has a diameter of about 50 miles. Although only 14 Trojans have been discovered, there may be many more that are too small and faint to be detected.

9.7 THE ORIGIN OF THE ASTEROIDS

Three important hypotheses have been presented to explain the origin of the asteroids. The first is that asteroids are fragments of a large planet or several small planets which disintegrated from either a collision with one another or excessive rotational speeds. According to the second theory, asteroids are bits of the original material from which the solar system was formed which for some reason failed to condense into a satellite, coalesce with either or both of the planets Mars and Jupiter, or form into a separate planet. The third hypothesis is that asteroids may be the nuclei of large comets.

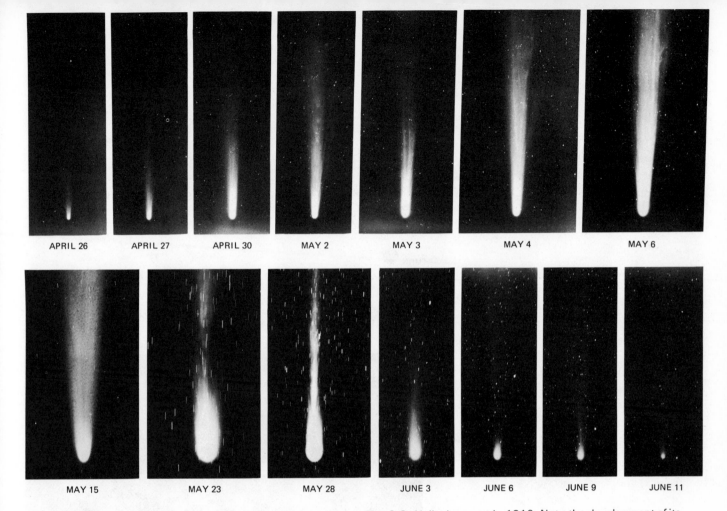

APRIL 26 APRIL 27 APRIL 30 MAY 2 MAY 3 MAY 4 MAY 6

MAY 15 MAY 23 MAY 28 JUNE 3 JUNE 6 JUNE 9 JUNE 11

9.8 COMETS

Of all the astronomical bodies that are visible to the unaided eye, comets are probably the most awesome because of their unexpected appearances, spectacular changes in brightness and shape, and long tails, if present, that fan out behind them. According to Webster, the word "comet" is derived from the Greeks, who called these bodies "kometes," which means "long-haired." Most comets, however, do not have tails.

Since time immemorial, comets have been regarded as the most puzzling and mysterious of the astronomical bodies. Their appearance caused fear among the people, who regarded them as omens of some great calamity. When Halley's comet appeared in 1066, many people assumed it to have been directly responsible for the death of King Harold at the Battle of Hastings and the conquest of England by the French.

Fig. 9.3 Halley's comet in 1910. Note the development of its tail as the comet approached the sun and its decline as the comet receded from the sun. (Photograph from the Hale Observatories)

The fear of comets that accompanied the belief that they are a part of the earth's atmosphere was lessened when Brahe showed that the 1577 comet was a body revolving around the sun at a greater distance than Venus. This concept was firmly established when Edmund Halley predicted the reappearance of the comet that bears his name. After noting the similarity of the orbits of the comets that appeared in 1456, 1531, 1607, and 1682, he concluded that it was a single comet traveling around the sun in an elliptical orbit once every 75 or 76 years. He predicted its reappearance in 1758. The earliest record of its appearance is 467 B.C.

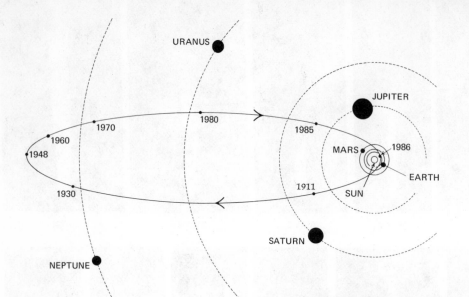

Fig. 9.4 The orbit of Halley's comet

Fig. 9.5 Comet Ikeya-Seki, November 1965. (NASA photograph)

Its last appearance was in 1910, when it appeared to the unaided eye as a faint, hazy object on April 19, 1910 at the U. S. Naval Observatory. One month later (Fig. 9.3) it became a magnificent spectacle—a spot with a beautiful tail that was as bright as the Milky Way. Halley's comet will appear again in 1986 (Fig. 9.4).

9.9 THE DISCOVERY OF COMETS

Many of the visual discoveries of comets (such as the Comet Ikeya-Seki, which was discovered in 1965, Fig. 9.5) are made by amateurs using wide-field, low-power telescopes. When an astronomer discovers a comet, it usually appears on a photographic plate which was taken for other purposes.

The temporary designation of newly discovered comets is made by the year of their discovery, followed by a letter which indicates the order of their discovery, e.g., Comet 1973b designates the second comet discovered in 1973. The permanent designation is made by the order of their passage of perihelion. Comet 1973 II designates the second comet to pass perihelion in 1973.

9.10 ORBITS

About 75% of the observed comets for which there is sufficient and reliable information have orbits that are either parabolic or hyperbolic; the remaining have elliptical orbits. Although it has been assumed that the comets with parabolic or hyperbolic orbits are visitors from beyond the solar system, no definite information has been presented to substantiate this assumption. In fact, the available information supports the theory that comets originate within the solar system. An analysis of their parabolic orbits reveals that they initially moved in highly eccentric elliptical orbits which were altered when the comets made a close approach to either Jupiter or Saturn. There is also the possibility that if more time were available to observe the individual comets and to calculate their orbital elements more accurately, it would reveal that they follow an elongated elliptical rather than a parabolic or hyperbolic orbit.

From a statistical study of the known cometary orbits and their distribution in space, the Dutch astronomer Jan Oort in 1950 proposed a hypothesis for the source of comets. His work indicates that the sun is capable of holding a cloud of orbiting comets at a distance of about 150,000 a. u. The gravitational attraction of a passing star perturbs these comets and alters some of their orbits so that they make a close approach to the sun in an elliptical, parabolic, or hyperbolic orbit.

Of the nearly 200 comets that have been observed with elliptical orbits, about 85 have periods of less than 200 years, and about 40 have been observed to pass perihelion at least twice. These are called periodic comets. Their orbital characteristics are different from those of the planets in that generally they are more eccentric and have inclinations that are less than $30°$ to the plane of the ecliptic. Most of them move in the same direction as the planets, although a few of them retrograde.

A periodic comet with a most unusual orbit was discovered by Schwassmann and Wachmann at the Hamburg Observatory in 1927, two years after it had passed perihelion. Its orbit is more like that of a planet—nearly circular with a small inclination to the plane of the ecliptic ($9\frac{1}{2}°$). Another unusual feature about its orbit is that it lies completely outside of Jupiter's orbit, between the orbits of Jupiter and Saturn. The comet also shows remarkable fluctuations in brightness. In one day its brightness was observed to increase over 100 times, and during a two-month period in 1945, it increased over 2500 times from causes that are still not known. Comet Oterma has an eight-year period in the most nearly circular orbit known.

A few comets have orbital periods that are less than Jupiter's 12-year period. These are believed to have been "captured" by Jupiter and are referred to as Jupiter's family of comets. When a comet makes a close approach to Jupiter, the planet's gravitational attraction is sufficient to alter the comet's orbit by retarding it, thereby placing it in a smaller orbit with a shorter period (Fig. 9.6). There are about 45 comets that have periods between 5 and 10 years. They all move in a direct motion in orbits that are inclined less than $45°$ to the plane of

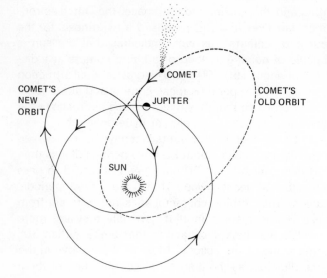

Fig. 9.6 The mechanics for the possible "capture" of a comet by Jupiter and the reversal of the direction of its orbital motion

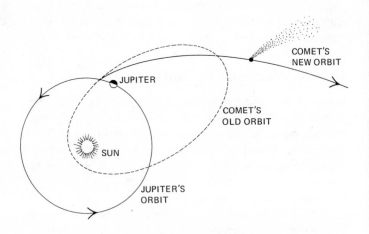

Fig. 9.7 The mechanics for the possible "expulsion" of a comet by Jupiter

the ecliptic. Their orbits are oriented in space so that their aphelion and either of their nodes are close to Jupiter's orbit. The one notable exception is Encke's comet, which has the shortest period of any known comet, 3.3 years. Its perihelion distance of 32 million miles (51 million km) places it within the orbit of Mercury.

Jupiter is also capable of "expelling" a comet from the solar system. At a close approach, Jupiter's gravitational attraction can accelerate the comet, thereby placing it in a larger orbit with a longer period (Fig. 9.7). Successive similar encounters could change the comet's orbit from elliptical to parabolic or hyperbolic, thus causing the comet to leave the solar system.

9.11 THE STRUCTURE OF COMETS

A complete comet has a head and a tail. The head consists of a star-like nucleus (frozen particles) surrounded by a hazy, luminous, spherical coma (gas cloud). The tail is a faint streak of luminous material which stretches

away from the head and away from the sun. The nuclei, from which the coma and the tail are derived, are extremely small—less than 10 miles (16 km) in diameter. The head diameters range from about 10,000 miles (16,000 km) to nearly 1.5 million miles (2.4 million km). The average head is 80,000 miles (129,000 km), which is approximately the diameter of Jupiter. Tail lengths range from a few million miles to more than 100 million miles (161 million km). With such values, a comet is easily the largest object in the solar system.

The extremely small mass of a typical comet has been estimated to be less than that of a very small asteroid. Comets have been observed to pass within 1.5 million miles (2.4 million km) of the earth and very close to planetary satellites without the slightest effect on their orbits. From these observations, the upper limit for the mass of a typical comet has been established at less than 1/10,000 that of the earth. With a very low mass and a very large volume, the density of a typical comet is extremely low—so low that the comet appears trans-

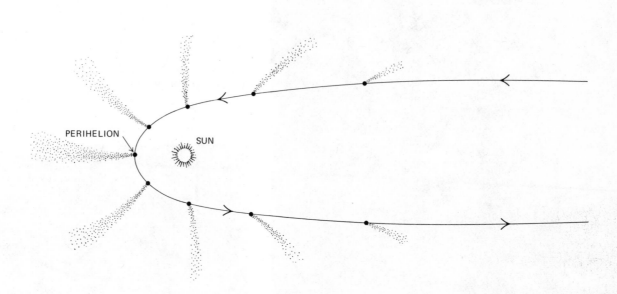

Fig. 9.8 The formation of a comet's tail, which always points away from the sun

parent. When Halley's comet appeared in 1910, the stars were clearly visible through its 50,000-mile (80,000 km) head, and when it passed between the sun and the earth, no trace of its nucleus was visible against the background of the solar disk. Also, the outer portions of the comet's tail swept across the earth without any noticeable effects.

9.12 THE SPECTRA OF COMETS

The average comet becomes visible at about 3 a. u., when the frozen particles in the nucleus (ammonia, methane, and water) begin to reflect sunlight. This is indicated by its spectrum, which is a faint replica of the solar spectrum. As the comet approaches the sun, its particles begin to vaporize and flow as the result of the sun's radiation, producing in the comet's spectrum the bright bands of carbon (C_2 and C_3), cyanogen (CN), methylene (NH), amide (NH_2), and hydroxyl (OH). All are formed from the four abundant elements: carbon,

hydrogen, oxygen, and nitrogen. When the comet is near perihelion, the bright emission lines of the metals chromium, iron, nickel, and sodium become visible in the spectrum. The spectrum of a comet's tail reveals the presence of positively charged molecules of carbon monoxide (CO^+) and nitrogen (N_2^+).

9.13 A COMET'S APPEARANCE

Faint comets are the general rule, bright comets are very few, and extremely bright comets are rarities. A typical comet is visible for only a few days, some are visible for several weeks, and a relatively few are visible for several months. Usually a comet is first seen telescopically as a faint, hazy spot of light. As it approaches the sun, its brightness and size appear to increase, and quite often a bright, star-like nucleus is visible within the coma. Although many comets never produce a tail, those that do appear to form the tail when the comet is about 2 a. u. from the sun (Fig. 9.8). The tail reaches its

Fig. 9.9 Comet Mrkos, 27 August 1957. (Photograph from the Hale Observatories)

Fig. 9.10 Comet Arend-Roland, 27 April 1957, with its unusual, sharp spike pointing toward the sun. (Photograph from the Hale Observatories)

maximum length and brightness soon after the comet has passed perihelion; then the tail gradually decreases as the comet recedes from the sun. The tail always extends away from the sun, so that when the comet approaches the sun, its tail follows the head. When the comet moves away from the sun, its tail precedes the head.

Two forces act on the particles in the comet's nucleus which cause the formation of the comet's tail—the solar wind and the solar-radiation pressure. The solar wind is a hot, low-density gas of charged atomic particles (a hydrogen plasma of protons and electrons) that continuously streams outward from the sun and out into space. The interaction of the solar wind with the particles in the nucleus produces the tail; however, it is not fully understood how this is accomplished. When the solar-radiation pressure exceeds the solar gravitational force, the particles in the comet's nucleus are forced out away from the sun, forming the comet's tail. This occurs when the surface area of a particle is greater than its mass. The radiation pressure acts on a particle in the same way that the wind acts on a sail.

The tails of comets may be classified into three important types: ion, dust, and spike. The ion and dust tails are clearly visible in the remarkable Comet Mrkos, which was discovered in 1957 (Fig. 9.9). The ion tail consists of ionized particles projected in a stream away from the sun. Excitation by solar radiation makes the ions luminous. The dust tail consists of small dust particles which curve backward in the plane of the comet's orbit. The dust particles are luminous because of reflected and scattered sunlight.

In April 1957 Comet Arend-Roland (Fig. 9.10) displayed not only a normal tail streaming away from the sun, but also a long, straight, slender, bright tail pointing directly toward the sun. This unusual tail appeared like a "spike" because it consisted of gas and dust particles that were diffused from the comet's head into a thin sheet that was lying completely in the comet's orbital plane. Actually, the "spike" was pointing away from the sun, but its position in space made it appear to be pointing toward the sun.

Fig. 9.11 This time-exposure photograph shows the zodiacal light beyond the observatory dome and the star trails moving down in the western sky. (Yerkes Observatory photograph)

9.14 THE ZODIACAL LIGHT

On a clear, moonless, spring evening at the end of twilight, the zodiacal light can be seen extending above the western horizon; just before twilight on an autumn morning, it can be seen extending above the eastern horizon. It appears as a faint, diffuse, conical-shaped patch of light. The zodiacal light's head base lies on the horizon, its axis coincides approximately with the ecliptic, and its hazy tip extends to a great height (Fig. 9.11). This means that in spring, the zodiacal light appears to make a large angle with the horizon; in autumn, the angle is small.

Fig. 9.12 Meteor trail among the stars in the constellation of Orion. (Yerkes Observatory photograph)

The zodiacal light appears to come from an edge-view of a lens-shaped cloud of small particles centered around the sun and lying close to the plane of the ecliptic. It is believed that the particles are probably the material ejected from comets and the debris from colliding asteroids which eventually spiral toward the sun because of their small size. The light appears bright along its axis; it fades gradually outward and becomes so diffused that it is difficult to establish its edges. Its spectrum is similar to the solar spectrum, indicating that it is either reflected sunlight or light scattered by small particles. Since the zodiacal light is slightly polarized and is not red, small particles such as atoms and gas molecules have been eliminated as its source. To produce the observed brightness, particles with diameters of about 0.01 inch and albedoes of about 7% would be required.

A smaller, extremely faint, nearly circular patch of light called the *gegenschein* (counterglow) appears in the night sky opposite the sun. Although its true nature is not known, it is believed to be the end-on view of the earth's tail, which is similar to that of a comet, is produced by solar radiation, and is made visible by reflected sunlight.

9.15 METEORS

Almost everyone has seen star-like objects shoot across the evening sky. They are called meteors and are popularly known as shooting stars (Fig. 9.12). The term "meteor" does not refer to the actual body, but rather to the luminosity that is produced as it passes through the earth's atmosphere. The body which produces the

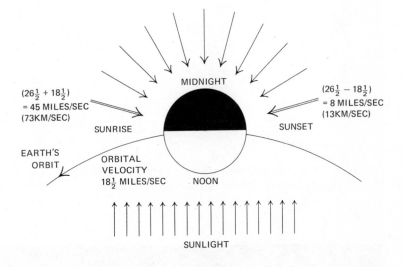

$(26\frac{1}{2} + 18\frac{1}{2})$
= 45 MILES/SEC
(73KM/SEC)

$(26\frac{1}{2} - 18\frac{1}{2})$
= 8 MILES/SEC
(13KM/SEC)

MIDNIGHT

SUNRISE

SUNSET

EARTH'S
ORBIT

ORBITAL
VELOCITY
$18\frac{1}{2}$ MILES/SEC

NOON

SUNLIGHT

Fig. 9.13 The velocity of meteoroids entering the earth's atmosphere. Head-on maximum velocity is 45 miles per second; overtaking maximum velocity is 8 miles per second.

meteor is called a meteoroid. Occasionally, when a meteor is bright enough to be visible in the daytime or to cast shadows at night, it is called a fireball; and more rarely, when it explodes in the atmosphere and produces thunder-like sounds, it is called a bolide. A meteoroid that is large enough to survive its flight through the earth's atmosphere and fall on the earth's surface is called a meteorite. When a meteorite seen to fall is re-covered, it is called a fall; when an unknown meteorite is discovered, it is called a find.

Many people confuse meteors with comets. Me-teors are very small bodies, usually about the size of pebbles, which become visible for only a few, fiery seconds as they pass through the earth's atmosphere. Comets are the largest bodies in the solar system and are visible for several weeks as hazy spots of light. Although comets move rapidly through space, their apparent motion relative to the stars is very slow.

There are two possible sources for meteors—either inside or outside the solar system. If meteors were produced by bodies within the solar system, they would travel at speeds ranging from about 8 (13 km) to 45 miles (72 km) per second; if produced by bodies out-side of the solar system, they would travel much faster. Since the velocity of escape from the sun (velocity in a parabolic orbit) at a distance of 93 million miles (150 million km) is about 26.5 miles (42.7 km) per second and since the earth's orbital velocity is 18.5 miles (29.8 km) per second, a meteoroid's maximum velocity as it enters the earth's atmosphere head-on (Fig. 9.13) is 45 miles (72.4 km) per second (26.5 + 18.5). If the meteo-roid overtakes the earth, its velocity is 8 miles (12.9 km) per second (26.5 − 18.5). No meteor has been ob-served with a velocity greater than 45 miles (72 km) per second, which indicates that meteors come from within the solar system rather than from interstellar space.

9.16 OBSERVATIONS

An observer on a clear, dark evening may be able to see from six to ten meteors per hour. More are visible after midnight than before, and the number increases to a maximum just before dawn. This is understandable when the orbital and rotational motions of the earth and the

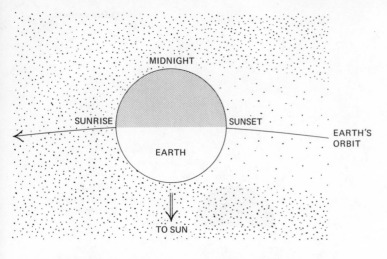

Fig. 9.14 There are fewer meteors in the earth's wake; therefore, more meteors are visible from midnight to sunrise

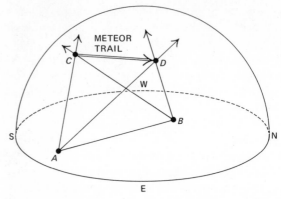

Fig. 9.15 Simultaneous photographs of a meteor taken from two stations (A and B) can establish the initial point (C) and the final point (D) of its trail

Fig. 9.16 This is the bright, interrupted meteor trail of the Lost City meteorite fall, 7 January 1970. (Photograph from the Smithsonian Institution Astrophysical Observatory)

motion of the meteors are considered. Between sunset and midnight (Fig. 9.14), the observer is on the side of the earth that is moving away from the meteors; therefore, only those meteors that overtake the earth will be visible. After midnight, the observer is on the side of the earth that is moving head-on into the meteors; therefore, he will see more meteors, and they will appear brighter because they are entering the earth's atmosphere with higher velocities.

The average meteor becomes visible when it is about 60 miles (97 km) above the earth's surface; it has been completely consumed by the time it reaches a height of about 50 miles (80 km). However, if the meteor is brighter than either Venus or Jupiter, it will remain visible to height of about 30 miles (48 km). It has been estimated that nearly 200 million meteors become visible to the unaided eye over the entire earth's surface during a 24-hour period. There are also many more that are visible telescopically. Their average total mass has been estimated at about 100 tons (90,720 kg). Only about one ton is deposited on the earth; the rest is consumed in the earth's atmosphere.

Two important techniques, photography and radar, are used to determine the direction and velocity of a meteor. In the photographic technique (Fig. 9.15), simultaneous photographs of the meteor trail (CD) are taken with wide-angle telescopic cameras from two stations (A and B) that are about 25 miles (40 km) apart. When the meteor is first observed, the simultaneous photographs show the initial point of the meteor trail with respect to the stars from each station. From the photographs the spatial position for the beginning of the meteor trail (C) is established by triangulation. The end of the meteor trail (D) is established in the same manner. The velocity of the meteor is determined by a shutter placed in front of each camera which rotates at a uniform rate and interrupts the meteor trail at 20 breaks per second. Figure 9.16 shows the segments of the interrupted image. When the segments are measured, the angular and meteor velocities can be determined.

In the radar technique, developed after World War II, microwaves from 3 to 100 meters that are easily reflected by the ionized gases in the meteor trail

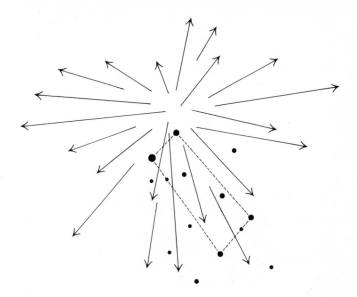

Fig. 9.17 The Geminids, a beautiful meteor shower that reaches its maximum rate of 55 meteors per hour about December 14. The meteors appear to radiate from a common point (the radiant) in the constellation of Gemini the Twins.

are sent out and received by the radar transmitter. With this technique the range, direction, and velocity of the meteor can be measured. The results, however, are less accurate than those derived from the photographic technique. The most important advantage of the radar technique is its ability to detect faint meteors when they enter the earth's atmosphere in the daytime.

9.17 METEOR SHOWERS

The meteors that have been discussed are called sporadic because they have no common point of origin, that is, they appear at any time and at any place in the sky. When meteors appear to radiate from a common point in the sky, they are called meteor showers. The common point (radiant) is one of perspective. Since the meteors in a shower move along parallel paths, they appear to radiate from the radiant (Fig. 9.17), in the same manner

Table 9.2 Maximum visual display of meteor showers

Shower	Date	Radiant R.A.	Dec.	Hourly rate	Associated comet
Quandrantids	Jan 3	230°	48°	30	—
Lyrids	Apr 21	270	33	5	1861 I
Aquarids	May 4	336	0	5	Halley
Perseids	Aug 12	46	58	35	1862 III
Draconids	Oct 10	254	54	(periodic)	Giacobini-Zinner
Orionids	Oct 22	94	16	15	Halley
Taurids	Nov 1	52	21	5	Encke
Leonids	Nov 17	152	22	5	Temple
Geminids	Dec 14	113	32	55	—
Ursids (Ursa Major)	Dec 22	206	80	15	Tuttle

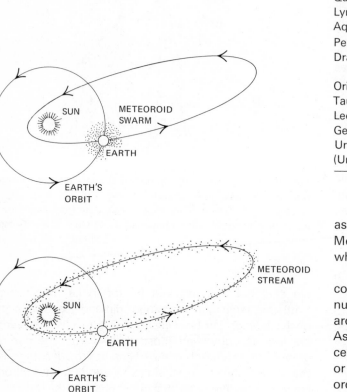

Fig. 9.18 An annual meteor shower occurs when the earth is at the intersection of its orbit and the orbit of the meteoroid stream. A periodic shower occurs when the earth and the meteoroid swarm are both at the intersection.

as a road appears to diverge from a common point. Meteor showers are identified by the constellation in which the radiant appears to be located (Table 9.2).

Many of the meteor showers are associated with comets. The particles that have been ejected from the nucleus by solar radiation pressure move in an orbit around the sun that is very close to the cometary orbit. As shown in Fig. 9.18, these particles may be either concentrated in a pile (meteoroid swarm) behind the nucleus or distributed over the entire orbit of the comet (meteoroid stream). A meteor shower occurs every year when the earth crosses the meteoroid stream. Periodic showers occur when the earth passes through a meteoroid swarm.

9.18 METEORITES

In Joshua 10:11, we find "... and it came to pass, as they fled from before Israel, and were in the going down to Beth-horen, that the Lord cast down great stones from heaven upon them unto Azekah, and they died." The philosopher Anaxagoras and the Chinese scholars have also eloquently described stones falling from the sky. Even though this phenomenon was observed, for cen-

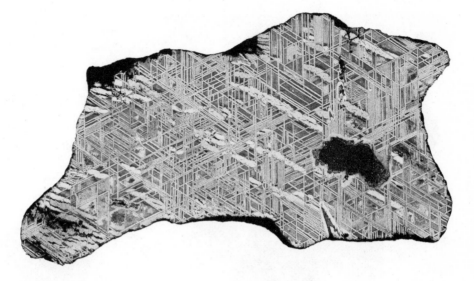

Fig. 9.19 Widmanstätten figures. The polished, etched surface of a section of the Edmonton, Kentucky iron meteorite clearly shows the low nickle crystalline structure of kamacite as white bands. (Photograph from the Smithsonian Institution Museum of Natural History).

turies scholars chose to believe that it was an impossibility and that it had to be an earthly phenomenon. Only at the beginning of the nineteenth century did man first begin to put together the pieces which convinced him that they were truly stones from the sky.

9.19 COMPOSITION

Meteorites are classified into three major categories: iron, stones, and stony-irons. It is interesting to note that from the study of the known meteorites, about 95% of the falls are stones and 65% of the finds are irons. Despite the fact that the stones are more abundant in space, more of the finds are irons; the stones are more difficult to differentiate from terrestrial rocks, and they decompose more rapidly.

The average composition by weight of the important elements in iron meteorites is 90% iron and 8.5% nickel; in stone meteorites it is 36% oxygen, 24% iron, 18% silicon, and 14% magnesium. The stony-iron meteorites are composed of iron and stone in equal amounts by volume, with the stony material imbedded in a sponge-like mass of iron. The irons are usually heavy,

nearly three times heavier than a terrestrial rock of the same size. The stone meteorites are similar to terrestrial rocks and are composed of silicate materials, nickel, and aluminum. Most of the iron meteorites can be identified by their unusual and distinctive internal structure, which was discovered by Alois de Widmanstätten and bears his name. When a small surface area of an iron meteorite is ground, polished, and etched, the beautiful Widmanstätten figures are usually revealed. They consist of large, parallel, intersecting crystalline bands of low nickel kamacite formed by slow cooling (Fig. 9.19).

The stones are further classified as chondrites and achondrites (Fig. 9.20). The chondrites consist mostly of silicate materials, similar to terrestrial rocks, and contain tiny, almost spherical drops of glass (magnesium and iron silicates) called chondrules. Their composition is variable, indicating that they must have evolved from different materials, but under similar conditions. The two dominant minerals in chondrites are olivine and orthopyroxene. The abundance of iron in the chondrites is also quite variable. The achondrites, which are also similar to terrestrial rocks, do not contain chondrules or nickel-iron.

(a)

(b)

Fig. 9.20 (a) Plainview, Texas chondrite is six inches long and clearly shows regmaglyphs (thumbprint-like depressions); (b) Pasamonte, New Mexico achondrite is two inches long and shows thread lines. (From the collections of Ronald A. Oriti, Griffith Observatory; photographs by James E. Klein)

9.20 APPEARANCE

Most people are surprised to learn that a moderately sized meteorite is not flaming hot when it strikes the earth's surface; rather, it is cool enough to touch, does not burn for days, and does not make a glowing crater. Beyond the earth's atmosphere, meteoroids are very cold. When they pass through the atmosphere, friction heats them to incandescence; however, their flight through the atmosphere is but a few seconds so that only their surfaces become hot enough to melt. Also, much of the melted material is swept away into the earth's atmosphere so that when the meteoroid strikes the earth's surface, it is relatively cool. A meteorite that has just fallen is usually covered with a very thin, dark crust, the molten material that has solidified rapidly toward the end of its flight through the earth's atmosphere. Many meteorites show flow-lines (threads or small ridges) where the molten material has flowed

because of the meteorite's forward motion. Weathering quickly changes the color of the crust to a dull gray or brown.

9.21 SPECTACULAR METEORITES

The largest known meteorite fall ever observed in the United States was the 2000-pound stone meteorite that fell in Furnas County, Nebraska on February 18, 1948. Recovered six months later, it is now on display at the University of New Mexico (Fig. 9.21). The second largest was the 800-pound stone meteorite which fell near Paragould, Arkansas on February 14, 1930. It was recovered one month later and placed on display at the Chicago Natural History Museum.

The largest meteorite find in the United States was the Willamette meteorite (15 tons), which was discovered in 1902 near the Willamette River, Portland, Oregon

Fig. 9.21 The Furnas County, Nebraska stone meteorite. (Photograph from the Institute of Meteoritics, Department of Geology, University of New Mexico)

Fig. 9.22 The Ahnighito-Cape York iron meteorite (about 34 tons). (Courtesy of the American Museum of Natural History)

and is on exhibit at the Hayden Planetarium, New York. It is conical-shaped, probably because it did not tumble as it passed through the earth's atmosphere, and it has several large cavities on one of its surfaces.

In 1894 the arctic explorer Commodore R. E. Peary discovered three iron meteorites near Cape York, Greenland: "The Ahnighito" (34 tons) (Fig. 9.22), "The Woman" (2500 pounds), and "The Dog" (1000 pounds). They were brought to the United States in 1897 and are on exhibit at the Hayden Planetarium.

In this century, Soviet territory has been hit twice by great meteorites—first on June 30, 1908 in central Siberia, and second on February 12, 1947 north of Vladivostok. The great Siberian meteor of 1908 fell in a forest near the Tunguska River and was seen by many people over an area of several thousand square miles. It first appeared above the southern horizon at 7:00 A.M. and moved northward along a meridian line at great speed. One observer described it as "like a piece broken off the sun"; another said that "the ground suddenly rose and fell like a wave." Seismographs and micro-

barographs throughout Europe recorded the tremor and the pressure waves. After the Russian Revolution, an investigation of the site revealed more than 100 depressions, which indicated that a cluster of meteorites rather than a single one had hit the earth. In spite of all this evidence, no one has ever been able to find a single meteorite in the entire area. Soviet scientists have concluded that a small comet struck the earth, because the comet's nucleus, which contains frozen water, ammonia, methane, and carbon dioxide would have completely evaporated on contact with the earth's surface.

One of the finest meteorite craters is the Barringer, located near Winslow, Arizona. It is a nearly circular depression with a diameter of 4200 feet (12,802 meters) and a depth of 600 feet (183 meters) from its rim. The rim rises about 130 feet (40 meters) above the surrounding plain and appears somewhat upturned, similar to the appearance of lunar craters (Fig. 9.23). Over 30 tons of iron meteoric material have been found on the floor of the crater and for several miles around it. The largest single fragment weighs over 1400 pounds (6350

Fig. 9.23 An aerial view of the Bar-ringer meteorite crater in Arizona. (Yerkes Observatory photograph)

kg). It is believed that the crater was formed about 50,000 years ago by a meteorite whose mass has been estimated to range from 63,000 tons, or 57,166 metric tons (by E. M. Shoemaker) to 2,600,000 tons, or 2,359,240 metric tons (by E. J. Öpik). These estimates are based on theoretical reasoning and calculation.

9.22 MICROMETEORITES

A large number of very tiny particles, or micrometeorites (about 0.0001 inch), enter and pass through the earth's atmosphere, especially during a meteor shower. Because of their small size, they pass through the earth's atmosphere at low speeds, thereby reaching the earth without vaporizing.

9.23 TEKTITES

Small glass-like stones (tektites) have been found in large numbers in a few scattered places in Indo-China, Java, Philippines, Australia, United States (Texas and Georgia), Czechoslovakia, and the Ivory Coast of Africa. A chemical analysis has revealed that they are rich in silicates and are dissimilar in composition to any of the rocks in the area in which they were found. When they were first observed on the ground, they appeared as dirty brownish or greyish rocks; however, when they were scrubbed and cleaned, they were black and shiny. Their shapes fall into three general groups: roughly spherical, disk, and tear-drop, which indicates that they were all involved in a flight through the earth's atmosphere (Fig. 9.24).

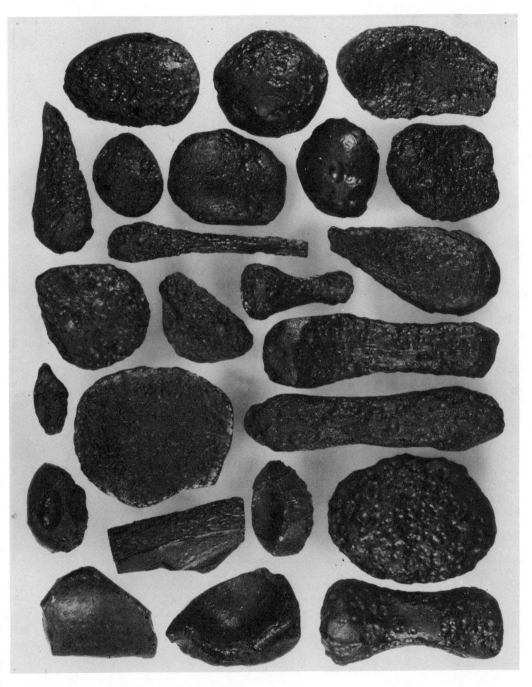

Fig. 9.24 Tektites from Thailand. (Dean R. Chapman, NASA/
Ames Research Center photograph)

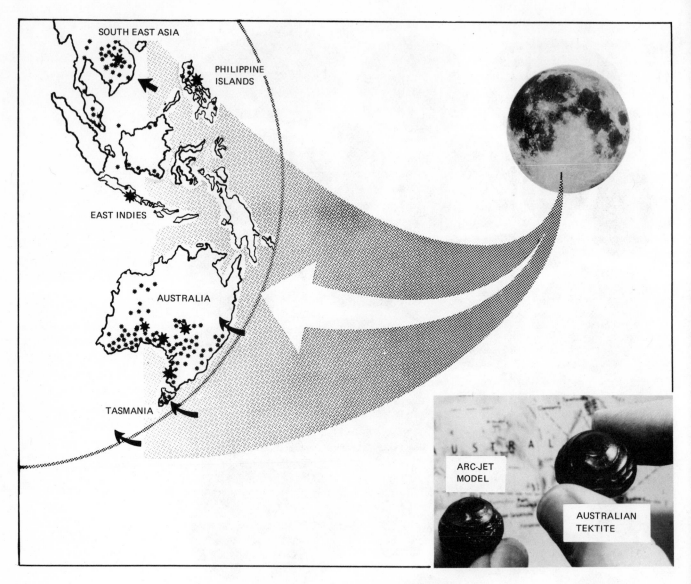

SOUTH EAST ASIA

PHILIPPINE ISLANDS

EAST INDIES

AUSTRALIA

TASMANIA

ARC-JET MODEL

AUSTRALIAN TEKTITE

Fig. 9.25 Tektite landing pattern. (NASA/Ames Research Center photograph)

Although the ages of the tektites over the world vary considerably, the ages of those in any one area are identical. The oldest tektites (34 million years) are found in the United States. Others range in age from 15 million years (Czechoslovakia) to 700,000 years (Australia).

Their distribution on the earth suggests that they may be lunar particles ejected from the moon by large meteoric impacts. The theory that they may be of terrestrial volcanic origin has been rejected as there is no evidence of a large crater in any of the tektite areas.

Dean R. Chapman of NASA's Ames Research Center in California has determined that a similarity exists between tektites found in Australia (Australites) and the rocks found near the rim of the moon crater Tycho Brahe which were analyzed by Surveyor 7 when it landed there in 1968. Chapman also analyzed the position pattern of the Australites and proposed that they could have been produced by moon particles ejected from the crater Tycho (Fig. 9.25). He also proposed that the Czechoslovakia and the United States tektite areas could have been produced by other great meteoric impacts on the moon which occurred 15 and 34 million years ago.

REVIEW

1. What is Bode-Titius rule? Is it valid? How are the asteroids related to this rule?
2. Discuss the location, distribution, orbits, size, and mass of the asteroids.
3. List two theories to account for the origin and formation of the asteroids.
4. What is the nature of a comet?
5. List the characteristics of cometary orbits.
6. What is Jupiter's family of comets? Describe how they might have been "captured" by Jupiter.
7. Describe and explain the changes that may occur in the appearance of a comet as it approaches and leaves perihelion.
8. Explain how the tail of a comet is formed and describe its shape and size. Do all comets have tails? Why? Can a comet develop more than one tail? If so, how is this accomplished? Give an example.
9. Name and describe a comet which had a tail directed toward the sun. What term applies to such a phenomenon? Is this a contradiction of the fact that comets' tails always point away from the sun?
10. Discuss what would happen if the earth were to (a) pass through a comet's tail (b) collide with a comet's head.
11. Explain the nature of the zodiacal light and the counterglow. When are the most favorable times for viewing the zodiacal light? Explain.
12. Halley's comet will appear about 1986. At the present time: (a) near what planetary orbit is it the closest; (b) how far is it from the earth; (c) is it visible with a telescope? Why?
13. What source has been proposed for comets? Explain what three possible paths may be followed by a comet.
14. What bodies not native to the earth, other than lunar rocks, are available for study and analysis? What can be learned from such bodies?
15. Cite one evidence that meteors come from within the solar system.
16. Explain why a meteor appears as a bright streak of light.
17. What is a meteor shower? What is meant by the radiant of a meteor shower? Name three of the most prominent annual meteor showers and state when their maximum is visible.
18. What is the composition of meteorites?
19. Discuss the origin, distribution, and age of tektites.

10
The Sun—Earth's Nearest Star

From its prominent position in the sky, the sun has exerted a hypnotic influence on man's consciousness. Early in history, man recognized that the yellow disk he saw moving across the sky every day was the key to his existence on earth. It provided the heat that allowed the crops to grow; it dispelled the foreboding darkness of the night and the fears that lurked in the shadows. The sun had a tremendous impact on the psyche of man—the human imagination began to associate the concepts of creator, father, heaven, and life with this body. In Chinese thought, the sun was seen as the male principle of the universe, Yang; the moon, with its delicate sun-derived light, was the female principle, Ying.

Until the emergence of science, the sun was worshipped as a god, a powerful deity that man could little afford to ignore. The Egyptians worshipped the sun in many forms; one such representation depicted it as an egg which was laid each morning by the sky-goose. The Greeks, who called the sun god Helios, believed that he rose from the swamps of Ethiopia every day, traveled across the sky in a chariot, and set in the land of the Hesperides. The Aztecs sacrificed captives to their sun god, Tezcatlipoca, in the hope that they would keep the sun from collapsing.

Although we have eliminated myths from our ideas of the sun, we recognize that it contains over 99% of the solar system's mass and dominates everything that comes within its influence. The very presence of the solar system would be impossible without the binding grip of the sun's gravitational force. Life on earth is dependent on the sun—eliminate it and life would

By permission of Johnny Hart and Field Enterprises, Inc.

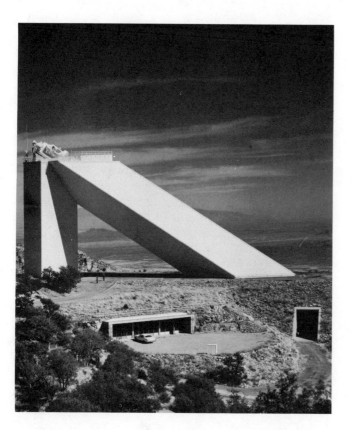

cease to exist in a very short period of time. From a physical perspective, ancient man's worship of the sun was not as naive as one might believe.

10.1 PHYSICAL PROPERTIES

Let us take a closer look at the dominant body of the solar system. At 92,960,000 miles, the sun is earth's nearest star. The next nearest star (Proxima Centauri) is over $\frac{1}{4}$ million times farther away. These distances can be better understood when one realizes that the light from the sun takes only 8 minutes to reach the earth, while the light from Proxima Centauri reaches earth in about 4.2 years. The sun is the only star close enough to

Fig. 10.1 The world's largest 60-inch solar telescope is located at the Kitt Peak National Observatory near Tucson, Arizona. The heliostat is mounted at the top of the vertical tower. The optical tunnel is slanted to permit the instrument to be oriented to the north celestial pole in order to facilitate the daily tracking of the sun. The major portion of the instrument is located in the subterranean chamber under the telescope. ("Kitt Peak" National Observatory photograph)

the earth to allow its features to be observed and studied in detail (Fig. 10.1). The knowledge of its structure and behavior provides the information which enables man to better understand the star in general.

The sun is a gaseous sphere whose visible surface has a linear diameter of about 864,400 miles (1,391,079 km) and an angular diameter of just under 32 minutes. Although recent observations indicate that the sun may have an extremely small equatorial bulge, its shape, for all practical purposes, can be considered spherical. The sun's mass, which is 2.2×10^{27} tons, is about one-third million times greater than the earth's. Its volume is over one million times greater than the earth's; therefore, its average density of 1.41 grams per cubic centimeter is about one-fourth that of the earth.

The movement of the solar surface features reveals that the sun rotates from west to east, in the same direction as the earth's rotation, and that its equator is inclined about 7° to the plane of the ecliptic. A careful observation of these features reveals that the sun does not rotate as a solid body, but as a gaseous sphere. The sunspots near the equator move faster than those in the higher latitudes. Since sunspots do not normally appear in latitudes greater than about 45° or near the equator, the rotational period for these latitudes is determined from the Doppler shift in the sun's spectrum. The spectra of the approaching and receding edges are taken simultaneously. The spectral lines of the approaching edge are shifted toward the violet and those of the receding edge toward the red. The apparent rotational velocity at any latitude is one-half the difference between the spectral shifts at that latitude. The actual rotational period is determined by dividing the circumference of the sun at that particular latitude by the apparent rotational velocity. The sun's rotational period is about 25 days at the equator, 27 days at 35° latitude, 33 days at 75° latitude, and about 35 days near the poles.

The energy that the sun emits comes from thermonuclear reactions (Chapter 15.5) that occur in its core (Fig. 10.2). Energy is transferred to the sun's surface within the radiative zone by radiation; within the convective zone, which is close to the sun's surface, by convection. The earth intercepts an extremely small

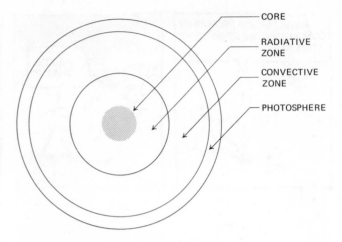

Fig. 10.2 The sun's interior

amount of the total energy emitted by the sun. On one square centimeter of surface that is perpendicular to the solar beam, the earth receives about two calories per minute. This is called the solar constant.

By Wien's law the sun's surface temperature is about 6164°K; by Stefan's law, about 6000°K. These values differ because they are based on different characteristics of the energy distribution curves. If the sun is a perfect radiator, the effective temperature of its surface, which is the average temperature of the entire disk, is 5750°K. The temperature of the sun's interior rises rapidly to an estimated value of 15,000,000°K at the center.

10.2 COMPOSITION

Solar radiation produces an absorption spectrum characterized by dark lines superimposed on a continuous spectrum, which shows the sun to be a sphere of very hot gases (the continuous spectrum) surrounded by cooler gases (the absorption spectrum). The composition of the sun is determined by comparing its spectrum with the spectra of the known elements (Fig. 10.3).

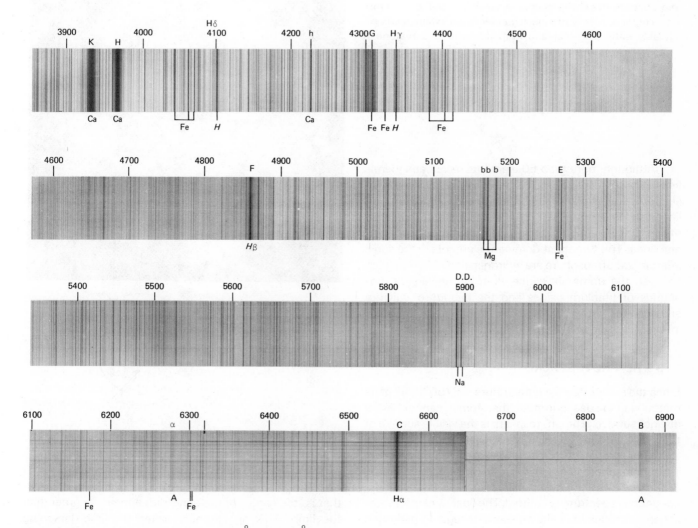

Fig. 10.3 The solar spectrum from 3900 Å to 6900 Å taken with the 13-foot spectroheliograph. (Photograph from the Hale Observatories)

195

Fig. 10.4 The darkening of the sun's limb. Light at the sun's limb comes from a shallow depth, where it is cooler; light at the sun's center comes from a much greater depth, where it is considerably hotter. (Photograph from the Hale Observatories)

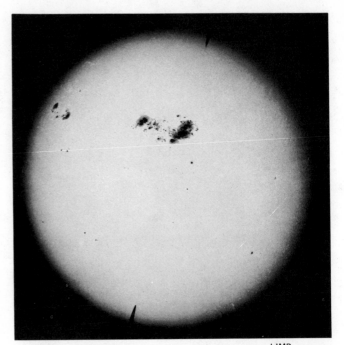

Although more than 60 elements have been identified in the solar spectrum, it is believed that all the known elements are present, since there are many absorption lines that have not as yet been identified, and the quantities of some elements are insufficient to produce absorption lines. The two most dominant elements in the sun's interior and atmosphere are hydrogen and helium, which are also the dominant elements in the universe. Compounds of titanium oxides and the hybrids of calcium and magnesium have also been identified in the sun's interior.

10.3 THE PHOTOSPHERE

Since the sun's effective temperature is 5750°K, all of its matter is in the gaseous state; therefore, it cannot have a distinct surface. The photosphere is the visible surface of the sun. The term "surface" as applied to the sun means the highest layer of its gases visible to the human eye. The photosphere is an envelope of glowing gases about 300 miles (483 km) in depth. It is from this layer that the continuous spectrum is emitted. The opacity of the photosphere is produced by the presence of negative hydrogen ions (hydrogen atoms that have acquired an extra electron). These ions absorb the wavelengths of visible light so effectively that the photosphere appears almost completely opaque. Above the photosphere is the sun's atmosphere (chromosphere and corona), in which the gases are less dense and emit so little radiation by comparison that the region is transparent.

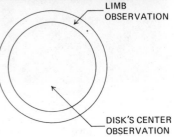

LIMB OBSERVATION

DISK'S CENTER OBSERVATION

The photosphere appears to be unevenly illuminated, that is, the center of the sun's disk appears brighter than the limb. This appearance, called the limb-darkening effect, occurs because the observer sees at the limb a short distance into the sun's atmosphere, whereas he sees much deeper at the center of the disk, where the material is hotter and brighter (Fig. 10.4).

When seen through a telescope, the photosphere appears mottled (granulated). The bright, irregular granules, whose diameters range from about 150 to

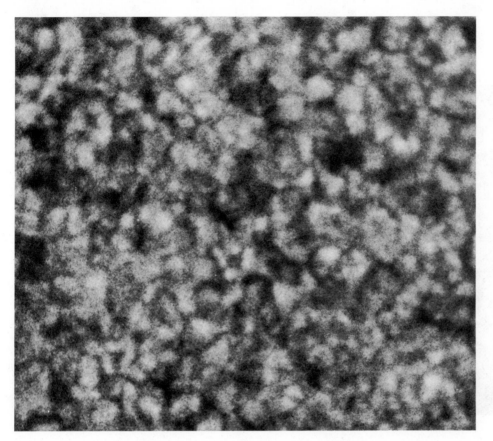

Fig. 10.5 A highly magnified section of the sun's surface showing the solar granulations. (Photograph from the Hale Observatories)

800 miles (241 to 1287 km), resemble rice grains (Fig. 10.5). These bright patches are $50°-100°$K hotter than the photosphere and are produced by the gases that rise convectively from below. The average granule remains visible for a few minutes, whereas a large granule remains visible for hours until it cools to the temperature of the photosphere. The process which produces the convective motions of the gases takes place in the region directly below the photosphere, in a layer called the hydrogen convective zone. When a hydrogen ion in this zone combines with an electron, the tremendous amount of energy released causes the gases to rise to the sun's surface.

10.4 THE CHROMOSPHERE

The chromosphere is a layer of heterogeneous, nearly transparent gases whose height extends to about 8000 miles (12,874 km). The density decreases rapidly, and the temperature increases slowly outward in the lower part of the atmosphere. The opposite occurs in the upper part— the density decreases slowly, and the temperature increases very rapidly. The hydrogen in the lower part is nearly neutral, whereas in the upper part it is nearly ionized.

During a total solar eclipse, the chromosphere becomes visible for a very brief moment. When the moon

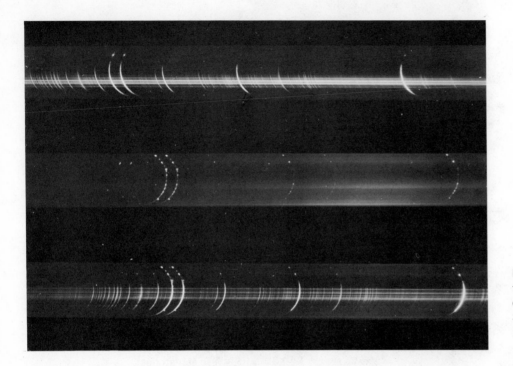

Fig. 10.6 The flash spectrum of the sun's chromosphere, taken during the total eclipse of 24 January 1925, Middletown, Connecticut. (Photograph from the Hale Observatories)

completely covers the sun's photosphere, the chromosphere appears as a red, irregular fringe of light around the moon's disk. When this occurs, the absorption spectrum of the photosphere changes abruptly to a bright-line emission spectrum (Fig. 10.6), or flash spectrum. Each crescent in the flash spectrum represents the radiation in one wavelength. The brightest and strongest 'ines are those of hydrogen, calcium, and helium—the elements that produce these lines are more effective at greater heights above the photosphere. The hydrogen produces the characteristic red color of the chromosphere.

A permanent feature of the chromosphere are the many fine, hair-like luminous threads (spicules) about 325 miles (523 km) in diameter and 8000 miles (12,874 km) in height which are visible in the lower part of the chromosphere. Each spicule lasts for several minutes; however, since there are so many of them, they are always visible near the sun's limb. They also appear to rise vertically above the level of the photosphere at speeds of about 12 miles (19 km) per second. United States Orbiting Solar Observatories 5 and 6, launched in 1969, and the others that have followed have provided the opportunity for further observation and study of the temperature and behavior of the gases in the chromosphere.

10.5 THE CORONA

The corona, the tenuous outer layer of the sun's atmosphere, is visible during a total solar eclipse as a faint,

Fig. 10.7 Composite photograph of the sun's inner and outer coronas. (NASA/Ames Research Center photograph)

pearly halo whose brightness is comparable to that of the full moon. Since the invention of the coronograph (an instrument which produces an artificial solar eclipse), the corona can be observed and studied whenever the sun is visible.

The corona is divided into inner and outer parts (Fig. 10.7). The inner corona displays a continuous spectrum, which results from the scattering of the radiation from the photosphere by the free electrons in the corona. Throughout the continuous spectrum there are several bright emission lines whose wavelengths do not coincide with the Fraunhofer lines. For years, astronomers believed that they were the spectral lines of a new element, "coronium." In 1914 the Swedish physicist B. Edlén resolved the problem when he discovered that the emission lines were produced by atoms of known elements that were highly ionized rather than by a new element. To obtain the high degree of ionization, the temperature of the corona has been estimated at 1,500,000°K. (This is a kinetic rather than a radiation temperature.) The coronal green line at 5303Å is produced by the ionized iron atom with 13 of its electrons missing, and the coronal red line at 6374Å is produced by the ionized iron atom with 9 of its electrons missing. Other spectral lines have been identified as having been produced by ionized atoms of argon, calcium, and nickel. The presence of the coronal emission lines indicates that the corona's density is extremely low. Even with an extremely high temperature, the corona thus contains very little heat. Ionization is produced by the impact of electrons moving at high speeds. The outer corona displays a continuous spectrum with many absorption lines, which is similar to the solar spectrum. The visible part of the outer corona extends to a height of about 1,000,000 miles (1.6 million km) above the chromosphere.

The structure of the corona varies with sunspot activity. During sunspot maximum it is more uniform and concentric around the sun's disk, whereas during sunspot minimum it shows streamers extending to great heights above the solar equator.

10.6 THE SPECTROHELIOGRAPH

One of the most important instruments used to study the solar structure and atmosphere is the spectroheliograph, invented independently by George E. Hale and H. Deslandres in 1890. It is an adaptation of the spectrograph (Chapter 4) with two slits which permit the sun to be photographed in the light of a single wavelength. The sun's image is brought to a focus at the first slit by a telescope objective. The light passes through the slit and then through a prism or a grating which produces the solar spectrum on the surface of a mirror. The mirror reflects the spectrum to a second slit, located in front of a stationary photographic plate. By rotating the mirror, any single spectral line can be permitted to pass through the second slit. If the image of the sun is allowed to move across the first slit while the photographic plate is moved at the same rate across the second slit, the image of the sun is photographed in the light of the single wavelength which passes through the second slit. These photographs are called spectroheliograms. Hydrogen and calcium spectroheliograms are preferred because these two elements produce the stronger lines at the higher levels of the sun's atmosphere. Figure 10.8 shows photographs of the sun in white light, in the light of the alpha line of hydrogen, and in the light of ionized calcium. Spectroheliograms in the light of the alpha line of hydrogen and the K line of ionized calcium display regions of bright light called plages, or faculae (Fig. 10.9). They are associated with sunspots, becoming visible just before the spot appears, and remaining visible for several

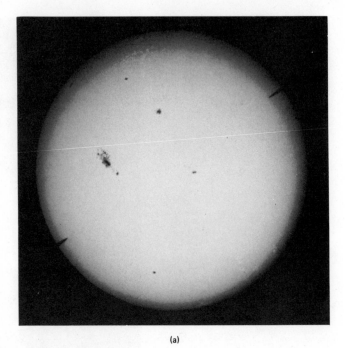

(a)

Fig. 10.8 Four views of the sun: (a) white light (ordinary photograph); (b) hydrogen alpha line; (c) calcium K line (calcium spectroheliogram); (d) enlarged hydrogen spectroheliogram (hydrogen alpha line) showing a sunspot group. (Photograph from the Hale Observatories)

(b)

(c)

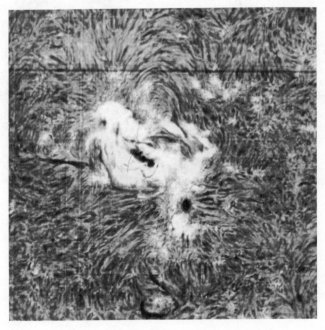

(d)

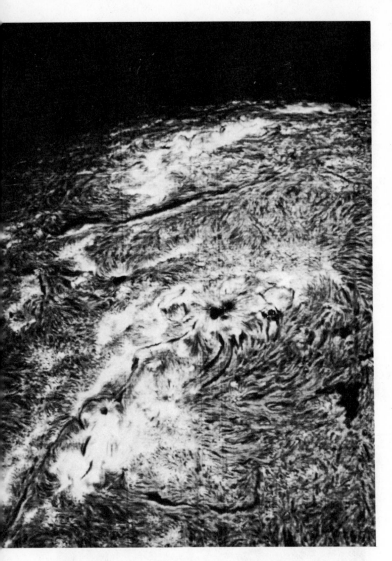

Fig. 10.9 Spectroheliogram. A detailed, greatly magnified section of the sun's surface taken in red light of the hydrogen alpha line, which shows the bright regions of the faculae. (NASA/Ames Research Center photograph)

days after the spot has disappeared. Faculae appear to be regions that are denser, hotter, and brighter than the photosphere; when they disappear, they blend slowly and smoothly into the photosphere.

10.7 SUNSPOTS

When the sun is active, the photosphere is marred by the appearance of dark splotches called sunspots. References to unaided-eye sunspot observations are found in Chinese, Japanese, and Greek literature. The first telescopic observation of sunspots was made in 1610 by Galileo, who suggested that they might be clouds in the sun's atmosphere. Astronomers have been investigating these occurrences for over 300 years to determine what causes them and as yet, no final answer has been found. Herschel believed that they are openings in the bright solar surface which enable man to see into the sun's dark interior. Some astronomers believed that they are openings caused by the gases' rising from the interior to the surface as the result of explosive action. Others believed that the sunspots are great, whirling fountains of gases flowing toward the center of a low-pressure area. None of these theories appears to fulfill the observed conditions. The present theory is that a spot is produced by a strong magnetic field and that the gases flow alongside magnetic lines of force that exist in a spot.

Before a sunspot becomes visible, a magnetic field is recorded on a magnetogram (Chapter 10.10). An increase in the size of a spot follows an increase in the magnetic field. Doppler studies have revealed that the gases within spots move radially outward at the lower levels and radially inward at the higher levels.

When studied by either direct visual observation or photography in hydrogen light, the gases in a sunspot are seen to move rapidly along curved lines that are similar to those formed by iron filings placed along a magnet. The gases appear to flow away from the spot at the photosphere and toward the spot at the chromosphere level. This phenomenon, named after the Indian astronomer who discovered it while measuring the Doppler displacement of the spectral lines near the edge of the sunspots, is known as the Evershed effect.

When first observed a sunspot appears as a small dark area (pore) with an average diameter of 1000 miles and an average life span of a few hours. It appears dark because its temperature is about 1500°K cooler than the photosphere; however, if it could be seen alone, it would appear brighter than many stars. The pores that persist increase their size and darkness and eventually develop into the umbra of the spot (inner dark core). When the umbra is fully developed, the penumbra (lighter area) appears to surround the umbra. When the sunspot begins to decay, the penumbra makes inroads into the umbra and divides it into smaller spots. This process continues until it completely obliterates the umbra. A spot has a rapid growth and a relatively slow decay. Its average life span is about two weeks. The longest life span recorded was nearly $1\frac{1}{2}$ years.

10.8 SUNSPOT GROUPS

Sunspots usually appear in groups of two or more. When several spots are in a group, there are usually two, large spots that dominate the group, called principal spots. The large spot which becomes visible first as the sun rotates is called the leading spot and is usually the largest spot in the group (Fig. 10.10). The other principal spot is called the following spot. Principal spots are usually oriented in an east-west direction, whereas the other spots in the group are distributed randomly around the two.

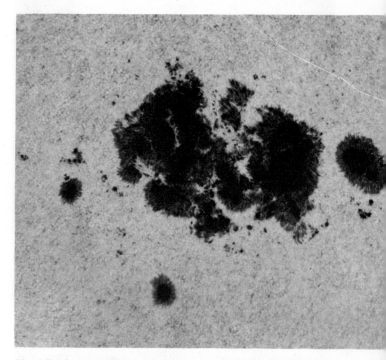

Fig. 10.10 An enlarged view of an exceptionally large sunspot group. (NASA/Ames Research Center photograph)

10.9 THE SUNSPOT CYCLE

The number of spots visible on the sun's disk varies daily and annually. After nearly 20 years of maintaining a systematic record of the number of spots appearing daily on the sun's disk when it was visible, the German apothecary Heinrich Schwabe in 1843 announced the discovery of a sunspot cycle of approximately 11 years. During the cycle, the number of visible spots increases from 0 to a maximum (more than 100 spots), then decreases to 0. From actual observations, the cycle appears to be most irregular—during the past 70 years, it has ranged from about $7\frac{1}{2}$ to 16 years, with an average of 10 years.

At the beginning of a cycle, several spots appear at approximately 30° north and south latitudes. As the cycle progresses, the old spots die and are replaced by new spots. Their number increases, and their average position shifts toward the equator, reaching a maximum number at approximately 15° north and south latitudes. At sunspot maximum, the number of visible spots may range from about 50 to nearly 200. After the maximum number has

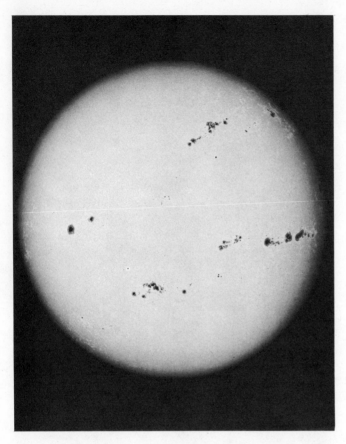

Fig. 10.11 The sun at sunspot maximum, 21 December 1957, showing sunspots, faculae, granular structure, and limb-darkening effect. (Photograph from the Hale Observatories)

spots. The spot's magnetic field is oriented perpendicular to the sun's surface in the spot's center and becomes more tangential as the distance from the center increases until it disappears at the edge of the penumbra.

By means of a scanning process which allows the sun's image to move across the slit of a spectrograph, a magnetogram is produced (Fig. 10.12). This is a series of traces that are parallel to the sun's equator and show the position, intensity, and polarity of the magnetic fields over the entire solar disk. An upward deflection on the magnetogram indicates a north polarity; downward deflection, a south polarity. Spots or spot groups that exhibit either an upward or a downward deflection (same polarity) are called unipolar groups. Two spots or magnetic fields that are quite close together and exhibit both an upward and a downward deflection (opposite polarities) are called bipolar groups. Spots that have opposite deflections irregularly distributed are called complex groups. Nearly 90% of the spots are in the bipolar group; less than 1% are in the irregular group.

During a sunspot cycle, the leading spots in each group in one hemisphere are of one polarity. When the leading spots in each group in the northern hemisphere are positive, their following spots are usually negative. At the same time, the leading spots in the southern hemisphere are negative, and their following spots are positive. When a new cycle begins, a complete reversal in the polarities of the spots occurs in both hemispheres. Based on the changes in the polarity, the sunspot cycle becomes 22 years—twice the length of the cycle based on the maximum-minimum number of spots.

been reached, the number begins to decrease, and the spots' positions shift toward the equator, reaching a minimum number or completely disappearing at approximately 8° north and south latitudes. Spots rarely appear near the equator or between 45° latitude and the poles (Fig. 10.11).

10.10 THE ZEEMAN EFFECT

In 1896 the Dutch physicist P. Zeeman discovered that when a source of light is placed in a magnetic field, its spectral lines are split into two or more components and that the degree of splitting is proportional to the magnitude of the magnetic field. In 1908 the American astronomer George E. Hale discovered the presence of magnetic fields when he observed the zeeman effect in the spectra of spots. The strength of the magnetic fields of sunspots ranges from about 100 gauss (a unit of magnetic field intensity) for small spots to nearly 4000 gauss for large

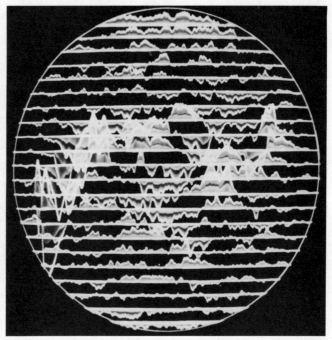

1953 JULY 18	1953 JULY 19

Fig. 10.12 Solar magnetograms showing the location, intensity, and polarity of weak magnetic fields in the sun's photosphere on July 18–19, 1953. Each strip represents a scan across the sun's disk by the magnetometer. The small deflections of opposite magnetic polarity near the north and south poles indicate the sun's "general magnetic field." The extended fields near the equator arise from bipolar magnetic regions that sometimes produce sunspots. (Photograph from the Hale Observatories)

10.11 SOLAR PROMINENCES

Photographs taken in monochromatic light of the solar disk show long, dark, thread-like filaments around the faculae and sunspot groups. When they are seen on the solar limb, they are called prominences and display a wide variety of forms (streamers, loops, arches, and hedges) and activity (quiescent and eruptive).

The eruptive prominences occur around active sunspot groups during the early period of the growth of the spots (Fig. 10.13). They are characterized by hot, luminous gases that appear elevated above the photosphere and the chromosphere to average heights of

50,000 miles (80,465 km). Some are so active that they appear more than 1 million miles (1.6 million km) above the photosphere. At first it was believed that the motion of the gases in the prominences was generally upward from the photosphere; however, motion picture photography has revealed that in most prominences the motion is downward.

Quiescent prominences, found around faculae and sunspot groups about one month after the first spot has appeared, are characterized by hot, luminous gases that seem to remain motionless above the solar surface, i.e., their general shapes remain the same for several hours to several months before they start to dissipate. Although

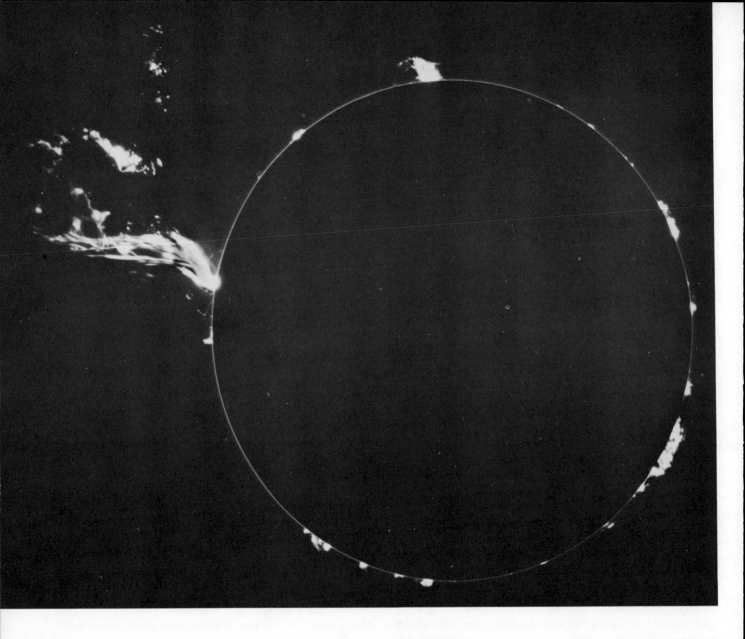

Fig. 10.13 The spectacular eruptive prominence of 1 March 1969, which appeared on the sun's western limb, was photographed from the University of Hawaii's Mount Haleakala Observatory. Its maximum visible height above the solar surface was nearly 375,000 miles. The prominence was associated with a solar flare. Many lesser prominences are also visible along the limb. (Photograph from the Institute of Astronomy, University of Hawaii)

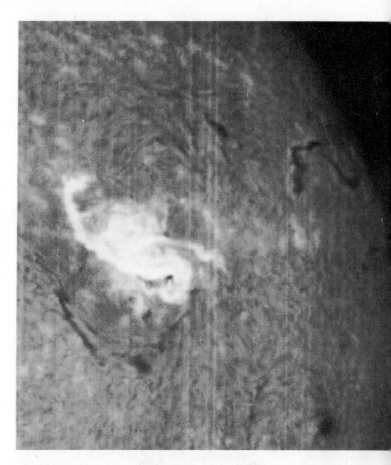

Fig. 10.14 A solar flare photographed in red light of the hydrogen alpha line, 16 July 1959. Bright faculae and dark filaments are also visible. (Photograph from the Hale Observatories)

they appear to be motionless, they are actually in great turbulence.

Coronal prominences originate high in the corona above centers of activity where the material is higher and denser than the rest of the corona. The material appears to condense around these regions. When a sufficient amount has condensed and the magnetic field in the sun's atmosphere can no longer support it, the material starts to rain downward on the chromosphere. It is believed that the changes in the prominences result from the abrupt changes that occur in the sun's magnetic fields. The process by which this is accomplished is not yet understood.

10.12 SOLAR FLARES

Flares are outbursts of unusually high-intensity light which occur near large, active, complex sunspot groups. They are best seen in hydrogen and calcium light; however, when the bursts are very intense, they are visible in white light (Fig. 10.14). Their light curves show that they rise rapidly to maximum intensity, remain there for a short period of time, then drop slowly to minimum intensity. The duration of the flares varies from several minutes to several hours. At sunspot maximum, the frequency of the flares reaches a maximum of about four each day.

Flares involve more energy than does any other solar activity. Since they are about 10 times brighter than the photosphere, flares are the brightest objects visible on the solar surface. Flares produce mass motions of high-energy particles in space, which disturb the earth's atmosphere, produce aurora borealis, and inter-

fere with short-wave radio transmission. Although the cause of flares has not been determined, it is known that their high energies cannot be derived from either the mass motions of the high-energy particles or thermal sources.

10.13 THE EARTH-SUN RELATIONSHIP

All points of solar disturbances are called centers of activity and are the sources of solar electromagnetic and corpuscular radiation. Since solar electromagnetic radiation moves away from its source in straight lines and

Fig. 10.15 A view of the aurora borealis as seen from Alaska. (Photograph by Gustav Lamprecht, College, Alaska)

in all directions, it affects only the daylight side of the earth's surface. Since corpuscular radiation is a continuous emission of highly charged particles which can be deflected by the earth's magnetic field, it affects the earth's entire surface.

10.14 COMMUNICATION DISTURBANCES

With the appearance of a brilliant solar flare within a large sunspot group, excessive amounts of ultraviolet, X-ray, and radio radiation, and streams of highly charged particles are emitted. The electromagnetic radiation travels at the speed of light and reaches the earth in about eight minutes; the charged particles travel at about 1800 miles (2897 km) per second and reach the earth in about one day. The ultraviolet electromagnetic radiation disrupts the ionized layers of the earth's upper atmosphere and causes radio fadeouts that often last for several hours. The charged particles produce magnetic storms in the ionosphere and induce electrical current within the earth, which create noise in long-range radio transmission and disrupt telegraph and telephone communications.

10.15 THE AURORAS

Streams of highly charged particles produce the aurora borealis and the aurora australis (the northern and southern lights), which are visible within a region about 40° from the north and south magnetic poles. Maximum auroral activity occurs within a region about 20° from the magnetic poles at altitudes of 60 miles (97 km). More and brighter auroras appear after sunspot maximum. The auroras appear just above the horizon in the early evening as one or more arches of soft red, green, and violet lights accompanied by streamers, which are visible to a height of about 40° above the horizon (Fig. 10.15). Their position and brightness appear to be in a constant state of flux.

The spectra of auroras show that the hydrogen alpha line has a Doppler shift which corresponds to velocities from several hundred to several thousand miles per second. Since the atoms in the earth's atmosphere cannot produce either the hydrogen-alpha emission line or the Doppler shift, it is believed that auroras are produced by the interaction of highly charged particles (predominantly protons and electrons) with ionized atoms of oxygen and molecules of nitrogen in the upper atmosphere.

10.16 THE AIRGLOW

Even when the sun is quiet—when there are no centers of activity visible—it is continuously emitting charged particles which produce a permanent "airglow" over the entire sky. The airglow provides almost twice as much light as the stars, although both serve as sources of night-sky illumination when the moon is not visible. The spectrum of the airglow shows that its light comes mainly from oxygen and sodium atoms and hydroxyl (OH) molecules.

REVIEW

1. Draw a cross-sectional view of the sun's interior. Label the zones and indicate their thickness, temperature, and dominant method of energy transfer.

2. What are the apparent shapes, sizes, and colors of the sun's disk at noon and when near the horizon? Explain why these differences occur.

3. Explain the darkening effect of the sun's limb.

4. What is the chromosphere and how can it be observed?

5. Describe the changes that occur in the appearance of the corona during the sunspot cycle.

6. Do all parts of the sun rotate at the same rate? Explain what this indicates.

7. Describe the development and decline of a sunspot group.

8. What causes sunspots to appear to move across the sun's disk from east to west, even though the sun rotates from west to east?

9. Discuss the number of sunspots and the shifting of the sunspot zones during the sunspot cycle.

10. Describe the magnetism of sunspot groups in both hemispheres of the sun, from one cycle to another.

11. What are solar prominences? Describe the important types. When and where are they visible?

12. What are solar flares? What terrestrial effects are associated with the appearance of solar flares?

13. How are auroras produced? Do the aurora borealis and the aurora australis appear at the same time?

14. What is the Zeeman effect? Who discovered it? How is it detected?

15. What is a flash spectrum? What does it reveal about the sun's atmosphere?

16. What is the corona? When is it visible? Explain the nature of its light. What are the coronal emission lines? Explain their origin.

17. Explain the operation of the spectroheliograph.

11
The Properties of Stars

Early man regarded stars as fiery objects located at an equal distance from the earth on the underside of a large, inverted dome which was suspended over the earth. He believed that the stars were "fixed" because they maintained their positions with respect to the other stars. Aristotle reasoned that if the earth revolves around the sun, the shifting of the nearer stars in relation to the more distant stars would be visible. Since he was not able to detect such motion, he concluded that the earth is stationary. Later, when the sun-centered Copernican system of the universe was established, efforts to observe the apparent motion of the stars were still unsuccessful; however, it was concluded that the stars were too far away from the earth for such motion to be detected.

11.1 STELLAR PARALLAX

In 1838 the German astronomer Friedrich W. Bessel observed and measured the apparent motion of star 61 Cygni in relation to the more distant stars. His discovery made it possible to measure the distance to the nearer stars by a simple method which was greatly simplified in 1903, when F. Schlesinger added the technique of photography. A star's apparent motion was measured from photographs taken of the area around the star at intervals of six months for at least two years. Although the average angular value (P) represented the annual apparent shift (parallax) in the position of the star (Fig. 11.1), the parallax of a star has been taken at one-half this value (p) and is defined as the angle at which the star subtends the radius of the earth's orbit (1 a. u.). When the star's parallax has been determined, its distance can be found from the proportion: the star's distance is to the

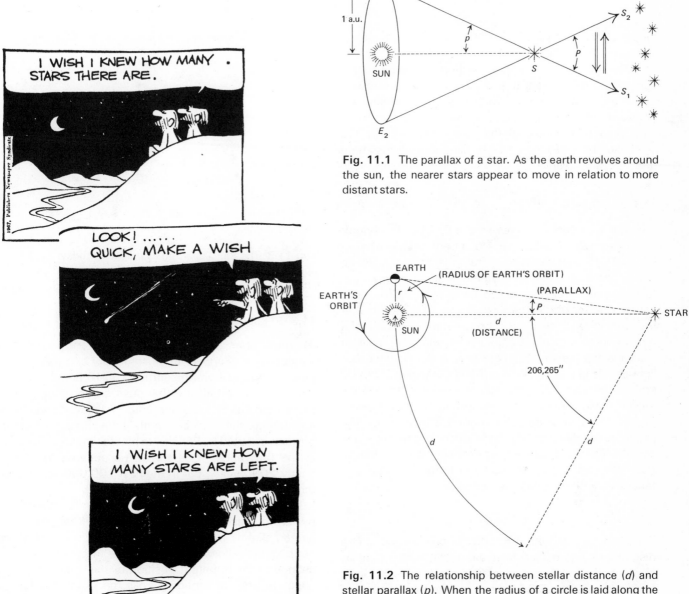

Fig. 11.1 The parallax of a star. As the earth revolves around the sun, the nearer stars appear to move in relation to more distant stars.

Fig. 11.2 The relationship between stellar distance (d) and stellar parallax (p). When the radius of a circle is laid along the circumference, it subtends an angle of 206,265 seconds. If the star's parallax is known, its distance can be determined from the proportion: star's distance (d) is to the radius of the earth's orbit (r) as 206,265″ is to the star's parallax (p).

By permission of Johnny Hart and Field Enterprises, Inc.

radius of the earth's orbit as 206,265″ is to the star's parallax (Fig. 11.2).

The use of the parallax method is limited to the several thousand stars that are near the sun, because the more distant stars produce small displacement angles on photographic plates that are difficult to measure accurately. Some of the other methods that are available for measuring stellar distances of the more distant bodies will be presented later in the text.

11.2 DISTANCE UNITS

The star 61 Cygni has a parallax of 0″.293. The bright, first-magnitude, double star Alpha Centauri has a parallax of 0″.75, and its distance from the earth is 4.3 light years. The faint eleventh-magnitude star Proxima Centauri has the largest observed parallax of 0″.76 at 4.2 light years, making it the nearest star to the earth after the sun. Stellar distances become more meaningful when two new distance units are introduced—the light year and the parsec. The light year is the distance that light travels in one year at about 186,000 miles (299,000 km) per second. The light year is equivalent to nearly 6 million million miles (9.7 million million km). Proxima Centauri is at a distance of about 4.2 light years. The parsec is the distance of a body when its parallax is one second. The word parsec is a *portmanteau* word derived from the words "parallax" and "seconds." Star distances vary inversely as their parallax,

$$d = 1/p.$$

Therefore, a star with a parallax of one second is at a distance of one parsec, whereas a star with a parallax of one-half second is at a distance of two parsecs. Since one parsec equals 3.26 light years, the relationship between distance in light years and parallax in seconds becomes

$$d = 3.26/p.$$

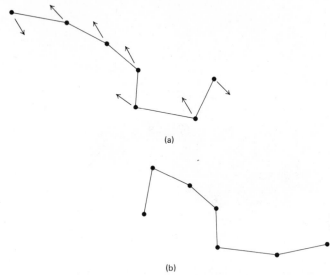

Fig. 11.3 The Big Dipper: (a) as it appears today; (b) as it will appear in 100,000 years. Arrows indicate stellar directions and magnitudes of their proper motions.

11.3 STELLAR MOTIONS

Although stars move at great speeds and in different directions, they appear to be stationary because of their great distances from the earth. In 1718 Edmund Halley was the first to indicate that stars are in motion when he pointed out that the star Sirius had moved about one-half degree, the apparent width of the full moon, from its position as listed by Ptolemy in his star catalog. The stars in the Big Dipper have shown no apparent motion in nearly 2000 years, but in the next 100,000 years, their motion will be quite obvious (Fig. 11.3).

The apparent position of a star can be determined by its right ascension and declination. This position is altered slightly by precession and other motions of the earth. When allowance is made for these changes, the change in the apparent position of the star, that is, the apparent angular motion across the observer's line of sight, expressed in seconds of arc per year, is called its proper motion. "Barnard's star," named after the astronomer who recognized its fast motion, has the largest known proper motion, 10″.25 per year, which is about

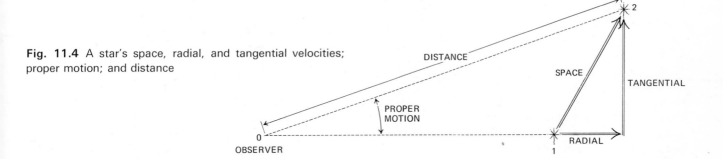

Fig. 11.4 A star's space, radial, and tangential velocities; proper motion; and distance

1° in 350 years. Proper motion varies inversely as the distance; therefore, a star's distance can be determined from its proper motion. The value derived by this method is less accurate than that determined by the parallax method.

Proper motion can be resolved into two component velocities: radial and tangential. In Fig. 11.4, the radial velocity (V_r) is in the direction of the line of sight of the observer and is expressed in miles per second. Its value is obtained from the Doppler shift in the star's spectrum. A shift of the spectral lines toward the violet indicates that the star is moving toward the observer; a shift toward the red indicates that it is moving away from the observer. The amount of the displacement is directly related to and a measure of the star's velocity. The tangential velocity (V_t) is perpendicular to the line of sight and is expressed in miles per second. Its value in astronomical units per year can be determined by dividing the star's proper motion by its parallax.

A star's motion in space—its velocity with respect to the sun—is called space velocity (V_s). When the radial and tangential velocities of a star are known, its space velocity can be determined by using the Pythagorean theorem in the solution of a right triangle.

$$V_s^2 = V_r^2 + V_t^2.$$

11.4 STARLIGHT MEASUREMENT

The most basic quantity used in the study of the structure and behavior of stars is the light that these bodies emit. Several methods are used to measure the intensity of this light. Since many students own or use telescopes, the simple but imprecise method which uses the light-gathering power of a telescope will be explained. This method was proposed by William Herschel and is based on the principle that the light-gathering power of a telescope is proportional to the area of its objective lens or mirror. This is expressed algebraically by

$$B = \pi r^2,$$

where (B) is the brightness of the image and (r) is the radius of the objective. Since the radius is one-half of the diameter $(d/2)$, the relation can be expressed:

$$B = \pi r^2$$

$$B = \pi(d/2)^2 = \pi(d^2/4)$$

$$B \sim d^2.$$

Therefore, the light-gathering power of a telescope is proportional to the square of the diameter of its objective. This means that a telescope gathers more light with a large objective than with a small one. This can be illustrated by comparing a 5-inch telescope to a 7-inch telescope. The light-gathering power of the 5-inch telescope is 25; that of the 7-inch is 49, which means that the amount of light gathered by the 7-inch telescope is nearly twice that of the 5-inch. Now, let us point both telescopes in the same direction in the sky. Suppose that in the field of view of the 7-inch there are two stars visible, one bright and the other just barely visible. In the field of view of the 5-inch telescope, the brighter star is just barely visible. Since the 7-inch telescope receives as much light as the 5-inch telescope, the brighter star is twice as bright as the dimmer star.

Another, more precise method uses either of two photographic procedures: (1) two different time exposures of a star field are made on the same photographic plate and the size of the star images are compared, or (2) a single star image is recorded on a photographic negative and its blackness is measured. Both methods are simple, although the first method is normally used. However, the second method will be explained here to give the student an idea of how star intensity is measured. The degree of blackness of a star's image on a negative increases as the star's brightness increases; therefore, the image of a bright star is blacker than the image of a dim star. The degree of blackness is measured by passing a light beam through the negative with the star image in its center. A bright star image will filter out the light beam more effectively than will a faint star, and the amount of light filtered is a measure of the star's brightness.

The best and most precise method for measuring the brightness of a star is the photoelectric method, which makes use of photomultiplier. Starlight is brought to a focus at the focal point of a telescope, passed through a small hole in a metal plate, and projected onto the surface of a photomultiplier. The brightness of the star is determined by the current produced in the photomultiplier.

11.5 THE LUMINOSITY AND BRIGHTNESS OF A STAR

The size and temperature of a star determine its luminosity, the rate at which the star radiates electromagnetic energy. If two stars are of equal size, the hotter star will radiate the greater energy. If two stars are of equal temperature, the larger one will radiate the greater energy.

The luminosity and distance of a star determine its brightness, that is, the way it appears to an observer. If two stars are of equal brightness, the more distant star is the more luminous. The brightness of a star follows the inverse square law, which states that light varies inversely as the square of its distance. A star at a given distance with a brightness of 1 will be only $\frac{1}{4}$ as bright when its distance is doubled, and only $\frac{1}{9}$ as bright when its distance is tripled.

11.6 APPARENT-MAGNITUDE SCALE

As one views the evening sky, it is obvious that stars differ considerably in their apparent brightness. In the second century B.C., Hipparchus was the first astronomer to devise a system for identifying stars according to their apparent brightness. He compiled a list of over 1000 stars and assigned numbers from 1 to 6 to indicate their apparent brightness. The smaller the number on the magnitude scale, the brighter the star. First magnitude was assigned to the several brightest stars that were visible, sixth magnitude to those that were just barely visible. Second, third, fourth, and fifth magnitudes were assigned to stars between these two extremes.

In 1856 Norman Pogson proposed the present magnitude system, which is based on the works of Fleckner and Herschel. The physiologist Fleckner pre-

Table 11.1 Light ratios

Magnitude difference	Light ratio
1	2.512
2	6.3
3	15.9
4	39.8
5	100.0
10	10,000.0
20	100,000,000.0
25	10,000,000,000.0

Table 11.2 Magnitudes of familiar celestial bodies

Celestial body	Magnitude
Sun	−26.5
Moon (full)	−12.5
Venus at its brightest	− 4.2
Jupiter at its brightest	− 2.5
Mars at its brightest	− 2.0
Sirius	− 1.4
Arcturus	− 0.1
Vega, Capella	0.0
Aldeberan	+ 0.9
Polaris (north star)	+ 2.0

sented what is known as Fleckner's law, which states that equal differences in the perception of light by the human eye correspond to equal ratios in the intensity of light. Astronomer Herschel developed the relationship that a first-magnitude star is approximately 100 times brighter than a sixth-magnitude star. Pogson proposed that the ratio of brightness between any two consecutive magnitudes be the fifth root of 100, which is equal to 2.512. This means that the difference in brightness between any two consecutive magnitudes is 2.512, or approximately 2.5. In Table 11.1 the light ratios for the various magnitudes are listed. A first-magnitude star is 2.512 times brighter than a second-magnitude star, $(2.512)^2$, or 6.3 times brighter than a third-magnitude star, $(2.512)^3$, or 15.9 times brighter than a fourth-magnitude star, and $(2.512)^5$, or 100 times brighter than a sixth-magnitude star. The magnitude of a star is only a measure of its brightness and does not take into consideration its size, temperature, or distance.

The apparent-magnitude scale has been extended at both ends, and its reference point (zero magnitude) has been established by means of several stars whose brightnesses have been determined very accurately. Zero magnitude is 2.512 times brighter than first magnitude, and − 1 magnitude is $(2.512)^2$, or 6.3 times brighter than first magnitude. Sirius, one of the original first-magnitude stars, was found to be about 10 times brighter than the average first-magnitude star, or − 1.4

magnitude on the extended scale. The sun's magnitude is −26.5.

Optical aids can extend man's vision from the unaided-eye limit of + 6 magnitude to + 23.5. A pair of binoculars brings into view stars of + 10 magnitude; the 6-inch telescope used by many amateur astronomers brings into view stars of + 13 magnitude; and the 200-inch Hale telescope brings into view stars of + 20 magnitude (when used optically) and + 23.5 magnitude (when used photographically). This is the present limit, because the residual night-sky light which comes from starlight, zodiacal light, and other sources is brighter than the light from stars of lesser magnitudes.

Table 11.2 lists the magnitudes of some of the most conspicuous and familiar celestial bodies.

11.7 ABSOLUTE-MAGNITUDE SCALE

Since the brightness of a star depends on its luminosity and distance, the apparent-magnitude scale cannot be used to compute the actual amount of light that stars emit. To accomplish this, the absolute-magnitude scale was introduced. The absolute magnitude of a star is the magnitude that it would have when seen from the earth at a standard distance of 10 parsecs (32.6 light years). This means that when all the stars are placed at this arbitrary standard distance and their brightnesses are

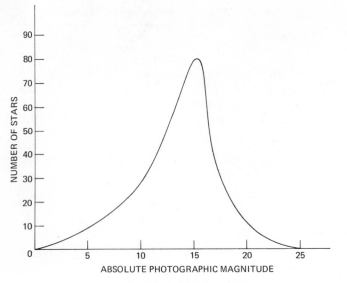

Fig. 11.5 Stellar luminosity function, the number of stars in a given volume of space for each absolute magnitude

A comparison of the 10 nearest stars with the 20 brightest stars reveals that the sun is the most luminous of the 10 nearest stars, except for Sirius and Alpha Centauri. Of the 20 brightest stars, all are more luminous than the sun. From this, we could conclude that the nearest stars are generally faint and that the brightest stars are intrinsically bright. We could also infer that the intrinsically bright stars are more abundant in space than those that actually appear bright. The number of stars in a given volume of space for each absolute magnitude is called the luminosity function, which is shown in Fig. 11.5.

11.8 THE COLORS OF STARS

The brightness of a star depends on the color that is used to observe it. Stars emit energy in all wavelengths, but not in equal amounts. Because the human eye is more sensitive to the yellow-green light, a star which emits its maximum energy in blue-violet light, for example, will appear dimmer than a star which emits its maximum energy in yellow-green light.

This indicates that the brightness of a star can be measured in several ways. When a star is observed visually, its brightness is called visual magnitude. When a photographic plate with an emulsion sensitive to blue-violet is used, the brightness of the star is called photographic magnitude. Since the human eye is not a reliable instrument for measuring the brightness of a star, a photographic emulsion was developed which is sensitive to yellow-green light. When such a plate is used, the

compared, those beyond 10 parsecs appear brighter, while those that are less than 10 parsecs appear dimmer. The sun, with an apparent magnitude of -26.5, is closer to the earth than 10 parsecs; therefore, when placed at the standard distance, the sun would appear as just another faint star, with a magnitude of $+4.9$. A sixth-magnitude star, which is already at the standard distance, would have identical apparent and absolute magnitudes.

From the inverse square law of light, the relationship between the apparent magnitude, absolute magnitude, and distance can be expressed by the proportion

$$L(10)/L(r) = (r/10)^2,$$

where $L(10)$ is the luminosity of a star at 10 parsecs, $L(r)$ is the star's luminosity at a distance of r parsecs, and r is the star's distance in parsecs. A sixth-magnitude star at a distance of 100 parsecs placed at the standard distance of 10 parsecs would appear 100 times brighter, with a magnitude of $+1$.

$$\frac{L(10)}{L(r)} = \left(\frac{r}{10}\right)^2 = \left(\frac{100}{10}\right)^2 = 100.$$

brightness of a star is called photovisual magnitude. Since a blue star appears brighter photographically than visually, the difference between the two methods for measuring brightness can be used to measure the colors of the stars.

The difference between the photographic and photovisual magnitudes is the color index of the star. In the magnitude scale, the smaller numbers represent the brighter stars; therefore, the color index of a star is negative when the photographic magnitude is numerically smaller than the photovisual and positive when it is larger. Therefore, stars of different colors have different temperatures. A blue star has a higher surface temperature than a red star. On the color-index scale, 0 has been assigned to blue stars (10,000°K). The color indices range from −0.6 for blue-white stars (25,000°K) to +2.0 for red stars (3000°K).

All the methods that have been described for measuring the magnitude of stars use the limited range of wavelengths of visible light. When all the wavelengths of the electromagnetic energy are used, the brightness of a star is called bolometric magnitude. Since this magnitude cannot be observed directly (much of a star's energy is absorbed by the earth's atmosphere), the magnitude is determined theoretically.

11.9 THE SPECTRA OF STARS

The spectroscopic analysis of starlight provides important information about the surface temperatures, sizes, distances, and motions of stars. Most stars produce absorption spectra which indicate that they have hot interiors surrounded by cooler atmospheres. Their spectral lines are identical with those of terrestrial elements, indicating that matter in the stars is the same as that on the earth.

Stellar spectra were first observed in 1824 by the Bavarian optician Joseph Fraunhofer, when he discovered that the stellar absorption lines are similar to those in the solar spectrum. About 40 years later, the Italian astronomer Pietro Secchi was able to classify stellar spectra into four general groups. When photography was applied to the study of stellar spectra, the

Harvard University astronomers instituted a program for classifying stellar spectra which reached its culmination with the publication of the *Henry Draper Catalogue*, the most extensive catalogue of stellar spectra with nearly 225,000 stars catalogued. The production and development of this catalogue in its present form is largely the lifetime work of Miss Annie J. Cannon of the Harvard College Observatory.

11.10 THE HENRY DRAPER STELLAR SPECTRA CLASSIFICATION

The Henry Draper classification organizes the stars into a continuous sequence according to the appearance of their spectra. The great majority of the stars are grouped into seven principal classes designated by the letters O, B, A, F, G, K, and M. The order of the sequence can be easily remembered by the first letters of the words in the phrase "Oh, be a fine girl, kiss me." The O stars (blue-white) have high temperatures, whereas the M stars (red) have low temperatures. Since each spectral class blends with the adjacent classes, a refinement was achieved by dividing each class into 10 subclasses and numbering them from 0 to 9. A star of spectral class F7 indicates that its spectrum is located seven-tenths of the way from spectral class F0 to G0.

The differences in the stellar spectra are due primarily to the differences in the temperatures of the gases in the outer layers of the stars' atmospheres. In the spectra of the hottest stars, only the lines of highly ionized atoms are visible. In the F stars, located in the middle of the spectral sequence, lines of neutral metals appear because the temperatures are lower. In the M stars (with the lowest temperatures) lines of neutral metals and simple compounds are most prominent. Table 11.3 lists the spectral classes and important features of some of the conspicuous and familiar stars.

In addition to the seven important spectral classes, there are several classes for unusual stars. Spectral class W has been assigned to the Wolf-Rayet stars. Since these stars are extremely hot and show strong emission lines of ionized helium, this spectral class

Table 11.3 Familiar stars in the spectral sequence

Star	Spectral class	Temperature (° K)	Important features
—	O	25,000	Ionized helium, oxygen, nitrogen, and carbon
Spica	B1	15,000	Ionized oxygen, nitrogen, helium, and hydrogen
Sirius	A1	10,000	Ionized calcium, hydrogen at maximum strength
Procyon	F5	7,000	Strong lines of ionized calcium, strong lines of ionized metals
Capella	G1	6,000	Strong lines of neutral metals
Sun	G2		Strong lines of ionized calcium
Arcturus	K2	4,500	Lines of neutral metals
Betelgeuse	M2	3,000	Strong lines of neutral metals, molecular bands of titanium oxide

has been placed before spectral class O. At the other end of the sequence, after spectral class M, are classes R, N, and S. The R and N stars show extensive bands in their spectra with strong molecular bands of carbon. The spectra of S stars show metallic lines and strong bands of zirconium oxide.

11.11 THE HERTZSPRUNG-RUSSELL DIAGRAM

Probably the most significant diagram drawn in astronomy was developed independently by the Danish astronomer Ejnar Hertzsprung and the American astronomer Henry N. Russell. They discovered the relationship between the luminosity of a star, its spectral class, and its color (Fig. 11.6). The Hertzsprung-Russell diagram, named in honor of the two astronomers, shows the position of several thousand stars by plotting their absolute visual magnitude against their spectral class or color index. The stars are not distributed randomly, but appear to be concentrated in several regions. The prominent feature is that most of the stars lie on a narrow diagonal band, called the main sequence, which runs from the upper left to the lower right of the diagram. The stars on this band are called main-sequence stars. Those at the upper left of the main-sequence band are hotter, larger, more luminous, and more massive than those at the lower right. Average stars, like the sun, are located in the center of the main-sequence band.

A few of the stars (yellow and red giants) appear to be concentrated on a shorter band, located above and to the right of the main sequence. Since these stars have the same spectral class and temperature as the main-sequence stars, but higher luminosities, they are considerably larger and have lower densities. Their red color indicates a low surface temperature, and their high luminosity indicates a large diameter and surface area. The very few stars that appear to be sprinkled across the top of the diagram are the supergiants, which represent the largest, most luminous stars.

Below the main sequence and in the lower left of the Hertzsprung-Russell diagram are the white dwarf stars. Their position on the diagram indicates that they are very hot with low luminosities. This implies that their total radiation, size, and surface area are extremely small—some are even smaller than the earth. The masses of several of the white dwarfs have been determined and are comparable to that of the sun.

11.12 THE LUMINOSITY CLASSIFICATION

Upon closer analysis of the spectra of two stars in the same spectral class, differences in the intensity of certain spectral lines are observed. When W. Morgan and P. Keenan of Yerkes Observatory recognized that certain spectral characteristics could be correlated to the star's

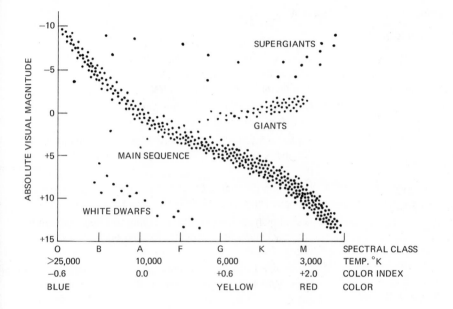

Fig. 11.6 Hertzsprung-Russell diagram

luminosity, they established what is known as the Morgan-Keenan system, which divides the stars (with the exception of the white dwarfs) into five luminosity classes. This vertical refinement in the classification of stars is shown in Table 11.4 and Fig. 11.7.

Table 11.4 The Morgan-Keenan luminosity classification

Star	Description	Class
Rigel, Deneb	Most luminous supergiants	I_a
Antares	Least luminous supergiants	I_b
Canopus	Bright giants	II
Arcturus, Capella, Aldeberan	Normal giants	III
Procyon, Altair	Subgiants	IV
Vega, Sirius, Sun	Main sequence (dwarfs)	V

11.13 STELLAR DIAMETERS

The diameter of a star can be estimated when its spectral class and absolute magnitude are known. The spectral class provides the star's surface temperature, which is used to determine the radiation that the star emits from

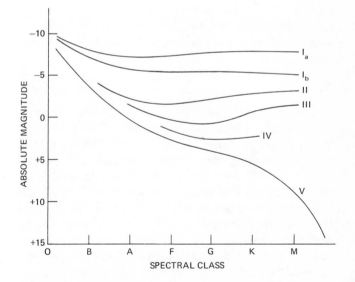

Fig. 11.7 The Morgan-Keenan luminosity classification

Table 11.5 Interferometer diameters of red giants

Star	Angular diameter	Diameter (sun = 1)
Arcturus (Alpha Bootis)	0.020″	22
Aldeberan (Alpha Tauri)	0.020″	45
Beta Pegasi	0.021″	90
Betelgeuse (Alpha Orionis)	0.034″–0.054″	400–600
Mira (Alpha Ceti)	0.056″	460
Alpha Hercules	0.030″	500
Antares (Alpha Scorpii)	0.040″	640

one square centimeter of its surface every second. The absolute magnitude is used to determine the total radiation that the star emits per second. Dividing the total radiation by the radiation from one square centimeter of surface gives the total surface area of the star; from this, its diameter can be easily determined.

A star's diameter can also be determined when its angular diameter and parallax are known by the relationship

$$D = d/p,$$

where D is the star's diameter expressed in astronomical units, d is its angular diameter, and p is its parallax in seconds of arc. Even with the 200-inch Hale telescope, the largest stars cannot be seen as perceptible disks. Theoretically, this telescope should be able to show these stars as disks; however, optical aberrations and atmospheric disturbances prevent this. The measurement of stellar angular diameters, achieved in 1920 by Albert A. Michelson with an interferometer (Chapter 4), produced results that are in close agreement with the estimates based on spectral class and absolute magnitude. The diameters of some of the red giants that were measured with the interferometer are shown in Table 11.5.

REVIEW

1. Define parallax. If a star at a distance of one parsec has a parallax of one second, and one parsec = 3.26 light years, what is the parallax of the nearest star (Proxima Centauri, at a distance of 4.2 light years)?

2. Describe the principle of the parallax method for determining stellar distances.

3. Explain why the parallax method for determining stellar distances is rather limited. List other methods that are used.

4. If a star's parallax is 0″. 30 of arc, what is its distance in (a) light years and (b) parsecs?

5. Distinguish among a star's proper motion, tangential velocity, and radial velocity. Explain how each is determined.

6. List several methods for measuring the intensity of starlight. Which is the most precise? Explain how it is determined.

7. Distinguish between the brightness and the luminosity of a star. Which one can be observed? Explain.

8. What is the difference between the apparent and the absolute magnitude of a star?

9. If two stars are of equal brightness but different distances, which one will appear more luminous? Explain.

10. Why do stars appear to be of different colors?

11. State the stellar spectral class in which the following spectral features are present: (a) intense hydrogen lines, (b) strong lines of neutral metals, (c) intense helium lines, (d) molecular bands. Explain why these differences occur.

12. Describe the Henry Draper stellar spectra classification and the important characteristics of each spectral class.

13. Explain how the luminosity classification of stars was determined from their spectra.

14. Describe the graph of the Hertzsprung-Russell diagram and show the relationship that exists between spectral class, absolute temperature, color, and color index.

12
Multiple Star Systems

Although most stars appear to the unaided eye as single points of light, many stars belong to multiple star systems—stars that are held together by mutual gravitational force. Such star systems range from two stars, called binaries, to star clusters of hundreds to thousands of stars.

The discovery of multiple star systems was made by Giovanni Riccioli in 1650, when he observed that the star Mizar in the handle of the Big Dipper appeared as a double star in his telescope. By 1777 Christian Mayer had observed over 100 double stars and concluded that the fainter star in each "double" was a planet revolving around the "true" star. His conclusion caused quite a discussion among astronomers. The astronomer Father Hell in Vienna disagreed with Mayer's conclusion and explained that the fainter star was simply an optical illusion. Both were wrong.

William Herschel's work with double stars helped to establish certain characteristics about them. They differ in size and brightness, and both are in motion. Herschel also differentiated between apparent and real double stars. An apparent double (optical double) is two stars which appear to be close together, but actually are not physically associated. A real double (physical binary) is two stars that revolve around their barycenter under the influence of their mutual gravitational force.

Binaries have been classified according to the technique that was used in their discovery. Visual binaries are those whose stars are so far apart that they can be detected visually as two stars either through a telescope or on a photographic plate. Eclipsing binaries are those whose orbits are nearly in the line of sight of the observer (so that each eclipses the other) and are detected by a periodic variation in brightness. Spectroscopic binaries

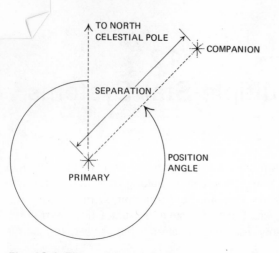

Fig. 12.1 The position angle and separation of binary stars

are discovered spectroscopically from the variations of the star's radial velocities, indicated by the variation in the Doppler shift of their spectral lines.

12.1 VISUAL BINARIES

The position and motion of the stars in a visual binary system can be determined by observing the motion of the fainter (companion) star as it moves about the brighter (primary) star and measuring the position angle and the separation of the stars. The position angle (Fig. 12.1) is the angle measured from the north celestial pole eastward around the primary to the companion. The separation is the angular distance between the two stars. The position angle and the separation are measured with a filar micrometer or on a photographic plate. Three prominent visual binaries and their periods of revolution are Procyon (21 years), Sirius (50 years), and Castor (420 years).

12.2 SPECTROSCOPIC BINARIES

Many binaries appear in the largest telescopes as single stars; however, their binary status is clearly apparent from the periodic variation in their spectra. These stars are called spectroscopic binaries. The first to be discovered was the brightest star of the double star Mizar in 1889 by E. Pickering. Among the brightest of the spectroscopic binaries are Capella in Auriga the Charioteer and Spica in Virgo the Virgin.

When the two stars of a spectroscopic binary system are about equal in brightness, they can be detected by their Doppler displacements. As shown in Fig. 12.2, when both stars are moving at right angles to the observer's line of sight, the spectral lines are superimposed. When one star is receding and the other is approaching the observer, the spectral lines appear double, that is, the spectral lines of the receding star are displaced toward the red and those of the approaching star toward the violet (Fig. 12.3). Many of the spectroscopic binaries show a single spectrum, which indicates that the primary is much brighter than its companion, consequently drowning out the spectrum of the dimmer

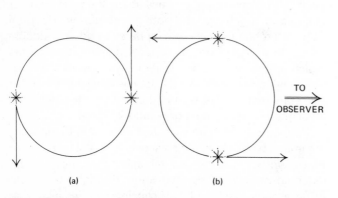

Fig. 12.2 Spectroscopic binary star system: (a) stars are moving at right angles to the observer (spectral lines are superimposed); (b) stars are approaching and receding from the observer (spectral lines appear double)

SPECTRAL TYPE A2   PERIOD 20.5 DAYS

λ4415.1   λ4528.6

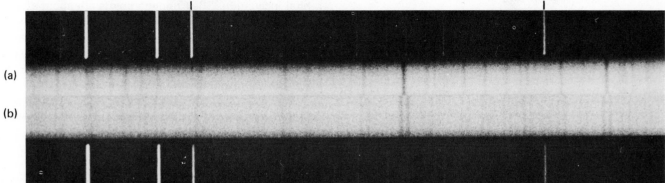

(a)

(b)

Fig. 12.3 Spectrum of a spectroscopic binary star, Zeta Ursa Majoris (Mizar): (a) lines of the two components are superimposed on 11 June 1927; (b) lines of the two components are separated by a difference in orbital velocity of about 87 miles per second on 13 June 1927. (Photograph from the Hale Observatories)

star. The periodic variation in the spectrum indicates the presence of two stars revolving around their barycenter. When the companion is too close to the primary and very faint, its presence can be detected by its gravitational effect on the motion of the primary. It causes the primary to move along a wavy path (Chapter 12.5). This was first detected by Bessel when he observed that the line of Sirius' path is slightly wavy rather than straight. Such star systems are called astrometric binaries.

12.3 ECLIPSING BINARIES

The orbital plane of an eclipsing binary lies very close to the observer's line of sight, so that each star appears to periodically eclipse the other. The first to be discovered, and probably one of the finest examples of an eclipsing binary, is the star Algol, the "blinking demon" located in the constellation of Perseus the Hero. The companion has a diameter that is about 20% greater and a brightness that is three magnitudes less than the primary. The two stars are about 13 million miles (21 million km)

apart, and their orbital plane is inclined about 8° to the observer's line of sight. The bright star revolves around the dim star in about 2 days and 21 hours. During each revolution the companion passes between the observer's line of sight and the primary star, partially eclipsing it for nine hours, and at maximum eclipse, reducing the light of the binary system to one-third its normal brightness.

12.4 LIGHT CURVES OF ECLIPSING BINARIES

By plotting the brightness of an eclipsing binary against time, one can obtain a light curve of the binary. The light curve of Algol is shown in Fig. 12.4. The maximum and minimum points on the curve represent maximum and minimum brightnesses; the difference between the two brightnesses is called the amplitude; the interval between two consecutive maximum or minimum points is called the period.

A study of the light curve of an eclipsing binary reveals the binary system's orbital period, the inclination

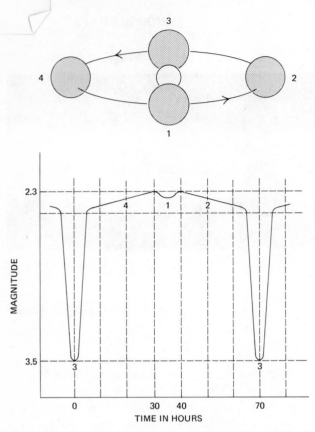

Fig. 12.4 The Algol (β Persei) eclipsing binary and its light curve

Fig. 12.5 Light curves of eclipsing binaries: (a) two stars of equal size, magnitude, and small orbital inclination; (b) two stars of equal size and small orbital inclination—star 1 is brighter than star 2

of its orbit, and the size and luminosity of its stars. Figure 12.5(a) represents the light curve of two stars that have approximately the same size and luminosity, and a slight orbital inclination. Their minima points are about equal. Figure 12.5(b) represents the light curve when the luminosity of star 1 is greater than that of star 2. When star 1 eclipses star 2, its minimum is smaller than when star 2 eclipses star 1. The pointed minima indicate that total eclipse lasts for only a moment.

Figure 12.6(a) represents the light curve when the size and luminosity of star 1 are greater than those of

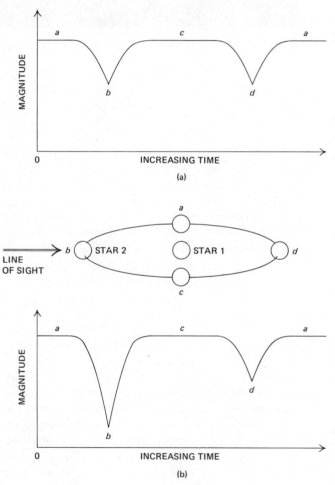

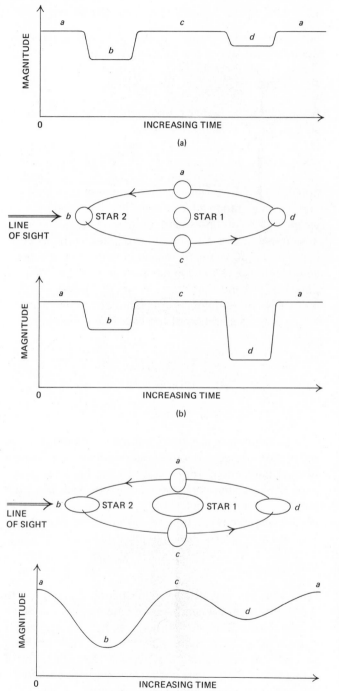

Fig. 12.6 The light curves of eclipsing binaries: (a) star 1 is larger and brighter than star 2; (b) star 1 is larger but dimmer than star 2

star 2. When the more luminous star 1 eclipses star 2, the minimum is less than when the less luminous star 2 eclipses star 1. The minima are flat, because total eclipse is not momentary, but has a definite period of duration. Figure 12.6(b) represents the light curve when star 1 is less luminous than star 2. When star 1 eclipses star 2, the minimum is greater than when the more luminous star 2 eclipses star 1.

When the two stars in a binary system are very close together, enormous tides result from their mutual gravitational force. This distorts the stars into elliptical shapes and causes the light curve to appear wavy (Fig. 12.7). Between eclipses, the stars are seen lengthwise; just before and after an eclipse, they are seen end-on.

Fig. 12.7 The light curve of an eclipsing binary whose stars are so close together that enormous tides result from their mutual gravitational force, distorting the stars into elliptical shapes and producing a wavy light curve

225

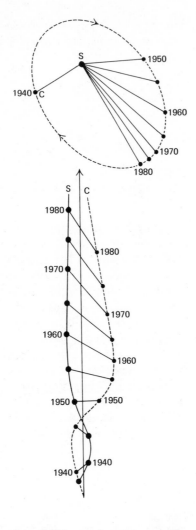

Fig. 12.8 The proper motion of Sirius and companion. The straight line represents the barycenter of the system, the solid line is the path of Sirius, and the dotted line is the path of the companion.

12.5 THE MASS OF A BINARY SYSTEM

We learned in Chapter 2 that Newton generalized Kepler's third law of planetary motion as

$$P^2 = a^3/(M + m),$$

where (P) is the body's orbital period in years, (a) is the semimajor axis of its orbit in astronomical units, and ($M + m$) is the sum of the masses of the two bodies as compared to the sun's mass. With this formula it is possible to find the sum of the masses of the two stars in a binary system by observing their period of revolution (P) and the separation of the stars (a). For example, the visual binary of Sirius and its companion, which are designated as Sirius A and Sirius B, has an orbital period (P) of about 50 years. By measuring the binary's angular semimajor axis ($7''.7$) and its distance from the sun (2.6 parsecs), we find that their product (7.7)(2.6), or 20.0, is the system's semimajor axis (a) in astronomical units, which is the separation of the two stars. Therefore,

$$P^2 = a^3/ (M + m)$$

$$(M + m) = a^3/P^2 = (20.0)^3/(50)^2$$

$$= 3.2 \text{ solar masses.}$$

To determine the individual mass of each star, we must take into consideration their motions with respect to their barycenter. The barycenter lies on a line which joins the two stars, and the distance of each star from the barycenter is inversely proportional to its mass, that is, the more massive body is closer to the barycenter. This is expressed by the relationship

$$m_1/m_2 = d_2/d_1.$$

(This situation was discussed in Chapter 7 in relation to the earth-moon system.) As the binary system of Sirius A and Sirius B moves through space, its barycenter follows a uniform path, and the two stars oscillate around it in varying degrees. In Fig. 12.8, the paths of Sirius A and Sirius B are shown as wavy lines around the straight line which represents the path of the bary-

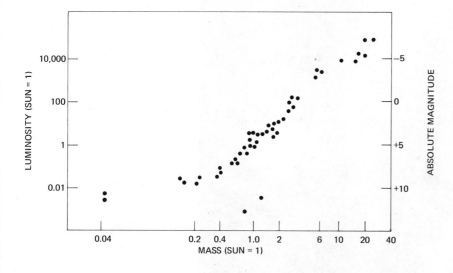

Fig. 12.9 Mass-luminosity relation

center. The ratio of their distances from the barycenter (d_2/d_1) is 2.2, which means that Sirius B is orbiting about 2.2 times farther from the barycenter than is Sirius A. Therefore, the mass of Sirius B is equal to the sun's mass, and the mass of Sirius A is 2.2 times greater.

12.6 THE MASS-LUMINOSITY RELATIONSHIP

In 1924 the English astrophysicist Arthur S. Eddington discovered one of the most important and significant relationships in astronomy—the mass-luminosity relationship (Fig. 12.9). By plotting the mass of stars (in terms of the sun's mass) against their absolute bolometric magnitudes, he discovered that most of the stars plotted were on a narrow band which extended from the lower left to the upper right of the diagram. This indicated that a definite relationship exists between the star's mass and its luminosity and that luminosity increases as mass increases. The mass-luminosity relationship, which holds true for most stars except white dwarfs, indicates that mass is a significant stellar property. From this relationship the masses of most stars can be determined approximately from their absolute magnitudes. There is no known star with a mass greater than 100 times that of the sun.

12.7 STAR CLUSTERS

We have learned that stars appear in space independently and in multiple star systems. They also appear in clusters of two major types: galactic (open) and globular (closed). A star cluster is a physically related group of stars. Its grouping is an apparent one because actually, the stars are widely separated and their numbers range from a very few to so many that the largest telescopes are not able to resolve many of them. The stars in a cluster move in nearly parallel paths so that they appear to converge or diverge from a common point in the sky, similar to meteors in a meteor shower. Their motions suggest that they have a common origin and age. With these characteristics, clusters become very interesting objects for studying the evolution of stars.

12.8 GALACTIC CLUSTERS

Nearly 800 galactic clusters have been discovered. They are located almost exclusively in the center of the spiral arms of the Milky Way. It is believed that tens of thousands of these clusters exist but that they have escaped detection because the dust and gas particles in the plane of the Milky Way are obscuring them. The number of stars in a cluster ranges from about 10 to nearly 1000.

Fig. 12.10 The Pleiades, NGC 1432, a typical galactic cluster in Taurus, which shows reflection nebulosities. Photographed with the 100-inch telescope. (Photograph from the Hale Observatories)

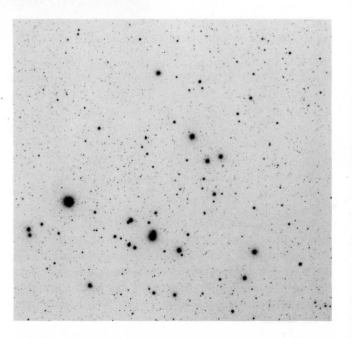

Fig. 12.11 The V-shaped Hyades cluster, a galactic cluster in the constellation of Taurus (Lick Observatory photograph)

The well-known Pleiades and Hyades in Taurus the Bull are excellent examples of galactic clusters visible to the unaided eye. The Pleiades (Fig. 12.10) appear as a small group of six stars that are imbedded in bright nebulosity. The bright nebulosity is dust and gas clouds reflecting starlight and appearing luminous against the darker background. Seen with the 200-inch Hale telescope, the cluster reveals the presence of several hundred stars. The Hyades appears as a V-shaped arrangement of stars which marks the head of Taurus the Bull (Fig. 12.11). The galactic cluster of the Praesepe in Cancer the Crab is visible to the unaided eye as a very faint, hazy spot of light. It is often referred to as the "Beehive," because it resembles a swarm of bees when seen telescopically. The Hyades and Praesepe are examples of star clusters without nebulosities.

12.9 THE DISTANCE OF GALACTIC CLUSTERS

When the apparent magnitude of the stars in a cluster are plotted according to their color index (Fig. 12.12), we obtain a color-magnitude diagram. It is similar to the H-R diagram, but with the addition of a vertical scale of the age of stars in years. Since the stars in a cluster are at approximately the same distance from the sun, the modulus distance (the difference between the apparent and the absolute magnitudes of each star $(m - M)$) is constant; therefore, star distances can be easily determined from the color-magnitude and H-R diagrams, as will now be explained. Superimpose the color-magnitude diagram on the H-R diagram so that the two color-index scales coincide. Then move the color-magnitude diagram vertically until its main sequence coincides with that of the H-R diagram. With the diagrams in this position, the absolute magnitude of the stars can be obtained; from the distance modulus, their distances can be determined.

12.10 ASSOCIATIONS

Since the turn of the century it has been known that O and early B stars occur in the Milky Way in stellar groups in which the stars are farther apart than those in

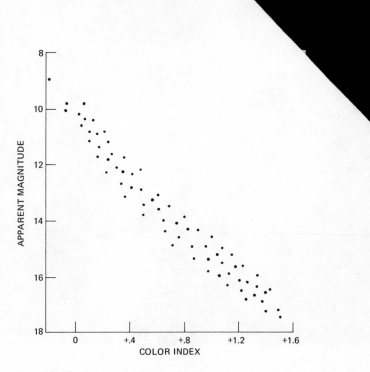

Fig. 12.12 Color-magnitude diagram of a hypothetical open cluster (similar to the Praesepe cluster)

galactic clusters. After studying the T-Tauri stars and later the O and early B stars in groupings in the Milky Way, the Soviet astronomer V. A. Ambartsumian in 1949 presented the first explanation of their nature. He observed that the shapes of the groupings are nearly spherical and that the stars are moving at great speeds away from the center of the grouping. Ambartsumian called these groupings "associations," because his study led him to believe that the stars in a grouping must have had a common origin, that is to say, they did not come together by chance but are associated. The stars are also extremely young, possibly still in the formative stage; otherwise, they would not appear in groupings. From further studies it has been concluded that the associations are temporary, because in time the stars would become so scattered that they would no longer appear in groupings. An excellent example of an association is the cluster of stars in the center of the great nebula in Orion.

Assoc

Fig. 12.13 The globular cluster NGC 6205 (Messier 13), in Hercules, photographed with the 200-inch telescope. (Photograph from the Hale Observatories)

12.11 GLOBULAR CLUSTERS

At present, there are about 120 known globular clusters in the Milky Way. They appear to be concentrated in the direction of the constellation Sagittarius, which marks the center of the galaxy, and form a spherical shell around the galactic center. In contrast to galactic clusters, globular clusters are larger, more compact, spheroidal in shape, more distant (the nearest is about 6000 parsecs), and contain thousands of stars that move at high velocities.

The few globular clusters visible to the unaided eye appear as faint, hazy spots of light. In the southern hemisphere, the two brightest, Omega Centauri and 47 Tuscanae are visible; in the northern hemisphere, the brightest and best known is M13 in the constellation of Hercules the Kneeler. A long-exposure photograph of M13 (Fig. 12.13) reveals it to be a most beautiful celestial object. Not even the largest telescopes can resolve the stars in the center of M13, which are at a distance of over 9000 parsecs. The appearance of this

great concentration of stars in the center of the cluster is misleading, because the star density is less than 1000 stars per cubic parsec of space.

12.12 CLUSTERS AS DIAGNOSTICS OF EVOLUTION

The H-R diagrams of star clusters are important in the study of both the composition of clusters and stellar evolution. The diagrams of most of the globular clusters are quite similar, whereas those of the galactic clusters vary considerably. The diagram of a typical globular cluster, M3 in our galaxy, (Fig. 12.14) shows that its stars have left the upper part of the main sequence, indicating that the very hot, highly luminous, and short-lived stars are not present in globular clusters. These stars have aged and have moved to other parts of the diagram, indicating various stages of evolution. Some might have evolved into supernovae and disappeared from the diagram.

The diagram shows that the following stars are present in a typical cluster: small, less luminous, cool

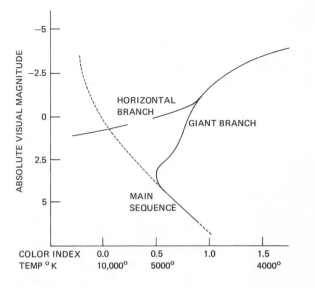

Fig. 12.14 The H-R diagram for the stars in M3 globular cluster

stars in the lower part of the main sequence whose lifespans are much longer than those in the upper part of the main sequence; large, red, luminous giants with absolute magnitudes up to − 3; and blue, hot stars on the horizontal branch that extends from the giant branch. The gap in the horizontal branch indicates the region of the RR Lyrae variable stars, which are also present in globular clusters.

REVIEW

1. What is the difference between an optical double binary?

2. What is a spectroscopic binary? Explain how we can tell from its spectrum that the object is a true physical binary. Why do some spectroscopic binaries show single spectra?

3. What is an astrometric binary? How can it be detected? Give a famous example of an astrometric binary.

4. What is an eclipsing binary? Draw the light curve of the eclipsing binary Algol and explain the physical characteristics of the two stars and the system which produce the curve.

5. Describe and explain how the different light curves of eclipsing binaries are produced.

6. How can the light curve of an eclipsing binary be used to determine the sizes of the two stars?

7. Explain how the stellar masses of a binary system are determined.

8. What is the mass-luminosity relation? Who discovered it? Does it hold true for all stars?

9. What are galactic clusters? Give several examples. Where in the Milky Way are they located? How are the stars in the cluster distinguished from those that are not?

10. Explain how the distance to a galactic cluster is determined.

11. What are stellar associations? Are they stable? Compare them with clusters.

12. What are globular clusters? Compare them with galactic clusters.

13. Explain why clusters are referred to as diagnostics of stellar evolution.

13
Variable Stars

There are many stars whose luminosities appear to vary considerably. We have already discussed binary stars—two stars that revolve around their barycenter under the influence of their mutual gravitational force. Binary stars are not true variables: their variation in brightness is caused extrinsically by the periodic eclipsing of one star by the other. On the other hand, the variation in brightness of intrinsic variable stars is caused by actual physical changes that occur within the stars. These are the true variables (Figs. 13.1, 13.2).

Two general types of intrinsic variable stars can be identified: pulsating variables and eruptive (explosive) variables. Most of the pulsating variables are giants, and a few are supergiants of spectral classes B to N. Some show irregular fluctuations in brightness, but most of them have a fairly regular rhythmic period which ranges from about one hour to three years. The pulsating variables include the Cepheid variables, RR Lyrae stars, red irregular variables, and flare stars.

The eruptive variables are stars which display sudden, unexpected outbursts of energy. In novae stars, the increase in brightness may be as much as 12 magnitudes, with a period of about two weeks. In supernovae stars, the increase is so enormous that the star is clearly visible in the daytime sky for a period of several months.

Variable stars are designated by one or two Roman letter combinations within each constellation. The first variable discovered in a constellation is assigned the letter R. Thus, the first star discovered in the constellation of Coronae Borealis is designated as R Coronae Borealis. Subsequent discoveries are assigned letters S, T, . . . ,Z; then two-letter combinations, RR, RS, . . . , RZ; SS, St, . . . ,SZ; and so on to ZZ; then AA, AB, . . . ,

Fig. 13.1 WW Cygni, eclipsing Algoltype variable star, photographed at maximum and minimum brightness. This is a double-exposure photograph with a slight displacement. The variable is seen in the center of the photograph. (Photograph from the Hale Observatories)

Fig. 13.2 A field of variable stars in the Andromeda Galaxy (NGC 224) with two variables marked. Photographed with the 200-inch telescope. (Photograph from the Hale Observatories)

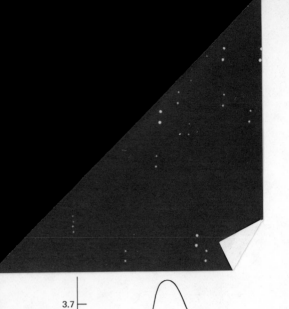

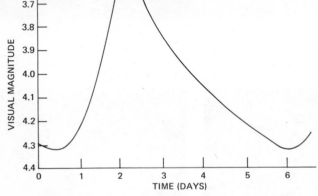

Fig. 13.3 The light curve of Delta Cephei, a typical Cepheid

AZ; BB, BC, . . . , BZ; and so on to QZ, with the letter J omitted. This system accommodates 334 variable stars in each constellation. With additional discoveries, the letter V, followed by Arabic numbers, is used, and the variable is designated V335,..., and so on. In Cygnus, for example, the 335th variable is designated as V335 Cygni.

13.1 CEPHEID VARIABLES

The prototype of the pulsating variables are the Cepheids, which derive their name from the star Delta Cephei, the first to be discovered. Nearly 600 Cepheids have been discovered in our galaxy, and all lie very close to the galactic plane within the layer of dust and gas. They are the yellow supergiants of spectral classes F or G at maximum brightness, with periodic light variations that range from 1 to 50 days (average period is about 6 days).

The light curve of Delta Cephei, a typical Cepheid, is smooth and asymmetrical (Fig. 13.3). It shows that the star brightens very rapidly from an apparent magnitude of 4.4 to 3.7, then fades at a slower rate back to 4.4. This light curve is typical for the Cepheids with periods up to about five days. Those with longer periods show a definite hump on the fading portion of the curve, which is probably caused by shock waves as the star pulsates. The average variation in brightness for the Cepheids is one magnitude. Polaris, the north star, is a Cepheid variable with a short period of four days and a variation in brightness of only 0.1 magnitude, which can be easily observed with binoculars.

A spectroscopic analysis of the light from a Cepheid variable shows that changes occur in the radial velocity of the star and in the spectral class with a variation in brightness. Figure 13.4 shows the relationship between the Cepheid's light curve, spectral class, radial velocity, and size. The variation in brightness is interpreted as a periodic rise and fall (pulsations) of the star's radiating surface evidenced by the Doppler shift in the spectrum. The radial velocity curve is a mirror-image of the light curve; for a typical Cepheid, its total range is about 24 miles (39km) per second.

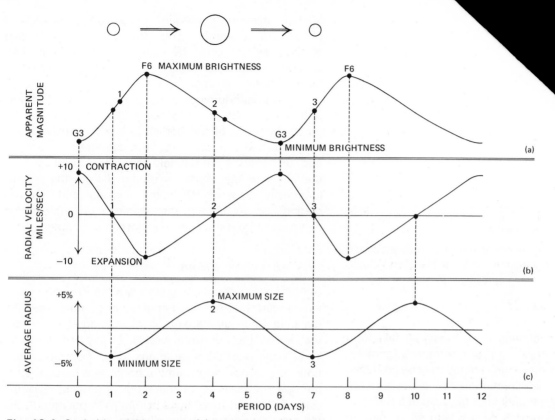

Fig. 13.4 Cepheid variable curves: (a) light curves; (b) radial velocity curve; (c) radius curve

When the star is in position 1 on the light curve, its radial velocity is zero (no Doppler displacement), and its size is minimum. As the star expands, its spectral lines shift to the violet, because the star's surface approaches the observer, and its size reaches a maximum (2) when the radial velocity becomes zero. During the expansion period, the total change in the star's radius from minimum to maximum is about 10% of the average radius of a typical Cepheid. As the star contracts, its spectral lines shift to the red, because the star's surface recedes from the observer, and its size reaches a minimum (3) when the radial velocity becomes zero again.

If a Cepheid reacted like a typical star, part of the energy released during the contraction period would radiate into space, and the rest would increase the kinetic energy of the star's atoms, resulting in increased luminosity, with maximum occurring when the star's size became minimum. However, the light curve of a Cepheid does not follow this pattern. Maximum luminosity occurs when the star is expanding at its maximum radial velocity and after it has reached its minimum size. Minimum luminosity occurs when the star is contracting at its maximum radial velocity and after it has reached its maximum size. A variation in the brightness of a

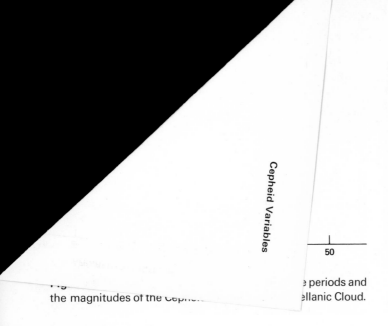

Cepheid Variables

50

Fig. ... periods and the magnitudes of the Cephe... ...ellanic Cloud.

Cepheid produces a change in the spectral class from G at minimum brightness to F at maximum brightness, thus indicating that maximum energy may be produced when the star's size is minimum, but its effect does not reach the star's surface until later because of a time lag. Since maximum brightness occurs with an increase in the wavelength of the light, it appears that as the star's brightness decreases at the shorter wavelengths, it continues to increase at the longer wavelengths.

13.2 THE PERIOD-LUMINOSITY RELATION

When Henrietta Leavitt of Harvard College Observatory plotted the periods of the Cepheids in the Small Magellanic Cloud against their apparent magnitudes in 1912, she discovered a significant relationship, as shown in Fig. 13.5. When the periods of the Cepheids increase, their apparent magnitudes also increase. Since a star's apparent magnitude depends on its absolute magnitude and distance, she assumed that the stars in the Cloud are at approximately the same distance from the earth, because the size of the Cloud in relation to its distance from the earth is relatively small; therefore, the dif-

ference between the absolute and apparent magnitudes of each star is constant. Thus, the apparent magnitudes of the Cepheids could be taken as a measure of their absolute magnitude, thereby establishing the period-luminosity relationship.

The period-luminosity relationship is most important, because it provides the tool for measuring the great distances of the bodies in the universe. This is accomplished by observing the apparent magnitude and the period of the Cepheid variable. With the period, the absolute magnitude is obtained from the period-luminosity diagram. When the apparent and absolute magnitudes are known, the Cepheid's distance can be determined from the inverse square law (Chapter 11.7).

13.3 RR LYRAE STARS

Another group of pulsating stars are the RR Lyrae stars, which were first observed in globular clusters. They are the blue-white giants with absolute magnitude of zero that lie on the horizontal branch of the H-R diagram. Their periods of light variations range from about one hour to one day. At maximum brightness most of them are spectral class A; at minimum brightness, spectral class F. The RR Lyrae stars belong to Population II, the old stars found in globular clusters around the galactic center and in the galactic plane. A few of them belong to Population I, young stars found in the galactic disk; however, they remain there for only a brief period in their lives. (Stellar populations are discussed in Chapter 14.3.)

Since the RR Lyrae stars are of about the same absolute magnitude and are present in clusters, the cluster's distance and the size and shape of the galaxy it is in can be determined. Unfortunately, the RR Lyrae stars are too faint to be detected, even in our nearest spiral galaxies; therefore, their use is restricted to our own galaxy and its immediate neighborhood.

The RR Lyrae stars have provided man with the means of expanding the universe's known limits. In 1952 Walter Baade, assuming that the distance scale was correct, determined that the Andromeda galaxy is about 750,000 light years from the sun and that its structure is similar to that of our own galaxy. He con-

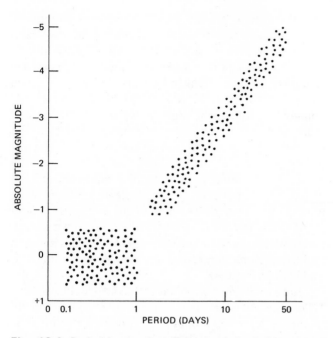

Fig. 13.6 Period-luminosity diagram of Cepheids and RR Lyrae stars, from which W. Baade concluded that the RR Lyrae stars are a continuation of the Cepheid variable stars

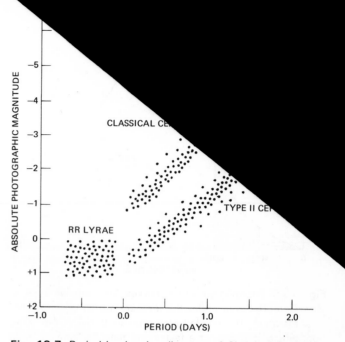

Fig. 13.7 Period-luminosity diagram of Classical Cepheids, Type II Cepheids, and RR Lyrae stars

cluded that if the RR Lyrae stars are a continuation of the Cepheid variables, they should therefore be detectable in the Andromeda galaxy at a distance of 750,000 light years (Fig. 13.6).

Baade was not able to find a single RR Lyrae star; however, he did observe that there are only red giants in the center of the Andromeda galaxy and mostly blue giants in its disk. This indicated two types of stars of different characteristics. He designated the blue giants as Population I and the red giants as Population II stars. He also observed that Population II stars located in the globular clusters around the center of the Andromeda galaxy have a period-luminosity relationship that is similar to the Classical Cepheids (whose prototype is the star Delta Cephei), but magnitudes about 1.5 lower. He concluded that the Classical Cepheids are 1.5 magnitudes brighter than what had been established by

Henrietta Leavitt; therefore, this increased the brightness of the original Cepheids and doubled the distance scale. The distance of the Andromeda galaxy was extended to over two million light years, which placed the RR Lyrae stars beyond the range of their visibility. The period-luminosity relationship for the Classical Cepheids (Population I), Type II Cepheids (Population II), and the RR Lyrae stars, based on Baade's work, is shown in Fig. 13.7.

13.4 RED VARIABLE STARS

After the RR Lyrae stars, the red variables are the most common variable stars in our galaxy. These red giants and supergiants are of two types—long-period variables (Mira-type), and irregular variables. Both types show variability in brightness and surface temperature.

... with a five-magnitude change in brightness, ...adiates 100 times more energy at maximum ...ness than at minimum. This large increase in radi- ...with only a 600° rise in temperature can be partially ...unted for and explained by the energy-distribution ...es for Mira at 2600°K and 2000°K (Fig. 13.8). The ...iation in visible light (represented by the shaded area ...der each curve) increases at a greater rate than the ...tal radiation; therefore, a considerably larger amount ...f light is visible at the higher temperature than at the ...ower. Also, during pulsations, the diameter of Mira increases by about 20%, which results in a 50% increase in its surface area. Since the increase in the visible light at the higher temperature and the increase in the surface area do not account for the increase of five magnitudes in brightness, something else, still not known, occurs to produce this increase.

Among the most irregular of the red variables are the R Coronae Borealis stars, which remain at maximum brightness for many months and sometimes years, then suddenly decrease their brightness by two to seven magnitudes. They remain at minimum brightness for a very brief period, then return slowly and erratically back to maximum brightness. The spectra of the R Coronae Borealis stars reveal that they are rich in carbon and are highly luminous.

The T Tauri stars also display erratic fluctuations. Many studies have been made which show that these stars are found in dust clouds and interstellar nebulosity, which suggests that they may be extremely young stars in the condensing stage of their development. It is believed that their erratic fluctuations result from their interaction with the nebulosity.

The flare stars are another type of erratic variable. They are generally main-sequence stars that display sudden outbursts of energy that last only minutes and often double the brightness of the star. It is believed that the flares represent localized outbursts of energy (small surface areas) from below the star's surface similar to the flares that occur on the sun's surface. The prototype of flare stars is UV Ceti. Its outbursts occur at about $1\frac{1}{2}$-day intervals, with increases in brightness of about two magnitudes. Other examples of flare stars are Krueger 60 and Proxima Centauri, the star nearest the earth.

The long-period variables have low densities, are of spectral classes M, R, N, or S, and have magnitudes that range from less than 2 to 7 and periods of 90 to 700 days. The prototype of the long-period variables is the remarkable red supergiant Mira Ceti, which is about 300 times larger than the sun. During an average period of 331 days, its visual magnitude changes from between 3 and 5 at maximum brightness to between 8 and 10 at minimum brightness, and its spectral class varies from M6 at maximum to M9 at minimum. Its surface temperature varies from 2600°K at maximum to 2000°K at minimum.

Stefan's law states that the total energy radiated by a unit area of a star's surface is proportional to the fourth power of the temperature (Chapter 3.8). Therefore, since the ratio of Mira's maximum and minimum surface temperatures (2600/2000) is 1.3, one square centimeter of its surface should radiate $(1.3)^4$, or nearly three times more energy at maximum brightness than at minimum.

(a)

(b)

Fig. 13.9 Nova Hercules 1934, showing a large increase in brightness in two months: (a) 10 March 1935; (b) 6 May 1935. (Lick Observatory photograph)

13.5 ERUPTIVE VARIABLE STARS

In 1572 Tycho Brahe observed a star that had never been seen before. By the following day, it had become as bright as Venus so that it was clearly visible in the day-time. This convinced him that it was a "nova stella" (new star). Today, we know that a nova is not a new star, but a faint, preexisting subdwarf, smaller and denser than the sun, which unexpectedly and abruptly increases its brightness 12 to 13 magnitudes (60,000 to 150,000) in less than two days. As it slowly returns to its prenova brightness, it experiences several irregular fluctuations. When these have disappeared, the nova appears to have returned to being a faint star.

It is now believed that a nova is an unstable star which at times generates more energy than its surface can radiate into space. The excess energy is ejected into space by an explosion which involves only the star's thin outer shell. When the outer shell has dissipated, the star appears in its prenova form. During the very brief period when the nova is increasing in brightness, its spectrum shows absorption lines greatly displaced toward the violet, indicating that the star's outer shell is moving rapidly outward and toward the observer. After maximum brightness has been attained, the outer shell is no longer opaque, so that the light from all parts of the shell is visible. The spectrum is most complex, the bright lines from the back side are shifted toward the red, the lines from the front are shifted toward the violet, and the lines from the sides are not displaced. Figure 13.9 shows Nova DQ Hercules 1934, a slow nova, which remained at maximum brightness for three months.

Most novae have been seen to erupt only once. The few that have been observed to erupt several times are called recurrent novae and are similar to novae except for their change in brightness, which is only about nine magnitudes. After each explosion, the nova appears to return to its former condition, except for a slight loss in its mass. A prominent recurrent nova is T Coronae Borealis, a faint, blue star in a binary system which

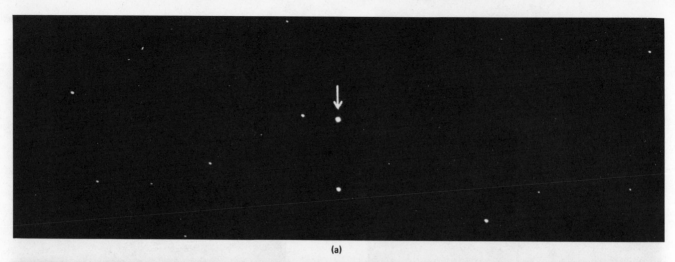

(a)

(b)

(c)

erupted once in 1866 and reached a brightness of magnitude 2, and erupted again in 1946 and reached a magnitude of 3. Prior to the 1946 outburst, its brightness was observed to vary slightly and erratically. At the present time, the star is showing similar activity.

Dwarf novae are stars that exhibit some of the basic characteristics of a nova star, but to a lesser degree. Their light curves show that the outbursts occur with a very rapid increase in brightness every few months, followed by a slower decline. During minimum brightness, many small but constant fluctuations have been observed. The range of brightness is about four magnitudes. Although their spectra are similar to those of the novae stars, they do not show the displacement of the bright lines at minimum brightness in the direction of the observer, which suggests that rather than being ejected into space, their outer shells expand and contract. Two well-known dwarf novae are SS Cygni and U Geminorium.

13.6 SUPERNOVAE STARS

The most spectacular eruptive variable star is the supernova. Cataclysmic explosions equal to at least one solar mass eject gaseous material into space at speeds above 3000 miles (4828 km) per second. Its brightness can increase millions of times and reach an absolute magnitude of -17 (Fig. 13.10).

Although more than 200 supernovae have been recorded in other galaxies, they are rare in our own galaxy. The average rate of their appearance is still being debated. According to F. Zwicky, one supernova appears in each galaxy about once every 300–400 years, a conservative estimate. However, since many are so remote, detection is impossible. J. S. Shklovsky's estimate is one every 45 years.

Fig. 13.10 A supernova in IC4182, a galaxy in Virgo photographed with the 100-inch telescope: (a) 23 August 1937, maximum brightness, 20-minute exposure; (b) 24 November 1938, faint, 45-minute exposure; (c) 19 January 1942, too faint to observe, 85-minute exposure. (Photograph from the Hale Observatories)

Three supernovae have been recorded in our galaxy. The first appeared in 1054 in the constellation of Taurus and was recorded by the Chinese and Japanese as a "guest star." It became several times brighter than Venus and was clearly visible in the daytime. The remnant of this supernova is visible today as an expanding nebulosity (Crab Nebula) in the constellation of Taurus. The second supernova was observed in 1572 by Brahe in the constellation of Cassiopeia. It was visible for nearly two years and at maximum was brighter than Venus. The third supernova was observed in 1604 by Kepler in the constellation of Ophiuchus.

Supernovae appear to fall into two definite groups: Type I and Type II. Type I supernovae become brighter by about two magnitudes and show a more rapid decline in brightness than do Type II supernovae. Their spectra show that hydrogen is prominent in Type II and rather weak in Type I. An interesting and prominent feature of their spectra is the extremely broad emission lines—an indication of the violent explosion that has occurred in the star. An analysis of these broad emission lines is most difficult, and only a few of them have been identified.

13.7 THE CRAB NEBULA

An excellent example of the remnant of a supernova is the "Crab Nebula" in Taurus, which consists of a homogeneous, shapeless, central mass surrounded by a complex network of fine filaments (Plate 19). Its central mass, which shows a continuous spectrum of strongly polarized light, and the radio emission of energy suggest synchrotron radiation, that is, radiation emitted by extremely high-velocity electrons revolving in a magnetic field. At the present time the nebula has a radius of about 180'', and its present rate of expansion is about 0''.21 per year. The outer parts of the nebula are moving away from the center at about 800 miles (1287 km) per second. The nebula is a strong source of both radio and x-ray emissions. The spectrum of the filaments shows emission lines of hydrogen, neutral and ionized helium, and other elements found in the spectra of planetary nebulae.

Fig. 13.11 "The Owl" nebula in Ursa Major, photographed with the 60-inch telescope. (Photograph from the Hale Observatories)

13.8 PLANETARY NEBULAE

Many stars eject material with no visible outbursts, in a less violent and more continuous manner than the novae and supernovae. These are extremely hot stars with extended atmospheric shells. The presence of the shell is revealed by the very broad emission lines, or bands, that are superimposed on a continuous spectrum. The continuous spectrum is produced by the central star, and the broad emission lines are believed to be produced by the gases in the semitransparent shell—the gases nearest the observer are approaching and show a Doppler shift toward the violet, whereas those on the opposite side are receding and show a Doppler shift toward the red. Examples of stars with extended atmospheric shells are the P Cygni, the Wolf-Rayet, and the planetary nebulae. The spectra of the P Cygni and Wolf-Rayet stars show lines of ionized nitrogen and silicon in various levels of ionization—their surface temperatures range up to 60,000°K. The large Doppler shifts in the spectral lines of the Wolf-Rayet stars indicate that the gases in the shells are moving out at speeds up to 2000 miles (3219 km) per second.

Planetary nebulae are stars with larger and more massive atmospheric shells. The name is derived from their resemblance to the telescopic disks of planets. Over 500 are known, and many of the faint ones were discovered by R. Minkowski. The studies of central stars of planetary nebulae indicate that they are small, dense, and extremely hot. Some have temperatures of nearly 200,000°K, which places them among the hottest stars known. The gas shells of planetary nebulae have diameters that range up to 200,000 astronomical units. Since the material in a shell is expanding at the average speed of 20 miles (32.19 km) per second, the gases would eventually become too tenuous for the shell to be visible. Excellent examples of planetary nebulae are "The Ring" in Lyra (Plate 20), Planetary Nebula in Aquarius (Plate 21), "The Owl" in Ursa Major (Fig. 13.11), and "The Dumbbell" in Vulpecula (Plate 22).

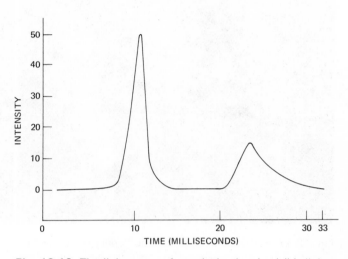

Fig. 13.12 The light curve of a typical pulsar in visible light. There is a double flash during each period.

13.9 PULSARS

A variable star emitting extremely short, stable pulses of radio radiation was discovered in 1967 by A. Hewish and J. Bell of the Mullard Radio Astronomy Observatory, Cambridge, England. Since then, nearly 50 of these stars, with periods that range from 30 milliseconds to about 3 seconds, have been discovered. These pulsating radio stars were named pulsars. The first pulsar was designated CP 1919—the CP stands for Cambridge Pulsar (named after the observatory where it was discovered), and 1919 is its position in right ascension (19 hours 19 minutes).

The light curve of a typical pulsar (Fig. 13.12) shows that during each period there is a double flash, with an interval between the flashes equal to about one-half of the period. Theoretically, these periodic radio pulsations are caused by the very rapid rotation of a body that is extremely small (about 10 miles or 16 km, in diameter), extremely dense, and with an unusually large

magnetic field, such as a white dwarf or a neutron star. As they rapidly rotate, these bodies generate radio waves and eject material into space. Therefore, the phenomenon of pulsars is believed to be associated with that of neutron stars (Chapter 15.11).

In 1968 D. H. Staelin and E. C. Reifenstein III at the National Radio Astronomy Observatory discovered Pulsar NP 0532 in the Crab Nebula with an extremely short period of 0.033 second. The extremely fast phenomenon suggests that the radio source might be a neutron star. If this is correct, the rotational rate of the pulsar should decrease gradually as it loses its energy into space and increases its period of pulsation. This situation was verified when several pulsars were observed with daily increasing periods. This has also provided the clue to the source of energy for the synchrotron radiation observed in the Crab Nebula.

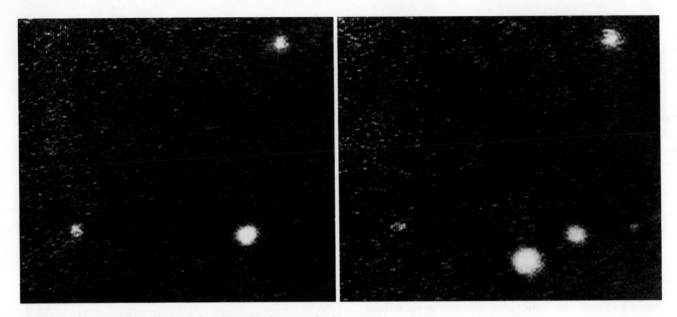

Fig. 13.13 Pulsar NP 0532 in the Crab Nebula, photographed with the 120-inch telescope with a special rotating disk. In the photograph on the left, the pulsar is almost invisible; in the photograph on the right, the pulsar is near maximum brightness. (Lick Observatory photograph)

In 1969 a tremendous breakthrough was achieved by a team of astronomers at the University of Arizona when they observed the pulsations of NP 0532 optically in ordinary light. They discovered that the light pulsations are exactly synchronous with the radio periodicity. Using a special rotating optical device, astronomers at Lick Observatory were able to photograph the optical variability (Fig. 13.13) showing that the pulsar is "on" in one picture and "off" in the other. The current consensus is that this pulsar is the first neutron star to be identified (Chapter 15.11). The remarkable, exciting pulsars may furnish us in the 1970s with many more surprises, which may help us to better understand the formation and evolution of stars and our Milky Way.

REVIEW

1. What is a variable star? Define the two main types of variable stars.

2. Describe the light curve of a Cepheid variable.

3. What is the relationship between the period and luminosity of a variable star? Who first established this relationship? Who revised this relationship and for what reasons?

4. How is the period-luminosity relation used to measure stellar distances?

5. What is the difference between an extrinsic and intrinsic variable? Give examples.

6. Explain what happens to the spectrum of a variable star as its brightness changes.

7. Explain how the light and velocity curves of a Cepheid variable show that it is not an eclipsing binary.

8. What are the properties of a RR Lyrae star? What part did they play in the modification of the period-luminosity relation? What change was made to the period-luminosity relation? What was its most important effect?

9. Describe the characteristics of irregular variable stars. Where are they usually found? How does the environment in which they are located explain their irregular variability?

10. What are flare stars?

11. What kind of a star may become a nova? What are dwarf novae? Give examples. What are recurrent novae? Give examples.

12. What are the differences between novae and supernovae?

13. What is the Crab Nebula?

14. What are planetary nebulae? What are the characteristics of the central star? Why were these nebulae named planetary? Give examples of planetary nebulae. Is there a relationship between planetary nebulae and novae?

15. Distinguish between pulsating stars and pulsars.

16. Describe the pulsar that was found in the Crab Nebula.

17. How far out have pulsars been found? Why are they believed to be rotating rapidly? Why are they considered to be extremely small objects?

14
Galaxies

14.1 THE MILKY WAY

When the constellation of Cygnus the Swan is directly overhead on a moonless summer evening in the northern midlatitudes, a diffusely glowing, narrow band of light appears that completely encircles the sky. This band of light is an immense assemblage of random star systems (our own solar system is a minor member) known as the Milky Way. The Milky Way passes from the northeastern horizon through Cassiopeia, Cepheus, and Cygnus, where it divides into two branches. The eastern branch, which is wider and brighter, moves through Aquila, Sagittarius, and Scorpius to the southwestern horizon. The western branch passes through Lyra, almost completely disappears in Ophiuchus, and reappears in Scorpius. The dark region between the two branches, called the Great Rift, is a dust and gas cloud that obscures the many stars that are located in this part of the sky. Since the earth is located within the Milky Way, no single complete picture of the Milky Way can be obtained. Figure 14.1 shows a mosaic of several photographs of the Milky Way between the constellations of Cassiopeia and Sagittarius.

When the constellation of Auriga the Charioteer is directly overhead on a winter evening in the northern midlatitudes, the Milky Way passes from the northwestern horizon through Cepheus, Cassiopeia, Auriga, Taurus, Gemini, Orion, and Canis Major, to the southeastern horizon. In winter the Milky Way appears narrower, dimmer, and less spectacular than it does in summer. In the southern hemisphere in winter, the Milky Way, with its brilliant star clouds in Norma and Carina, presents a most impressive sight. The Milky Way passes through the constellations of Sagittarius, Scorpius, Centaurus, and Crux (Southern Cross).

Fig. 14.1 Mosaic of the Milky Way from Sagittarius to Cassiopeia. (Photograph from the Hale Observatories)

In 1785 William Herschel extended our knowledge of the Milky Way when he observed with his telescope that the star count in the center of the hazy band of light is greater than at its edges. He observed that toward the center of the Milky Way, where the star count is the greatest, the stars are at great distances, because many of them are very faint and appear to the unaided eye as hazy spots of light. In the direction away from the Milky Way, where the star count is the least, the stars are nearer. He concluded that the Milky Way is elliptically shaped and that our sun is in the center of the system. In 1917 this concept was changed when Harlow Shapley's research showed that the globular clusters form a spheroidal system with the sun at a distance of about 30,000 light years from the center.

14.2 THE STRUCTURE OF THE MILKY WAY

Observations with optical and radio telescopes reveal that the Milky Way is a flat, disk-shaped system of about 100 billion stars with a spheroidal central region (Fig. 14.2). The diameter of the disk is about 100,000 light years, and its central region is about 10,000 light years. Unfortunately, the central region of the Milky Way is not visible optically because of the presence of great clouds of interstellar gas and dust; however, radio observations of the region show evidences of the presence of a small, bright nucleus where the stars are more closely packed than those in the spirals. Around this nucleus is a halo of globular clusters.

In 1951 W. W. Morgan and his associates at Yerkes Observatory determined from photographs the positions and distances of emission nebulae (luminous gas clouds) in the Milky Way. By plotting these distances, they obtained the first evidence that the Milky Way is a galaxy with spiral arms. Figure 14.3 shows the results of their work.

Three main spiral arms were plotted: the inner arm at a distance of about 18,000 light years from the center of the galaxy; the middle arm at about 27,000 light

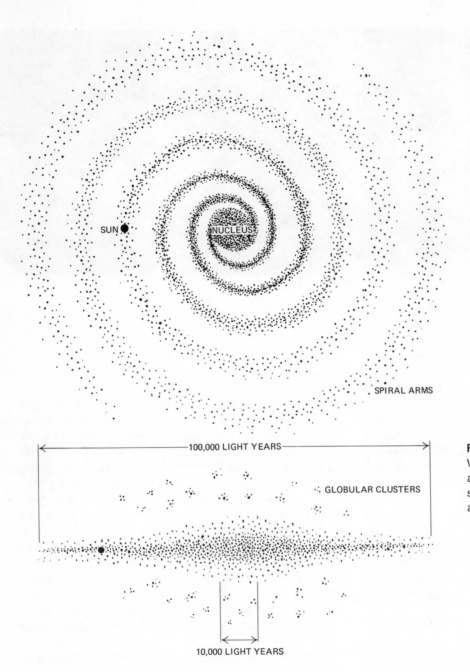

SUN

NUCLEUS

SPIRAL ARMS

100,000 LIGHT YEARS

GLOBULAR CLUSTERS

10,000 LIGHT YEARS

Fig. 14.2 The structure of the Milky Way. Schematic model developed from an analysis of radio signals. Edge-on view shows spirals to be rather thin. Spiral arms in top view appear almost circular.

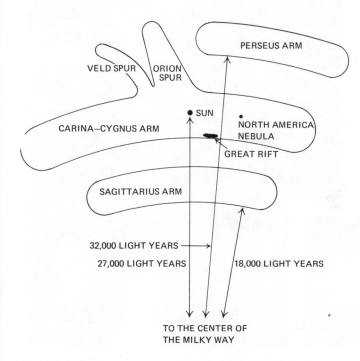

PERSEUS ARM

VELD SPUR ORION
SPUR

● SUN

NORTH AMERICA
NEBULA

CARINA–CYGNUS ARM

GREAT RIFT

SAGITTARIUS ARM

32,000 LIGHT YEARS ⟶

27,000 LIGHT YEARS

18,000 LIGHT YEARS

TO THE CENTER OF
THE MILKY WAY

Fig. 14.3 Optical view of the structure of the spiral arms near the sun, as developed by W.W. Morgan of Yerkes Observatory.

The Milky Way provides a new system of coordinates for the orientation of the celestial bodies. The reference line in this system of orientation is the galactic plane, which lies approximately on the center-line of the Milky Way. The great circle formed by the galactic plane, which divides the Milky Way into two equal parts, is called the galactic equator. It is inclined to the celestial equator and to the earth's equator by about 63°. The north galactic pole lies in the constellation of Coma Berenices, and the south galactic pole is in the constellation of Sculptor. The reference point used in the measurement of galactic longitude is the point on the galactic equator in the direction of the constellation of Sagittarius, which is the densest part of the Milky Way. Longitude is measured in a counterclockwise direction, as seen from the north galactic pole, through 360°. The galactic latitude is measured north or south from the galactic equator to 90°.

14.3 STELLAR POPULATIONS

Throughout the entire Milky Way—in the spiral arms, nucleus, and halo—are found such objects as Type II Cepheid variables, RR Lyrae variables, red irregular variables of the Mira type, novae, planetary nebulae, and main-sequence stars of low luminosity. Such objects as Type I Cepheid variables, open clusters, main-sequence stars of high luminosity, and supergiants are found only in the spiral arms of the galaxy. The globular clusters are found primarily in the nucleus and the halo of the galaxy.

Although the composition of nearly all the stars appears to be hydrogen and helium, an analysis of the spectra of stars reveals a difference in the amounts of heavier elements that are present. The strength of the spectral lines of the heavy elements in the sun, in the stars near the sun, and in the stars in the galactic clusters shows that the maximum abundance of the heavier elements is at about 4% of the total stellar mass, whereas it is only 0.1% in the stars in the globular clusters.

years; and the outer arm at about 32,000 light years. In the outer arm is the double cluster in Perseus. In the middle arm are the sun (appears to lie close to the inner edge), the North American Nebula, Coal Sack, and the Great Rift. One end of the middle arm extends in the direction of the constellation Carina, and the other end extends toward the constellation Cygnus. This arm has two spurs, the Orion and the Vela. Since the inner arm (in which lies Sagittarius) is not easily seen in the northern hemisphere, B. J. Bok and his associates observed and studied it from the southern hemisphere.

Fig. 14.4 Stellar Populations I and II. Left: a section of the spiral arms of the Andromeda Nebula photographed in blue light shows giant and supergiant stars of Population I. The hazy patch at the upper left consists of unresolved Population II stars. Right: NGC 205, the companion of the Andromeda Nebula, photographed in yellow light, shows stars of Population II. The brightest stars are red and 100 times fainter than the Population I blue giants. The very bright, uniformly distributed stars in both pictures are in the foreground and belong in our Milky Way system. (Photograph from the Hale Observatories)

This difference in the chemical composition of stars was explained by W. Baade in 1944 as representing two types of stellar populations, each having different characteristics and existing in different parts of the Milky Way. He classified the stars into Population I and Population II (Fig. 14.4). Population I stars lie near the galactic plane (where most of the interstellar matter is located) and in the spiral arms of the galaxy. A few of them also lie in the galaxy's center. They are the young stars that are rich in the metallic elements and have low velocities. Population I stars include the main-sequence stars of spectral classes A to M and the blue giants and

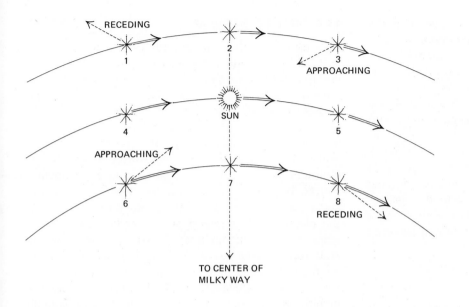

Fig. 14.5 Stars in the sun's neighborhood. Stars closest to the center of the Milky Way have greater velocities than those farther out. The rotation of the galaxy produces differential velocities in the stars.

supergiants found in the galactic clusters. Population II stars are found in globular clusters around the nucleus of the Milky Way and in the halo. They are the older stars that are weak in the metallic elements and move at high velocities in eccentric, highly inclined orbits.

14.4 GALACTIC MOTIONS

Statistical studies of the radial velocities and proper motions of the stars in the neighborhood of the sun reveal that the sun and the solar system are moving in the direction of the constellation Hercules at about 12 miles (19 km) per second. The direction toward which the sun is traveling in space is called the apex of the sun's motion (right ascension 18 hours, declination +30°), and the opposite direction from which the sun is moving is called the antapex. The stars appear to be moving toward the antapex and away from the apex. This is similar to the way a long, straight highway appears to converge in the direction in which one is traveling and to diverge in the opposite direction.

Although the galaxy is rotating, it does not rotate as does a wheel. Stars closer to the center of the galaxy rotate faster than those farther away. If this were not so, the galaxy would eventually collapse under the gravitational attraction of its parts. The sun and the stars in its neighborhood are moving in almost circular, parallel paths around the galaxy's center at a speed of about 150 miles (241 km) per second. Thus, they complete one revolution once every 200 million years. These stars are called low-velocity stars because their space velocities are about 12 miles (19 km) per second, and their nearly circular orbits lie close to the galactic plane. The few stars that move in very eccentric orbits which are highly inclined to the sun's orbital path are called high-velocity stars because their space velocities are greater than 40 miles (64 km) per second. As shown in Fig. 14.5, the stars in the neighborhood of the sun are moving in circular paths around the galaxy's center. The stars closest to the center are moving faster than those farther away. This differential rotational velocity of the galaxy affects the radial velocities of the stars. Stars that are moving at about the same speed as the sun and in the same direction, such as stars 4 and 5, show no radial motion. Stars that are on the radial line with the sun and the galaxy's center, such as stars 2 and 7, have no motion away from or toward the sun and therefore show no radial motion. Star 8, with the faster speed, and star 1, with its slower speed, are both increasing their distance from the sun; therefore, they show radial velocities. Star 6, with the fastest speed, and star 3, with its slower speed, are both decreasing their distance from the sun; they also show radial velocities.

If we assume that most of the mass of the galaxy is concentrated in the center of the galaxy and that the sun revolves around it, the galaxy's mass can be determined by substituting the sun's distance from the galaxy's center (30,000 light years) and its orbital period around it (200 million years) in Kepler's third law of planetary motion as modified by Newton:

$$(M_{galaxy} + m_{sun})(P_{sun})^2 = K(a_{sun})^3.$$

Although this method is one of oversimplification, it produces a fairly good approximation of the galaxy's mass of about 200 billion times that of the sun. When more precise values are used for the sun's motion, the galaxy's mass is about 150 billion times that of the sun.

14.5 INTERSTELLAR MATTER

In addition to the stars, which occupy a very small fraction of its total volume, the Milky Way contains large quantities of gas and dust particles (very fine, solid matter). This interstellar matter is concentrated in enormous clouds (diffuse nebulae) whose diameters range up to several parsecs. These clouds are located in the spiral arms of the Milky Way and have an average density of one atom of gas per cubic centimeter and 100 particles of dust per cubic mile of space. When the diffuse nebulae become luminous because of the presence of stars within or near the nebulae, they are called bright nebulae. When the gas and dust particles are so dense that the clouds appear dark, they are called a dark nebula. Most of the gases in the nebulae, which are cold and nonluminous, become visible by the process of emission and reflection. The solid particles become visible by increased density, general obscuration, reddening, reflection, and polarization of starlight.

14.6 DIFFUSE NEBULAE

On a clear, very dark evening, the Great Nebula in Orion is visible to the unaided eye as a very faint haze around the middle star in Orion's sword. Telescopically, this diffuse nebulae is one of the most beautiful of celestial bodies (Plate 23). It is a mass of interstellar gases which become luminous by the excitation of groups of extremely hot, luminous O- and BO-type stars imbedded in the nebula. This is an excellent example of a bright-emission nebula. The hydrogen gas in the nebula is ionized by the ultraviolet radiation from the hot stars, and light is emitted when the protons recombine with the electrons. This region of interstellar space around stars, which contains ionized hydrogen, is called the H II region, whereas the one which contains neutral hydrogen is called the H I region.

The Orion emission nebula, at a distance of approximately 500 parsecs, has a diameter of about 30 light years. The central region appears bluish green because the photograph has been overexposed to reveal the faint outer details. The blue light is caused by ionized oxygen, and the red light is caused by hydrogen. Other excellent examples of diffuse emission nebulae are the Lagoon Nebula in Sagittarius (Plate 24)[1] and the North America Nebula in Cygnus.

The collision of hydrogen atoms can also produce luminescence in a nebula if their speeds and impacts are tremendous. The Veil Nebula in Cygnus is an excellent example of such a nebula (Plate 25). Not a single hot, luminous star has been found near the nebula to account for its luminosity. The nebula is expanding at the rate of about 0".03 per year, and the luminosity occurs when the expanding filaments of gas collide with the low-density gas of the interstellar medium.

When a star near a nebula is cooler than type BI, the dust particles in the cloud scatter the starlight, and the nebula becomes visible. This is called a reflection nebula. Although emission nebulae also reflect starlight, the amount of light reflected in comparison to the amount emitted is negligible. The nebulosities around

---

[1] Plates 24–31 appear following p. 256.

the important stars of the Pleiades are excellent examples of reflection nebulae (Plate 26).

A cloud of interstellar matter that is too far away from a bright star to emit or reflect light is called a dark nebula. Some are so dense that they are clearly visible as dark objects obscuring many of the stars, whereas others are detected by their dimming of the stars in the background. The average dark nebula is irregular in shape and is less than 10 parsecs in diameter. An excellent example of a dark nebula is the "Horsehead" in Orion (Plate 27). The dark cloud at the left obscures the emission nebula which is in the background. Only a few of the bright stars are visible through the dark nebula. The outline of the horse head is simply an extension of the dark nebula. Other examples of dark nebulae are the Great Rift, which runs lengthwise in the Milky Way, dividing it into two parts, and the Coal Sack in both the Northern Cross and the Southern Cross. The smallest of the dark nebulae are the "globules," about 10,000 astronomical units in diameter, that are found in several nebulae such as the Lagoon. They are believed to be stars in the formative stage.

14.7 GENERAL OBSCURATION

In addition to being concentrated in the dark nebulae, the dust particles are more or less uniformly distributed throughout the spiral arms of galaxies, where their presence causes the stars to appear dimmer and more distant than they actually are. Another evidence of general obscuration is the apparent distribution of galaxies in space. This effect is similar to the dimming of starlight when the star is observed near the horizon. The dimming is proportional to the distance through which the light passes. E. P. Hubble at Mount Wilson Observatory discovered that it is almost impossible to observe galaxies in the plane of the Milky Way. The number of observable galaxies increases as the distance increases from the plane of the Milky Way. Hubble called the region in the plane of the Milky Way the "zone of avoidance." Today, we know that galaxies are difficult to detect in the zone of avoidance because of the increase in the concentration of the dust and gas particles and because of the increase in the absorption of light.

14.8 INTERSTELLAR REDDENING

The degree of interstellar obscuration depends on the wavelength of the light emitted by the body. The shorter wavelengths of visible light (blue, violet) are obscured more effectively than the longer wavelengths (yellow, red). This means that more of the shorter wavelengths have been absorbed by the interstellar material from a beam of visible light, so that the starlight appears to be redder. The reddening effect is present when the spectrum of a visibly dim, red, cool star of spectral class K shows it to be in actuality a bright, hot, blue star of spectral class B.

Interstellar reddening provides a simple, effective method for estimating the degree of starlight obscuration. The obscuration of visible light is inversely proportional to its wavelength. This means that since the wavelength of visible light varies from about 4000 to 8000 angstroms, the interstellar dust obscures starlight of 4000 Å wavelength twice as effectively as starlight of 8000 Å wavelength.

14.9 INTERSTELLAR REFLECTION

The nebulosity of the bright stars in the Pleiades, an excellent example of a reflection nebula, is produced by the dust particles in the nebula reflecting the starlight. Even though interstellar dust has a very high albedo, that is, 75% of the light that falls on its surface is reflected, a very bright star is required to illuminate the nebula sufficiently for it to be visible. Therefore, most of the reflection nebulae appear blue. If they appear red, it is due to interstellar absorption and the reddening of the starlight.

14.10 INTERSTELLAR POLARIZATION

Light consists of many electromagnetic waves, each vibrating in its own plane perpendicular to the direction of propagation. Generally, the waves vibrate in all planes, and the light is called unpolarized. Under certain conditions, the waves are aligned and vibrate in only one plane, producing polarized light. When polarized light strikes a Polaroid filter (this type of filter transmits light in only one plane) which is oriented so that the plane of vibration coincides with the plane of polarization, the light will pass through the filter. If the filter is rotated, less light will pass through. When the filter is oriented at right angles to the plane of vibration, no light will pass through the filter. This provides the means for determining the degree of polarization of starlight.

Starlight is polarized by interstellar matter. In this process the gas particles are more effective than the dust particles. Polarization has been verified in a number of ways. It is not present in the light from stars that are near and unobscured, whereas it is present at varying degrees from stars that are more distant and whose light has been affected by interstellar absorption and reddening. Also, the stars that are observed through the same cloud display about the same degree of polarization and in the same direction. These observations indicate that polarization is produced by the interstellar matter rather than by the stars themselves. It has also been observed that the light from stars near the plane of the Milky Way is polarized parallel to the galactic plane. The fact that the interstellar matter polarizes starlight indicates that the interstellar particles must be elongated, that is, needle-shaped. Also, the alignment parallel to the galactic plane suggests the presence of a magnetic field parallel to the galactic plane that aligns the needle-shaped particles uniformly.

14.11 COSMIC RAYS

At the turn of this century, most astronomers believed that the ions present in the atmosphere resulted from the radiation emitted by the radioactive substances found on the earth. If this were true, the ionization would decrease with an increase in altitude. In 1912 the Austrian physicist Victor Hess conducted balloon-borne experiments and found that ionization increases with altitude, which showed that the radiation producing the ionization, named cosmic rays, comes from outer space. When these rays are traveling in space, they are referred to as primary cosmic rays; when they enter the earth's atmosphere, they are referred to as secondary cosmic rays.

Primary cosmic rays are principally protons (hydrogen nuclei); there are also a few helium nuclei (alpha particles), and still fewer nuclei of the heavier elements such as carbon, iron, and nitrogen. They possess tremendous amounts of energy and move at almost the speed of light. It has been estimated that more than one billion billion primary cosmic rays bombard the earth's upper atmosphere every second. The cosmic rays with lower energies are deflected by the earth's magnetic field toward the poles and to the higher latitudes. The rays with greater energies and higher speeds strike the earth's entire surface; some are trapped by the earth's magnetic field in the Van Allen radiation belts.

When the primary cosmic rays enter the earth's atmosphere, they collide with the air molecules of nitrogen and oxygen and produce secondary cosmic rays which shower the earth's surface. The important secondary rays are protons, neutrons, mesons, electrons, and gamma rays. The mesons that reach sea level, called mu mesons, are very unstable, may be either positively or negatively charged, and have a mass that is greater than an electron's. When a mu meson decays, it forms either a positron or an electron and converts its excess mass into a neutrino, which is a particle of energy with no mass.

The origin of the cosmic rays is still controversial. The sun does not appear to be the primary source for cosmic rays, because investigations have revealed that the total cosmic radiation received by the earth is increased only slightly even after great outbursts of solar flares. Neither is an extragalactic origin considered to be a primary source, because of the great distances that are involved. The source would have to be tremendous to account for the cosmic radiation received by the earth. Most astronomers now believe that the primary source of the cosmic rays is from the supernovae in the Milky Way. Even though these stars are not a common occurrence, it is believed that the materials they eject at great velocities into space might have been stored in the galaxy.

14.12 GALAXIES

The few, faint, luminous patches of light located in the sky away from the Milky Way that were observed before the invention of the telescope were believed to be inter-

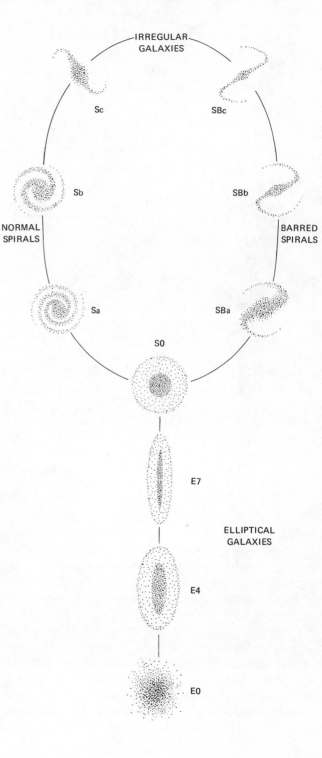

Fig. 14.6 Hubble's famous "tuning fork" diagram for classifying galaxies according to their appearance

stellar clouds (nebulae) within the Milky Way. With the introduction of the telescope, more of these supposed nebulae were discovered, and by 1781 they had been catalogued by the French astronomer Charles Messier. His famous list of nebulae made no distinction between actual nebulae, star clusters, and galaxies. For example, the Andromeda galaxy was listed as the Andromeda nebula. There were a few men who disagreed with Messier's catalogue. The German philosopher Immanuel Kant and the English astronomer William Herschel, for example, speculated that these nebulae were actually star systems like our own Milky Way, that is, "island universes."

The breakthrough occurred in 1924, when Edwin Hubble at Mount Wilson Observatory identified Cepheid variables in the Andromeda nebula. By measuring their apparent brightnesses, their periods of light fluctuations, and by using the period-luminosity relation, the present, corrected value for the distance to the Andromeda nebula was established as slightly over two billion light years. Their discovery established the "nebulae" as individual galaxies far beyond the limits of the Milky Way.

In 1926 Edwin Hubble classified the galaxies according to their apparent rather than actual shapes: elliptical, spiral, and irregular, which he presented in his famous "tuning fork" diagram (Fig. 14.6).

Fig. 14.8 Elliptical galaxy NGC 205, E5 type, a satellite of the Great Galaxy in Andromeda. Taken in red light with the 200-inch telescope. (Photograph from the Hale Observatories)

Fig. 14.7 The NGC 4486 (Messier 87) Galaxy in the Virgo cluster, a source of radio radiation, photographed with the 200-inch telescope. (Photograph from the Hale Observatories)

14.13 ELLIPTICAL GALAXIES

The apparent forms of elliptical galaxies range from spheres to ellipsoids whose lengths are about three times longer than their widths. The elliptical galaxies are designated by the letter E, followed by a number which indicates the galaxy's degree of ellipticity. There are eight classes that range from the spherical (EO, Fig. 14.7) to the elliptical (E7, Fig. 14.8). They all have bright centers, with luminosities that gradually diminish toward the edges. Generally free of dust, these stars are members of Population II.

14.14 SPIRAL GALAXIES

About three-fourths of the bright galaxies are spirals. Generally, they consist of a bright nucleus and two spiral arms that extend from opposite ends of the nucleus and wind around it. They are classified as normal spirals (S) and barred spirals (SB), according to the shape of their nuclei. The normal spirals have nuclei that are either spherical or elliptical, whereas those of the barred spirals are bar-shaped. The spirals are further divided into three classes (a, b, and c) according to the size of their nuclei and the tightness with which their spiral arms are wound around the nuclei. The (a) designation indicates the largest nucleus, with thin spiral arms that are wound the tightest around the nucleus; the (c) designation indicates the smallest nucleus, with wide spiral arms that are wound the loosest around the nucleus. Examples of each type are shown in Fig. 14.9.

Fig. 14.9 Classification of galaxies: (a) normal galaxies; (b) barred galaxies. (Photograph from the Hale Observatory) ▶

Plate 28 (preceding page) The Andromeda Galaxy. This great, spiral galaxy, about two million light-years away, is the nearest to the Milky Way. Two elliptical satellite galaxies, NGC 205 and NGC 221, are visible near the Andromeda Galaxy; one is below it, and the other is above and to the right of it. Photographed with the 48-inch Schmidt telescope. (Photograph from the Hale Observatories)

Plate 29 (above) Irregular Galaxy in Ursa Major, NGC 3034, Messier 82. This type of galaxy appears to lack symmetry, contain large amounts of interstellar dust, and stars (if present) too faint to be resolved. (Photograph from the Hale Observatories)

Plate 30 (right) The Trifid Nebula in Sagittarius appears to be divided into three parts by interstellar dust. The nebula contains very small dark spots (globules) which are believed to be stars in the formative stage. (Photograph from the Hale Observatories)

Plate 31 (overleaf) The Rosette Nebula in Monoceros, NGC 2237. (Photograph from the Hale Observatories)

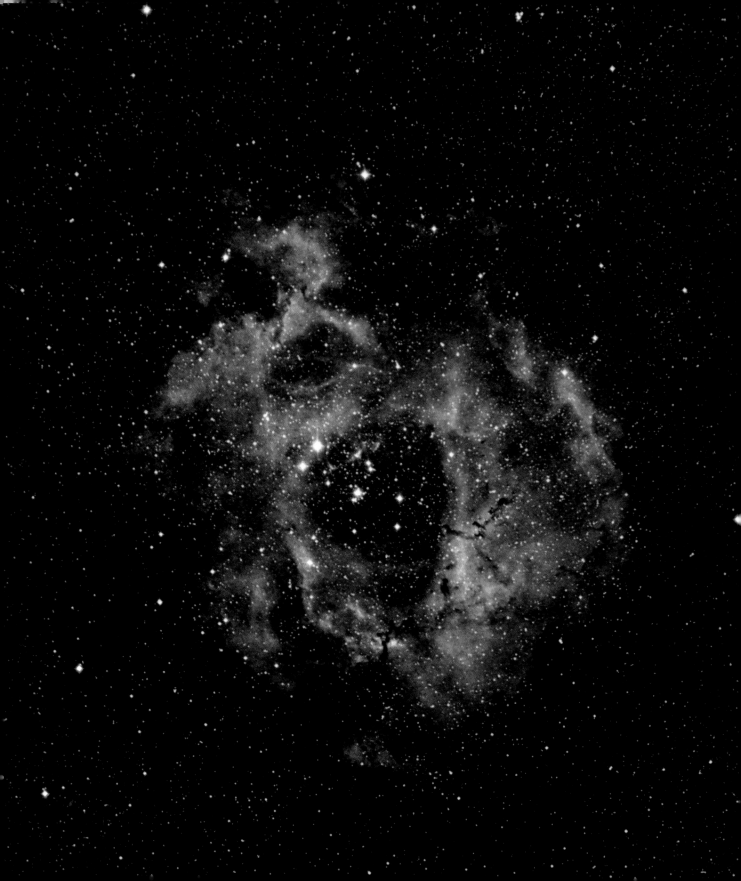

NGC 1201   TYPE S0

NGC 2811   TYPE Sa

NGC 488   TYPE Sab

NGC 2841   TYPE Sb

NGC 3031   M81   TYPE Sb

NGC 628   M74   TYPE Sc

(a)

NGC 2859   TYPE SB0

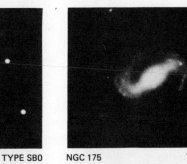

NGC 175   TYPE SBab(s)

NGC 1300   TYPE SBb(s)

NGC 2523   TYPE SBb(r)

NGC 1073   TYPE SBc(sr)

NGC 2525   TYPE SBc(s)

(b)

257

Population I-type stars are in the spiral arms of the Sb and Sc galaxies. They are the blue giants and supergiants of spectral classes O and B. No star has been resolved in the spiral arms of Sa galaxies. Population II-type stars are in the nuclei and in the globular clusters in the halo.

The Andromeda galaxy, at a distance of over two million light years, is probably the best known and most famous of all the spiral galaxies. It was observed by the ancient astronomers and as early as A.D. 964 was recorded as another "fixed star" by the Persian stargazer Al Sufi. Andromeda is clearly visible to the unaided eye as a small, elongated nebulosity of fourth magnitude located to the west of the Andromeda constellation. When it is seen through binoculars, this galaxy appears as a small disk, smaller than the moon; when seen through a telescope (Plate 28), it appears as a great elliptical object with several spiral arms. Studies reveal that it is larger and more massive than the Milky Way, with spiral arms that appear to be tightly wound. It is interesting to note that to an observer in the Andromeda galaxy, the Milky Way would appear like the Andromeda galaxy appears from the earth.

14.15 IRREGULAR GALAXIES

The irregular galaxies, which are few in number, display no symmetry of form. The stars are distributed around a central cloud whose form is most chaotic. The Large and Small Magellanic Clouds, typical irregular galaxies, contain luminous stars of spectral class O and B (Population I stars), globular clusters, and RR Lyrae stars (Population II stars). The Large Magellanic Cloud, located in the constellation of Dorado, appears as a detached portion of the Milky Way (Fig. 14.10). Its actual diameter is about 30 light years, but at an estimated distance from the earth of 160,000 light years, its apparent diameter is about 12°. Although it is classified as irregular, it shows a central bar which consists of stars surrounded by large, irregular clusters of bright stars. The cloud also contains interstellar matter. The Small Magellanic Cloud, located in the constellation of Tuscana, is about 180,000 light years away and has an actual diameter of about 25 light years. Although it contains gas particles, it appears to lack dust particles.

Another type of irregular galaxy recognized by Hubble is M82 (Plate 29). In this type, no star or star cluster is visible in the cloud. However, it is believed that stars do exist, but that they are too faint to be resolved. The large amounts of interstellar material displayed by M82 and its high red shift suggest that a cataclysmic explosion might have occurred.

The S0-type galaxy was later introduced in the "tuning-fork" diagram at the point where the elliptical spirals end and the two branches of the normal and barred spirals begin. Hubble described the new type as lenticulars, that is, disk-shaped spirals with a nucleus and without spiral arms. At present, they are regarded as old, elliptical galaxies that are located in rich clusters.

14.16 EVOLUTION OF GALAXIES

Hubble's "tuning-fork" diagram has the galaxies arranged in a sequence from elliptical systems with predominantly old stars, through spiral systems, to irregular systems with predominantly young stars. The sequence simply serves as a means of identifying the general types of galaxies as to their apparent appearance and does not indicate the general evolution of the galaxies. However, some astronomers have speculated from this sequence that galaxies start as elliptical spirals that are almost spherical in shape. Then, as their rotational velocities increase, they become more elliptical and eventually develop into irregular spirals. Others have speculated that the evolution occurs in the reverse direc-

Fig. 14.10 The Large Magellanic Cloud, a satellite of our Milky Way. Its brightness is equivalent to a star of zero magnitude (visual). (Lick Observatory photograph)

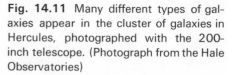

Fig. 14.11 Many different types of galaxies appear in the cluster of galaxies in Hercules, photographed with the 200-inch telescope. (Photograph from the Hale Observatories)

tion, that is, they start as irregular galaxies of young stars and eventually evolve into elliptical galaxies of old stars. Yet others believe that galaxies do not evolve from one type to another. They reason that since galactic forms are determined primarily by their masses and angular momentum, a galaxy's present form is basically its original form.

14.17 DISTRIBUTION OF GALAXIES

The photographic survey conducted by Hubble at Mount Wilson Observatory shows that the galaxies do not appear to be uniformly distributed on the celestial sphere. The greatest number are found at the galactic pole regions. They decrease with latitude and become almost nonexistent at the galactic equatorial regions. This is due to the fact that the tremendous amounts of interstellar material in the galactic plane obscure any object that might be there.

The galaxies appear to group, or cluster, in certain regions of the sky. Figure 14.11 shows a part of the clusters of many different types of galaxies in the constellation of Hercules. The Milky Way is a member of a group which contains 17 galaxies (Table 14.1). This cluster, known as the Local Group, occupies an ellipsoidal region in space, with the two main galaxies, Milky Way and Andromeda, located near the ends of its major axis. The plot of the Local Group is shown in Fig. 14.12.

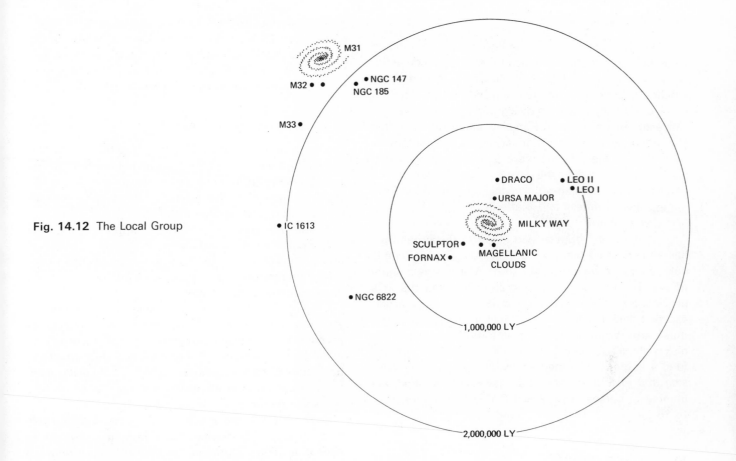

Fig. 14.12 The Local Group

Table 14.1 The Local Group

Galaxy	Type	Distance (light years)	Linear diameter (light years)
Milky Way	Sb		100,000
Large Magellanic Cloud	Irr.	160,000	30,000
Small Magellanic Cloud	Irr.	180,000	25,000
Ursa Minor (dwarf)	E3	220,000	3,000
Sculptor (dwarf)	E3	270,000	7,000
Draco (dwarf)	E2	330,000	4,500
Fornax (dwarf)	E3	800,000	15,000
Leo II (dwarf)	E0	750,000	5,000
Leo I (dwarf)	E4	900,000	5,000
NGC 6822	Irr.	1,500,000	9,000

Galaxy	Type	Distance (light years)	Linear diameter (light years)
Andromeda Galaxy (M31)	Sb	2,200,000	130,000
NGC 205	E5	2,200,000	16,000
NGC 221 (M32)	E3	2,200,000	8,000
NGC 147	E6	1,900,000	10,000
NGC 185	E2	1,900,000	8,000
NGC 598 (M33)	Sc	2,300,000	60,000
IC 1613	Irr.	2,200,000	16,000

14.18 MAFFEI

In 1968 the Italian astronomer Paolo Maffei noted two faint, blurred, elliptical patches between the constellations of Perseus and Cassiopeia. The fact that these patches appeared on infrared film but not on standard film led to an investigation by a group of scientists at the University of California at Berkeley and at the California Institute of Technology. In January 1971 they tentatively decided that the patches were probably two vast galaxies located almost on the galactic equator at a distance of about three million light years from the sun. They named them Maffei I and Maffei II after the man who first viewed them.

Maffei I, the brighter and larger of these galaxies, has an estimated diameter of 75,000 light years and is believed to be an elliptical galaxy; Maffei II is a spiral galaxy. The two objects are so close together that it is possible that their edges may overlap. These objects had escaped detection because of their location. Their light must pass through heavy concentrations of dust in the disk of the Milky Way before it reaches the earth. Therefore, it is greatly dimmed and reddened. If the conclusion that these two objects are galaxies is verified, the number of bodies in the Local Group will be increased to 19.

14.19 OTHER GROUPS

Moving beyond the Local Group to a distance of about 70 million light years, we find several thousand similar groups of galaxies, which George Abell divided into two categories: regular and irregular. The regular clusters are spherical in shape, centrally concentrated, rich in numbers, and consist primarily of elliptical galaxies. The Coma Berenices and the Corona Borealis are typical examples of regular clusters. The irregular clusters show no symmetry, no central concentration, and consist of practically all types of galaxies. The number of galaxies in an irregular cluster ranges from a few, as in the Local Group, to more than 1000, as in the Virgo cluster. Studies made by C. D. Shane and his associates at the Lick Observatory show that the distribution of faint and distant galaxies is similar to the distribution of the bright and nearer galaxies. Similar conclusions were reached by George Abell from his study and analysis of the National Geographic-Mount Palomar Sky Survey plates taken with the 48-inch Schmidt telescope.

14.20 SPECTRA OF GALAXIES

The spectrum of a distant galaxy is produced by the composite light from all the stars and interstellar matter in the galaxy. From its spectrum we obtain its average stellar composition; for example, the general color of the spectrum will be blue if the stars in the galaxy are predominantly blue. In spite of the composite light, the spectra of many distant galaxies show strong, distinct H and K lines of ionized calcium, which is understandable when we remember that these lines are also prominent in the spectra of many stars.

Elliptical galaxies are of classes G or K spectra and show no emission lines. Thus, the source of light comes primarily from Population II stars. The spectra of spirals, which show a wide range of spectral classes from A to G, have stars of both Population I and II, whereas the spectra of irregular galaxies, which resemble those of class A stars, have only Population I stars.

The spectra also reveal that the galaxies are not only rotating but also moving away from the observer at speeds in direct proportion to their distances from the observer. This will be explained when we consider the red-shift phenomenon (Chapter 16.2).

14.21 RADIO GALAXIES

The new and exciting field of radio astronomy developed from the 1931 discovery that strong radio waves are being emitted from the region of Sagittarius (the center of the Milky Way), the construction of the first radio telescope in 1936, and the 1946 identification of the first radio source from an object outside the solar system. At first it was believed that "radio stars" were emitting radio energy. Later, it was found that the radiation was coming not from radio stars, but from regions located within and beyond the Milky Way. In 1951 R. Minkowski

Fig. 14.13 The double radio source Cygnus A, photographed with the 200-inch telescope. (Photograph from the Hale Observatories)

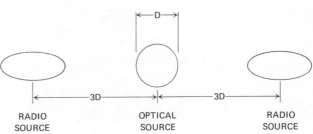

Fig. 14.14 Optical and two radio sources

and W. Baade were the first to associate a radio source beyond the Milky Way with an optically visible object. They discovered that the radio source of Cygnus A coincided with a galaxy nearly 700 million light years away. Cygnus A is the most intense extragalactic radio source, emitting radiation in radio frequencies nearly one million times greater than the radiation emitted by the entire Milky Way (Fig. 14.13). At first, it was believed that its tremendous energy was derived from the collision of a pair of galaxies within a cluster of galaxies. Later, however, it was determined that the radio emission was coming from two sources on either side of the optical object (Fig. 14.14).

Another strong radio source is the galaxy NGC 5128 in the constellation of Centaurus (Fig. 14.15). As can be seen from the photograph, the optical object appears as an elliptical galaxy with a dark, broad, irregular dust lane running across its center. It is believed that this may also be the collision of two galaxies—one a spiral seen edgewise; the other, an elliptical galaxy. Its two radio sources come from opposite sides of the elliptical galaxy, a not unusual situation. Many have been observed, and

Fig. 14.15 The unusual galaxy NGC 5128, associated with the bright radio source Centaurus A, photographed with the 200-inch telescope. (Photograph from the Hale Observatories)

EV 200°

EV 290°

EV 245°

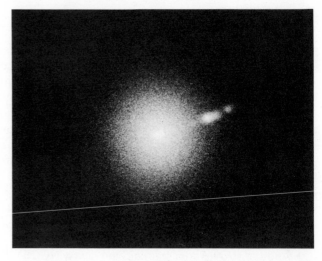

EV 335°

Fig. 14.16 Four views of the elliptical galaxy NGC 4486 (M87) showing the "jet" in polarized light. The direction of the electric vector of radiation recorded in each view is indicated. Photographed with the 200-inch telescope. (Photograph from the Hale Observatories)

the radio sources appear to be much larger than the optical.

A different radio source is shown (Fig. 14.16) in the elliptical galaxy NGC 4486 (M87). The light of the jet-like protrusion is highly polarized, which indicates that it might be synchrotron radiation, that is, the radiation produced when electrons spiral in a magnetic field at nearly the speed of light. This could be the result of some kind of cataclysmic explosion within the galaxy. A similar situation is found in the Crab Nebula in the constellation of Taurus (Chapter 13.7), where a strong radio source is accompanied by synchrotron radiation.

14.22 SEYFERT GALAXIES

In 1943 Carl Seyfert at Mount Wilson Observatory discovered a class of galaxies (Seyfert galaxies) similar to spirals, yet definitely different. Their distinguishing feature is the small, sharp, intensely bright nucleus which appears almost star-like, as shown in a negative print of the Seyfert galaxy NGC 4151 (Fig. 14.17). Almost all of the Seyfert galaxies are strong radio sources; some emit tremendous amounts of energy in the infrared region of the spectrum, and others emit greater amounts of ultraviolet radiation than is normally emitted by stars. Their spectra reveal very broad emission lines, indicating that the atoms in the nucleus are in a high state of excitation. In the spectrum of NGC 4151, lines produced by highly ionized iron have been observed. This is a notable feature, because identical lines are observed in the spectrum of the solar corona.

14.23 QUASARS

The peculiar, controversial, and fascinating radio sources that are not associated with galaxies were discovered in 1960. They are referred to as quasi-stellar radio sources, because they appear optically as point sources of light, similar to stars. The quasars are peculiar because their emission lines show a tremendous Doppler shift toward the red region of the spectrum, controversial because what causes these large spectral redshifts is not fully understood, and fascinating because each new investigation produces the unexpected.

Fig. 14.17 A Seyfert-type galaxy, NGC 4151, photographed with the 200-inch telescope. (Photograph from the Hale Observatories)

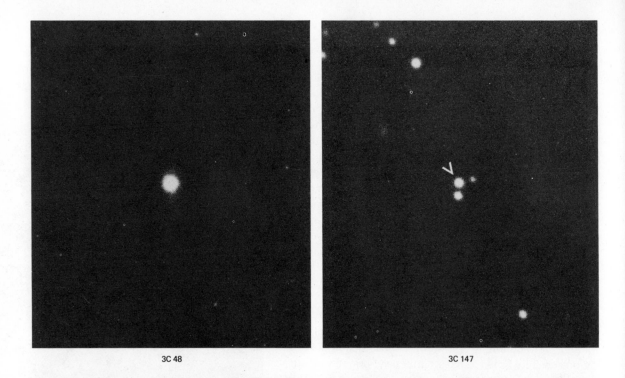

3C 48

3C 147

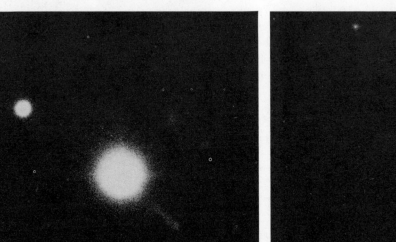

3C 273

3C 196

Fig. 14.18 Quasi-stellar radio sources photographed with the 200-inch telescope. Note the jet that appears in 3C273. (Photograph from the Hale Observatories)

The following data are revealed from their spectra: (1) broad emission lines which are produced by highly excited atoms; (2) spectral lines of elements which give the quasars a composition similar to that of the stars and the gaseous nebulae in the Milky Way; and (3) large spectral red shifts, indicating that the quasars are at extreme distances from the Milky Way. Some of the spectra also show strong absorption lines, caused when the radiation is absorbed by cooler material between the emitting source and the observer.

The light curves of quasars show erratic fluctuations in both optical brightness and radio energy output, with periods of several months and, in some cases, only several days. This indicates that the quasars are extremely small objects of light months or light days in diameter. If a quasar had a diameter of 10 light years, light variations between the sides nearest and farthest from the observer would show a light period of 10 years. If a quasar had a diameter of one light day, any light variation would show a maximum period of one day. Since light fluctuations are visible in months and days, the size of quasars must be extremely small.

The first quasar was discovered by Allan Sandage at Palomar Observatory and is called 3C48 (radio source number 48 in the third Cambridge Catalogue). Later, 3C273 was discovered, which is the brightest and probably the nearest of the quasars (Fig. 14.18). Maarteen Schmidt at Palomar Observatory detected from its spectrum that several faint hydrogen lines of the Balmer series had shifted toward the red end of the spectrum by about 16%. He also noticed that the magnesium and oxygen lines had shifted the same amount. There are two explanations for this red shift: the quasar is either receding at a great speed or emitting its light in extremely strong gravitational fields. The second explanation must be rejected because with such strong gravitational fields, the quasar would theoretically collapse to a very small body with an enormous density, and such a collapse has not been observed spectroscopically. If the first explanation is accepted, the spectral red shift indicates that the quasar is moving away from the observer at a speed of nearly 30,000 miles (48,000 km) per second. If the quasar follows Hubble's velocity-distance relation (Fig. 14.19 and Chapter 16.2) for galaxies, its distance would be about 1.5 billion light years. The most distant quasar shows a red shift of about 82%, which indicates that it is receding at a speed of about 152,000 miles (245,000 km) per second and is now at a distance of approximately seven billion light years. If the red shift is a measure of the quasar's distance, its energy output is considerably greater than the brightest galaxy containing billions of stars. This is a fantastic situation that is not easy to either visualize or accept.

Other explanations for the red shift have been suggested. James Terrell at Los Alomos Scientific Laboratories has proposed that they might be objects ejected

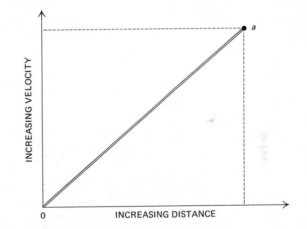

Fig. 14.9 Hubble's law—the velocity-distance relation. The radial velocities of galaxies increase as their distances from the observer increase. The fastest moving galaxy, represented by point *a* on the diagram, has a speed of about 152,000 miles per second, or about 82% of the speed of light.

from the center of the Milky Way and thus are relatively close to the earth. Halton C. Arp at Palomar Observatory has presented photographic evidence that shows quasars are in the vicinity of "peculiar" galaxies, which suggests that they might have been ejected from these galaxies. The collision of two galaxies or the cataclysmic explosion of several supernovae have also been proposed as explanations for the red shift in the spectra of quasars.

Another theory, involving antimatter, has been proposed to explain the tremendous energy outputs of the brightest quasars. Nuclear physicists working with nuclear accelerators have observed short-lived particles similar to normal matter but of opposite electrical charge. For example, an antielectron (positron) has the same mass as an electron, but its electrical charge is positive. When antimatter collides with normal matter, both are anihilated with the release of a tremendous amount of energy. This anihilation process is presented as a possible explanation for the tremendous energy outputs of the quasars.

Striking similarities have been observed between quasars and Seyfert galaxies. Both have bright compact nuclei and are strong in the infrared and ultraviolet, indicating that their gases are highly excited and moving at great speeds. They also display variability in light and radio output, and their radiation is polarized. These similarities suggest that the phenomena which produce them might also be similar.

REVIEW

1. What is the Milky Way? Describe the principle that Herschel used to determine and explain the structure of the Milky Way.

2. What is the approximate shape, size, and structure of the Milky Way?

3. What are the two important types of stellar populations? Explain their differences. Who first classified them in this manner? How are these two populations distributed in the Milky Way?

4. Give evidence that the Milky Way is rotating. How was the center of the Milky Way determined?

5. Where in the Milky Way is the sun located? What are its two principal motions within the Milky Way?

6. Explain how the differential rotational velocity of the Milky Way affects the radial velocities of the stars in the neighborhood of the sun.

7. Explain how the mass of the Milky Way can be determined from the sun's orbital velocity and its distance from the center of the galaxy.

8. How was the spiral structure of the Milky Way discovered?

9. How does the interstellar material affect the appearance of the Milky Way? How can its presence be detected?

10. Explain what produces the luminosity of the diffuse nebulae. Give examples.

11. What is a dark nebula? Give one famous example.

12. What is interstellar reddening? How is it produced? How is it used in estimating the degree of starlight obscuration?

13. To what does Hubble's term "zone of avoidance" refer? Was he correct? Why,

14. What is meant by interstellar polarization? How was polarization verified? What does interstellar polarization indicate about the characteristics of interstellar particles?

15. What comprises the "halo" around the Milky Way?

16. What are the two main types of cosmic rays? What are their sources? How were they discovered?

17. What criteria did Hubble use in his classification of galaxies? What are the names of the three major types of galaxies in his classification?

18. Compare the three major types of galaxies as to structure, shape, and size.

19. Discuss the distribution of galaxies in space. Give evidence of clustering.

20. Discuss the speculation that has been made about the evolution of galaxies. Give reasons for your answers.

21. What is the Local Group of galaxies? How many galaxies does it contain? What is its shape and size? Which of the three major types of galaxies is the most prevalent in the Local Group?

22. What is the nature of the light which produces the spectra of distant galaxies? What information about the galaxies do the spectra reveal?

23. What is an irregular galaxy? Which one is nearest to the Milky Way? Describe its structure and composition.

24. Discuss the historical sequence in the discovery and observations of radio sources within and beyond the Milky Way.

25. What is the radio source of Cygnus A?

26. What is meant by synchrotron radiation? Give several examples.

27. What are the characteristics of a Seyfert galaxy?

28. What are quasars? Explain why they are considered peculiar and controversial.

29. What do the light curves of quasars reveal?

30. Discuss the various explanations that have been suggested for the extremely large red shift in quasars.

15
Stellar Evolution: The Aging Process In Stars

What goes on four legs in the morning, two legs at noon, and three legs in the evening?

Riddle of the Sphinx

The answer to the ancient riddle is man: he crawls on his hands and knees as a baby; he walks on two legs as an adult; and he uses a cane as an old man. In this riddle we see an encapsuled view of the stages of a man's life from birth to death. Aging is a process which all matter undergoes. Stars are no exception to the vagaries of time.

Before we can comprehend the stages in a star's life, we must first recognize certain processes which occur in its interior. Although the interior of a star is inaccessible to direct observation, a great deal of information about its composition, structure, temperature, pressure, and energy has been accumulated from the knowledge of gas laws, hydrostatic and thermal equilibrium, methods of heat transfer, and methods of generating energy. Most of the stars are in a state of stable equilibrium, which means that at any point within the star, its temperature, pressure, and density are constant so that the star is neither expanding nor contracting.

15.1 THE GAS LAWS

Since a star is under tremendous pressures and temperatures, it is completely gaseous, and its molecules, which are in constant motion, continually collide with one another. These collisions produce the gas pressure, which is proportional to the temperature and density of the gas. The relationship of gas pressure, density, and temperature is summarized in three laws. Boyle's law states that the pressure of a gas at constant temperature is inversely proportional to its volume, or directly proportional to its density. Charles' law states that the pressure of a gas at constant volume is proportional to the temperature. When these two laws are combined, the result is the perfect gas law, which states that the pressure of a gas is proportional to the product of its temperature and density. Even though the stellar gas is highly compressed, it reacts like a gas because at extreme temperatures, its atoms have been ionized and their sizes reduced considerably.

15.2 HYDROSTATIC EQUILIBRIUM

The mutual gravitation between the masses within a star produces tremendous forces which act inwardly toward the regions of greatest density. These forces tend to cause the star to collapse toward the center. For a stable star, this gravitational inward pressure is balanced by an internal force acting outwardly which is produced by the gas pressure and by the radiation pressure. The gas pressure is produced by the force exerted by the gas particles, whereas the radiation pressure is produced by the high internal temperatures. A stable star is in hydrostatic equilibrium when its gravitational inward pressure equals the gas pressure and the radiation pressure.

15.3 THERMAL EQUILIBRIUM

Since a star emits energy from its surface and energy flows from a hot to a cold region, it can be concluded that the star's temperature is highest at its core. If the energy at the core is not replaced, the star's temperature would gradually decrease. However, this energy is replaced by nuclear reactions. A stable star is in thermal equilibrium when the rate at which energy is produced equals the rate at which it is emitted into space.

15.4 TRANSFER OF ENERGY

The transfer of energy within a star can be accomplished by the processes of conduction, convection, and radiation. The process of conduction, the direct passing of energy from one atom to another, is slow and inefficient except in white dwarfs, where the molecules are very close together. For this reason, conduction is not significant in most stars. Convection, the actual movement of atoms from a hotter to a cooler region, is an efficient means of heat transfer. For the greater part of a star's life, convection generally occurs in certain layers where the gas temperatures increase at a faster rate than the pressures. However, during the formative stages in a star's evolution (the convective stage), convection plays the predominate role in the transfer of energy.

The transfer of energy in most stars occurs by radiation, the actual movement of electromagnetic energy from one atom to another. This is true even though the process is not very efficient. When an atom which has become excited by absorbing a photon of energy that is moving outward returns to its previous state, it emits a photon whose chances of moving outward are extremely small, since it can be emitted in any direction.

15.5 NUCLEAR REACTIONS

The source of solar energy had been a riddle to scientists for years, because no known source could have kept the sun emitting its steady light for the past several billion years. In 1854 the German physicist H. von Helmholtz presented the first reasonable explanation when he suggested that solar energy is derived from the compression of its gases as they move inward due to gravitational attraction. Although this view was widely accepted, this process alone could keep the sun shining at its present rate for only several million years. The answer to the riddle was finally provided when the discovery of radioactivity made known the tremendous energy within an atom's nucleus. Stellar energy is derived from the excess mass created in the process of building elements of heavier atomic weight from elements of lighter atomic weight.

A star is an atomic reactor. Its energy is derived from two sources: the fusion of hydrogen into helium by the proton-proton reaction, and the carbon cycle. The proton-proton reaction is the simpler and more direct of the two. The steps are indicated by the following reactions:

$$_1H^1 + {_1}H^1 \rightarrow {_1}H^2 + e^+ + v + \gamma$$

$$_1H^2 + {_1}H^1 \rightarrow {_2}He^3 + \gamma$$

$$_2He^3 + {_2}He^3 \rightarrow {_2}He^4 + {_1}H^1 + {_1}H^1.$$

In this reaction, two protons ($_1H^1$) combine directly to form heavy hydrogen, or deuteron, ($_1H^2$), with the release of a positron (e^+), neutrino (v), and gamma ray (γ). The deuteron combines with another proton to form a helium isotope ($_2He^3$), with the release of a gamma ray. Two helium isotopes combine to form an ordinary helium nucleus ($_2He^4$) and two protons.

The concept of the carbon cycle was proposed independently in 1938 by the American astronomer H. Bethe and the German astronomer C. von Weizsacker. The steps are indicated by the following reactions:

$$_6C^{12} + {_1}H^1 \rightarrow {_7}N^{13} + \gamma$$

$$_7N^{13} \rightarrow {_6}C^{13} + e^+ + v$$

$$_6C^{13} + {_1}H^1 \rightarrow {_7}N^{14} + \gamma$$

$$_7N^{14} + {_1}H^1 \rightarrow {_8}O^{15} + \gamma$$

$$_8O^{15} \rightarrow {_7}N^{15} + e^+ + v$$

$$_7N^{15} + {_1}H^1 \rightarrow {_6}C^{12} + {_2}He^4.$$

In the carbon cycle, a carbon nucleus ($_6C^{12}$) combines with a proton to form an unstable, radioactive form of nitrogen isotope ($_7N^{13}$) and the release of a gamma ray. The nitrogen isotope almost immediately releases a positron and a neutrino and is converted into a stable form of carbon ($_6C^{13}$). The stable carbon combines with a proton to form ordinary nitrogen ($_7N^{14}$) and the release of a gamma ray. The ordinary nitrogen combines with a proton to form unstable, radioactive oxygen isotope ($_8O^{15}$) and the release of a gamma ray. The oxygen isotope disintegrates by releasing a positron and a neutrino and forming nitrogen ($_7N^{15}$). The nitrogen combines with another proton to form the original carbon ($_6C^{12}$), helium nucleus ($_2He^4$).

In this cycle, four protons have combined to form one helium nucleus. The atomic weight of one proton is 1.008 units. Four protons weigh 4.032 units, whereas one helium nucleus weighs 4.003 units. Thus, in both the proton-proton reaction and the carbon cycle, approximately 0.029 mass units are converted into various forms of energy. The carbon cycle, which requires a considerably higher temperature than does the proton-proton reaction, is the main source of energy in the hotter stars, whereas the proton-proton reaction supplies most of the energy in our own sun and in the cooler stars.

15.6 THE BIRTH OF STARS

The H-R diagram has proved a valuable tool in the study of the evolution of stars (Chapter 11.11). Although we do not know the complete evolutionary track of a star from its birth to death, we can plot certain observable stages in the development of stars on the H-R diagram, and from these we can formulate an overall picture, which is still quite speculative.

Most of the luminous stars that are visible today can sustain themselves for only several million years at the present rate at which they are using their "fuel." These stars could not have been created five billion years ago when the earth was created. This means that stars are being created continuously.

Young stars are found in clouds of interstellar matter. These clouds are located in the spiral arms of

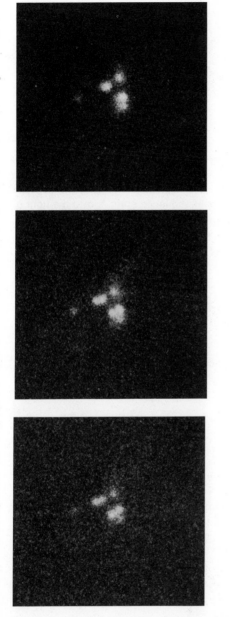

Fig. 15.1 The Herbig-Haro objects, photographed with the 120-inch telescope from 1947 to 1958, show what astronomers hope is the evolutionary process in the birth of a star. (Lick Observatory photograph)

galaxies, in nebulosities, and in dark nebulae. Such locations indicate that interstellar matter might be a prerequisite for the birth of stars. In the early stages of stellar evolution, these clouds of interstellar matter became so dense that the gas and dust particles begin to move under the influence of their mutual gravitation to form centers of condensations. When the condensation becomes visible as a dark "globule," it is called a "protostar." Evidences of such objects are visible in nebulae such as the Lagoon (Plate 24) and the Rosette (Plate 31). The appearance of a "star" in the Orion association where none was visible in earlier photographs was reported by G. Herbig at the Lick Observatory (Fig. 15.1).

As the protostar contracts, its density, pressure, and temperature increase. The increase in temperature results from the energy released by the gravitational fall of the matter which is absorbed by the cloud. When thermal equilibrium is established, the temperature is sufficient for the star to shine and be visible. At this stage, according to the Japanese physicist C. Hayashi, the star is completely convective, that is, energy from the interior is carried to the surface by convection. Its position on the H-R diagram is within a nearly vertical, narrow band to the right of the areas occupied by the red giants and supergiants (Fig. 15.2). The Hayashi theoretical evolutionary track for a convective star shows that it moves downward on the H-R diagram, because as the star collapses, its luminosity decreases, with very little change in temperature. During this period, which lasts about one million years, the core density increases.

When the transfer of energy in the core changes from convection to radiation, the star turns abruptly and moves horizontally to the left on the H-R diagram. It reaches the main-sequence line when the core temperature is high enough to start and support a nuclear reaction (the synthesis of hydrogen into helium), and this point in the star's evolutionary track is called age-zero main sequence. The star's position on the main-sequence line is determined by its mass and chemical composition (Fig. 15.3). A less massive star remains in the convective stage longer; therefore, it moves farther down the Hayashi band and joins the main-sequence line at the

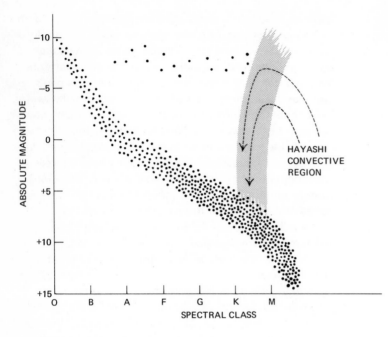

Fig. 15.2 Hayashi convective region, located above the main-sequence stars and to the right of the giants. As a protostar contracts, its density, pressure, and temperature increase (dashed line). As it moves downward, it is completely convective. Protostars to the right of the Hayashi region are unstable.

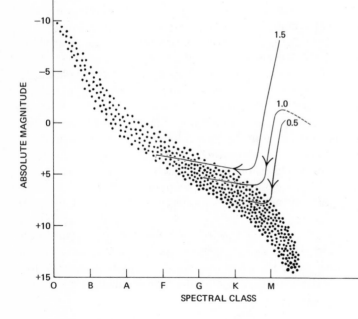

Fig. 15.3 Evolutionary tracks for stars of solar masses 0.5, 1.0, and 1.5. The abrupt turn to the left in the Hayashi evolutionary track indicates that the star's core temperature is sufficient to start and maintain a nuclear reaction.

lower right portion. The time that it takes a star to reach the main sequence is several million years for the most massive and several hundred million years for the least massive.

The core of a more massive star transfers energy by radiation earlier than does a less massive one; it moves, therefore, higher horizontally on the H-R diagram and joins the main-sequence line at the upper left portion. The stars at the lower end of the main-sequence line are believed to be about one-tenth as massive as the sun. This represents the minimum mass necessary to sustain a nuclear reaction. The stars at the upper end of the main-sequence line are about 100 times more massive than the sun. Stars of greater mass are believed to be unstable.

15.7 MAIN-SEQUENCE STARS

A main-sequence star is in equilibrium because it generates its energy almost exclusively from nuclear reactions in the core at the same rate as its surface radiates energy into space. Most of a star's evolutionary time is spent on the main-sequence line. A more massive and luminous star leaves the main sequence earlier than does a less massive, dimmer star, because it converts hydrogen into helium at a tremendously higher rate. As more hydrogen is converted into helium, the star's core becomes denser and hotter, which causes an increase in the star's nuclear reaction rate and luminosity. This is indicated on the H-R diagram in the star's evolutionary track by a vertical rise within the main-sequence band of less than one magnitude.

15.8 RED GIANT STARS

When the hydrogen in the core has been almost completely converted into helium, the star begins to contract gravitationally because the hydrogen necessary to maintain the nuclear reaction has been exhausted. The star's energy is now derived from the nuclear reactions that occur in the hydrogen-rich shell around the core and by the potential energy released by the gases as they collapse gravitationally toward the star's center. Part

of the potential gravitational energy and the radiation pressure of the gases in the outer layers of the star force the star to expand. As its size increases, its surface temperature decreases. Since the internal structure of the star has been altered, its evolutionary track shows it moving upward and to the right of the main-sequence line. Eventually, the increase in size and decrease in surface temperature cause the star to become what is known as a red giant or a red supergiant (Fig. 15.4).

In its final stage, as a red giant or supergiant, the star's size has increased tremendously, and its core temperature is about 100 million degrees absolute. At this point in its evolutionary track, it is the reddest and most luminous. It is believed that the high temperature triggers an explosion (helium flash), which starts the triple-alpha nuclear reaction process, in which three helium nuclei combine to form one carbon nucleus. The energy released by the triple-alpha process causes the core to expand and thus to reverse the expansion of the

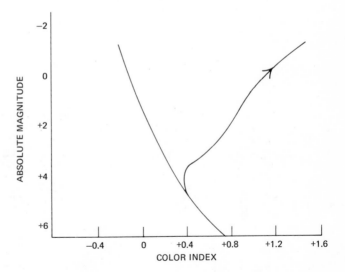

Fig. 15.4 Evolutionary track of a solar star from main sequence to red giant. As more hydrogen is converted to helium, the star rises vertically within the main-sequence band in its evolutionary track. When hydrogen in the core is almost completely exhausted, the star moves upward and to the right on the H-R diagram.

outer layers of the star. As the star contracts, its surface temperature increases and causes the star to move horizontally to the left on the H-R diagram in its evolutionary track (Fig. 15.5).

15.9 COLOR-MAGNITUDE DIAGRAMS

Figure 15.6 shows the color-magnitude diagrams of several galactic clusters superimposed. Since a cluster is a group of stars of different masses but of one origin, composition, and age, a comparison of their color-magnitude diagrams serves as an indicator of their age and stellar evolution. The youngest is the Double Cluster in Perseus, and the oldest is Messier 67 in Cancer. Their ages correspond to the position where the evolutionary track of each cluster breaks away from the main-sequence line.

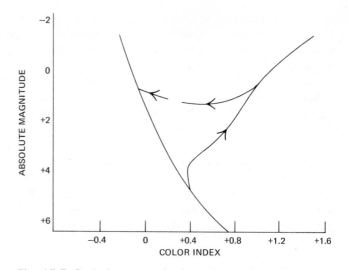

Fig. 15.5 Evolutionary track of a solar star from giant along the horizontal branch of the H-R diagram. The "gap" in the horizontal branch represents the location of the RR Lyrae stars.

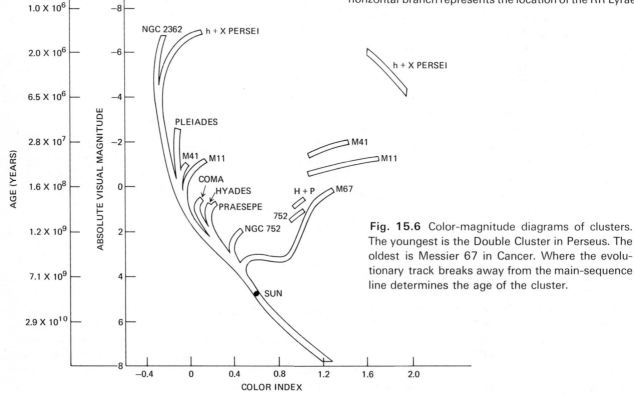

Fig. 15.6 Color-magnitude diagrams of clusters. The youngest is the Double Cluster in Perseus. The oldest is Messier 67 in Cancer. Where the evolutionary track breaks away from the main-sequence line determines the age of the cluster.

Color-magnitude diagrams of globular clusters show that they lie on the horizontal branch of the H-R diagram. The "gap" in the horizontal branch is occupied by the RR Lyrae stars. It appears that as a star evolves, it must pass through this gap as an unstable variable star. Between the end of the horizontal branch and the main sequence, a star is unstable and pulsates.

15.10 WHITE DWARF STARS

When a star has finally exhausted all of its sources of nuclear energy and its source of potential energy due to gravitational collapse and has contracted to its smallest possible size, it has become a white dwarf—a star of fairly high temperature, low luminosity, and great density. The white dwarf's enormous density derives from the almost completely ionized atoms; therefore, the atoms, nuclei, and electrons can occupy a much smaller space. Even in this condition, however, the free electrons are in the gaseous state, behave like a gas, and are referred to as a degenerate gas.

The quantum theory states that the number of free electrons that can be packed in a given space is limited. This minimum possible space is determined by the velocity of the free electrons. As their velocities decrease, a larger minimum space is required. When a white dwarf has been compressed to its minimum space, no further contraction is possible, because the tremendous central pressure prevents it. If further contraction were possible, the velocity of the electrons would have to increase. This is impossible, because the white dwarf has no energy available to produce the increase in the velocity of the electrons.

The English physicist A. Eddington and the American astrophysicist S. Chandrasekhar laid the foundation for the theory of the structure of white dwarfs. Eddington was the first to learn that some of the electrons in white dwarfs have speeds that approach the speed of light, and Chandrasekhar was the first to apply the theory of relativity to the structure of white dwarfs. From his theoretical equations, Chandrasekhar found that the radius of a white dwarf is related to its mass. This theoretical relationship is shown in Fig. 15.7. As the mass of

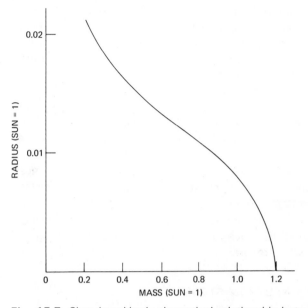

Fig. 15.7 Chandrasekhar's theoretical relationship between the masses and radii of white dwarf stars

a white dwarf increases, its radius decreases. According to his theory, the maximum mass possible for a white dwarf is 1.2 times the solar mass. About 100 white dwarfs have been discovered, but the mass of only three (the companions of Sirius, Procyon, and 40 Eridini)

A white dwarf's only source of energy is thermal. As the velocity of the nuclei of the atoms in a white dwarf decreases, the thermal energy that is released is conducted to the star's surface by the free electrons and then radiated into space. Since a white dwarf cools at an extremely slow rate, its evolutionary track on the H-R diagram is indicated by a diagonal line below and to the left of the main-sequence line.

If all stars eventually evolve into white dwarfs, some mechanism must be present that reduces their mass. The ejection of matter by stars has been observed in shell, Wolf-Rayet stars, novae, supernovae, and others. Although it has never been observed, the planetary nebulae are believed to be evidences of an important mass-ejection mechanism. An excellent example of a planetary nebula is the Ring Nebula in Lyra (Chapter 13.8). A planetary nebula is a shell of gas that has been ejected from and is expanding around an extremely hot star. A typical shell is spherical and hollow; therefore, it appears brightest at its edges, where the line of sight has its greatest depth. Recent studies have shown that the diameters of the shells seem to be correlated with the physical appearance of its central star. Planetary nebulae with small shells have very luminous central stars, whereas those with large shells have stars that are considerably less luminous (comparable to the most luminous white dwarf stars). Although not all the stars become planetary nebulae, studies show that the formation of a planetary nebula is an important mass-ejection mechanism which may be the step before the formation of a white dwarf.

15.11 NEUTRON STARS

Another possibility is that a white dwarf star may evolve into a neutron star. This possibility was strengthened with what is believed to be the first observational evidence of a neutron star, which occurred in 1969 when Baade's star, near the center of the Crab Nebula, was found to be the source producing the flashes associated with Pulsar NP0532.

It is currently believed that continued compression within a white dwarf star produces a neutron star at its center. Normally, free neutrons are unstable and decay into protons and electrons; however, under extremely high temperatures, neutrons are stable. Thus, with the high temperatures and enormous pressures which exist in white dwarfs and supernovae, the electrons could be forced into the nuclei, where they could combine with the protons to form neutrons. The neutron star would then consist entirely of neutrons.

As was suggested in Chapter 13.9, the neutron star is believed to be associated with a pulsar. A possible explanation is that an extremely small, dense neutron star is rotating at an extremely high rate within a large and intense magnetic field (Fig. 15.8). The star ejects material which rises to the surface in two beams generating radio waves called synchroton radiation. The extremely rapid rotation causes the particles and radia-

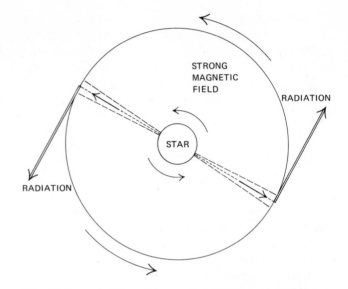

Fig. 15.8 A possible neutron-star model of a pulsar. The diameter of the neutron star is 10–20 miles (16–32 km), and the magnetic field is about 2400 miles (3862 km). It is believed that the radiation is emitted in the direction in which the magnetic field is rotating.

tion to concentrate at the poles, where they are ejected into space in the direction of rotation. As these beams of radiation sweep the earth, the typical energy pulse profile of a pulsar is observed.

15.12 SUMMARY OF STELLAR EVOLUTION

A summary of the evolutionary track of a star is shown in Fig. 15.9. It is believed that the dust and gas particles within a dense region of interstellar matter begin to contract under their mutual gravitational attraction to form condensations. A condensate visible as a dark "globule" is called a "protostar." Thermal equilibrium is established at point a on the diagram when the temperature is sufficient for the star to shine and be visible. Since the energy at this stage is transferred convectively to the star's surface, the star moves downward on the diagram, maintaining a fairly constant temperature, but gradually decreasing its luminosity. When the star begins

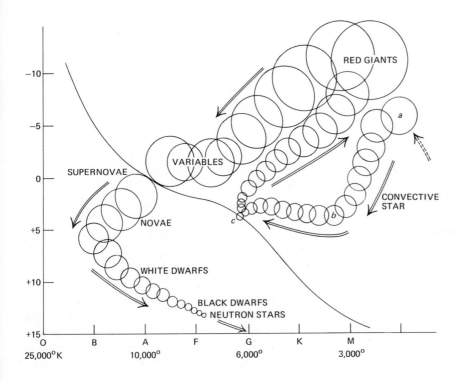

Fig. 15.9 The evolutionary track of a star slightly more massive than the sun from the convection star stage to the black dwarf on neutron star stage.

to transfer energy within the core by radiation and its core temperature is sufficient to start and maintain a nuclear reaction, the star's evolutionary track abruptly changes and moves to the left (point *b*). It hooks onto the main-sequence line at point *c* when the star becomes stable, that is, when it generates energy at the same rate at which it emits it into space. This point is called age-zero main-sequence. Practically its entire life is spent as a stable, main-sequence star. As it converts hydrogen into helium, the star moves about one magnitude vertically within the main-sequence band. When almost all of the hydrogen in the core has been exhausted, it begins to contract gravitationally. Part of the gravitational potential energy is used to expand the outer layers of the star. Since the star's internal structure has been changed, it begins to move above and to the right of the main-sequence line and eventually becomes a red giant, with a core temperature of about 100 million degrees absolute. This enormous temperature triggers an explosion

which starts the triple-alpha nuclear reaction—the conversion of three helium nuclei into one carbon nucleus. This reverses the expansion process, and the star begins to contract. During this stage, the star becomes unstable (a variable star) and fluctuates considerably in size and luminosity. Its instability could produce an explosion so that the star would become either a nova or a supernova. The final stages in its evolutionary track are the white dwarfs and ultimately, either a black dwarf (cold mass that does not shine) or a neutron star.

15.13 ORIGIN OF THE SOLAR SYSTEM

All men are intensely interested in their origins. As little children, they ask their parents where they came from. Some of the world's greatest literature (Fielding's *Tom Jones* and Proust's *Remembrance of Things Past*, for example) had dealt with men trying to discover their past in an attempt to establish their place in the world.

The astronomer, in attempting to explain the origin of the solar system, is following a similar drive—he wants to establish man's place in the universe. This search has been long and arduous, and the final answers have yet to be learned.

The astronomer's search must be carried out within certain limitations. Thus, any hypothesis explaining the origin of the solar system must conform to known physical laws and observable facts. Moreover, it must take into account the general ideas concerning the evolution of stars. Because the origin of the solar system is a historical event, the astronomer can only hope that neither the conditions of the solar system as they appear today nor the physical laws which govern matter have changed since the system came into existence.

Since the major bodies in the solar system (planets) rotate about their axes and revolve around the sun, the angular momentum of a revolving body becomes an important consideration in the development of any hypothesis for the origin of the solar system. A body in circular motion possesses angular momentum, which is defined as the product of the body's mass, its distance from the center of motion, and its angular velocity. The principle of the conservation of angular momentum states that the total angular momentum of an isolated system is always the same. This means that if the total angular momentum of an isolated system is to remain the same, one of the variables must decrease when another is increased. A well-known example of this principle is found in a figure ice-skater who spins very rapidly when she holds her arms close to her body and spins very slowly when she extends them. Since the angular momentum always remains the same, when the distance of the mass is increased by extending the arms, the angular velocity must decrease. Not only must the total angular momentum be taken into consideration, but so must its distribution within the system. For example, Jupiter accounts for 60% of the total angular momentum of the solar system.

The nebular hypothesis was first presented in brief form by the German philosopher Immanuel Kant in 1755 and later in more detail by the French mathematician Pierre Simon, Marquis de Laplace, in 1796. They visualized that the solar system originated from a slowly rotating cloud of gas which was slightly greater in size than the distance to the last known planet at that time. According to the principle of the conservation of angular momentum, as the cloud contracted under the influence of its own gravitational attraction, its rotational velocity increased. Laplace postulated that at certain stages in the contraction process, rings of gas were left behind, each rotating about itself and revolving around the center of the main cloud. Eventually, the material in each ring condensed into a planet, and the material at the center of the main cloud condensed into the sun. As the rings contracted and condensed to form the planets, smaller rings of gas were left behind and eventually condensed into the satellites.

The nebular hypothesis was widely accepted for many years. Today, it is difficult to accept, because it violates many basic physical principles. In an attempt to eliminate some of these difficulties in the nebular hypothesis, Chamberlain and Moulton proposed the planetesimal hypothesis, according to which a star passed very close to the sun and produced great tides on the solar surface which erupted into tremendous gas clouds. These clouds cooled into smaller clouds (planetesimals), which in turn condensed into planets. The gravitational force of the star provided the necessary angular momentum to start the planetesimals revolving around the sun.

The planetesimal hypothesis came under attack when H. N. Russell presented proof that a passing star is incapable of providing the necessary angular momentum and that the gas clouds ripped from the sun would never condense but would disperse into space. These and other violations made the nebular hypothesis unacceptable.

The present approach to the origin of the solar system is based on the concept that the sun and the planets are condensations of clouds of interstellar gas and dust. This thinking is based on the evidence that stars evolve from interstellar gas and dust clouds, that other planetary systems may possibly exist, and that both of these phenomena occur frequently. Because of these considerations, interest in the nebular hypothesis has been revived.

A version of the nebular hypothesis was presented in 1945 by the German physicist C. von Weizsacker, who assumed that the sun was formed before the rest of the solar system came into existence. Rotating around the sun was a large gaseous disk. The planets and satellites evolved from the eddy currents produced by turbulence within the gas cloud. The proposed mechanism by which this was accomplished raised difficult problems. Therefore, in 1949 G. Kuiper presented his protoplanet hypothesis, which considerably modified Weizsacker's model.

According to the protoplanet hypothesis, the rotating gas nebula contained sufficient material to both produce the sun and the other bodies and account for the tremendous losses in mass suffered by the terrestrial planets as they evolved into their present state. The mass of the gas nebula was so great that as it contracted, it separated into several large segments, each with sufficient mass to maintain its position and identity against the gravitational attraction of the more massive central body, the sun.

Although the protoplanet hypothesis explains the spacing, rotation, and revolution of the planets and their satellites, it fails to explain the distribution of angular momentum and the overlapping of the protoplanet nebulae. To eliminate these difficulties, W. McCrea proposed his accretion theory. The original gas cloud consisted of several large masses of dust and gas particles, each moving at a different speed. The masses in the center coalesced to form the sun, whereas the outer ones, those moving slowly, formed the planets and satellites. The fast-moving masses escaped from the gravitational attraction of the system.

A question which has increasingly intrigued astronomers is whether our solar system is unique. Although there is no conclusive evidence that establishes the existence of similar systems in the universe, most astronomers agree that the probability of their existence is extremely high. In 1963 Peter van de Kamp of the Sproul Observatory observed an oscillatory motion in Barnard's star as it traversed the celestial sphere. After many observations, one possible interpretation for the cause of the oscillation is that Barnard's star might be revolving around the barycenter of a system composed of the star and one or more companion bodies of planetary mass. This may ultimately prove to be man's first glimpse of another solar system; for the present, however, it must be emphasized that the search for other solar systems is still in the speculative phase.

A companion question usually raised when discussion turns to the possibility of other systems is whether life similar to that on the earth exists elsewhere. In order for life to start and continue, a source of energy (a star) must remain steady long enough to permit life to evolve on a nearby body which is in orbit around the star. Also, the basic chemicals necessary for the synthesis of amino acids, the building blocks of life, must be present. The law of probability indicates that there must be a large number of stars that could provide a habitable zone for life to evolve on a nearby body. Moreover, some of the basic chemicals, such as water vapor, hydroxyl molecules (OH), and formaldehyde (H_2CO) have been detected through microwave studies of certain dust clouds. Also, amino acids have been found on two meteorites. Although the search for life beyond the earth has just begun, early findings indicate that the earth may not be an isolated source of life in the universe.

REVIEW

1. What is meant when a stable star is in (a) hydrostatic equilibrium (b) thermal equilibrium?

2. List and describe the three mechanisms by which energy is transferred within a star. In what part of the star is each the dominant mechanism?

3. Describe the proton-proton reaction in the production of stellar energy.

4. What is being converted in the carbon cycle? What is being produced? What part does the carbon nucleus play in this reaction?

5. In what part of the star does the proton-proton reaction and the carbon cycle occur? Why?

6. What observational evidence indicates that interstellar matter may be a prerequisite in the formation of a star?

7. Explain what a change in a star's position on its evolutionary track on the H-R diagram indicates.

8. Explain what has occurred within a star, according to Hayashi, when it starts to shine and becomes visible. Where is it located on the evolutionary track on the H-R diagram?

9. What has occurred when the evolutionary track of a star abruptly starts to move horizontally on the H-R diagram toward the main sequence? What occurs when it has reached the main sequence?

10. Explain what determines the star's position on the main sequence.

11. What is a main-sequence star? In the evolution of a star, how much of its life is spent as a main-sequence star?

12. Two stars reach the main-sequence line at the same time. If one is spectral class K and the other is spectral class B, which one will leave the main-sequence line first? Why?

13. In the evolutionary process of a star from main sequence to red giant, why does the star's surface cool as it expands? Explain.

14. What is the triple-alpha reaction? At what point in the star's evolutionary track does it occur? What happens to the star as the result of the triple-alpha process? How is this indicated on the H-R diagram?

15. Compare the color-magnitude diagrams of an open cluster and a globular cluster. How do they differ? What does each reveal about the cluster?

16. What are white dwarf stars? Explain what is meant by degenerate gas.

17. Explain Chandrasekhar's theory for the structure of white dwarfs.

18. Explain how the color-magnitude on the H-R diagram is used in estimating cluster distances.

19. What is a neutron star?

20. Discuss and describe the development of the protoplanet hypothesis for the origin of the solar system.

21. What conditions appear to be necessary for life to start and continue? Discuss the possibility that these conditions exist on other bodies in the universe.

16
Cosmology

16.1 THE MYSTERIOUS

The night sky has always held a strange, disquieting fascination for man. Standing alone, away from the artificial lighting of modern civilization, he can look into a darkness that is broken by a single, illuminating disk and thousands of tiny, flickering lights. If he allows his imagination to run free, he can fall into the immensity of space. Rushing onward, stars, star systems, galaxies, and interstellar matter speed by, but the end is never reached. Even the wildest imagination is incapable of visualizing the ultimate conclusion of such a trip, and no living man has ever reached the universe's end (if in fact it does end) and returned.

Man, refusing to be cowed by the seeming futility of his search, has never ceased in his attempts to discern the structure of the universe. Astronomy has painstakingly developed an impressive body of knowledge about the structure of that part of the universe nearest the earth. Man, however, is not content to merely establish the laws that govern the celestial bodies; he also wants to discover the ultimate nature of the universe itself. In coming to grips with the universe as a whole, the astronomer must face several basic questions. What is the extent and shape of the universe? What was the cause of its creation? What is its age? What will be its final end? What, if anything, lies beyond the universe? Although these questions touch at the very core of existence, man may never find the answers.

Many of the early ideas about the origin and nature of the universe were woven together in the religions of man. One of these is found in the Bible in the book of Genesis, which tells us that the physical universe is a product of God's mind: "In the beginning God created the heavens and the earth; 2. The earth was waste, and void; darkness covered the abyss, and the spirit of God was stirring above the waters. 3. God said, 'Let there be light,' and there was light. God saw that the light was good." (Gen. I:1–3). Since the Christian church was the dominant force in Europe during the medieval period, its beliefs about the origin and nature of the universe were generally accepted by the philosophers, who simply tried to show that these beliefs were just and reasonable. The Christian universe was finite and bounded. Beyond the physical universe was the infinity of God. This concept began to crumble with Copernicus' suggestion that the placement of the sun at the center of the cosmos would simplify the computations for the movements of the planets. In 1576 Thomas Diggs took the step which Copernicus had avoided when he wrote that the infinity of the universe was a distinct possibility.

Man's conception of the universe was beginning to expand. Giordano Bruno, who was burned at the stake in 1600, believed that there was not just one world but an infinity of worlds. In the middle of the eighteenth century, the German philosopher Immanuel Kant conceived of an infinity of space populated by "island universes." With the advent of new instruments and methods, cosmology, the study of the origin, structure, and evolution of the universe, became an important branch of astronomy.

Elaborate scientific theories have been postulated in an attempt to answer the basic questions about the universe. While scientists try to remain within the safe pale of objectivity and base their theories on facts, cosmology pushes the human mind to its farthest limits. At this point, science moves back again into the realm of philosophy and religion. Cosmology may well be the limit beyond which man will never be able to extend his knowledge. Yet the probe will assuredly continue, for as Albert Einstein wrote:

The fairest thing we can experience is the mysterious. It is the fundamental emotion which stands at the cradle of true art and true science. He who knows it not and can no longer wonder, no longer feel amazement, is as good as dead, a snuffed-out candle . . . Enough for me the mystery of the eternity of life, and the inkling of the marvelous structure of reality, together

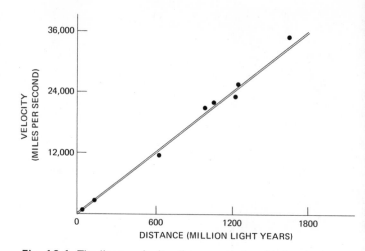

Fig. 16.1 The linear velocity-distance relationship for clusters of galaxies illustrates the relationship between the red shifts of galaxies and their distances.

with the single-hearted endeavor to comprehend a portion, be it ever so tiny, of the reason that manifests itself in nature.[1]

16.2 OUR VIEW OF THE UNIVERSE

The optical universe, the portion of the universe that man can see, is revealed by the optical telescope. The physical universe, which extends beyond the optical and includes those things that man is not able to see but which he knows exist because of their effects on visible objects, is revealed by the radio telescope.

Our observations show that the distant galaxies and clusters of galaxies are uniformly distributed in space. The red shifts noted in their spectral lines, if due to the Doppler effects, indicate that the galaxies are moving away from us at an increasing rate. In 1912 V. M. Slipher first observed and measured the red shift in the spectrum of a galaxy. By 1929 Hubble had discovered that the radial velocities of galaxies are in direct proportion to their distances from the observer. From this, he established the velocity-distance relationship, which

[1]Albert Einstein, *The World As I See It*, translated by Allan Harris, New York: Philosophical Library, 1949, p. 5.

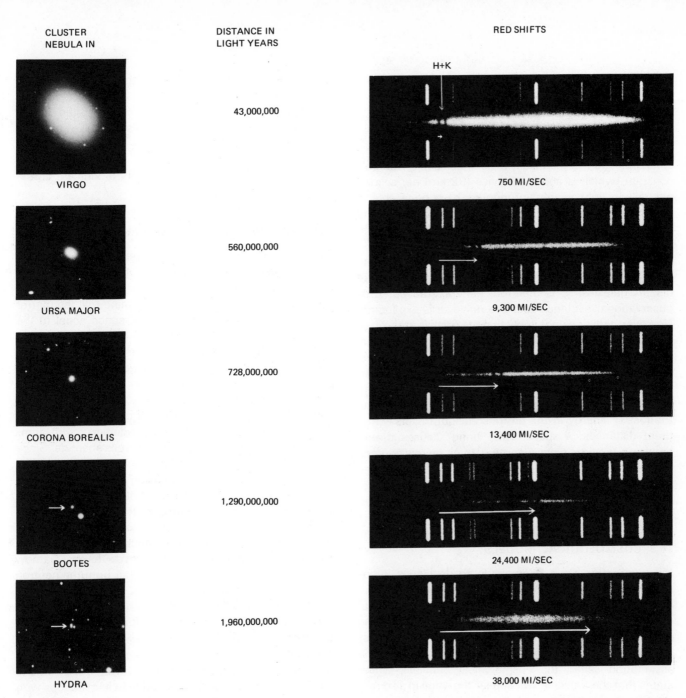

CLUSTER NEBULA IN	DISTANCE IN LIGHT YEARS	RED SHIFTS

H+K

VIRGO

43,000,000

750 MI/SEC

URSA MAJOR

560,000,000

9,300 MI/SEC

CORONA BOREALIS

728,000,000

13,400 MI/SEC

BOOTES

1,290,000,000

24,400 MI/SEC

HYDRA

1,960,000,000

38,000 MI/SEC

Fig. 16.2 Relation between red shift and distance for galaxies. Each galaxy shown on the left is a member of a cluster of galaxies in the constellation indicated. The red shift of the two absorption lines of ionized calcium in their spectra shown on the right is indicated by arrows. The red shifts are expressed in miles per second. The more distant galaxies show greater red shifts. (Photograph from the Hale Observatories)

is known as the Law of the Red Shifts, or Hubble's law. This linear relationship is shown in Fig. 16.1 and is expressed algebraically as

$$V = Hr,$$

where V is the velocity of the galaxy, H is Hubble's constant, and r is the galaxy's distance. Using Hubble's constant, which is about 20 miles (32 km) per second per million light years, astronomers have been able to determine the distance of galaxies. The photographs and spectra of five galaxies with distances that range up to about two billion light years are shown in Fig. 16.2.

The Doppler shift is the only verifiable cause that can account for the observed red shifts in the spectra of distant galaxies. It is therefore generally accepted as observational evidence that the universe is expanding. However, this does not imply that the earth is at the center of the universe, nor does it imply that the individual galaxies are expanding.

Some scientists who have not accepted the interpretation that the red shift indicates an expanding universe have suggested that the red shift is caused by the loss of energy in the protons as light travels across great distances of space. This "tiring" causes the increase in the light's wavelength. Others merely contend that something not yet discovered is causing the red shift. These and other suggestions that have been proposed are not supported by either theoretical or observational evidence.

16.3 COSMOLOGICAL MODELS

Many attempts have been made to develop a hypothetical model that would explain the nature of the universe. These models are based on mathematical equations, because mathematics is the only language capable of adequately describing the complicated cosmological situation. These equations are based on the assumption called the cosmological principle, which states that the universe will appear the same in all directions to all observers, regardless of their location in space. When the principle is extended to uniformity in time, that is, to an observer anywhere in space, the universe will appear the same regardless of time; this is called the perfect cosmological principle.

In Einstein's theory of relativity, the cosmological equation predicts the possibility of many types of universes, depending on the values assigned to the several variables. The two important models that have appeared since Einstein presented his theory of relativity are the evolutionary and the steady-state models. Both have accepted the theory that the red shifts indicate an expanding universe.

16.4 THE EVOLUTIONARY MODEL

The evolutionary model was first proposed by the Belgian cosmologist Georges Lemaitre in 1927. He suggested that the universe originated from an explosion of a "primeval nucleus" which contained all the matter in the universe within a volume of space equal to the diameter of the earth's orbit around the sun. The mechanics of how the universe was started from the "primeval nucleus" was developed by the American physicist George Gamow in his "big bang" theory (Fig. 16.3). According to Gamow, the universe was concentrated in a dense cloud of gas which consisted of neutrons and high thermal radiation, with temperatures estimated at 10 billion degrees absolute. Since the cloud was at a tremendous temperature and at an enormous pressure, an explosion occurred, ejecting its material into space at great velocities. During this expansion period, the neutrons decayed into protons and electrons. As the expansion continued, the temperature dropped sufficiently, which permitted the protons to capture neutrons and to form deuterons. Gamow theorized that the elements were built from the neutron capture process within 30 minutes.

Although the theoretical curve based on the neutron capture is in general agreement with the curve based on the observed relative abundances of the elements, some investigators doubt that the elements were formed in this manner, because the process would have come to a halt with the formation of unstable helium isotope with an atomic weight of 5. Since the unstable helium isotope immediately decays to the stable helium element with an atomic weight of 4, how were the heavier elements produced? Gamow's explanation was that since 98% of the universe consists of the low atomic weight

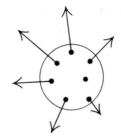

Fig. 16.3 According to the "big bang" theory, the universe originated from a tremendous explosion. The galaxies are moving away from the hypothetical center. The universe is expanding, and the space between galaxies is increasing.

elements, hydrogen and helium, these two elements were formed immediately after the explosion by the neutron-capture process, whereas the heavier elements were and are still being synthesized within the interior of stars that are evolving.

16.5 THE STEADY-STATE MODEL

The steady-state model of the universe, proposed by H. Bondi, T. Gold, and F. Hoyle, was developed because they questioned whether the universe had, as the evolutionary model required, a definite beginning and a finite age. In the steady-state model, the universe has always been and always will remain as it appears today, that is, its density remains the same, regardless of time. In this theory, the universe has no beginning and will have no end (Fig. 16.4). Because the expansion of the universe was established by the red shift, the steady-state model was forced to account for it so that the density of the universe would remain constant. Hoyle accomplished this by introducing his famous continuous-creation-of-matter hypothesis, which states that matter is created continuously at a sufficient rate to replace the matter that is moving outward. This controversial hypothesis is the basic weakness of the steady-state theory, because it postulates the creation of matter from nothing.

One evidence against the validity of the steady-state theory was produced in 1965 by Arno Penzias and Robert Wilson of the Bell Telephone Laboratories when

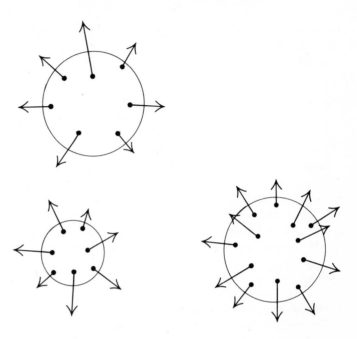

Fig. 16.4 According to the steady-state theory, the universe always has been and always will be as it appears today, that is, its density is the same, regardless of time. Since the universe is expanding, new matter is continuously being created.

they discovered, by using conventional radio telescopes, low-energy cosmic radio radiation coming from all directions. It appeared as though the entire universe was filled with this radiation, which was characteristic of the radiation emitted by a "black body," a perfect radiator, at a temperature of about $3°K$.

This universal cosmic radiation was predicted by George Gamow and the American physicist Robert Dicke. As early as 1948, Gamow said that if the universe started from an explosion of a "primeval nucleus," one should be able to detect radiation from it at the present time. The "primeval nucleus" was originally extremely hot and dense. As it expanded, it cooled and eventually permeated throughout the entire universe. Gamow implied from this theory, that the present-day temperature of the radiation should be about $3°K$, which is

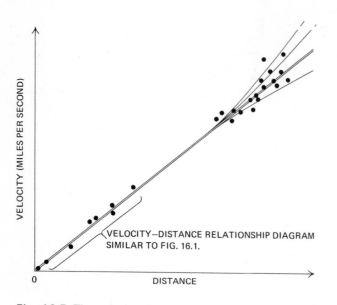

Fig. 16.5 The velocity-distance relationship extended to the more distant cluster galaxies and radio galaxies

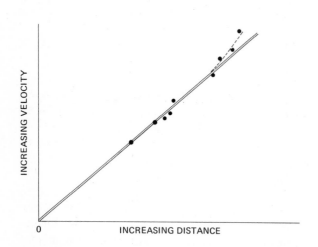

Fig. 16.6 The solid line represents Hubble's law. According to Allan Sandage at Palomar Observatory, recent observations show that bright, distant galaxies do not conform to Hubble's law. Their appearance above the line has been suggested as evidence of a pulsating universe.

what it actually turned out to be. The discovery of this radiation was a devastating blow to the steady-state theory. Since the steady-state universe never existed in a dense state, it could never have created a "black body" radiation.

16.6 THE PULSATING UNIVERSE

Plottings of recent observations of bright, distant clusters of galaxies and radio galaxies on a velocity-distance relation diagram (Fig. 16.5), have shown that these galaxies do not conform to the pattern established by Hubble's law; rather, they have an upward tendency, that is, they appear to lie above the line. The upward curve indicates that the galaxies are decelerating, which has been interpreted by Allan Sandage at Palomar Observatory as an indication of a pulsating universe—one which starts to contract when it reaches its maximum permissible expansion and then starts to expand again when it reaches its maximum permissible density (Fig. 16.6).

This is a continuous process. Allan Sandage has suggested that the period of pulsation is about 80 billion years. The deceleration of galaxies would occur if the galaxies are moving at velocities less than the escape velocity of the universe. Eventually, the gravitational force exerted by their combined masses would stop the expansion of the universe and start the process of contraction. This is not easy to test observationally, because since light from distant galaxies reaches the observer at different times, he sees a composite picture of the universe. Also, the faintness of these objects makes it very difficult to determine their distances accurately.

16.7 AGE OF THE UNIVERSE

In order to estimate the universe's age, we must assume that the universe had a definite beginning. Keeping this assumption in mind, we can try to determine the lapse of time between its beginning and its present state. We know that the oldest stars, located in globular clusters, have an age greater than 10^{10} years. Moreover, red-shift studies yield a comparable time for the expansion of the universe. Thus, with our present knowledge, the universe appears to be about 10 billion years old.

16.8 CONCLUSION

Although the observational evidence, such as the $3°K$ background radiation, points to the abandonment of the steady-state model and the acceptance of the big-bang model, we should not conclude that the latter model is the definitive one. Cosmological models are like all other models—they are reconstructions of the universe along lines prescribed by the observational data available. Cosmology presents a number of difficult problems to an astronomer who attempts to construct a reasonable model of the universe. Because of the great distances involved, facts become somewhat tenuous. Thus, the most essential evidence for the expanding universe— the red shifts—continues to have its detractors. As long as such doubts remain, no model can be said to be proved. In spite of the problems, Gamow's model presently provides the most efficient means of accounting for the given data. Continuing studies into quasars and pulsars may radically alter the situation in the near future. The "mysterious" still beckons.

REVIEW

1. How is the red shift related to the subject of cosmology?

2. Since the red shift is generally accepted as observational evidence of an expanding universe, does this imply that (a) the earth is at the center of the universe and (b) the galaxies are expanding? Explain your answers.

3. What other interpretations for the cause of the red shift have been proposed?

4. Explain what is meant by the perfect cosmological principle.

5. Who first proposed the evolutionary theory of the universe? Briefly outline the origin and evolution of the universe by this theory.

6. Explain the steady-state theory of the universe. What is considered to be its basic weakness? What observational evidence has been produced against the steady-state theory?

7. What is meant by the $3°K$ background radiation? Who first predicted its presence? Has it ever been observed? How is it related to the evolutionary theory?

8. Explain Hubble's law of the red shifts.

9. How was the age of the universe estimated? What is its value?

Appendixes

Appendix 1
Constellations

Few people ever notice the magnificent pagent than unfolds in the sky every night. Yet many hours of enjoyment and pleasure are readily available to anyone who is willing to do one simple thing—look. The task of learning and understanding the stars is not as formidable as it may appear, because although the number of stars in the universe has been compared to the number of grains of sand on all the earth's coasts, the stars visible to the unaided eye number less than 3000.

The initial step in becoming acquainted with the stars is to scan the sky and observe that the colors and brightnesses of stars differ considerably (Chapter 11). The colors range from blue (hottest) to red (coolest), and the brightnesses range from -1 magnitude (brightest) to $+6$ magnitude (just barely visible). For simplicity in observing the stars with the unaided eye, the following symbols and their magnitudes have been adopted.

Symbol

Magnitude -1 0   1   2   3   4

There are about 100 stars that are either bright enough or of sufficient interest to be identified by a proper name. Three of these are Polaris, the north pole star, which is almost directly above the earth's north pole; Sirius, the brightest star in the sky; and Vega, the fourth brightest star, which marks the general direction in space toward which the sun and the solar system are moving at about 12 miles (19 km) per second.

At first glance, the stars appear to be randomly distributed; on closer scrutiny, some of them appear to

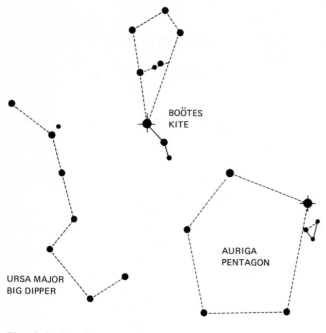

Fig. A.1 Asterisms

visualized by first locating their asterisms, then (with a little imagination) tracing the constellation pictures around the asterisms.

Constellations acquired a new meaning in 1927 when astronomers divided the entire sky into definite, irregular areas around the 88 constellations and assigned the name of the constellation to the respective area in which it is located. This produced a map of the sky on which the celestial bodies and events can be easily and quickly located by reference to the constellations.

1 NORTH CIRCUMPOLAR CONSTELLATIONS (CHART A.1)

The starting point for locating the constellations in the northern hemisphere is Polaris, the north star. To the unaided eye it is the nearest star to the celestial north pole (CNP), an imaginary point that marks the projection of the earth's north pole to the celestial sphere. At the present time. Polaris is less than one degree from the celestial north pole. When the observer faces the north point on the horizon, which is directly below Polaris, the stars appear to move in a counterclockwise direction around Polaris, which appears to remain stationary.

Five constellations revolve around Polaris—Ursa Major the Big Bear, Ursa Minor the Little Bear, Cepheus the King, Cassiopeia the Queen, and Draco the Dragon. These are called circumpolar constellations because they are visible every night at any time to observers located north of about 40° north latitude.

To locate the five circumpolar constellations, refer to Chart A. 1, in which Polaris is in the center and the five constellations are around it. The circumference of the circle is divided into 12 equal parts to represent the 12 months of the year. It is also divided into 24 equal parts to represent the hours in each day. To orient the chart with the sky for any evening at 8:00 P.M., face Polaris and hold the chart so that the proper month appears on the bottom.

Polaris, which marks the end of the handle of the Little Dipper and the tip of the tail of the Little Bear, locates the constellation of Ursa Minor. This constellation is easy to locate, because its clear, bright asterism is

be in geometrical shapes, such as straight lines, triangles, squares, and rectangles; others appear to be in definite groupings. Ancient man recognized these shapes and groupings and used them to form the constellations—the outlines of the people, animals, and physical objects that were in his primitive religion. Although the ancient Greeks recognized 48 constellations and many of them have Greek names, they were originated several thousand years earlier by the people living in the Tigris and Euphrates river valleys. Most of the star groupings are not even fair approximations of the constellation pictures they are supposed to represent; therefore, their recognition from the groupings is not easy. This problem was simplified when the few bright stars within the constellations were connected by straight lines to form asterisms—simple pictures which everyone can easily recognize. In Fig. A. 1, the asterism for Ursa Major the Big Bear is the Big Dipper; for Boötes the Bear Driver, it is the Kite; and for Auriga the Charioteer, it is the Pentagon. The constellations can be

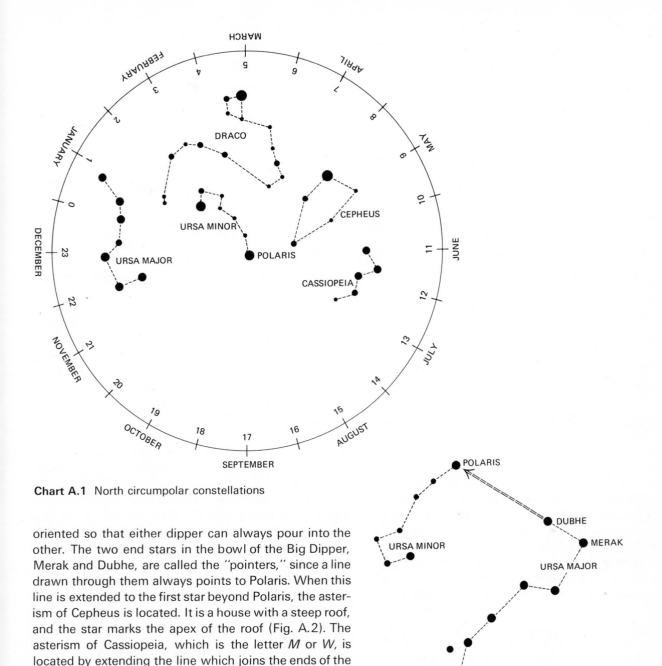

Chart A.1 North circumpolar constellations

oriented so that either dipper can always pour into the other. The two end stars in the bowl of the Big Dipper, Merak and Dubhe, are called the "pointers," since a line drawn through them always points to Polaris. When this line is extended to the first star beyond Polaris, the asterism of Cepheus is located. It is a house with a steep roof, and the star marks the apex of the roof (Fig. A.2). The asterism of Cassiopeia, which is the letter *M* or *W*, is located by extending the line which joins the ends of the handles of the two dippers to the first star beyond Polaris. This star marks one end of the asterism. When another star is included in the asterism, the outline of the chair on which Cassiopeia is seated can be easily visual-

Fig. A.2 Locating Polaris in Ursa Minor

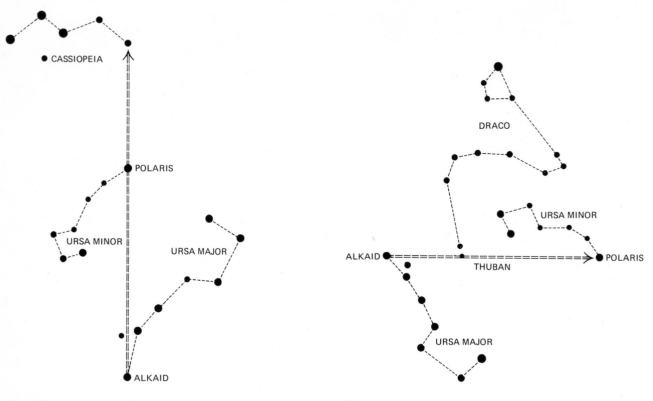

Fig. A.3 Locating Cassiopeia

Fig. A.4 Locating Draco

ized (Fig. A.3). The constellation of Draco is located by dividing the line which joins the ends of the handles of the two dippers into three equal parts. Two-thirds of the way on the line from Polaris is the star Thuban, which marks the tip of the dragon's tail. Draco has no asterism, because its arrangement of stars very clearly outlines the head, body, and tail of the dragon (Fig. A.4).

2 THE SEASONAL CHARTS

As an aid to identifying and learning the constellations, four seasonal charts have been drawn—autumn, winter, spring, and summer—which show the constellations as they appear about 9:00 P.M. on the first day of autumn (September 21), winter (December 21), spring (March 21), and summer (June 21). When using a chart, face one of the horizons, hold the chart vertically, and turn it so that the direction in which you are facing appears at the bottom. The observer's meridian is an imaginary vertical line which passes from the northern to the southern horizon and passes through Polaris and the zenith point of the observer (marked by a cross (+) on the chart).

3 AUTUMN CONSTELLATIONS (CHART A.2)

Three beautiful constellations are visible almost directly overhead in the autumn months. They are Cygnus the Swan, Lyra the Harp, and Aquila the Eagle, and they all lie in the Milky Way. The brightest star in each of these

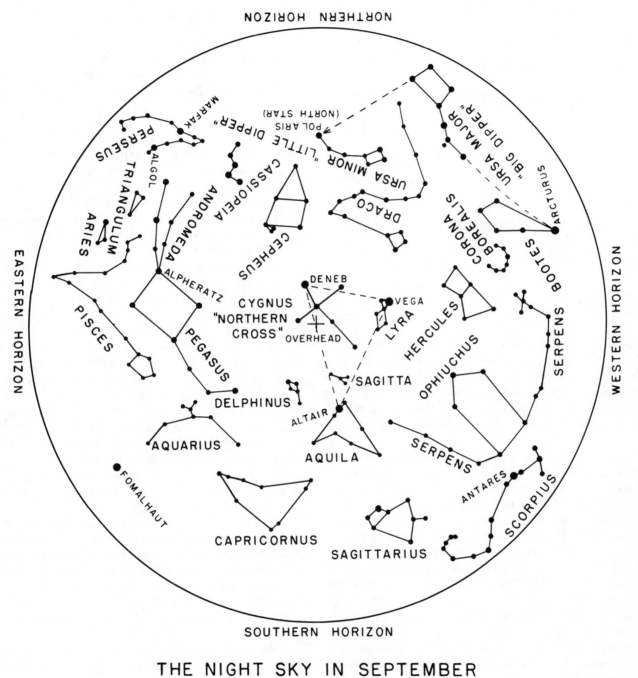

THE NIGHT SKY IN SEPTEMBER

Chart A.2 The autumn constellations. (Courtesy Griffith Observatory)

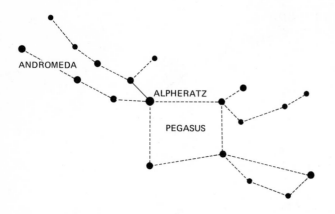

Fig. A.5 The constellations of Pegasus and Andromeda

4 WINTER CONSTELLATIONS (CHART A.3)

The winter hunting scene, the most outstanding feature of the winter sky, comprises several constellations—Orion the Mighty Hunter; his two dogs, Canis Major the Big Dog and Canis Minor the Little Dog; his adversary, Taurus the Bull; and his prey, Lepus the Hare. The asterism of Orion is the Hour Glass. The star Betelgeuse, which marks the right shoulder, is over one-third billion miles in diameter and was first measured with the interferometer by Michelson. The star Rigel marks the left foot. Orion wears a belt of three stars, with the top star, Mintaka, lying almost on the celestial equator. The curved row of stars in front and to the west of Orion represents the lion, which Orion is holding with his left hand. Below Orion is Lepus, and following the mighty hunter, to the east, are his two dogs. Canis Major has no asterism, because the outline of a dog can be easily visualized from the arrangement of the stars. The brightest star in the sky is Sirius, which marks the nose of the Big Dog. The constellation of Canis Minor is difficult to visualize, because most of its stars are very dim. Its brightest star, Procyon, together with Sirius and Betelgeuse form the winter triangle. Completing the scene is Taurus, a zodiacal constellation, which is in front and to the west of Orion. Its asterism is the open cluster of stars (the Hyades) which marks the head of the bull. Only the front part of the bull's body is visible, because the Greeks imagined that the bull was swimming in the Mediterranean Sea. The right eye of the bull is the bright star Aldebaran. The open cluster of the Pleiades is located in the left shoulder of the bull.

The three zodiacal constellations are Aries the Ram, Taurus the Bull, and Gemini the Twins. The asterism of Aries is a small triangle, and Hamal is its brightest star. The asterism of Gemini is two nearly parallel rows of stars. The twin sons of Jupiter are represented by the stars Castor and Pollux. Castor is located at the top of the western row of stars; Pollux, at the top of the eastern row.

Above the winter hunting scene are the two beautiful constellations of Auriga the Charioteer and Perseus the Hero. The asterism of Auriga is a five-sided figure, with Capella its brightest star. The asterism of Perseus

constellations—Deneb in Cygnus (the tail of the swan), Vega in Lyra (one corner of the small triangle), and Altair in Aquila (the middle star in the straight line)—form the summer triangle, which is almost a right triangle. The asterisms are the Northern Cross for Cygnus, a rectangle and triangle for Lyra, and a straight line of three stars for Aquila.

The three zodiacal constellations—Capricornus the Sea Goat, Aquarius the Water Carrier, and Pisces the Fishes—are visible low in the autumn sky between the southern and eastern points on the horizon.

Above the eastern horizon, the constellation of Pegasus the Winged Horse can easily be located by its asterism, the Great Square. The square represents the body of the horse, which is upside down, and only the front half is visible. The dim stars to the west of the square form the head and the two front legs of the animal. The star Alpheratz, which is located at the northeast corner of the square, is common to two constellations—Pegasus and Andromeda the Chained Lady. The asterism of Andromeda is two rows of stars diverging from Alpheratz and curving toward the constellation of Cassiopeia (Fig. A.5).

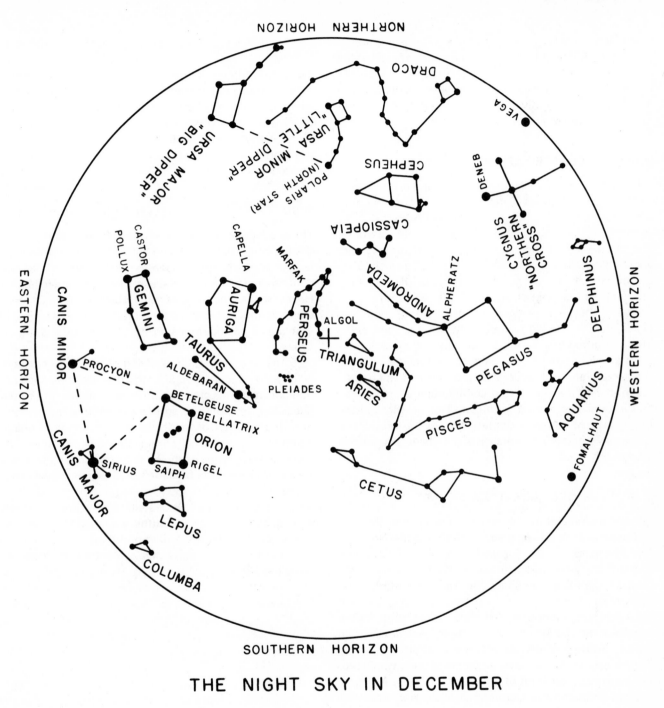

THE NIGHT SKY IN DECEMBER

Chart A.3 The winter constellations. (Courtesy Griffith Observatory)

resembles a wishbone, and its most interesting star is Algol, the "Blinking Demon." In the southern part of the sky are two, long, indistinct constellations that can be located and traced on a clear moonless evening. These are Eridanus the Po River and Cetus the Whale. Eridanus meanders in the region between Cetus, Orion, and Lepus.

5 SPRING CONSTELLATIONS (CHART A.4)

The prominent constellations in the spring are the three zodiacal constellations Cancer the Crab, Leo the Lion, and Virgo the Virgin. Dominating the entire southern sky is the long, faint constellation Hydra the Sea Serpent. The brightest and most beautiful constellation is Leo, and its asterism is a sickle and a triangle. The sickle represents the head of the lion; the triangle, its hind quarters. To the west of the sickle is a hazy spot of light visible to the unaided eye (the nebula of Praesepe, also called the "Beehive") located between two faint stars. This star group marks the constellation of Cancer, whose stars are very dim. To the east of the triangle in Leo is the constellation of Virgo. The location of this constellation is also marked by the continuation of the curved line through the handle of the Big Dipper, through the bright star Arcturus in Boötes, and to the bright star Spica in Virgo. Spica represents the sheaf of wheat in Virgo's left hand.

6 SUMMER CONSTELLATIONS (CHART A.5)

There are several prominent summer constellations: Boötes the Bear Driver; Corona Borealis the Northern Crown; Hercules the Kneeler; Ophiuchus the Serpent Carrier; and the zodiacal constellations of Libra the Scales, Scorpius the Scorpion, and Sagittarius the Archer.

The continuation of the curved line through the handle of the Big Dipper locates the star Arcturus, which marks the bottom of the kite, the asterism of Boötes. To the east of Boötes is a semicircle of stars which represent the constellation of Corona Borealis the Northern Crown. To the east of Corona Borealis is Hercules, who appears upside down in the sky. He is referred to as the kneeler, because he appears in a kneeling position. Its asterism is the letter *H*. The asterism of Ophiuchus is a triangle on top of a large vertical rectangle which represents the body of Ophiuchus. Around his body is the constellation Serpens the Serpent. The most prominent of the three zodiacal constellations is Scorpius. Its arrangement of stars clearly outlines the head, body, and tail of the scorpion. Its brightest star, Antares, marks the heart of the scorpion.

7 SOUTH POLAR CONSTELLATIONS (CHART A.6)

The south polar constellations are shown in Chart A.6. At the present time, there is no south celestial pole star. In fact, the area in comparison to that shown in Chart A.1 contains fewer stars and less prominent constellations. However, the area contains several brilliant stars: Canopus, which is one of the most beautiful, and two bright stars that are close together and point toward the Southern Cross.

The largest, most interesting southern constellation is the ship Argo, named after the famous ship which carried Jason and his crew to Colchis in search of the golden fleece. Since there are so many stars in this constellation, it has been divided into several smaller constellations that represent various parts of the ship—the constellation Carina is the keel, Puppis is the stern, and Vela is the sails. The brilliant star Canopus marks Argo's rudder.

A famous, fabled constellation is Crux Australis, whose asterism is the Southern Cross. The asterism, which looks more like a diamond than a cross, appears to many to be less impressive than the large, beautiful Northern Cross.

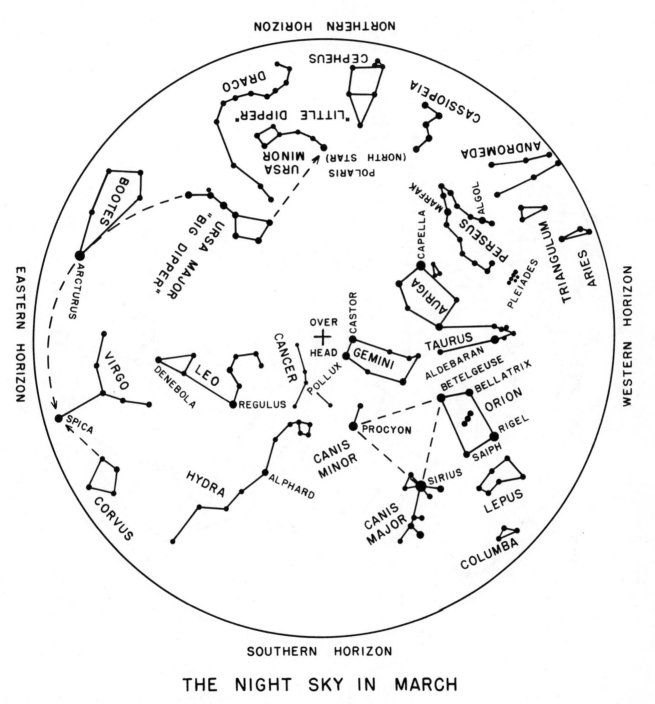

THE NIGHT SKY IN MARCH

Chart A.4 The spring constellations. (Courtesy Griffith Observatory)

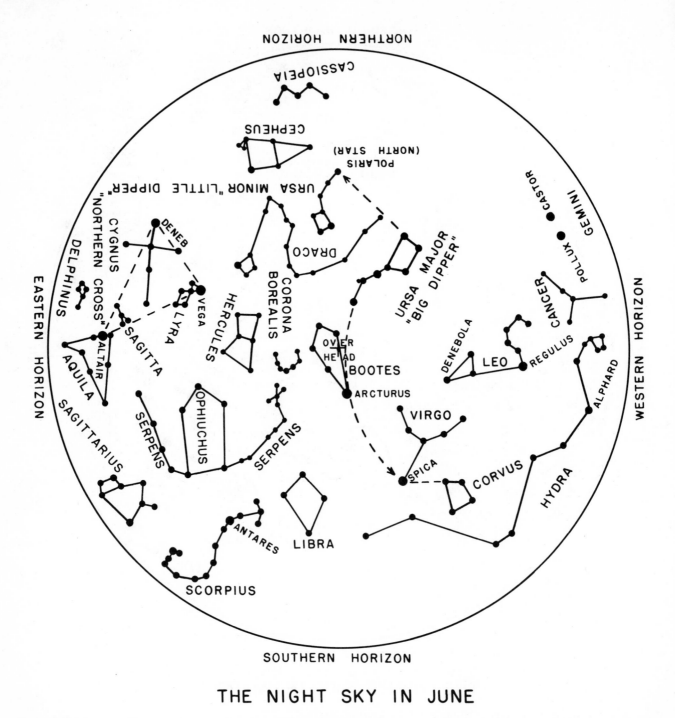

Chart A.5 The summer constellations. (Courtesy Griffith Observatory)

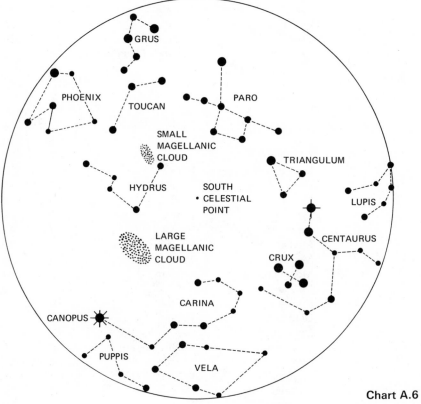

Chart A.6 South polar constellations

8 THE 88 CONSTELLATIONS

The 88 constellations are listed in the following table by their Latin and English names and their approximate position in the sky.

Constellation Table

Latin name	English name	Sky position R.A. (hours)	Decli-nation (de-grees)
Andromeda	Princess of Ethiopia	1	+40
Antila	Air pump	10	−35
Apus	Bird of paradise	16	−75
Aquarius	Water carrier	23	−15
Aquila	Eagle	20	+ 5
Ara	Altar	17	−55
Aries	Ram	3	+20
Auriga	Charioteer	6	+40
Boötes	Bear driver	15	+30
Caelum	Graving tool	5	−40
Camelopardus	Giraffe	6	−70
Cancer	Crab	9	+20
Canes Venatici	Hunting dogs	13	+40
Canis Major	Big dog	7	−20
Canis Minor	Little dog	8	+ 5
Capricornus	Sea goat	21	−20
Carina	Argo's keel	9	−60
Cassiopeia	Queen of Ethiopia	1	+60
Centaurus	Centaur	13	−50
Cepheus	King of Ethiopia	22	+70
Cetus	Whale	2	−10
Chamaeleon	Chameleon	11	−80
Circinus	Compasses	15	−60
Columba	Noah's dove	6	−35
Coma Berenices	Berenice's hair	13	+20
Corona Australis	Southern crown	19	−40
Corona Borealis	Northern crown	16	+30
Corvus	Crow	12	−20
Crater	Cup	11	−15
Crux	Southern Cross	12	−60
Cygnus	Swan	21	+40
Delphinus	Dolphin	21	+10
Dorado	Swordfish	5	−65
Draco	Dragon	17	+65

Latin name	English name	Sky position R.A. (hours)	Decli-nation (de-grees)
Equuleus	Little horse	21	+10
Eridanus	Po river	3	−20
Fornax	Furnace	3	−30
Gemini	Twins	7	+20
Grus	Crane	22	−45
Hercules	Hercules (Zeus' son)	17	+30
Horologium	Clock	3	−60
Hydra	Sea serpent	10	−20
Hydrus	Water snake	2	−75
Indus	Indian	21	−55
Lacerta	Lizard	22	+45
Leo	Lion	11	+15
Leo Minor	Little lion	10	+35
Lepus	Hare	6	−20
Libra	Balance	15	−15
Lupus	Wolf	15	−45
Lynx	Lynx	8	+45
Lyra	Harp	19	+40
Mensa	Table mountain	5	−80
Microscopium	Microscope	21	−35
Monoceros	Unicorn	7	− 5
Musca	Fly	12	−70
Norma	Level	16	−50
Octans	Octant	22	−85
Ophiuchus	Serpent carrier	17	0
Orion	Mighty hunter	5	+ 5
Pavo	Peacock	20	−65
Pegasus	Winged horse	22	+20
Perseus	Hero	3	+45
Phoenix	Phoenix	1	−50
Pictor	Easel	6	−55
Pisces	Fishes	1	+15
Piscis Austrinus	Southern fish	22	−30
Puppis	Argo's stern	8	−40

Latin name	English name	Sky position R.A. (hours)	Declination (degrees)
Pyxis	Argo's compass	9	−30
Reticulum	Net	4	−60
Sagitta	Arrow	20	+10
Sagittarius	Archer	19	−25
Scorpius	Scorpion	17	−40
Sculptor	Sculptor's tools	0	−30
Scutum	Shield	19	−10
Serpens	Serpent	17	0
Sextans	Sextant	10	0
Taurus	Bull	4	+15
Telescopium	Telescope	19	−50
Triangulum	Triangle	2	+30
Triangulum Australis	Southern triangle	16	−65
Tucana	Toucan	0	−65
Ursa Major	Big bear	11	+50
Ursa Minor	Little bear	15	+70
Vela	Argo's sail	9	−50
Virgo	Virgin	13	0
Volans	Flying fish	8	−70
Vulpecula	Fox	20	+25

REVIEW

1. Give two definitions for the term "constellation." What is an asterism?

2. What star is nearest the north celestial pole? How can it be located? What is its magnitude? What type of star is it?

3. What are circumpolar constellations? Name those at your latitude.

4. What is the significance of the "pointers" in the asterism of the Big Dipper?

5. What is the asterism of the following constellations: (a) Auriga (b) Crux (c) Cygnus (d) Leo (e) Pegasus?

6. What stars make up the (a) winter triangle (b) summer triangle?

7. Explain how the vernal equinox can be located.

8. In what constellation is the Hyades located? What does this group of stars represent? Is the bright star Aldebaran which appears in this group part of the Hyades?

9. What are the Pleiades? Where are they located? How many stars are visible to the naked eye? How many have been observed in the Pleiades?

10. In what constellation is each of the following located: (a) the eclipsing binary Algol, "the blinking demon" (b) the Andromeda galaxy (c) the Ring nebula (d) Capella?

11. What is the brightest star in the sky?

12. Name the five brightest stars with their magnitudes that appear in the winter sky at about 9:00 P.M. Name the two brightest stars that appear in the early hours in the summer sky.

13. The following examples represent three methods for designating stars: (a) Algol (b) Beta Persei (c) Kruger 60. Explain.

14. What constellations appear in the Milky Way in the summer sky? Where is the Coal Sack located? What is it? Describe and explain the Great Rift.

15. What constellations appear in the Milky Way in the winter sky? Compare the appearance of the Milky Way as to size and luminosity in summer and winter. Explain the difference with a diagram.

16. The constellations of Canis Major and Gemini appear to cross the observer's meridian at the same time. Do they rise on the eastern horizon at the same time? Explain.

Appendix 2
Scientific Notation

In astronomical work, very large and very small numbers are used. For example, the earth's distance from the sun is approximately 93,000,000 miles, or 15,000,000, 000,000 cm., and the wavelength of an x-ray is approximately 0.00000001 cm. Since the many zeros make it inconvenient to write these numbers, a simpler system involving the powers of ten is used. This system is called "scientific notation."

Powers of Ten

$$10^3 = 10 \times 10 \times 10 \qquad\qquad = 1000$$
$$10^2 = 10 \times 10 \qquad\qquad\qquad = 100$$
$$10^1 = 10 \qquad\qquad\qquad\qquad = 10$$
$$10^0 = 1 \qquad\qquad\qquad\qquad\quad = 1$$
$$10^{-1} = 1/10 \qquad\qquad\qquad\quad = 0.1$$
$$10^{-2} = 1/10 \times 1/10 = 1/100 \qquad = 0.01$$
$$10^{-3} = 1/10 \times 1/10 \times 1/10 = 1/1000 = 0.001$$

In scientific notation a number is usually written as the product of a number from 1 to 9 and a power of ten. The power of ten (exponent) indicates the number of places the decimal point must be moved to restore the number. If the power is positive, the decimal point must be moved to the right; if negative, it must be moved to the left.

Number	Scientific notation
15,000,000,000,000	1.5×10^{13}
93,000,000	9.3×10^7
69,600,000,000	6.96×10^{10}
0.00000001	1.0×10^{-8}
0.00000872	8.72×10^{-6}

The scientific notation is an important and useful technique because it expresses bulky numbers in simple terms so that they can be easily read and compared. It also simplifies the multiplication and division processes in calculations.

Appendix 3
Fundamental Metric
and English Units

Fundamental Units	Metric System	English System
Length	1 meter (m)	1 yard (yd)
Mass	1 kilogram (kg)	1 pound (lb)
Time	1 second (sec)	1 second (sec)

Units of Length

1 kilometer (km) = 1000 meters (m) = 0.6214 mile (mi)

1 meter (m) = 0.001 km = 100 centimeters (cm) = 1.094 yd = 39.37 inches (in)

1 centimeter (cm) = 0.01 m = 10 millimeters (mm) = 0.3937 in

1 millimeter (mm) = 0.001 m = 0.03937 in = 1000 microns (μ)

1 micron (μ) = 0.000001 m = 3.3937 $\times$ 10^{-5} in = 10,000 Angstroms (Å)

1 statute mile (mi) = 5280 feet (ft) = 1.6093 km

1 inch (in) = 2.5400 cm

Units of Mass

1 metric ton =1000 kilogram (kg) = 1.102 English tons

1 kilogram (kg) = 1000 grams (gm) = 2.2046 lb

1 gram (gm) = 0.0022046 lb = 0.0353 ounce (oz)

1 pound (lb) = 16 oz = 453.6 gm

1 ounce (oz) = 28.3495 gm

Appendix 4
Temperature Scales
and Conversions

Fahrenheit scale

| −459.0°F | 32.0°F | 212.0°F |

Centigrade (Celsius) scale

| −273.0°C | 0.0°C | 100.0°C |

Kelvin (absolute) scale

| 0.0°K | 273.0°K | 373.0°K |

| Absolute zero | Freezing point of water | Boiling point of water |

Conversions

$$°C = 5/9\,(°F - 32°) \qquad °C = °K - 273°$$
$$°F = 9/5\,(°C) + 32° \qquad °F = 9/5\,(°K) - 459°$$
$$°K = 5/9\,(°F + 459°) \qquad °K = °C + 273°$$

Appendix 5

Useful Physical Constants and Astronomical Quantities

Pi (π) = 3.14159 = 22/7

Radian (R) = 57°.3 = 206265 sec

Angstrom unit (Å) = 10^{-8} cm

Astronomical unit (a.u.) = 1.496 $\times$ 10^8 km = 9.3 $\times$ 10^7 mi

Velocity of light (c) = 2.99795 $\times$ 10^5 km/sec = 1.86 $\times$ 10^5 mi/sec

Light year (l.y.) = 9.461 $\times$ 10^{12} km = 5.9 $\times$ 10^{12} mi

Parsec (pc) = 206265 a.u. = 3.260 l.y.

Constant of gravitation (G) = 6.668 $\times$ 10^{-8} dyne. cm^2/gm^2

Solar constant (S) = 1.93 calories/$cm^2 \cdot$min (1.37 $\times$ 10^6 ergs/$cm^2 \cdot$sec)

Sun radius $(R_\odot)$ = 6.960 $\times$ 10^5 km = 4.32 $\times$ 10^5 mi

Earth radius (equatorial) $(R_\oplus)$ = 6378.16 km = 3963.20 mi

Sun mass $(M_\odot)$ = 1.991 $\times$ 10^{33} gm

Earth mass $(M_\oplus)$ = 5.977 $\times$ 10^{27} gm

Earth velocity of escape = 11.2 km/sec = 6.94 mi/sec

Proton mass (m_p) = 1.67 $\times$ 10^{-24} gm

Electron mass (m_e) = 9.11 $\times$ 10^{-28} gm

Hydrogen atom mass (m_H) = 1.673 $\times$ 10^{-24} gm

Appendix 6 Physical and Orbital Data for the Planets

	Mercury ☿	Venus ♀	Earth ⊕
Symbol			
Mean distance from sun (a.u.)	0.387	0.723	1.000
Mean distance from sun (miles)	3.6×10^7	6.7×10^7	9.3×10^7
Mean orbital speed (km/sec)	47.8	35.0	29.8
Synodic period (days)	115.9	583.9	—
Sidereal period (d, days; y, years)	88 d	224.7 d	365.26 d
Orbital eccentricity	0.206	0.007	0.017
Inclination of orbit to plane of the ecliptic	7°.0	3°.4	—
Inclination of equator to the orbital plane	?	23°	23°.5
Equatorial diameter (km)	4,880	12,110	12,742
Equatorial diameter (miles)	3,025	7,526	7,927
Diameter (earth = 1)	0.38	0.95	1.00
Mass (earth = 1)	0.056	0.815	1.000
Density (gm/cm³)	5.46	5.23	5.52
Escape velocity (km/sec)	4.3	10.3	11.2
Period of rotation	59 days	243 days retrograde	23 hours 56 minutes
Albedo	0.06	0.76	0.36

Mars ♂	Jupiter ♃	Saturn ♄	Uranus ♅	Neptune ♆	Pluto ♇
1.524	5.203	9.539	19.182	30.058	39.439
1.42×10^8	4.83×10^8	8.86×10^8	1.78×10^9	2.79×10^9	3.67×10^9
24.2	13.1	9.7	6.8	5.4	4.7
779.9	398.9	378.1	369.7	367.5	366.7
687.0 d	11.86 y	29.46 y	84.01 y	164.79 y	247.69 y
0.093	0.048	0.056	0.047	0.009	0.250
1°.9	1°.3	2°.5	0°.8	1°.8	17°.2
24°	3°	27°	98°	29°	?
6.790	143,000	121,000	47,000	45,000	5,600
4,218	88,700	75,100	29,200	27,960	3,500 ?
0.53	11.19	9.47	3.69	3.50	0.47 ±
0.107	318.0	95.2	14.6	17.3	0.11 ?
3.93	1.33	0.69	1.56	2.24	?
0.51	57.5	33.0	21.9	24.5	?
24 hours	9 hours	10 hours	10 hours	15 hours	
37 minutes	55 minutes	38 minutes	49 minutes	48 minutes	6.4 days
0.16	0.51	0.50	0.66	0.62	0.1 ?

Appendix 7 The Nearest Stars

Star	Right ascension (1970) h m	° Declination (1970) '	Distance (l.y.)	Proper motion (sec)	Radial velocity (km/sec)	Apparent visual magnitude	Absolute visual magnitude	Spectral class
Sun						−26.8		G2 V
α Centauri	14 37	−60 43	4.3	3.68	− 23	0.1	+ 4.4	G2 V
Barnard's star	17 56	+04 36	6.0	10.30	−108	9.5	+13.2	M5 V
Wolf 359	10 55	+07 13	7.6	4.84	+ 13	13.5	+16.8	M6 V
Lalande 21185	11 02	+36 10	8.1	4.78	− 86	7.5	+10.5	M2 V
Sirius	06 44	−16 41	8.6	1.32	− 8	− 1.5	+ 1.4	A1 V
Luyten 726	01 37	−18 07	8.9	3.35	+ 29	12.5	+15.4	M6 V
Ross 154	18 48	−23 51	9.4	0.74	− 4	10.6	+13.3	M5 V
Ross 248	23 40	+44 01	10.3	1.82	− 81	12.2	+14.7	M6 V
ε Eridani	03 32	−09 34	10.7	0.97	+ 15	3.7	+ 6.1	K2 V
Luyten 789−6	22 37	−15 31	10.8	3.27	− 60	12.2	+14.9	M6 V
Ross 128	11 46	+01 01	10.8	1.40	− 13	11.1	+13.5	M5 V
61 Cygni	21 06	+38 36	11.2	5.22	− 64	5.2	+ 7.5	K5 V
ε Indi	22 02	−56 55	11.2	4.67	− 40	4.7	+ 7.0	K5 V
Procyon	07 38	+05 18	11.4	1.25	− 3	0.3	+ 2.7	F51 V
Σ 2398	18 42	+59 35	11.5	2.29	+ 8	8.9	+11.1	M4 V
Groom. 34	00 17	+43 51	11.6	2.91	—	8.1	—	M1 V
Lacaille 9352	23 04	−36 02	11.7	6.87	—	7.4	—	M2 V
τ Ceti	01 43	−16 06	11.9	1.92	− 16	3.5	+ 5.7	G8 V
BD + 5° 1668	07 26	+05 28	12.2	3.73	+ 26	9.8	+11.9	M4 V

Appendix 8 The Brightest Stars

Star	Right ascension (1970) h m	Declination (1970) ° ′	Distance (l.y.)	Apparent visual magnitude	Absolute visual magnitude	Spectral class	Proper motion ″	Radial velocity km/sec
Sun				−26.73	+4.84	G2 V		
Sirius	06 43.8	−16 41	8.7	− 1.42	+1.45	Al V	1.324	−07.6
Canopus	06 23.3	−52 41	98.0	− 0.72	−3.1	FO Ib-II	0.025	+20.5
α Centauri	14 37.6	−60 43	4.3	+ 0.01	+4.39	G2 V	3.676	−24.6
Arcturus	14 14.3	+19 20	36.0	− 0.06	−0.3	K2 III	2.284	−05.2
Vega	18 35.9	+38 45	26.5	0.04	+0.5	AO V	0.345	−13.9
Capella	05 14.5	+45 58	45.0	0.05	−0.6	G8 III	0.435	+30.2
Rigel*	05 13.1	−08 14	900.0	0.14	−7.1	B8 Ia	0.001	+20.7
Procyon	07 37.7	+05 18	11.3	0.37	+2.7	F5 IV-V	1.250	−03.2
Betelgeuse*	05 53.5	+07 24	520.0	0.41	−5.6	M2 Iab	0.028	+21.0
Achernar	01 36.6	−57 23	118.0	0.51	−2.3	B5 IV	0.098	+19.0
β Centauri	14 01.7	−60 13	490.0	0.63	−5.2	B III	0.035	−12.0
Altair	19 49.3	+08 47	16.5	0.77	+2.2	A7 IV-V	0.658	−26.3
Aldebaran	04 34.2	+16 27	68.0	0.86	−0.7	K5 III	0.202	+54.1
Spica*	13 23.6	−11 00	220.0	0.91	−3.3	B IV	0.054	+01.0
Antares*	16 27.6	−26 22	520.0	0.92	−5.1	M IIb	0.029	−03.2
Pollux	07 43.5	+28 06	35.0	1.16	+1.0	KO III	0.625	+03.3
Fomalhaut	22 56.0	−29 47	22.6	1.19	+2.0	A3 V	0.367	+06.5
Deneb	20 40.4	+45 10	1600.0	1.26	−7.1	A2 Ia	0.003	−04.6
β Crucis	12 46.0	−59 32	490.0	1.28	−4.6	BO III	0.049	+20.0
Regulus	10 06.8	+12 07	84.0	1.36	−0.7	B7 V	0.248	+03.5
α Crucis	12 24.9	−62 56	370.0	1.39	−3.9	B IIV	0.042	−11.2

Note: Ia, most luminous supergiant; Ib, least luminous supergiant; II, bright giant; III, normal giant; IV, subgiant; V, main sequence; *, variable star.

Appendix 9 The Messier Catalogue of Nebulae and Star Clusters

Number M	NGC	Right ascension (1970)	Declination (1970)	Constellation	Apparent visual magnitude	Description
1	1952	5 32.7	+22 01	Taurus	11.3	"Crab" nebula; remains of supernova 1054
2	7089	21 31.9	−00 57	Aquarius	6.27	Globular cluster
3	5272	13 40.8	+28 32	Canes Venatici	6.22	Globular cluster
4	6121	16 21.8	−26 26	Scorpio	6.07	Globular cluster
5	5904	15 17.0	+02 13	Serpens	5.99	Globular cluster
6	6405	17 38.1	−32 11	Scorpio	6.0	Open cluster
7	6475	17 51.9	−34 48	Scorpio	5.0	Open cluster
8	6523	18 01.8	−24 23	Sagittarius		"Lagoon" nebula; diffuse nebula
9	6333	17 17.5	−18 29	Ophiuchus	7.58	Globular cluster
10	6254	16 55.5	−04 04	Ophiuchus	6.40	Globular cluster
11	6705	18 49.5	−06 19	Scutum	7.0	Open cluster
12	6218	16 45.6	−01 54	Ophiuchus	6.74	Globular cluster
13	6205	16 40.6	+36 31	Hercules	5.78	Globular cluster
14	6402	17 36.0	−03 14	Ophiuchus	7.82	Globular cluster
15	7078	21 28.6	+12 02	Pegasus	6.29	Globular cluster
16	6611	18 17.2	−13 48	Serpens	7.0	Open cluster with nebulosity
17	6618	18 19.1	−16 12	Sagittarius	7.0	"Swan" or "Omega" nebula; diffuse nebula
18	6613	18 18.2	−17 09	Sagittarius	7.0	Open cluster
19	6273	17 00.7	−26 13	Ophiuchus	6.94	Globular cluster
20	6514	18 00.6	−23 02	Sagittarius		"Trifid" nebula; diffuse nebula
21	6531	18 02.8	−22 30	Sagittarius	7.0	Open cluster
22	6656	18 34.6	−23 56	Sagittarius	5.22	Globular cluster
23	6494	17 55.1	−19 00	Sagittarius	6.0	Open cluster
24	6603	18 16.7	−18 27	Sagittarius	6.0	Open cluster
25	4725*	18 29.9	−19 16	Sagittarius	6.0	Open cluster
26	6694	18 43.6	−09 26	Scutum	9.0	Open cluster
27	6853	19 58.4	+22 38	Vulpecula	8.2	"Dumbbell" nebula; planetary nebula
28	6626	18 22.6	−24 52	Sagittarius	7.07	Globular cluster
29	6913	20 22.9	+38 25	Cygnus	8.0	Open cluster

Number M	NGC	(1970) Right ascension	Declination	Constellation	Apparent Visual magnitude	Description
30	7099	21 38.6	−23 18	Capricornus	7.63	Globular cluster
31	224	0 41.1	+41 06	Andromeda	3.7	Andromeda galaxy
32	221	0 41.1	+40 42	Andromeda	8.5	Elliptical galaxy (Sb); companion to M31
33	598	1 32.2	+30 30	Triangulum	5.9	Spiral galaxy (Sc)
34	1039	2 40.1	+42 40	Perseus	6.0	Open cluster
35	2168	6 07.0	+24 21	Gemini	6.0	Open cluster
36	1960	5 34.3	+34 05	Auriga	6.0	Open cluster
37	2099	5 50.4	+32 33	Auriga	6.0	Open cluster
38	1912	5 26.6	+35 48	Auriga	6.0	Open cluster
39	7092	21 31.1	+48 18	Cygnus	6.0	Open cluster
40	—	12 20.0	+59 00	Ursa Major		Double star
41	2287	6 45.8	−20 42	Canis Major	6.0	Loose open cluster
42	1976	5 33.9	−05 24	Orion		Orion nebula; diffuse nebula
43	1982	5 34.1	−05 18	Orion		Northeast portion of Orion nebula
44	2632	8 38.2	+20 06	Cancer	4.0	Praesepe; open cluster
45	—	3 45.7	+24 01	Taurus	2.0	The Pleiades; open cluster
46	2437	7 40.4	−14 45	Puppis	7.0	Open cluster
47	2422	7 35.1	−14 26	Puppis	5.0	Open cluster
48	2548	8 12.0	−05 41	Hydra	6.0	Open cluster
49	4472	12 28.3	+08 10	Virgo	8.9	Elliptical galaxy
50	2323	7 01.5	−08 18	Monoceros	7.0	Loose open cluster
51	5194	13 28.6	+47 21	Canes Venatici	8.4	"Whirlpool" galaxy; Spiral galaxy (Sc)
52	7654	23 22.9	+61 26	Cassiopeia	7.0	Loose open cluster
53	5024	13 11.5	+18 20	Coma Berenices	7.70	Globular cluster
54	6715	18 53.2	−30 31	Sagittarius	7.7	Globular cluster
55	6809	19 38.1	−31 01	Sagittarius	6.09	Globular cluster
56	6779	19 15.4	+30 07	Lyra	8.33	Globular cluster
57	6720	18 52.5	+33 00	Lyra	9.0	"Ring" nebula; planetary nebula
58	4579	12 36.2	+11 59	Virgo	9.9	Spiral galaxy (SBb)
59	4621	12 40.5	+11 50	Virgo	10.3	Elliptical galaxy
60	4649	12 42.1	+11 44	Virgo	9.3	Elliptical galaxy

Number M	NGC	Right ascension	(1970) Declination	Constellation	Apparent visual magnitude	Description
61	4303	12 20.3	+04 39	Virgo	9.7	Spiral galaxy (Sc)
62	6266	16 59.3	−30 04	Scorpio	7.2	Globular cluster
63	5055	13 14.4	+42 11	Canes Venatici	8.8	Spiral galaxy (Sb)
64	4826	12 55.2	+21 51	Coma Berenices	8.7	Spiral galaxy (Sb)
65	3623	11 17.3	+13 16	Leo	9.6	Spiral galaxy (Sa)
66	3627	11 18.6	+13 10	Leo	9.2	Spiral galaxy (Sb); companion to M65
67	2682	8 49.5	+11 56	Cancer	7.0	Open cluster
68	4590	12 37.8	−26 35	Hydra	8.04	Globular cluster
69	6637	18 29.4	−32 23	Sagittarius	7.7	Globular cluster
70	6681	18 41.3	−32 19	Sagittarius	8.2	Globular cluster
71	6838	19 52.4	+18 42	Sagittarius	6.9	Globular cluster
72	6981	20 51.8	−12 41	Aquarius	9.15	Globular cluster
73	6994	20 57.3	−12 46	Aquarius		Open cluster
74	628	1 35.1	+15 38	Pisces	9.5	Spiral galaxy (Sc)
75	6864	20 04.3	−22 01	Sagittarius	8.31	Globular cluster
76	650	1 40.3	+51 25	Perseus	11.4	Planetary nebula
77	1068	2 41.1	−00 07	Cetus	9.1	Spiral galaxy (Sb)
78	2068	5 45.3	+00 02	Orion		Small diffuse nebula
79	1904	5 22.9	−24 33	Lepus	7.3	Globular cluster
80	6093	16 15.2	−22 55	Scorpio	7.17	Globular cluster
81	3031	9 53.4	+69 12	Ursa Major	6.9	Spiral galaxy (Sb)
82	3034	9 53.6	+69 50	Ursa Major	8.7	Irregular galaxy
83	5236	13 35.3	−29 43	Hydra	7.5	Spiral galaxy (Sc)
84	4374	12 23.6	+13 03	Virgo	9.8	Elliptical galaxy
85	4382	12 23.8	+18 21	Coma Berenices	9.5	(SO) type galaxy
86	4406	12 24.6	+13 06	Virgo	9.8	Elliptical galaxy
87	4486	12 29.2	+12 33	Virgo	9.3	Elliptical galaxy
88	4501	12 30.4	+14 35	Coma Berenices	9.7	Spiral galaxy (Sb)
89	4552	12 34.1	+12 43	Virgo	10.3	Elliptical galaxy
90	4569	12 35.3	+13 19	Virgo	9.7	Spiral galaxy (Sb)
91?	—	—	—	—	—	—
92	6341	17 16.2	+43 11	Hercules	6.33	Globular cluster
93	2447	7 43.2	−23 48	Puppis	6.0	Open cluster
94	4736	12 49.6	+41 17	Canes Venatici	8.1	Spiral galaxy (Sb)
95	3351	10 42.3	+11 52	Leo	9.9	Spiral galaxy (SBb)
96	3368	10 45.1	+11 59	Leo	9.4	Spiral galaxy (Sa)

Number M	NGC	(1970) Right ascension	Declination	Constellation	Apparent visual magnitude	Description
97	3587	11 13.1	+55 11	Ursa Major	11.1	"Owl" nebula; planetary nebula
98	4192	12 12.2	+15 04	Coma Berenices	10.4	Spiral galaxy (Sb)
99	4254	12 17.3	+14 35	Coma Berenices	9.9	Spiral galaxy (Sc)
100	4321	12 21.4	+15 59	Coma Berenices	9.6	Spiral galaxy (Sc)
101	5457	14 02.1	+54 30	Ursa Major	8.1	Spiral galaxy (Sc)
102?	—	—	—	—	—	—
103	581	1 31.2	+60 32	Cassiopeia	7.0	Open cluster
104	4594	12 37.4	−11 21	Virgo	8.3	Spiral galaxy
105	3379	10 45.2	+13 01	Leo	9.7	Elliptical galaxy
106	4258	12 16.5	+47 35	Canes Venatici	8.4	Spiral galaxy
107	6171	16 29.7	−12 57	Ophiuchus	9.2	Globular cluster

*Index Catalogue number (IC)

Glossary

Glossary

Aberration of starlight The apparent shift in the direction of a star due to the orbital motion of the earth.

Ablation The vaporization of the surface material of a meteoroid due to the heat produced by friction as the body passes through the earth's atmosphere.

Absolute magnitude The apparent visual magnitude a body would have at a distance of 10 parsecs (32.6 light years).

Absolute zero The lowest temperature at which all molecular motion stops ($-273°$C, $-459°$F, or $0°$K).

Absorption spectrum Dark (absorption) lines superimposed on a continuous spectrum.

Acceleration A change in the velocity or direction of a body.

Achromatic lens A lens system of two or more components used to correct chromatic aberration—the spreading of the spectrum into its constituent colors.

Active sun The sun when it has many centers of activity—sunspots, prominences, flares, and other phenomena.

Airglow The fluorescence of the earth's upper atmosphere.

Albedo The reflecting power of a body. The percentage of the incident light that a body reflects.

Almagest The celebrated book of Claudius Ptolemy which summarized the astronomical work up to his time and presented his theories of planetary motions.

Alpha particle The nucleus of a helium atom. A positively charged particle consisting of two protons and two neutrons. Also a product of radioactivity.

Altitude The angular distance above the horizon of a celestial body measured along its vertical circle.

Angle of incidence The angle between the incoming ray of light and the normal (perpendicular) to the reflecting or refracting surface.

Angstrom unit A unit of length equal to 10^{-8} cm which is used to measure the wavelength of light. Its symbol is Å.

Angular diameter The angle subtended by the diameter of a body.

Angular momentum The momentum of a body moving about an axis or a point. It is the product of its mass, linear velocity, and distance from the center of motion.

Annular eclipse A solar eclipse when the sun's apparent disk is larger than the moon's apparent disk so that a ring of the sun's disk is seen completely around the moon.

Antimatter Matter that is made up of antiparticles which are identical with the particles in all respects except that they are opposite in electrical charge.

Aperture The diameter of the objective lens or mirror of a telescope.

Aphelion The point in the elliptical orbit of a planet or comet at which the body is at its greatest distance from the sun.

Apogee The point in the elliptical orbit of the moon or artificial satellite at which the body is at its greatest distance from the earth.

Apparent magnitude A measure of the visual brightness of a celestial body as observed from the earth.

Apparent noon The time when the sun's center is on the observer's meridian.

Emission line   A bright discrete line in a spectrum.

Emission nebula   A bright gaseous nebula whose light is derived from the ultraviolet light of a star within or near the nebula.

Emission spectrum   A series of bright lines (emission lines) produced by a low-pressure incandescent gas.

Energy levels of atoms   The possible energies above the least possible that an atom can have due to the absorption of radiation from external sources.

Ephemeris   A table that gives the positions of celestial bodies at regular intervals of time.

Epicycle   The small circle in the Ptolemaic system whose center moves along the circumference of the larger circle (deferent) while the planet moves along the circumference of the small circle.

Epoch   An arbitrary date selected as a point of reference to which astronomical observations are referred.

Equation of time   The difference between the apparent and mean solar time.

Equator   A great circle on the terrestrial sphere whose points are 90° from the north and south poles.

Equatorial mount   A telescope mount with one axis parallel to the earth's axis which rotates at the same rate as the earth by means of a clock drive.

Equinox   One of two intersections of the ecliptic and the celestial equator.

Erg   A unit of energy in the metric system. The amount of work accomplished by a force of one dyne moving a body a distance of one centimeter.

Escape velocity   The initial speed that a body must attain to overcome the gravitational pull of another body and escape into space.

Exosphere   The top layer of the earth's atmosphere where the molecules readily escape from the earth's gravitational pull.

Extragalactic   Outside or beyond the Milky Way.

Faculae   Extended bright regions ("little torches") seen near the sun's limb.

Filar micrometer   An instrument attached to the eyepiece of a telescope to measure the angle (separation) between two stars and their relative positions.

Fireball   An unusually bright meteor.

Flare   A very bright flash of light over a small area of the sun's surface, especially near an active sunspot, which is due to an intense outburst of energy.

Flare star   A star that suddenly and unpredictably increases its brightness for a short period of time.

Flash spectrum   The spectrum of the sun's limb which is a bright-line spectrum of the chromosphere visible for an instant just before totality in a solar eclipse.

Flocculi (plages)   Bright regions in the chromosphere in the magnetic fields around sunspots visible in spectroheliograms in monochromatic light.

Fluorescence   The absorption of radiation of one wavelength (especially ultraviolet) and its re-emission in another wavelength (visible light).

Focal length   The distance from the center of a lens or mirror to the focal point.

Focal ratio   The "f" number, or speed. The ratio of the focal length of a lens or mirror to its diameter.

Forbidden lines   Spectral lines not usually obtainable under laboratory conditions because their emissions result from atomic transitions that are most improbable.

Force   That which can change the speed or the direction of a body.

Fraunhofer line   An absorption (dark) line in the spectrum of the sun or a star.

Frequency   The number of waves that pass a given point in a unit of time.

Full moon   The phase of the moon when it is in opposition (opposite side of the sun from the earth) and its entire visible hemisphere is illuminated.

Fusion   The process by which heavier atomic nuclei are created from lighter ones.

Galactic cluster   An open cluster of stars found in the spiral arms of the Milky Way.

Galactic equator   The plane of the great circle on the

celestial sphere that locates the center line of the Milky Way.

Galactic poles The north and south galactic poles that are 90° from the galactic equator.

Galaxy A large assemblage of stars and interstellar material held together by gravitation. A galaxy usually contains from millions to hundreds of billions of stars. The Galaxy is the Milky Way.

Gamma ray The most energetic form of electromagnetic radiation with the shortest wavelength.

Gegenschein A faint diffuse patch of light (counterglow) seen opposite the sun in the sky. It is probably caused by the reflection of sunlight from very small particles in space around the earth.

Giant star A star of large radius and luminosity.

Gibbous A phase of the moon or a planet during which more than half but less than the whole disk appears illuminated.

Globular cluster A large spherical cluster of stars located in the halo which surrounds the Milky Way and other galaxies.

Globule A small, dark, relatively dense nebula that is believed to be a protostar.

Granules Small, bright spots in the sun's photosphere which give it a mottled appearance similar to rice grains. They are produced by hot gases rising from below the photosphere.

Gravitation The property of matter by which one mass exerts a force of attraction on another.

Great circle The curve formed on the surface of a sphere by the intersection of a plane which passes through its center. It divides the sphere into two equal parts.

Greenwich meridian The meridian which passes through a point at the Royal Greenwich Observatory in England is the reference, or "prime meridian," for determining longitude.

Gregorian calendar The calendar in common use today which was introduced by Pope Gregory XIII in 1582.

Ground state The lowest possible energy level of an atom.

H I region A region in space of neutral hydrogen.

H II region A region in space of ionized hydrogen.

Halo A region which surrounds the nucleus of a galaxy and contains globular clusters and stars.

Harmonic law Kepler's third law of planetary motion, which states that the squares of the sidereal periods of planets are proportional to the cubes of the semimajor axes of their orbits: $P^2 = a^3$.

Harvest moon The full moon nearest to the time of the autumnal equinox which rises after sunset on successive nights with the minimum delay.

Hayashi lines The theoretical evolutionary track on the Hertzsprung-Russell diagram of a convective star in its early stages of evolution.

Head of comet The principle part of a comet, which contains the nucleus and coma.

"Heavy" elements In astronomy, they usually refer to the elements whose atomic numbers are greater than that of helium.

Heliocentric system A system which is centered around the sun.

Helium flash An explosion-like ignition of the helium in the core of a red giant star which starts the triple-alpha nuclear process.

Hertzsprung-Russell (H-R) diagram A plot of the absolute magnitudes of stars against their spectral class, color index, color, or temperature.

Horizon system A system in which the coordinates azimuth and altitude are used to establish the position of a celestial body.

Hour angle The angle measured from the local (observer's) meridian westward along the celestial equator to the hour circle which passes through the body.

Hour circle A great circle on the celestial sphere which passes through the celestial poles and crosses the celestial equator at 90°.

Hubble constant   A number that relates the rate of recession of a galaxy to its distance.

Hyperbola   A conic section. An open curve formed by the intersection of a plane parallel to the axis of a circular cone.

Image   The optical representation of an object produced by the reflection or refraction of the light rays by a lens or a mirror.

Inclination of an orbit   The angle between the orbital plane of a body and usually either the plane of the celestial equator or the ecliptic.

Index Catalogue (I.C.)   A supplement to the New General Catalogue (NGC) of star clusters and nebulae.

Index of refraction   The ratio of the speed of light in a vacuum to its speed in a given transparent substance.

Inertia   The property of matter by which a body resists a change in its state of motion.

Inferior conjunction   The planetary configuration of an inferior planet (Mercury and Venus) when it is between the earth and the sun.

Inferior planet   A planet whose mean distance from the sun is less than the earth's. Its orbit lies between the earth and the sun.

Infrared radiation   Electromagnetic radiation whose wavelength is longer than that of visible red light and shorter than that of radio waves.

Insolation   The amount of the sun's radiation that falls on a unit area of the earth's surface in a unit of time.

Interferometer   An optical instrument which utilizes the principle of the interference of light waves to measure small angles and hence the diameter of stars.

International date line   An arbitrary line nearly coinciding with the 180° meridian across which the date changes by one day.

Interstellar lines   Absorption lines (dark spectral lines) on stellar spectra produced by diffuse gas in space.

Interstellar matter   Microscopic dust particles and diffuse gases in space between the stars.

Ion   An electrically charged atom produced by either the loss or gain of one or more electrons.

Ionization   The process by which atoms lose or gain electrons.

Ionosphere   The layer of the earth's atmosphere which contains many ionized atoms.

Irregular galaxy   A galaxy whose shape is not symmetrical—either an elliptical or spiral galaxy.

Irregular variable   A star whose energy output is not periodic.

Isotope   A different form of the same element whose atoms have the same atomic number but different atomic weight (mass).

Jovian planet   One of the four large, relatively low-density planets: Jupiter, Saturn, Uranus, and Neptune.

Julian calendar   A solar calendar introduced by Julius Caesar.

Julian day calendar   A calendar based on the system of the continuous numbering of the days beginning with January 1, 4713 B.C.

Kepler's laws   The three basic laws of planetary motion discovered by Johannes Kepler.

Kinetic energy   Energy caused by the motion of a body. It is expressed as one-half the product of its mass and the square of its velocity: K.E. $= \frac{1}{2}mv^2$.

Kirchhoff's laws   The three laws which explain the formation of continuous, emission (bright-line), and absorption spectra.

Kirkwood's gaps   The gaps in the spacing of the planetoids or the rings of Saturn.

Latitude   The angular distance on the terrestrial sphere measured from the equator, north or south, along the meridian which passes through the place.

Law of areas   Kepler's second law of planetary motion, which states that the radius vector (line joining the planet and sun) sweeps equal areas in its orbital plane in equal intervals of time.

Law of the red shift   The radial velocity of a distant

galaxy, which is measured by the red shift, is proportional to its distance; therefore, the red shift is a measure of the galaxy's distance.

Leap year A calendar year of 366 days which occurs every fourth year divisible by four except in century years not divisble by 400. 1900 was not a leap year. 2000 will be a leap year.

Libration A real or apparent oscillation of a body which permits the observer on the earth to see more than one hemisphere of the body during a given period of time.

Libration (latitudinal) The libration due to the moon's equator being inclined about $6\frac{1}{2}°$ to its orbital plane which permits the observer to see about $6\frac{1}{2}°$ beyond the north and south poles of the moon during one lunar month.

Libration (longitudinal) The libration due to the moon's constant rotational speed and its variable orbital speed which permits the observer on the earth to see over $7\frac{1}{2}°$ beyond the east and west limbs of the moon during one lunar month.

Light An electromagnetic radiation visible to the eye.

Light curve A plot of the variation of the magnitude of a variable star or an eclipsing binary against time.

Light-gathering power of a telescope The amount of light a telescope collects which is proportional to the area of its objective.

Light year The distance light travels in one year in space (vacuum), which is approximately 6×10^{12} miles, or 9.7×10^{12} km.

Limb The apparent edge of the sun, moon, or planet.

Limb darkening The sun's limb appears darker than the center of its disk because at the disk's center, the observer sees into deeper and hotter layers of the sun's photosphere.

Line broadening The phenomenon which increases the width of spectral lines.

Line of apsides The major axis of the elliptical orbit of a body.

Line of nodes The line which connects the ascending and descending nodes of an orbit which intersects a reference plane such as the ecliptic.

Local apparent time The local hour angle of the apparent sun plus 12 hours.

Local group The cluster of galaxies, including the Milky Way, that appears to form a group.

Local mean time The local hour angle of the mean sun plus 12 hours.

Local standard of rest The coordinate system in which the motions of the stars in the neighborhood of the sun average zero, that is, they appear to be at rest within the system.

Longitude The angular distance on the terrestrial sphere measured from the Greenwich meridian, east or west along the equator to the meridian that passes through the place.

Luminosity The rate at which a star emits electromagnetic radiation into space. It is usually expressed in terms of the sun's luminosity.

Luminosity function The relative number of stars of various absolute magnitudes in a unit volume of space.

Magnifying power The apparent increase in the size of a body when seen through a telescope over its size when seen with the unaided eye.

Magnitude A number which designates the brightness of a body. It is a measure of the light received from a body.

Main sequence A narrow band on the H-R diagram on which the majority of the stars lie. The band runs from the upper left to the lower right of the diagram.

Mantle The earth's layer which lies between the crust and the core.

Mare The Latin name for a sea-like lunar feature.

Mass-luminosity relation An empirical relationship which states that the luminosity of a star, primarily a main sequence or a giant, depends on its mass. The more massive stars are the more luminous.

Mean solar day The time between successive crossings of the observer's meridian by the mean sun.

Mean sun   An imaginary body that moves eastward along the celestial equator at a uniform rate and completes its circuit in the sky in the same period as the apparent sun.

Meridian   The great circle on the terrestrial sphere which passes through the observer's position and the earth's north and south poles. The great circle on the celestial sphere which passes through the observer's zenith and the celestial north and south poles.

Meson   A short-lived subatomic particle with a mass between that of a proton and an electron.

Messier catalogue   A catalogue of nebulae, star clusters, and galaxies compiled by Charles Messier in 1787. The bodies are designated by M and a number, e.g., M31 for the Andromeda galaxy.

Meteor   The bright streak of light that is visible when a meteoroid passes through the earth's atmosphere and is heated by friction between it and the air molecules.

Meteor shower   Many meteors that appear to radiate from a point in the sky, due to the earth's passing through a swarm or a stream of meteoroid particles.

Meteorite   A meteoroid that has survived its flight through the earth's atmosphere and has struck the earth's surface.

Meteoroid   The stony, metallic particle which produces the meteor when it passes through the earth's atmosphere.

Micrometeorite   An extremely small meteoroid whose size causes it to move very slowly through the earth's atmosphere so that it does not burn.

Milky Way   A faint, diffuse band of light which completely encircles the sky and consists of a vast number of stars and interstellar material.

Mohorovicic discontinuity   Moho for short. The boundary between the earth's crust and the mantle. Named for the Yugoslav scientist Andrja Mohorovicic.

Molecule   The smallest unit of a substance that retains the chemical properties of the substance. It is a combination of two or more atoms.

Monochromatic   Consisting of one color or wavelength.

n-body problem   The problem of determining the motion of a body that is interacting with two or more other bodies under their mutual gravitational attraction.

Nadir   The point on the celestial sphere that is 180° from the zenith and directly below the observer.

Neap tides   The lowest tides that occur each month when the moon is near the first- or third-quarter phase.

Nebula   A cloud of interstellar dust or gas.

Neutrino   A particle with zero mass when at rest and no magnetic field which carries away energy when it is emitted from a nuclear reaction.

Neutron   A subatomic particle without a charge and with a mass approximately equal to that of a proton.

New General Catalogue (NGC)   A catalogue of star clusters, nebulae, and galaxies compiled by J. Dreyer which succeeded the Messier Catalogue.

New moon   The phase of the moon which occurs when the longitude of the sun and the moon are the same and the moon's dark hemisphere is toward the earth.

Newtonian focus   A reflecting telescope which uses a secondary plane mirror placed near the top of the tube to divert the light rays from the primary mirror and bring them to a focus at the side of the tube, at right angles to the direction of the telescope.

Node   The intersection of the orbital path of a body with the reference plane, e.g., the celestial equator or the ecliptic. See ascending node and descending node.

Nova   A star that experiences some kind of a violent explosion, increasing its brightness several magnitudes, then fading gradually.

Nuclear fusion   See fusion.

Nucleus (atom)   The central part of the atom which contains protons and neutrons that comprise almost the entire mass of the atom.

Nucleus (comet)   The swarm of solid particles in the head of a comet.

Nucleus (galaxy)   The center of the galaxy where the star density is the greatest.

Nutation   As the earth's polar axis precesses, the

earth's pole wobbles about nine seconds of arc around its mean position.

Objective   The primary, light-gathering, image-forming lens or mirror of a telescope.

Oblate spheroid   A solid formed by rotating an ellipse about its minor axis. A spherical body that has been flattened by rotation.

Oblateness   A measure of the amount of flattening of a sphere. It is the ratio of the difference between the equatorial and polar diameters of the spheroid to the equatorial diameter.

Obliquity of the ecliptic   The $23\frac{1}{2}°$ angle between the planes of the ecliptic and the celestial equator.

Obscuration (interstellar)   The absorption of starlight by interstellar dust.

Occular   An eyepiece.

Occultation   When a smaller body passes behind a larger body. The occultation of a star by the moon. The occultation of Jupiter's satellites by the planet.

Opacity   The property of a body to stop the passage of light. The absorbing power of a nebula to obscure starlight.

Open cluster   A loose, unsymmetrical cluster of tens to several thousands of stars located in the disk or spiral arms of the Milky Way.

Opposition   The configuration of a planet when it is on the opposite side of the sun as viewed from the earth, that is, its elongation is 180°. This occurs only for planets whose orbits are larger than the earth's.

Optical binary   Two stars that appear to be close together, although they are neither in the same region of space nor gravitationally associated.

Ozone   Oxygen molecules composed of three atoms which are formed by the action of the sun's ultraviolet radiation on the oxygen molecules of two atoms found in the stratosphere.

Parabola   A conic section. An open curve formed by the intersection of a circular cone and a plane parallel to its side (surface of the cone).

Paraboloid   The surface generated by the rotation of a parabola about its axis. The shape of the surface of the primary mirror in most reflecting telescopes.

Parallax (stellar)   The apparent angular displacement of a nearby star with respect to the more distant stars due to the earth's orbital motion around the sun. It is the angle which subtends the radius of the earth's orbit (1 a.u.) at the star's distance.

Parsec   A unit of distance. The distance of a body when its stellar parallax is one second of arc. 1 parsec = 3.26 light years.

Penumbra   The portion of a body's shadow which is partially illuminated. It is the transition region between total obscuration in the umbra and total illumination outside of the shadow.

Penumbral eclipse   A lunar eclipse which occurs when the moon passes through only the penumbra of the earth's shadow.

Periastron   The point in the orbit of a star in a binary star system which is closest to the other star.

Perigee   The point in the orbit of an earth satellite which is closest to the earth.

Perihelion   The point in the orbit of a body revolving around the sun which is closest to the sun.

Period-luminosity relation   The empirical relationship between the absolute magnitude and the period of light variation of cepheid-variable stars.

Perturbation   The deviation in the orbital path of a body produced by a third body or an external force.

Phases   The progressive changes in the shape of the illuminated hemisphere of the moon or planet as seen from the earth.

Photoelectric cell   A vacuum tube in which electrons are ejected from the surface of a light-sensitive substance (cathode) when exposed to light and then are accelerated to the anode. This flow of electrons is an electric current which can be used to determine the amount of light which strikes the cathode.

Photographic magnitude   The magnitude of a body as

determined by a photographic plate sensitive to blue and violet light.

Photomultiplier A photoelectric cell in which the number of ejected electrons is increased by having the electrons strike in succession a series of light-sensitive surfaces. This amplifies the electric current generated so that it can be measured more easily and accurately.

Photon A discrete parcel of electromagnetic energy.

Photosphere The apparent luminous visible solar surface; the region from which nearly all of the light is emitted.

Photovisual magnitude The brightness of a body as determined by a photographic plate sensitive to green and yellow light; the spectral region to which the human eye is most sensitive.

Plage (flocculi) A bright region in the chromosphere, above and around a sunspot in its magnetic field, visible in a spectroheliogram.

Planetarium An optical instrument which electronically projects the celestial bodies visible to the unaided eye on a domed ceiling. It permits the observer to view from any position on the earth's surface a simulated but realistic sky of the present, past, or future.

Planetary nebula An extremely hot star surrounded by a large shell of rarefied gas that is slowly expanding. Telescopically, it appears like the planet Uranus; hence, the name planetary.

Planetoid A minor planet or an asteroid.

Polarized light The partial or complete alignment of the light waves so that they vibrate in one plane.

Positron A subatomic particle that is equivalent to an electron, but has a positive charge.

Precession The slow movement of the earth's rotation axis which causes the north celestial pole to sweep a circle of $23\frac{1}{2}°$ radius around the north ecliptic pole during a period of about 26,000 years.

Prime focus The point in the telescope tube where the image is formed by the objective (primary lens or mirror).

Prime meridian The meridian (great circle) that passes through the old Royal Observatory at Greenwich, England and is used as the standard reference for measuring longitude on the earth.

"Primeval nucleus" Lemaitre's single superdense sphere of matter (primeval atom) which exploded, expanded, and formed the present matter in the universe.

Prominence Luminous gas clouds of many different shapes and sizes visible on the sun's limb projecting upward from the chromosphere.

Proper motion The rate at which a star's direction in the sky changes. Usually expressed in seconds of arc per year.

Proton One of the two fundamental units that make up the nucleus of the atom. A subatomic particle of positive charge. It is the nucleus of the ordinary hydrogen atom.

Protostar A cloud of dust and gas which is condensing at an accelerating rate, decreasing in size, and increasing in temperature and is in the early stages of becoming a star.

Pulsar An extremely small, dense radio source that emits brief pulses of radiation at regular periods. It may be a neutron star.

Pulsating variable A variable star that periodically changes its brightness because it pulsates.

Quadrature The configuration of a planet when the angle between the planet and the sun as viewed from the earth is 90°. This occurs only for planets whose orbits are larger than the earth's.

Quarter moon The phase of the moon when only one-half of its illuminated hemisphere is visible from the earth. This occurs when the moon has traveled one-quarter or three-quarters of its orbit.

Quasars The abbreviated name for quasi-stellar radio sources. They are extremely large objects emitting light and radio energy, are stellar in appearance, highly luminous, and show large red shifts.

Quiet sun The sun when the number of centers of activity are at a minimum.

Radar telescope   A radio telescope that transmits a radio signal toward a celestial body. The body reflects part of the energy which the telescope picks up, amplifies, and records.

Radial velocity   The component of relative velocity of a body that is measured along the observer's line of sight.

Radiant   A point in the sky from which meteors in a meteor shower appear to radiate.

Radiation   The method of transferring energy through a vacuum (space). Also, the energy (electromagnetic or corpuscular) that is transmitted.

Radio telescope   A telescope which makes observations in radio wavelengths. A large paraboloidal antenna which collects radio energy emitted by a celestial source, a receiver which amplifies the signal, and a recorder which records the information.

Radioactive decay   The process by which a radioactive element decomposes into lighter elements and emits gamma rays and other subatomic particles. This radioactivity provides the means of determining the age of a body.

Radius vector   The imaginary line which joins a planet to the sun and moves as the planet revolves around the sun.

Rays (lunar)   A system of long, bright streaks which appear to radiate from some of the lunar craters.

Recurrent nova   A star that has been observed to erupt on several occasions. These outbursts occur on an average of once every 30 years.

Red giant   A large, cool, very luminous star. It is located above and to the right of the main-sequence line of the H-R diagram.

Reddening (interstellar)   The reddening of starlight as it passes through interstellar dust because the dust scatters the blue light more effectively than the red.

Red shift   The shift in the spectral lines toward the red end of the spectrum of remote galaxies which is attributed to the Doppler effect.

Reflecting telescope   A telescope which uses a mirror for its objective and the principle of reflection of light for its operation.

Reflection nebula   A cloud of interstellar dust and gas which is luminous because it reflects the light from a nearby star.

Refracting telescope   A telescope which uses a lens for its objective and the principle of the refraction of light for its operation.

Resolving power   The telescope's ability to resolve (separate) two objects which appear as a single source of light to the unaided eye.

Retrograde motion   The apparent westward motion of a planet with respect to the stars as a background.

Revolution   The motion of a body around a point in space or another body. The earth revolves around the sun. A star in a binary star system revolves around its barycenter and around the other star.

Right ascension   The angular distance measured from the hour circle which passes through the vernal equinox, eastward along the celestial equator to the hour circle which passes through the celestial body.

Rille   A crevasse (cleft or channel) on the lunar surface.

Roche's limit   The minimum distance at which a satellite cannot survive the gravitational force of a planet and therefore disintegrates. Saturn's rings are within Roche's limit.

Rotation   The motion of a body about its axis.

Saros   A cycle of about 18 years in which similar eclipses recur.

Satellite   A body that revolves around a larger body. The moon is the earth's satellite.

Schmidt telescope   A reflecting telescope which utilizes a spherical mirror and a correcting plate to compensate for the aberrations of the mirror. This system permits a large field of view to be photographed.

"Seeing"   A measure of the stability of the atmosphere which establishes the quality of the appearance of celestial bodies.

Seismic waves   Vibrations produced by earthquakes

or man-made subterranean explosions which travel through the earth's interior.

Semimajor axis One-half of the major axis of an ellipse. It also represents a planet's mean distance from the sun.

Separation The angular distance between two stars of a visual binary system.

Seyfert galaxy A spiral galaxy whose bright stellar nucleus emits strong ultraviolet and infrared radiation and some radio radiation. This type of galaxy was discovered by Carl Seyfert.

Shell star A star surrounded by a shell (sphere) of gas.

Shower (cosmic rays) Secondary high-energy cosmic particles produced by the collision of the primary cosmic ray particles with the molecules in the earth's atmosphere.

Shower (meteor) Meteors that appear to radiate from a common point (radiant) in the sky. The shower occurs when the earth passes through a stream or a swarm of meteoric material ejected by a comet and lying in the comet's path.

Sidereal day The interval of time between two successive transits of the observer's meridian by the vernal equinox of any given star.

Sidereal month The interval of time for the moon to complete one revolution around the earth, with a star or the vernal equinox as the reference.

Sidereal period The interval of time for one body to complete one revolution around another body, with a star or the vernal equinox as a reference.

Sidereal time It is star time and is defined as the local hour angle of the vernal equinox.

Sidereal year The interval of time for the earth to complete one revolution around the sun, with a star or the vernal equinox as the reference.

Small circle A closed curve formed on the surface of a sphere by the intersection of the sphere by a plane which does not pass through the sphere's center.

Solar activity A phenomenon such as a sunspot, plage, flare, or prominence that is visible on or above the solar photosphere.

Solar apex The point in the sky toward which the sun is moving. In this direction the stars appear to be moving toward the observer.

Solar constant The amount of solar radiation that a unit area normal to the sun's rays receives at a distance of 1 a.u. in a unit of time. Its mean value is 1.93 calories/cm^2·min (1.37×10^6 ergs/cm^2·sec).

Solar day The interval of time for the earth to complete one rotation with respect to the sun. The period for the sun to make two successive transits of the observer's meridian.

Solar parallax The angle which subtends the earth's equatorial radius at a distance of 1 a.u.

Solar system The sun's family. All the celestial bodies that are held together gravitationally by the sun (planets, satellites, minor planets, comets, etc.) and revolve around the sun.

Solar time The time based on the sun. It starts when the sun makes a lower transit of the observer's meridian. It is the local hour angle of the sun plus 12 hours.

Solar wind A tenuous gas of charged particles—ions and electrons—ejected by the sun that moves through space at high speeds.

Space velocity The star's velocity with respect to the sun expressed in miles or kilometers/sec.

Spectral class The classification of a star according to the characteristics of its spectrum.

Spectrograph The instrument for photographing the spectrum of a body.

Spectroheliogram A solar photograph taken in monochromatic light—usually hydrogen or ionized calcium.

Spectroscopic binary A binary star system which is revealed only by the shifting of its spectral lines.

Spectroscopic parallax (spectroscopic distance) A procedure for estimating the distance of a remote star by establishing its absolute magnitude from its spectral class and comparing it to its apparent magnitude.

Spectrum A band of colors, like a rainbow, from red to violet produced when light is dispersed by refraction or diffraction.

Speed   The ratio of distance to time expressed in miles/hour.

Spherical aberration   A major defect in a spherical lens or mirror. The light rays that strike the peripheral areas of the spherical surface have shorter focal lengths than those that strike near the optical axis.

Spicules   Bright, short-lived threadlike jets of material visible in the chromosphere over the entire solar limb.

Spiral galaxy   A flat, rotating galaxy with spiral arms that emerge from either a bright round or a bar nucleus.

Sporadic meteors   Meteors that are not associated with a shower. They appear at different times and places in the sky.

Spring tides   The highest tides during each lunar month when the sun, moon, and earth are in line. They occur when the moon is new or full.

Standard time   The time kept within a 15°-wide longitude zone based on the local mean solar time of the zone's central meridian.

Star cluster   A group of stars held together by mutual gravitation that are believed to have a common origin and velocity.

Steady-state universe   A cosmological theory according to which the shape and density of the universe have always been the same, that is, the universe had no beginning and will have no end. Since the principle of the red shift was accepted, the density was maintained by the continuous creation of matter.

Stefan's law   A formula which states that the rate at which energy is emitted from a unit area of a black body is proportional to the fourth power of its absolute temperature.

Stratosphere   The layer of the earth's atmosphere that lies between the troposphere and the ionosphere.

Subdwarf   A star whose luminosity is less than that of a main-sequence star of the same spectral class.

Subgiant   A star whose luminosity is less than a normal giant and greater than a main-sequence star of the same spectral class.

Summer solstice   The point on the ecliptic where the sun reaches its greatest angular distance ($23\frac{1}{2}°$) above the celestial equator. It marks the longest day of the year.

Superior conjunction   The planetary configuration of an inferior planet (Mercury and Venus) when the sun is between the planet and the earth.

Supernova   A star that temporarily increases its luminosity millions of times when it erupts and ejects a large amount of its material into space.

Synchrotron radiation   The radiation emitted by charged particles spiraling in a magnetic field at almost the speed of light.

Synodic month   The moon's period of revolution with respect to the sun, which is the period of its cycle of phases.

Synodic period   The interval of time between two similar successive planetary configurations.

Syzygy   A lunar configuration when the sun, earth, and moon are in line. This occurs when the moon is new or full.

T Tauri stars   Extremely young variable stars with erratic variations in brightness that are associated with interstellar material.

Tangential (transverse) velocity   A star's velocity with respect to the sun at right angles to the line of sight expressed in kilometers per second.

Tektites   Round glassy stones found on the earth that are believed to be molten lunar material ejected by meteoritic impacts.

Telluric lines   Spectral lines or bands produced by the absorption of light from a celestial body in the earth's atmosphere.

Temperature   A measure of the degree of motion of gas or liquid molecules.

Terminator   The line of demarcation between the illuminated and dark portions of the moon or a planet.

Thermal equilibrium   The rate at which energy is generated equals the rate at which energy is emitted into space by a star.

Thermocouple   A device which consists of a junction of two dissimilar metals used to measure the intensity of the radiation absorbed by the junction.

Thermonuclear reactions   The fusion of atomic nuclei under the influence of extremely high temperatures and pressures with the release of energy.

Tides   The deformation of a body produced by the differential gravitational force exerted on it by another body.

Total eclipse   A total solar eclipse occurs when the moon's disk completely obscures the sun's disk. A total lunar eclipse occurs when the moon is completely inside the umbra of the earth's shadow cone.

Totality   The interval of time during a total eclipse when the light of one body is completely obscured by another body.

Transit   The passage of a small body across the disk of a larger body, e.g., Mercury transiting the sun. The passage of a body across a meridian, e.g., the upper transit of the observer's meridian by the sun.

Triangulation   The method by which the distance to a remote (inaccessible) point can be determined by the solution of the elements of a triangle. The accessible elements are measured and the inaccessible are calculated by trigonometry.

Trojans   Two groups of asteroids that revolve around the sun in Jupiter's orbit—one is leading while the other is following the planet by an angle of 60° at the sun.

Tropic of Cancer—The parallel of latitude, $23\frac{1}{2}°$ north, which marks the northernmost position above the equator reached by the sun—June 21.

Tropic of Capricorn—The parallel of latitude, $23\frac{1}{2}°$ south, which marks the southernmost position below the equator reached by the sun—December 21.

Tropical year   The interval of time for the earth to complete one revolution around the sun with the vernal equinox as a reference. Numerically, it is equal to the ordinary year of approximately $365\frac{1}{4}$ days.

Troposphere   The lowest layer of the earth's atmosphere next to the earth's crust where most weather phenomena occur.

Twilight   The phenomenon of partial light visible after sunset and before sunrise which results from the reflection of sunlight from particles in the earth's upper atmosphere.

Ultraviolet radiation   The electromagnetic radiation whose wavelengths are shorter than the visible violet and range from about 4000 to 100 Å.

Umbra   The portion of the shadow cone of a body where the sun light is completely obscured. The central portion of a sunspot which appears the darkest.

Universal time   The local mean solar time on the prime meridian at the Royal Observatory, Greenwich, England.

Universe   The total space occupied by matter and radiation.

Upper transit   The instant of time when a body crosses the visible portion of the observer's meridian.

Van Allen radiation belt   Doughnut-shaped regions which lie in the plane of the earth's magnetic equator where high-energy charged particles are trapped in the earth's outer magnetic field and move from one magnetic hemisphere to the other.

Variable star   A pulsating star that increases and decreases its size rhythmically and exhibits changes in luminosity.

Vector   A quantity that has magnitude (amount) and direction.

Velocity—Speed in a given direction, e.g., miles per hour to the east or kilometers per second to the southwest.

Velocity of escape   The minimum velocity that a body must move to overcome the gravitational attraction of another body, enter into a parabolic orbit, and escape into space.

Vernal equinox   The intersection of the celestial equator and the ecliptic at the point where the sun crosses from south to north.

Vertical circle   A great circle on the celestial sphere which passes through the observer's zenith and intersects the horizon at 90°.

Visual binary   A binary star system in which the two stars are visible telescopically as two separate bodies.

Visual magnitude   The magnitude of a star based on its brightness as seen with the eye.

Volume   A measure of the space occupied by a body.

Walled plain (lunar)   The very large lunar craters that appear as depressions with hardly any outside walls.

Wandering of the poles   The actual shifting of the earth itself while its axis of rotation remains fixed with respect to the stars, that is, the north and south poles of the earth drift in relation to the earth's surface.

Waning moon   The moon between the full and new phase when its illuminated surface as seen from the earth is decreasing.

Wave   One method of describing how electromagnetic radiation is propagated.

Wavelength   The distance between two corresponding successive points in a wave motion, e.g., the distance between two successive crests or troughs.

Waxing moon   The moon between the new and full phase when its illuminated surface as seen from the earth is increasing.

Weight   The gravitational force between the earth and the body.

White dwarf   A star that has exhausted either all or most of its fuel, collapsed, and has become extremely dense, hot, and very faint. It is believed to be near its final stage of evolution.

Widmanstätten figures   A distinctive crystalline structure seen in a ground, polished, and etched surface of a meteorite.

Wien's law   The relationship between the temperature of a black body and the wavelength at which maximum radiation is emitted.

Winter solstice   The point on the ecliptic at which the sun reaches its greatest angular distance ($23\frac{1}{2}°$) below the celestial equator. It marks the shortest day of the year.

Wolf-Rayet stars   Very hot O-type stars that eject gas at high velocities.

World calendar   A proposed calendar whose year has been divided in four equal, identical quarters so that the same date of the month would fall on the same day of the week.

X-rays   The radiation of short wavelengths located between the ultraviolet and the gamma rays on the electromagnetic spectrum.

X-ray stars   Stars that emit radiation in the x-ray frequencies.

Year   A unit of time defined by the revolution of the earth. It is the interval of time for the earth to complete one revolution around the sun.

Zeeman effect   The broadening or splitting of spectral lines into several of slightly different wavelengths when the source is in a magnetic field.

Zenith   The point on the celestial sphere that is directly above the observer.

Zodiac   An 18°-wide belt which completely encircles the sky and centers on the ecliptic. It was divided by the ancients into 12 equal parts, each containing one constellation.

Zodiacal light   A faint glow of light visible along the ecliptic nearest the sun on the western horizon after sunset and on the eastern horizon before sunrise.

Zone of avoidance   An irregular region along the center of the Milky Way (galactic equator) where the interstellar dust is so dense that few, if any, exterior galaxies are visible.

Zone time (standard time)   The solar time within a 15°-wide zone as determined by the central meridian of the zone. Zone time is the local mean time of the central meridian. Zone time is kept at sea where the zone boundaries are meridians, and standard time is kept over land areas where the boundaries are irregular.

Index

Index